DIET NUGGETS
AND
WISDOM APPETIZERS

365 DAYS OF ENCOURAGEMENT FOR DIETERS

KATHLEEN KURLIN

Diet Nuggets and Wisdom Appetizers
365 Days of Encouragement for Dieters

By Kathleen Kurlin

Diet Nuggets and Wisdom Appetizers is an original work and many of the names that appear in the body of the book have been changed to protect identity.

All quotes used were copied from http://www.quotegarden.com. If no reference crediting the quote is given, the quote was written by me, Kathleen Kurlin.

Cover & Interior Design by Cory E. Olson, CEO Graphics

Back Cover Photo by Jim Fischer

Printed in the United States of America

ISBN-13: 978-1484871294

For my girls,
Lindsay and Kelsey
You are amazing, beautiful women.
I am blessed that God chose you for me.
And for all my sisters who struggle with
Weight, wanting nothing more than
to be comfortable in your own skin.
You are not alone!

PREFACE

I want to be clear from the get go – this is not a diet book, nor is this a Bible reference book. I am not a nutrition expert, a personal trainer, life coach or theologian. I am a writer, but more importantly, what I am, is a "regular woman" who has been battling weight issues since I was a child. I am a "Professional Dieter" and a woman who has struggled her ENTIRE life to be comfortable in her own skin; a woman who wants to love myself as I am regardless of my weight, yet unable to accept myself for who I am when I am continually unhappy with my weight.

My first "real" diet at the age of 14 lasted three months and resulted in the loss of the 30 pounds I was targeting. I successfully kept that weight off for four years until I married and slowly started regaining the weight. When I got pregnant and gave birth to my first child at the age of 23, my 60-pound pregnancy weight gain birthed my weight loss obsession which sent me straight to my first Weight Watchers® meeting. One year later I reached my goal weight and successfully maintained it to achieve my Lifetime Membership. A divorce and a few years as a single, working mom wreaked havoc on my emotional state, which exacerbated my hidden food addictions ... and so the cycle began in earnest.

Like countless other women, I've tried every fad diet, program, plan and pill in the endless pursuit of losing weight and keeping it off. I have been at my ideal weight and maintained that healthy weight for extended periods of time; even worked for a major weight loss company for several years during that maintenance time. Through all these programs and plans, I invariably regained the weight (and then some), which led to depression, binge eating, shame and guilt ... etc., perpetuating a lifetime cycle of yo-yo dieting.

Two years ago I made a decision to stop the vicious cycle of losing, gaining, depression, failure, guilt and shame and made a plan to get off the hamster wheel of diet insanity. I joined a year-long support group through my church called *Living Free*, which is similar to a Celebrate Recovery group based on a 12-step program. What I learned in that year was that I am serious food addict who suffers from bulimia and exercise bulimia. This didn't come as any real surprise to me. I'd been in denial for some time; reluctant to give voice to my obsessions, because knowledge leads to responsibility and responsibility invariably leads to accountability.

I have subscribed to several daily online devotionals that I've been reading for many years. These devotions have provided me with daily encouragement and spiritual insights for many of life's challenges including spiritual battles, financial difficulties, job struggles, parenting dilemmas and relationship trials. While I have benefitted from these devotionals, I have yet to find one that speaks specifically to my daily diet struggles. Because of my food addictions and exercise obsessions, I have made a career out of dieting, and I want – no I *need* regular, daily encouragement and spiritual enlightenment with this one, major area of my life.

I started thinking that *someone* should write a devotional that would provide readers with daily insights and encouragement that would speak specifically to weight loss needs and challenges. And then I thought that *someone* could be me since I'm a writer and I've got decades worth of experience at weight loss battles!

When I began the *Living Free* group I felt God speaking to me to chronicle my year-long journey in a daily online blog so that I could provide encouragement to my sisters in Christ walking this journey with me. This book is the result of my year-long journey to self-discovery; my journey to get healthy; my journey to a commitment to follow Jesus and truly LIVE FREE of the bondages of food addictions, exercise addictions and living cloaked under a mantle of shame and guilt.

My year long journey was like peeling back the layers of an onion. With every layer stripped away, God was ready and waiting to uncover yet another hurt, another scar, another triggered memory responsible for my life-long addiction to food. It wasn't a pretty journey, but in the end it was a pretty remarkable journey to see the amount of healing God brought to me.

This book isn't meant to cure anyone who suffers from food addictions, bulimia or any other eating or food related disorder. It's definitely not another diet regime. This book is meant merely to provide little *bites* (as in appetizer) of spiritual encouragement and little nuggets of diet truths to those seeking direction from someone who has been there; a sojourner who has not only walked this road, but fallen down repeatedly, only to push herself up time and time again.

The title of this book, **Diet Nuggets and Wisdom Appetizers** is intended to whet your appetite for the Savior while encouraging you as you walk the challenging road to weight loss, emotional health and spiritual growth. Two years after beginning my journey I can't say that I'm cured from my food addictions and diet obsessions as I don't believe any of us ever arrive at total victory or perfection this side of Heaven. I can say that I am stronger, more confident and at long last happy with the woman God created me to be.

My prayer is that through this year long journey, those who suffer with weight loss struggles and food addictions can begin to peel back some of their own layers and discover the road to healing. I pray you find that underneath those layers you discover the person God created you to be. I pray this book gives you hope.

Blessings in Christ,
Kathy K.

ACKNOWLEDGMENTS

First and foremost I must always give thanks and praise to my Lord and Savior for blessing me with the gift of words. I thank Him for speaking through me – and to me and for allowing me to use this gift and passion for writing He has placed in me to reach out to others. Through His mercy and healing, He has managed to use my trials and struggles to make my "mess" my message and my "tests," my "testimony." I'm not all the way there yet, but gaining ground daily. Life is hard, but with Christ as my center, He has made it more than bearable – He's made it rich in love and laughter.

Thank you to my "boys," my husband, Robert, my son Jordan and my grandson, Gage. Your constant and unwavering support has kept me going when I have doubted myself. My special thanks to Bob; I love you more than words can say which is odd for a girl who loves words so much. You've always encouraged me to pursue my dreams, even in the many lean years when there was barely enough money for groceries and gas. You rarely told me 'no' when it came to writing expenses and have always been my strongest supporter and greatest cheerleader.

I would be remiss if I didn't extend a special thank you to Cory Olson of CEO Graphics. You are a heaven-sent angel straight from God and your gifts and talents are beyond compare. You are a woman of high moral character and full of integrity; especially when the task given you was probably way more than you bargained for. Your commitment was unwavering and I appreciate you immensely! You have an amazing God-given talent!

Thank you also to Jen Chang for your willingness to help with the daunting task of editing and finding all my typos and errors. You are a heaven-sent angel as well and I appreciate your willingness to jump in and help out in the eleventh hour. BIG thanks to you!

To all my sisters in Christ who walked this difficult road with me in *Living Free* two years ago. Your stories, your struggles, your pain and your tears impacted my life significantly. Thank you to my accountability partners, Christina, Mona, Linda C. and Valerie. Thank you also to Joyce, Rebecca, Linda B., Judy, Tammy, Karen, Faye, Ellie, Brenda, Cara, Mary, Betty, Sue, and the countless others who came and went over my year in *Living Free*. You have all been a great source of inspiration and encouragement to me.

Last, but certainly not least, thank you to my beautiful daughters, Lindsay and Kelsey. I know I haven't always influenced your lives in a positive way with regards to your self-confidence and body image. I pray you can learn from my mistakes and truly embrace the beautiful women that you are. Take it from me, it doesn't matter what the scale says, you are not valuable because of what you weigh. You are valuable because you are compassionate women who love deeply, live passion-ately and embrace life with both laughter and common sense. Be well-balanced my beautiful girls ... go forth and "be responsibility," and love who God created you to be!

Thanks be to God ...

JANUARY 1
HAPPY YOU NEAR!

Here it is again ... the start of another New Year and that can only mean one thing: it's time for the proverbial New Year's Resolution. You've been here before and made the same resolution year after year (decade after decade). You tell yourself this year will be different. THIS will be the year you're going to lose those extra 10 (20, 40 or 100 lbs.) *once and for all*. If that were true, you wouldn't be here again, making that same resolution; no closer to losing the weight than you were a year ago.

Let's face it – most of us know resolutions don't work anymore than diets do. A diet, by its very nature is so restrictive, it quickly becomes unrealistic. So how can we expect this year to be different? Well first off, ditch the diet notion altogether and purpose in your heart to make several realistic changes. If you need a good program always start with a trusted health care physician for recommendations. There are many programs that work, but always remember that shortcuts are just that – they only work *short term*. Stick with a sound program that promotes slow, steady weight loss.

Don't go on a diet - make simple lifestyle changes. Walk more – move more; eat less. It's not rocket science and most of us have heard this all before. This year, take those extra steps; clean out the pantry and fridge TODAY. Rid your house of all the junk food; find an accountability partner or support group; keep a food/menu journal and most importantly – include God in ALL your plans – be it losing weight, getting out of debt or whatever your resolution may be this year. God wants to be part of EVERY aspect of your life! If you want to lose weight ... PRAY, PRAY, PRAY! And after you've done that – pray some more. Hopefully, by incorporating all these suggestions into your life you will achieve your New Year's goals and you'll uncover a brand new you. This year can be different! Don't fail at another resolution for a Happy New Year; but realize there's a Happy You Near!

After all is said and done, a lot more will have been said than done.
~ Author Unknown

Don't worry about anything; instead, pray about everything. Tell God what you need, and thank him for all he has done. Philippians 4:6 (NLT)

PRAYER FOR TODAY: *Father God, I know that I've tried to lose weight before and failed. I am asking You for divine guidance to help this year be the year that I finally succeed. Help me to release this false sense of control I think I have over this issue. I give You my burden of food addictions and weight issues. I lay it ALL down and ask that You would keep me from picking these burdens up again. I give You the control. In Your name I ask all these things, Lord Jesus. Amen.*

JANUARY 2
Turnover Leftovers

Weight loss resolutions continue to be the number one New Year's resolution year after year. At one time or another nearly everyone has experienced an unwelcome tightness of their clothes. It's so much easier to blame the snug feeling on dryer shrinkage rather than our own bad habits. The reality of resolutions is that by Valentine's Day, most people have already abandoned their weight loss efforts and reverted back to their old (bad) habits.

It's two days into the New Year and if your house is like mine, there may be an abundance of Christmas leftovers and goodies still hanging around. The temptation to overindulge and gobble down sugar cookies and fudge is overwhelming. My generation grew up as members of the "clean your plate club" being made to feel guilty about starving orphans in China. Throwing away perfectly good food is not in our nature. If you're serious about losing those unwanted pounds this year, not only will you need to change your eating habits, but your thoughts MUST change as well. Tear up your membership card to the "Clean Plate Club" and either throw away all tempting snack foods or give them away to someone else. Starving college students or the break room at work are great for unloading those snacks and goodies.

The urge to polish off the leftovers will be tough to resist. STOP before you give in to that instant gratification and ask God for strength to resist the temptation. *You have not, because you ask not!*

Don't dig your grave with your own knife and fork. ~ English Proverb

Those who know your name trust in you, for you, O Lord, have never abandoned anyone who searches for you. Psalm 9:10 (NLT)

PRAYER FOR TODAY: *Father God, I ask Your help in reshaping my thinking and age-old habits. I know I can't expect to change everything about my thinking overnight and real change will only come when I learn to rely on You one day at a time. Help me today, Lord! In Your name I ask all these things, Lord Jesus. Amen.*

JANUARY 3
Last Supper Failures

The last day of a long holiday season is what is commonly referred to as the "Last Supper" before hunkering down and getting really serious about this diet resolution business. Most diets start in earnest on the first Monday of January after the holiday season has officially passed. In the past it's become a race to see how much food one can consume before the "real diet" starts on that first January Monday.

"Last supper" thinking can conceivably add an extra two to five pounds of unwanted weight. The notion that diets can only begin on a Monday is simply another ploy of the enemy to keep us from achieving lasting weight loss success. If you want to change – changing your thinking must begin immediately. Attitude and lifestyle changes will not happen automatically as if by osmosis. A conscious effort must be made to change old eating habits and thought patterns. There should be no "last supper" bingeing. Eating healthier doesn't have to mean giving up everything we love. You don't have to say good-bye to fudge and cookies forever. But lifestyle changes will mean you simply cannot eat fudge and cookies *every day* of your life if you want to maintain a healthy weight and lifestyle.

Proper meal planning, portion control and moderate exercise need to become part of your everyday life. You can allow yourself occasional treats but they need to be planned treats. When the voice of the enemy tries to convince you that you can indulge today because tomorrow you will really begin in earnest … don't listen to him! Satan is a liar and he's a pro at convincing people to make bad decisions. Remember – greater is He that is in you than he that is in the world!

If you fail to plan, you plan to fail! ~ Benjamin Franklin

No weapon formed against you will prosper. Isaiah 54:17 (NIV)

PRAYER FOR TODAY: *Father God, I ask that You would help me not give in to the urge to finish all the holiday goodies in my house before I begin my lifestyle changes in earnest. Real change must start today and not after a long weekend binge. Begin today to change my thinking. In Your name I ask all these things, Lord Jesus. Amen.*

JANUARY 4
Put Up or Shut Up

Four days into the New Year and we're quickly exhausting all legitimate excuses for beginning our new lifestyle changes. It's time to put up or shut up. If you've made the decision to get on track to a healthier, lighter you – it starts now ... one day at a time. Looking ahead a few weeks or a few months, the journey before you can seem daunting. Perhaps you're overwhelmed and thinking, "What's the point? It'll take *forever* to lose this weight."

Realistically, did any of us simply wake up one morning to discover we'd gained 40 pounds overnight? No, of course not! Clearly, change will not happen overnight and the weight will not "magically" disappear overnight or in a couple of weeks – perhaps not even over a couple of months. If you've got a significant amount of weight to lose it can only happen one pound at a time. Ask for strength DAILY to keep your focus on getting healthy and not a particular number on the scale. Do not fixate on "the perfect weight!" There is no perfect weight, but there can be a healthy, realistic weight that is age or gender appropriate.

Don't worry about tomorrow or next month or where you hope to be weight-wise by a certain date. Focus only on today. The enemy will use all sorts of tricks to distract you and boredom ranks high on his attack list. Arm yourself from his attacks by knowing how to fight back with the Word of God – use those Scriptures as weapons! God is on your side and His word works. Set realistic, attainable guidelines for balanced eating and realistic goals for your weight loss. If you need to lose 100 pounds don't focus on the number as a whole rather look ahead to five or ten pounds at a time. As always, don't forget to include God in whatever plan or activity you choose. He loves to be included in every aspect of your life because He loves you and wants you to succeed!

I will not worry what I weigh but keep my focus, trust God and pray!

"So don't worry about tomorrow, for tomorrow will bring its own worries. Today's trouble is enough for today." Matthew 6:34 (NLT)

PRAYER FOR TODAY: *Father God, I feel overwhelmed with the amount of weight I need to lose. Please help me to focus on one day at a time and enjoy the journey of each new day rather than fixating on all the pounds I need to drop. Help me to love myself TODAY at this weight, just as I am. In Your name I ask all these things, Lord Jesus. Amen.*

JANUARY 5
Combat Ready

Research studies and plain old common sense tell us that if we take in more calories than we burn, we will gain weight. That's pretty much a given. When we're in the early stages of a lifestyle change sometimes it's necessary to treat the situation as if we're going to war. (Which really, isn't that what we're doing when we decide to get healthy and fit?) A soldier would never show up to a battle without being properly outfitted for the challenge. Likewise, if we're to experience any kind of weight loss success we need to have the proper weapons to endure the long fight ahead of us. We've already talked about using the Scriptures to combat the attacks of the enemy and of course, constant, daily prayer is a must. In addition, there are simple steps we can take to ensure success that doesn't have to include expensive weight loss programs or gym memberships.

One of the most effective strategies for losing weight includes finding an account-ability partner. Enlist the help of a friend, family member, spouse, or weight loss group (if you can afford it) and ask for their help along this journey. Your account-ability partner is someone you should call, text or email in those weak moments for encouragement, prayer and/or support. Secondly, when you're first starting out, write down everything that goes in your mouth. It's so easy to overlook those little BLTs (bites, licks and tastes). Don't overlook your BLTs at Costco on sample day! You can't be accountable for the calories that go in your mouth if you don't have an honest appraisal of exactly what they are. You may be surprised by how many (or how few) calories you actually consume over the course of a day. This is the only body we have and we only get one chance in this lifetime. Life rarely affords us "do-overs." Take care of your "temple" starting today before it's too late!

When in doubt, write it out. When doubt takes seed, it's a friend I need!

For we must all stand before Christ to be judged. We will each receive whatever we deserve for the good or evil we have done in our bodies. 2 Corinthians 6:10 (NLT)

PRAYER FOR TODAY: *Father God, help me to "suit up" with the necessary weapons to fight this ongoing weight-loss battle. I pray that You will help me to align myself with a trusted friend who I can be accountable to, as well as be a friend to them. I know my chances for failure are greater if I fight this battle alone. In Your name I ask all these things, Lord Jesus. Amen.*

JANUARY 6
Overwhelming Your Good Intentions

There is no denying that many of us are rooted and grounded in compulsive eating bondages and addictions to food. Perhaps you're one of the lucky few who simply need to shed a few pounds of baby weight or wants to lower your cholesterol. Whatever led you to your New Year's resolution to get healthier, journaling while you get healthy can be therapeutic and help you zero in on some of your compulsive behaviors. Because so many of us use food for comfort during times of stress, grief and celebration, undoing all of our bad behaviors will be a process and will not happen overnight. Many of us have been abusing food for years stemming all the way back to dysfunctional childhoods. Getting to the core of what triggers binge eating and the love/hate relationship we have with food may be a painful process but one you'll want to explore if you hope to experience true freedom. It's especially important to seek God's favor during this time in order to not only lose weight, but to purge our hearts from whatever led us to abuse food in the first place.

Including God in all your lifestyle changes and relying on the Word of God to bolster your efforts will improve your chances for success in any weight loss program. However, making too many lifestyle changes at one time can lead to an abrupt ending to your good intentions. Don't overwhelm your mind and daily routine with too many changes all at once. This journey is a marathon – not a sprint.

Simply because we do not run across goal lines, slam dunk basketballs, or hit home runs, doesn't mean we can't change the score. ~ Author Unknown

The thief's purpose is to steal and kill and destroy. My purpose is to give life in all its fullness. John 10:10 (NLT)

PRAYER FOR TODAY: *Father God, give me the strength I need today to make practical changes in my life. Help me to turn away from food for comfort and seek You instead. I pray You will take away my desire to satisfy my emotions with food. I know that apart from You, I can do nothing! In Your name I ask all these things, Lord Jesus. Amen.*

JANUARY 7
The PAMMI Curse

Congratulations, we've made it through the first week of getting healthy! Monitoring our progress by weighing ourselves helps us to chart our successes and/ or failures. However, it's important not to become a slave to the scale – or PAMMI, which is an acronym for: Personality Altering, Mood Monitoring Instrument. Letting the scale dictate our moods based on a loss or a gain may seem far-fetched, but if you're a woman, you know exactly what I'm talking about! Don't give in to the enemy whose sole job is to make you unhappy however he can.

Don't become fixated with the numbers on the scale and don't have unrealistic expectations. A two to five pound weight loss for the first week is excellent. If you lost more than that - hooray for you! But if you only lost one pound or less don't beat yourself up. Every pound lost is a victory. Numbers should not be able to steal our joy!

Weighing every day (or after every trip to the gym) quickly becomes just another bondage or addiction. A once-a-week weigh-in is realistic. Keeping a written record will help you stay accountable and on track. It's also a good idea to record your measurements with a measuring tape about once a month. Oftentimes the numbers on the scale aren't relaying what's really happening in our bodies. We may be losing inches that don't reflect on the scale. No change on the scale can oftentimes lead to discouragement and cause us to give up prematurely. The changes in your body may be too subtle to show up on the scale, but the measurements won't lie.

Avoid comparing your weight loss journey with someone else. You are a unique individual, specially created in the Father's image and we're all different. Even if you're following an identical program with your spouse, best friend or identical twin sister or brother, your DNA is different, so your weight loss is specific to YOU. If God has taken the time to number the hairs on your head, you can rest assured that He's got your number when it comes to losing weight! Keep up the good work! Tomorrow is a new day and new week!

A pound lost is a pound gone and hopefully one we'll never see again!

You made all the delicate, inner parts of my body and knit me together in my mother's womb. Psalm 139:13 (NLT)

PRAYER FOR TODAY: *Father God, thank You for a week of lifestyle changes and bringing me that much closer to my goal of healthy living. Grant me wisdom and common sense to incorporate even more changes with this new week. May I not be overwhelmed to the point of stress and may I not become complacent and fall into boredom so I revert back to my bad habits. Help me to overcome laziness in my thoughts and actions. In Your name I ask all these things, Lord Jesus. Amen.*

JANUARY 8
My Daily Low-Cal Bread

The first week of a new eating program may have you anxious to "jump start" your weight loss. Many of the nationally known weight loss programs offer such a program to get you in the door and losing weight quickly. There is nothing wrong with jump starting your weight loss efforts and if you can afford such a program, it may be something for you to check into. But as with anything, there needs to be common sense with sudden lifestyle changes. Physics will generally work in your favor if you've had no restrictions on your eating lifestyle prior to this week. Simply by changing little things such as switching from regular soda to diet soda (or better yet, water) you're already eliminating many unnecessary calories from your diet. Cutting your normal food portions in half can reduce your caloric intake considerably. You will lose weight if you make changes for the better.

It's important however, to resist the idea of fasting or starving yourself to lose weight. Many people assume that by not eating, they're guaranteed to lose weight. While that may be true initially, your body is smarter than you give it credit for. You will ultimately do more damage than good by starving yourself.

Fasting is not a bad thing when it's prompted by God for a spiritual discipline or when seeking direction about a particular spiritual need. However, starving yourself for the sole purpose of losing weight will in fact cause your fat burning metabolism to stop working completely. God designed our bodies to eat regularly. Don't be afraid to eat!

Never skip meals. You must eat to lose!

Do not be like them, for your Father knows what you need before you ask him.
Matthew 6:8 (NIV)

PRAYER FOR TODAY: *Father God, help me to keep all things in balance when it comes to my food and my eating habits. Help me to avoid the temptation to speed up my weight loss by using starvation or quick fixes through weight loss supplements. Keep me rooted and grounded in You and the promises set forth in Your Holy Word. In Your name I ask all these things, Lord Jesus. Amen.*

JANUARY 9
Exorcising Exercise Fears

If you're not making exercise a part of your daily schedule, don't pressure yourself to jump into a rigorous program just yet. It's okay to wait a couple of weeks while you're adjusting to many of the food changes you're making. As with any lifestyle change, if you're considering adding exercise to your routine, consult with your physician before beginning any program; especially if you've not exercised in a long time – *or ever*. Jumping into anything new without doing your research will derail you before you even have a chance to begin. Do your homework and check into different programs or routines before you settle on one specific workout plan.

For now if you feel like you need to get moving, simply make minor changes like parking your car a little farther out or taking the stairs rather than the elevator. Small steps are necessary when first beginning so you'll have the strength and endurance for the long haul.

Excess weight, food addictions and compulsive eating will not change by wishing it away. It's going to take work – hard work, in addition to careful planning and determination. It will be worth it in the long run if you believe in yourself. God already believes in you and wants you to enjoy life to the fullest!

If you want to change your life, you don't need *wish*bone, you need BACKbone!
~ Joyce Meyer

[Praise to God for a Living Hope] Praise be to the God and Father of our Lord Jesus Christ! In his great mercy he has given us new birth into a living hope through the resurrection of Jesus Christ from the dead. 1 Peter 1:3 (NIV)

PRAYER FOR TODAY: *Father God, I pray for direction and guidance as I consider starting an exercise program. I pray for wisdom to start slow and not take on more than I can handle. Give me a good attitude about exercise and guide me to something that will not only be fun, but be good for my mind and body as well. In Your name I ask all these things, Lord Jesus. Amen.*

JANUARY 10
Guard Your Mouth

Experts suggest that eating five or six small meals a day will fuel your body more efficiently and keep you burning calories all day rather than eating "three squares a day." Much the same way a camp fire will burn better with lots of smaller twigs and branches rather than throwing one giant log on it, your body will burn calories more efficiently if you eat small meals throughout the day rather than one giant binge. Never skip meals on purpose.

You should begin each day with a healthy, hi-fiber, hi-protein meal. You're most substantial meal should be first thing in the day because your body has been deprived of nutrition for 8-10 hours. Eat breakfast like a king with a larger meal, lunch like a prince with a smaller meal and dinner like a pauper with an even smaller meal.

Avoid going to bed on a full stomach. Ideally you should wait several hours after eating your evening meal before retiring for the evening. For your in-between meals, stay away from empty calories like chips or crackers and opt for something with fiber and/or protein that will fill you up. A glass of water with an apple or carrots and celery and 1 or 2 oz. of lean turkey will fill you up more than a cookie will. If you need the chips and salsa experience, substitute celery or green peppers with your salsa, or buy large carrots and slice them thin (like a chip) and dip in your salsa. Healthy options are always available if you're willing to put in a little effort.

God cares about what goes IN my mouth as well as what comes OUT of my mouth!

Set a guard over my mouth, LORD; keep watch over the door of my lips. Psalm 141:3 (NIV)

PRAYER FOR TODAY: *Father God, I ask that today You will help me to be aware of what I am putting in my mouth. May I eat only what I have planned for and help me not over-indulge in any area. I pray for balance in all things. In Your name I ask all these things, Lord Jesus. Amen.*

JANUARY 11
Sin-N-Out

Now that we're incorporating lifestyle changes into our daily nutrition, eating out should be looked upon as a very doable challenge. Unless we intend to lock ourselves away like reclusive hermits until we feel as though we've loss sufficient weight, regulated our blood pressure and/or have healthy cholesterol – we're going to have to figure out how to interact with the dining out population.

It's important to set healthy boundaries when eating out. Never confess to anyone that you can't eat there, because *"I'm on a diet."* Sadly, there are a lot of people who will take that as a personal challenge and do everything in their power to thwart your efforts. (Those are usually the well-meaning friends who weigh 90 lbs. or the ones who have stopped trying altogether and want everyone to be as miserable as they are.)

Most restaurants these days serve entrees with humongous portions. Enlist the aid of a friend or spouse to share an entree with you. If you have no takers on the sharing thing, ask the waitress for a "To Go" container IMMEDIATELY when you order your food. When the meal arrives IMMEDIATELY transfer half the portion to the Styrofoam container and save it for lunch the next day. Both of the options have just saved you HALF the calories.

Above all – plan ahead! Go online and study the menu of a restaurant BEFORE you arrive. Figure out healthy options and know what you want to order when you sit down. PLAN, ATTACK AND CONQUER and you'll be *In-n-Out* before you sin it out!

Obstacles are those frightful things you see when you take your eyes off your goal.
~ Henry Ford

So humble yourselves before God. Resist the Devil, and he will flee from you. Draw close to God, and God will draw close to you. James 4:7-8 (NLT)

PRAYER FOR TODAY: *Lord, help me resist the devil and all the slings and arrows he aims at me for my destruction. Help me to stand strong, make healthy choices and choose to do the right thing to care for this temple that You have entrusted to me. In Your name I ask all these things, Lord Jesus. Amen.*

JANUARY 12
Temple Housework

Eventually we are going to have to deal with "weekend" mentality. The temptation to take a "weekend off" from our healthy eating is bound to surface at some point along our journey. For some a weekend can start as early as Thursday night and last through Monday evening. The key to success is, do not buy into that logic. Too many "weekends" off is likely what got most of us to where we are now – overweight and unhappy with ourselves. If you must eat out on a weekend, use common sense. Try to stay away from entrees that have heavy sauces (cream or butter) and choose vegetables or salad as your sides rather than potatoes (mashed, fried or otherwise). When having salad, it's the cheese, croutons and fatty dressings that add the most calories. Opt for a low-cal dressing or vinegar and oil and always order dressings ON THE SIDE. Learn these words! They are your friends when eliminating useless calories.

Eating fast food doesn't have to be tough. Avoid any menu item that has the words "Grande," "Extra-Large," "Super-Size," or "Jumbo" in the description. These descriptions should tell you that these are big "no-no's" for anyone wanting to trim down. Substituting a side salad or plain baked potato is obviously going to be a healthier choice than jumbo fries.

No truer words were ever spoken than those by *Garfield the Cat*, who said, "Diet is *die* with a 'T' on the end. Amen, Garfield! We are not on a diet, but have chosen to clean house and get these temples of ours in better shape. If we're going to be around for the long haul and be about God's business, we need to take care of what He has entrusted to us today!

Discovering our powerlessness is the first step toward wholeness. ~ Taken from: The Twelve Step Life Recovery Devotional, Celebrate Recovery

Then David continued, "Be strong and courageous, and do the work. Don't be afraid or discouraged, for the LORD God, my God, is with you. He will not fail you or forsake you. He will see to it that all the work related to the Temple of the LORD is finished correctly." 1 Chronicles. 28:20 (NLT)

PRAYER FOR TODAY: *Father God, I ask for wisdom and common sense when eating out. Help me to avoid temptation by arming myself with a plan ahead of time before I dine out. You know all my weaknesses, so please strengthen me before I give in to my fleshly desires. In Your name I ask all these things, Lord Jesus. Amen.*

JANUARY 13
And Then He Rested

So we've been battling the bulge; wrestling with restaurant menus and meal planning; tackling the jobs of ridding the pantry of all non-healthy snacks. Hopefully, we're weighing and measuring our food portions; lifting our spirits with positive attitudes; attacking the stairs instead of using the elevator; parking a little farther from the door so we can power walk to the door. We're shoring up our defenses, toting that bale, lifting that hay, banging the drum … blah, blah, blah. Whatever your metaphor – I don't know about you, but all this work and I'm a little tired. It's been nearly two full weeks; shouldn't we take a break at some point? Well *yes and* no.

God did not design our bodies to be in work mode 24/7. Even He rested after all the work He'd done creating our wonderful Earth. Since we're in the very beginning stages of making lifestyle changes that will carry us through the rest of our lives, why not decide to set aside one day a week to rest our weary minds and bodies for the purpose of simple relaxation.

I suggest you relax your mindset in this "Get Fit" state of life. Keep in mind though, that relax is not a synonym for ABANDON. We're not quitting – merely resting. Whether your Sabbath is Saturday or Sunday, God purposely set aside one day a week for us to rest and regroup. Ideally God intended the day to be a day of spending in communion with Him with praise, prayer, worship and fellowship. Why not spend quality time today with loved ones, friends or family? Perhaps you simply need to enjoy some quiet reflection time to just sit and bask in inactivity and talk to God.

Regardless of how you spend your Sabbath, rest up for tomorrow is a new day. Pace yourself and sprinkle your weight loss program with realistic expectations and enough down time to give you strength to see your goals become reality.

He enjoys true leisure who has time to improve his soul's estate.
~ Henry David Thoreau

And God blessed the seventh day and declared it holy, because it was the day when he rested from his work of creation. Genesis 2:3 (NLT)

PRAYER FOR TODAY: *Thank You, Lord for a day of resting my mind, my body and my spirit. May I be rejuvenated and renewed to begin fresh tomorrow with a healthy attitude and mindset. May I enjoy all You have created, today and every day. Thank You for all the immeasurable blessings in my life. In Your name I ask all these things, Lord Jesus. Amen.*

JANUARY 14
KISS Your Weight Good-Bye

How many of us secretly hope to wake up and all of sudden find that we've lost 20 pounds magically overnight? After all – it's been two whole weeks! The cold, hard reality is that 14 days is barely enough time to make a significant change in the way we're feeling or looking. Changes at this point will be subtle. Believe it or not, there is a huge contingency of people who've already ditched their resolutions and fallen right back into old bad habits. Hopefully you aren't one of them.

In order to keep ourselves from becoming yet another weight-loss failure statistic, we must have tenacity for the boring day-to-day business of making lifestyle changes. Boredom is the number one reason most people quit any activity or program. Change things up. Try new recipes. Take a different route to the grocery store. If you've dropped even a couple of pounds find a way to treat yourself to something special that's not food related. A pedicure, a round of golf or a power walk at the mall to window shop might be a good way to re-energize your efforts.

If you've lost more than a couple of pounds rearrange your closet and move some of those smaller sizes towards the front so they're within easy reach. At some point you're going to want to start trying on some of those clothes you've outgrown with the intention that you'll be wearing them comfortably very soon. We've only just begun and once that initial "honeymoon" phase wears off, it quickly becomes all about the work we have yet to do. Remember to **KISS** your weight loss plan: **Keep It Simple Sisters OR Sons!**

The greatest discovery of my generation is that a human being can alter his life by altering his attitudes of mind. ~ William James (1842-1910)

And I am sure that God, who began the good work within you, will continue his work until it is finally finished on that day when Christ Jesus comes back again. Philippians 1:6 (NLT)

PRAYER FOR TODAY: *Father God, grant me unwavering focus regarding the goals I hope to achieve. Give me power over boredom and instill in me that fighter's spirit that will carry me through to the completion of this journey. In Your name I ask all these things, Lord Jesus. Amen.*

JANUARY 15
Walk the Talk

Perhaps it's time we mix it up a little and consider incorporating moderate exercise into our daily routine. (It's always recommended to check with your physician before beginning any new exercise regime.) Exercise doesn't have to be boring or expensive. A good pair of walking shoes can put you on the right track (literally). Hopefully you've already found a reliable accountability partner to help with your eating resolutions as you restructure your food choices. Why not enlist the help of an accountability partner to keep you accountable and committed to a workout program as well.

Don't overdo your first day of any new exercise program, especially if you haven't exercised in a while. Overdoing it too soon causes those underused muscles to rebel and keeps us from advancing any further. If you're not already exercising, pick a short walking route to begin with and choose a comfortable steady pace. (Try your neighborhood, a park, a high school track or the mall.) Ideally you want to challenge your body to walk farther and faster each day.

Check with your local high school or YMCA for public indoor pools. Swimming is a great exercise that won't impact your joints the way walking, jogging or cycling will. Dust off your bicycle or tennis equipment, golf clubs … or whatever will get you moving and off the couch. Maybe you'll want to invest in a Nintendo Wii Fit and make it a family affair. Your spouse and kids will love spending time with you and your body will thank you for it in the long run.

In a perfect world where money is no object, we'd all hire personal trainers and belong to a gym outfitted with every modern piece of exercise equipment. Since a lot of us don't have those options, we need to get creative. Hang tough and focus on what you can do today to make positive changes. Be it eating right, exercising more or studying God's Word for wisdom and strength - do what you have to do DAILY to endure to the finish. Boredom can only defeat you if you let it. Attitude is everything!

The only way to keep the devil from using your mind as a playground is to post a NO TRESPASSING SIGN!

If one person falls, the other can reach out and help. But someone who falls alone is in real trouble. Ecclesiastes 4:10 (NLT)

PRAYER FOR TODAY: *Lord, strengthen my body to begin a healthy exercise program. Help me to find something that's not only fun, but will be of great benefit to my body and my spirit. Thank You for the ability to move what I've got and helping me to do what I can right where I am at. In Your name I ask all these things, Lord Jesus. Amen.*

JANUARY 16
Whine and Crackers

Occasionally there will be one of *those days* when you just want to have a good old fashioned pity party because of your weight issues. It seems so unfair that we're surrounded by people who can eat anything they want and never gain a pound. It seems unfair that when we're working so hard to control our food portions and eating healthy foods, someone brings donuts to work. It seems unfair that we've got a friend doing the same program as we are and they're down a whole pants size while we're still squeezing into our fat girl jeans.

There are times I've even gone so far as to blame God for my weight problems, because after all, He made me this way. Some days it just feels easier to play the blame game rather than pointing that finger of accusation back at myself.

Playing the blame game or having a pity party proves two things – most of us have a terrible two-year-old living on the inside of us AND whining is easier than hard work. We need to reprimand that inner whiny two-year-old and get tough with ourselves. Besides … hosting a pity party is one party for which there are no complimentary hostess gifts!

Haven't we all told our children at one time or another "Life's not fair – suck it up!" Losing weight and getting healthy is the perfect time to remind ourselves *"Life's not fair, so suck it up!"* There will be "off" days. If losing weight were easy, it wouldn't be a billion dollar a year business. Don't let the *off days* discourage you to the point of throwing in the towel. One day soon you'll be the person your friends are whining about because you're looking so good. Quit your whining and suck it up! There are NO QUICK FIXES!

Obesity is a mental state, a disease brought on by boredom and disappointment. ~ Cyril Connolly, *The Unquiet Grave*

No matter what happens, always be thankful, for this is God's will for you who belong to Christ Jesus. 1 Thessalonians 5:18 (NLT)

PRAYER FOR TODAY: *Lord, forgive me for my self-absorption and my whining and complaining. I know there are people whose lives are far more tragic than mine and I am blessed. Thank You that I have food options. Forgive me and thank You for helping me to see the bigger picture. In Your name I ask all these things, Lord Jesus. Amen.*

JANUARY 17
A Loser is as a Loser Does

There is a realty show called *The Biggest Loser*. It's a weight loss show that follows the trials of severely obese people. It's a great show for motivating those of us at home to get off the couch and make changes in our lives. Few of us are afforded the luxury of being isolated on a weight loss ranch for months at a time with the singular goal of losing weight. Given the same exact circumstances, away from jobs, kids, school and day-to-day responsibilities and given the advantage of working out six or eight hours *each day*, we'd all lose massive amounts of weight in a short period of time. Real-life rarely allows that. That's not real life – but reality TV.

Most of us *do* have busy lives with jobs and households to run and we're lucky to squeeze in 30 minutes of exercise three or four times *a week*. It's okay to set goals with regards to our weight loss, but keep them realistic. Rather than focusing on a specific number like, "I'm going to lose 20 pounds by the end of the month if it kills me!" *(Oh really?)* Set your sights on something more easily attainable such as "At the end of one month, I want to be able to walk a mile without gasping for air." Or, "In one month I hope to be able to bend over and comfortably touch my toes without blacking out when I stand up." Keep it real.

Obviously your goals will change as your body and your weight changes. Set mini goals each week. Your goals can be as simple as "I will resist the temptation of eating the complimentary bread that comes before my meal." Or, "I will not give in to the urge to eat the candy sitting on the receptionist's desk at work this week." Resisting temptations are every bit as important as going to the gym or losing five pounds this week. Learning to say "no" to unwise food choices is half the battle of losing weight. Even if you only lose one pound this week, give yourself a pat on the back because you are blessed to be a "Loser!" Look at the realistic things you can accomplish this week – and then do them!

Learn from yesterday, live for today, hope for tomorrow. ~ Unknown Source

For I can do everything through Christ, who gives me strength. Philippians 4:13 (NLT)

PRAYER FOR TODAY: *I pray for the emotional and mental strength to resist temptations today. I pray for the time to be able to exercise today. I pray my body will function as You designed it and that my heart and my lungs will be strengthened by my efforts. Help my arms, my legs and my mind work in perfect harmony so I can maximize whatever exercise I get today. In Your name I ask all these things, Lord Jesus. Amen.*

JANUARY 18
Pinch a Penny – Squeeze a Quarter

Last week while hiking I had the pleasure of sharing the trail with a woman who was a personal trainer who gave me some valuable hiking tips. One of the greatest tips was that when walking downhill, try to clench your butt cheeks the entire downward slope like you're pinching a quarter. This helps to firm up those glutes and if practiced frequently, you'll eventually achieve those much sought after "Buns of Steel."

Since receiving that nugget of wisdom, I'm reminded to clench my glutes on the downhill slopes. Try to get a visual of squeezing a quarter between your butt cheeks and holding it there for the descent. I dare you to do this without laughing. If you're walking with a friend remind your hiking partner, *"Squeeze the quarter, girl!"*

"Squeezing quarters" isn't just for hiking. Try this "squeezing" technique throughout your normal daily routines, like walking to and from the car or around the office at work; up and down the stairs at home or while vacuuming the carpet. As long as the maximus is in fact, maximus, we should endeavor to do our best to reduce it to a minimus and pray that underneath that protective layer of gluteus maximus, we'll uncover those dormant Buns of Steel. Full steam ahead – each day brings us one day closer to walking in victory and pinching a quarter in your butt cheeks will help your victory walk look *fab-u-lous, dahling!*

If you don't make a total commitment to whatever you're doing, then you start looking to bail out the first time the boat starts leaking. It's tough enough getting that boat to shore with everybody rowing, let alone when a guy stands up and starts putting his life jacket on. ~ Lou Holtz

You are tempted in the same way that everyone else is tempted. But God can be trusted not to let you be tempted too much, and he will show you how to escape from your temptations. 1 Corinthians 10:13 (CEV)

PRAYER FOR TODAY: *Thank You, Lord for always challenging me to become a better person each and every day. Some days I feel like giving up, but I know You purposely put people in my life to encourage and support me. I'm getting too old to keep giving up and starting over. Please let THIS year, be the year of my success. In Your name I ask all these things, Lord Jesus. Amen.*

JANUARY 19
Food For Thought

If we've trained ourselves to be emotional eaters it's common to use food not just when we're depressed but in cases of sadness, worry, anxiety and stress. Many of us also use food in times of celebration. We are "Seafood" eaters. Or more appropriately "*See*-food," meaning if we see it – we eat it!

Using food to pacify wounded emotions will only lead to greater weight gain which only increases depression or anxiety. It's a vicious cycle that must stop. We don't want to keep repeating the same mistakes and patterns and never defeat this foe. Is this an area of your life that you are unwilling or unable to lay down? Even if we've experienced great success in the past but we're repeating self-destructive weight gain patterns, we need to get to the source of our emotional eating.

The first step towards healing is admitting there is a problem. The second step is working out these issues one at a time, facing our weaknesses head on and taking it one day at a time. The enemy would have us believe we're the only one who ever struggles with these suffocating addictions. The good news is – the enemy is a liar, and our Father in Heaven promises never to leave us or forsake us.

The definition of insanity is doing the same thing over and over again and expecting different results. ~ Albert Einstein

So let us come boldly to the throne of our gracious God. There we will receive his mercy, and we will find grace to help us when we need it. Hebrews 4:16 (NLT)

PRAYER FOR TODAY: *I confess my addiction to food to You, Lord. Forgive me for my weaknesses. Lift me up and make me strong when I am weak. Help me to resist temptation and trust in You to guide my paths. I'm afraid I'll continue to live this way unless You step in and change my temperament and my self-destructive habits. I cannot do this without Your constant help and intervention. Give me this day my daily bread and may that bread be enough to satisfy my spirit and my flesh. In Your name I ask all these things, Lord Jesus. Amen.*

JANUARY 20
Attitude is Everything

Ever had one of those days when you're afraid to get up and look at yourself in the mirror? If we've publicly admitted our weaknesses with food, the enemy may be working overtime to heap a load of guilt and shame upon us. He can make us feel like marked souls as though we should have a scarlet letter on our chests.

No one can make us feel shame unless we choose to pick that mantle up and carry it around, and that would be counterproductive to our New Year's resolution. We're not having any of that guilt or shame stuff, devil! You are a thief and a liar!

There is a certain freedom that comes with purging the soul. Now that the proverbial cat is out of the bag, so to speak, the only place left to go now is forward. No more slinking around letting that little voice creep into our heads that tells us we're no good because of our weight. At one time or another, most of us hear those little niggling voices of doubt whenever we feel like we've got a physical imperfection. Be it excess weight, bad acne, a giant nose, an overbite – or whatever "thorn in your flesh" the enemy uses against you to make you feel ugly or inadequate.

Rather than focusing on our negative features we must choose to adopt a healthier, more positive attitude. None of us knows how many days we'll have here on this Earth. We've wasted far too many days as it is crying over perceived physical imperfections. Today accept the things you can't change and truly commit to working towards the goal of changing the things you can change such as an obsession with food. Tell yourself, "one step at a time will eventually bring me one step closer to a healthier, happier me!"

The hardest part of any weight loss program is not what I put into my mouth – but what thoughts I put into my head. Attitude is everything.

*The entire law is summed up in a single command: "Love your neighbor **as yourself**."* [Emphasis added] Galatians 5:14 (NIV)

PRAYER FOR TODAY: *Lord, I've spent a lot of my life disliking who I am, so it's hard for me to obey Your Word to "love myself." I've been guilty of negative self-talk and I know that saddens You. Please forgive me and help me to dwell on all the positive qualities You've blessed me with. Help me to remember love is not based on physical appearance. In Your name I ask all these things, Lord Jesus. Amen.*

JANUARY 21
There Will Be Meltdowns

Occasionally life throws you an unexpected curve ball that spells disaster, and in one fell swoop you manage to undo three weeks' worth of hard work with regards to your eating program. Your computer freaks out and erases a bunch of your documents. One of your children has a full-blown crisis of epic proportions that you're unable to fix for them. Your checkbook is a disaster zone and you've got an unexpected bill to pay. You barely slept last night and had horrible nightmares when you finally did doze off.

Any one of these is enough to send you foraging in the pantry for something sweet, salty or crunchy. Pick your poison. Those dark-chocolate covered almonds your spouse hid in the pantry call your name and maybe you give in and have a full out binge. Of course, the almond binge is closely followed by bingeing's second cousin – Mr. Guilt. BEFORE you fall face down in a giant vat of chips, STOP! Before you fall completely off the weight loss wagon you need to pick yourself up before the wagon backs up and runs over you a few more times.

We're not perfect and sometimes life will just *be life* and there will be curve balls and disasters with your kids and bills and problems and ... *meltdowns*. Welcome to the real world. To counteract a meltdown, adjust your calories for the remainder of the day. Plan a small dinner with high protein and low carbs AND NO MORE SNACKING for the rest of the day!

Don't give the meltdown its due and keep it in perspective. Pray for the strength to survive the next meltdown (because there will always be meltdowns). Look for solutions for coping that don't include chocolate. Remember – God is still in control.

It is not enough for a man to know how to ride; he must know how to fall. ~ Mexican Proverb

So do not fear, for I am with you; do not be dismayed, for I am your God. I will strengthen you and help you; I will uphold you with my righteous right hand. Isaiah 41:10 NIV

PRAYER FOR TODAY: *Help me to keep things in perspective and help me to avoid sweating the small stuff. I know that You are in control – today and always. Forgive me for my meltdown and help tomorrow to be a new and better day. In Your name I ask all these things, Lord Jesus. Amen.*

JANUARY 22
How Feel You?

Most of us know we aren't supposed to live by our feelings, but some days *"feel"* harder than others. Compounding problems throughout our day coupled with nasty traffic or pounding headache and before you know it you *feel* like you want to eat your weight in Oreos. But, if we've resorted to this kind of logic in the past we know giving in to *feelings* only leads to self-loathing, self-hatred and intense feelings of failure and guilt. If we hope to keep those New Year's resolution, we need to do our best to ignore our *feelings*.

Feelings are fickle things that can have us do (or not do) all sorts of things if we let them control us. You make a promise to go and workout with a friend, but you *feel lazy* today, so you blow her off. You promise to visit a sick friend but you don't feel like driving and fighting traffic, so you don't go. You don't *feel* like weighing out your food portions today because you're short on time, so you simply guess at the amounts. You *do feel* like giving in to that urge to eat ice cream for dinner instead of 3 oz. of chicken and a salad because you had a bad day at work.

God designed us to be emotional beings, but he didn't intend for us to live our lives based solely on *how we feel*. Feelings will rarely line up with doing the right thing. *NOBODY* feels like working out or keeping a food diary or resisting donuts or visiting a sick friend or cutting up our charge cards … or fill in the blanks as you see fit.

Remember in the *Star Wars* movie when Yoda asked Luke Skywalker, *"How feel you?"* Well guess what? Don't give your feelings a chance to control you! Pray about decisions before you let your feelings convince you otherwise. Choose rather than *feel!*

Feelings are much like waves, we can't stop them from coming but we can choose which one to surf. ~ Jonatan Mårtensson

You will keep him in perfect peace all who trust in you, whose thoughts are stayed on you. Isaiah 26:3 (NLT)

PRAYER FOR TODAY: *Lord, help me not to live according to my feelings or make decisions based on how I feel, but rather on wise counsel, sound judgment, logic and facts. I pray for restful sleep, to be rejuvenated as I rest so I may wake refreshed with a clear mind and renewed spirit. In Your name I ask all these things, Lord Jesus. Amen.*

JANUARY 23
Stupid is as Stupid Does

I have a number of friends who embarked upon a month-long weight loss challenge that began on January 1st. I don't think any of them are calling this challenge a "resolution" per se, since the definition of resolution is, *the act or process of resolving or the action of solving.* The only thing to be solved at the end of their 30 days is who will walk away with the cash prize – the proceeds of which came from each of them through a minimum buy-in.

After 19 days, one contestant is boasting of their 20-pound weight loss, due primarily to a diet of nothing more than a liquid diet shake. Another contestant was heard proclaiming that "I'll kill myself or die trying in order to win that money." While yet another vowed "they were going to starve to lose weight and win the money."

Our bodies don't respond well to sudden, drastic drops in weight especially if it's done in a very unhealthy manner. It wreaks havoc on our fat-burning system. Science tells us fad diets don't work and weight quickly lost, quickly returns.

Set your goals on 1-2 pounds of weight loss per week. You may lose a little more or little less than that each week, but be realistic and don't get hung up on the numbers. Weight lost slowly over a longer period of time, ensures your ultimate success because you're being smart. Remember, don't be stupid – you have to eat, to lose!

"Momma always said, 'stupid is as stupid does.'" ~ **Forrest Gump**

Do not be wise in your own eyes; fear the LORD and shun evil. Proverbs 3:7 (NIV)

PRAYER FOR TODAY: *Thank You, Lord for wisdom and common sense. Help me not be overly anxious or in an unrealistic hurry to lose weight. I know that will cause me to do something stupid that won't be good for my body. I pray for patience to tackle this weight loss journey one day at a time. Thank You for all Your many blessings. In Your name I ask all these things, Lord Jesus. Amen.*

JANUARY 24
Mind Over Mouth

"Ugh … I look so fat in these pants. Could my butt be any bigger?" "This haircut is so hideous; it makes me look like a bowling pin." "I'm so fat and ugly! What was God thinking when He made me this way?"

Does any of this sound at all familiar? Self-loathing comments aren't limited to the facially challenged or reclusive misfits of society. Most people struggle with moments of weakness regarding their perceived physical shortcomings when they set out to lose weight. Maintaining a positive attitude for the long haul of this weight loss resolution is going to prove challenging, to say the least. All it takes is one little thought or misspoken word to upset the apple cart of our emotions – especially if we're prone to negative thoughts regarding our physical bodies.

Admitting we have a problem with food is the first step toward healing. A second important step is retraining our thoughts AND our mouths. We must stop the negative talk, self-loathing and self-hatred. As a parent, we'd be crushed if we heard one of our children speak ugly thoughts about themselves. In the same way, our ugly talk about ourselves grieves our Heavenly Father.

To achieve successful weight loss it's recommended that we get in the habit of weighing our food portions so we can control our calories. It's time to start weighing the words of our mouth by eliminating unhealthy talk from our vocabulary as well so we can have a healthy self-esteem!

One of the things I learned the hard way was that it doesn't pay to get discouraged. Keeping busy and making optimism a way of life can restore your faith in yourself. ~ Lucille Ball

What goes into a man's mouth does not make him 'unclean,' but what comes out of his mouth, that is what makes him 'unclean. Matthew 15:11 (NIV)

PRAYER FOR TODAY: *Forgive me, Lord, for my negative self-talk. Help me stop speaking the negative thoughts in my head. And while we're at it – help me to stop the negative thoughts before they even take form in my brain. I know You created me in Your image and You think I'm fabulous! In Your name I ask all these things, Lord Jesus. Amen.*

JANUARY 25
Get Thee Behind Me Satan

Some days it seems as though the universe, the devil and even well-meaning friends are all conspiring together to do battle against our willpower to succeed. Maybe by now you've found a good rhythm with healthy eating; you're keeping track of how many calories you're consuming. You're exercising three to five days a week and finding a little extra breathing room in your *fat-girl jeans*. Praise God for victories!

Within the span of a few short days however, the potential to undo all of that hard work looms, waiting to pierce our vulnerabilities like a giant thorn in the flesh. A trip to Costco on sample day; a baby shower or NFL football playoff party or even a sick day at home can quickly undue all of our hard work.

Okay, Universe … enough already! We're human after all – not SUPER-human! Unfortunately the world doesn't stop spinning on its axis simply because we've decided to adopt a healthier lifestyle.

Before we dive in on full attack mode, stop – think – and take a couple of deep breaths. Say a quick prayer and if you still want to sample, take a second to tug on the waistband of your pants. Can you breathe easier because you have room? Is your muffin top spilling over your jeans or is it finally shrinking? If the answer is "YES," isn't that feeling better than satisfying your sweet tooth? The more frequently you exercise your "no thank-you" response, the easier it becomes to exorcise your inner demons and banish your excess weight! Kick the enemy to the curb by telling him, "GET THEE BEHIND ME, SATAN!"

Faith makes things possible, not easy. ~ Author Unknown

I plead with you to give your bodies to God. Let them be a living and holy sacrifice – the kind he will accept. When you think of what he has done for you, is this too much to ask? Romans 12:1 (NLT)

PRAYER FOR TODAY: *Lord, I am so grateful for the willpower to resist the temptation of excess food. Strengthen my will to be able to say 'no' on a regular basis. Help me to take better care of my body and make it a holy habitation for Your Holy Spirit. In Your name I ask all these things, Lord Jesus. Amen.*

JANUARY 26
One Day Closer

We shouldn't be surprised to hear that a number of people have already ditched their New Year's resolutions to lose weight and get healthy. Three and a half weeks can feel like a lifetime when depriving ourselves of our favorite foods – especially since it may seem as though we've little to show for it yet.

If we're being diligent, it's important to realize that changes may be happening to our bodies that we can't see yet. We have to ask ourselves what we're hoping to truly accomplish with this resolution. Depending on our many moods, the answer is subject to change. Do we really want to get healthier or are we looking for a specific number on the scale?

Losing weight may remain at the top of the list, but at some point, we need to adjust our attitudes so at the end of the year, we can look at ourselves in the mirror and like who we are – regardless of the number. For many – that would be no big deal, but not all of us possess a healthy self-esteem so this may be a journey that will be difficult to traverse.

Hang in there. Hopefully, we've convinced enough friends to come along on the journey with us so we'll have company in our struggles. Thank goodness we can rest in the knowledge God is with us and will remain by our side indefinitely regardless of what we weigh.

I know not what the future holds, but I know who holds the future.
~ Author Unknown

"For I know the plans I have for you," declares the LORD, "plans to prosper you and not to harm you, plans to give you hope and a future. Then you will call upon me and come and pray to me, and I will listen to you. You will seek me and find me when you seek me with all your heart." Jeremiah 29:11 (NIV)

PRAYER FOR TODAY: *Thank You, Lord for seeing me through to this point. I pray You will help me to learn from any mistakes made this past week. May I continually move forward and conquer bad habits. I pray each day will bring me one day closer to a happier, healthier me. In Your name I ask all these things, Lord Jesus. Amen.*

JANUARY 27
Baby Steps

I've made mention of a support group that I attended through my church called *Living Free*. This was a group that used a 12-step program in dealing with food addictions. The following are the 12 steps used in many addiction recovery classes: *We ...*

1. We admitted we were powerless over our addictions and compulsive behaviors. That our lives had become unmanageable.
2. Came to believe that a power greater than ourselves could restore us to sanity.
3. Made a decision to turn our will and our lives over to the care of God.
4. Made a searching and fearless moral inventory of ourselves.
5. Admitted to God, to ourselves, and to another human being, the exact nature of our wrongs.
6. Were entirely ready to have God remove all these defects of character.
7. Humbly asked Him to remove all our shortcomings.
8. Made a list of all persons we had harmed and became willing to make amends to them all.
9. Made direct amends to such people whenever possible, except when to do so would injure them or others.
10. Continued to take personal inventory and when we were wrong, promptly admitted it.
11. Sought through prayer and meditation to improve our conscious contact with God, praying only for knowledge of His will for us and power to carry that out.
12. Having had a spiritual experience as the result of these steps, we tried to carry this message to others, and practice these principles in all our affairs.

These 12-steps won't magically cure us of our food addictions. If we have an unhealthy relationship with food there's no better place to start than with the first step. After that – we take another step and then another. They don't have to be big steps – baby steps will get us there.

Freedom lies in being bold. ~ Robert Frost

And I know that nothing good lives in me, that is, in my sinful nature. I want to do what is right, but I can't. Romans 7:18 (NLT)

PRAYER FOR TODAY: *Lord, I ask for the courage to take the steps necessary that will move me towards healing. I don't want to live in bondage to my flesh any longer. I know I cannot succeed unless You step in and help me. In Your name I ask all these things, Lord Jesus. Amen.*

JANUARY 28
Expect the Unexpected

It goes without saying that there will be unexpected derailments of your weight loss train once you've finally gotten yourself on track. Losing weight and getting healthy is a declaration of war on fat, sugar, carbohydrates and sloppy living. Every day there must be a renewing of your mind and attitude.

The enemy will try to subtly attack you on your weight loss journey because he wants you to fail. During these winter months cold and flu bugs lurk on every door handle or debit card machine waiting for a chance to launch an attack. It's important to listen to your body. If you need to adjust your diet for a cold or the flu, listen to your body and make sure you're eating sufficient calories to fight your illness.

Once your cold or flu has passed, get yourself right back on the weight loss New Year's resolution train and go full speed ahead. You may want to be slightly more restrictive the first few days after an illness to compensate for the extra carbs your body has been consuming during sickness. Getting back on track may seem harder than ever, especially if your body is in a slightly weakened state from illness. Resuming exercise will be especially tough, so do what you can without injuring your weakened body. Go slow at first; listen to your body.

Don't let an unexpected sickness derail you permanently. Otherwise, a year from now, you'll be in the same place as you are today – full of excuses and stuck at the dead end station of "Big Buttville" or "Backfat Junction" and no closer to your healthy goals or desired weight. Put on your armor and re-board the train immediately after your illness has passed. NO EXCUSES!

If your body's not right, the rest of your day will go all wrong. Take care of yourself. ~ V.L. Allineare

Don't become so well-adjusted to your culture that you fit into it without even thinking. Instead, fix your attention on God. You'll be changed from the inside out. Readily recognize what he wants from you, and quickly respond to it. Unlike the culture around you, always dragging you down to its level of immaturity, God brings the best out of you, develops well-formed maturity in you. Romans 12:2 (The Message Bible)

PRAYER FOR TODAY: *Thank You, Lord for bringing me through bouts of sickness. Being sick gives me a greater appreciation for good health. Help me to do my part to maintain optimum health as much as I'm able. Help me to get back on track and eat right, exercise and renew my mind, spirit and attitude. In Your name I ask all these things, Lord Jesus. Amen.*

JANUARY 29
She Who is Faith-Full

Reading the Scriptures opens our eyes to God's infinite power. God has the power to change situations including the will of people, control the climate and even the direction the sun moves. It can give us pause for thought wondering if God can cause the sun to actually stop moving in the sky (see Joshua 10:13-14) why doesn't He answer my simple prayer of "Lord, take away my craving for sweets?" There are times when it seems as though the more fervent our prayers – the more temptations we encounter. Does God have a really weird sense of humor? Is God mad at me? Is God treating me like an unloved step-child?

Of course the answers to all of these questions are a resounding "NO." God's Word is filled with reassuring words that God loves us, died for us and wants us to operate in the gifts of the Spirit (love, joy, peace, etc.). God however, is not some magical genie in a bottle that is waiting to grant our every wish. Nor is he, Monty Hall wanting to play *"Let's Make a Deal"* with us.

God is our loving Heavenly Father, and as a father, he knows our wants, needs and desires intimately. He wants the best for us, but He's not going to hand us everything on a silver platter. God wants us to trust in Him and lean not on our own understanding.

As a parent, we don't automatically give our children everything they desire, especially if we know that what they're asking for is something they aren't mature enough to handle. God designed our bodies to be unique and He knows what will work best for each of us. Clearly even with weight loss, there are lessons to learn. If God granted our every request, we'd have no need of faith at all. And without faith, we'd have no need of God.

Before you begin a thing remind yourself that difficulties and delays quite impossible to foresee are ahead. ... You can only see one thing clearly, and that is your goal. Form a mental vision of that and cling to it through thick and thin. ~ Kathleen Norris

And without faith it is impossible to please God, because anyone who comes to him must believe that he exists and that he rewards those who earnestly seek him. Hebrews 11:6 (NLT)

PRAYER FOR TODAY: Lord, forgive me for behaving like a spoiled child who always wants my own way. I want to be in Your perfect will – to learn what You have to teach me throughout this journey of weight loss. Give me the strength I need to resist temptation. Help me to walk in love, joy, peace, faith and especially self-control. Help me not to worry about tomorrow. In Your name I ask all these things, Lord Jesus. Amen.

JANUARY 30
Manna from Heaven

The book of Exodus contains so much *food for thought*. When the Israelites complained about all the good food they left back in Egypt, God supernaturally provided them with quail and manna to eat – enough for millions of people – and sufficient quantities of both manna and quail DAILY for 40 years. That's pretty huge!

Can you imagine eating the same thing – day in and day out, for 40 straight years? There are pros and cons of repetitive meals. While that would certainly make life easier without so many choices, it could eventually get boring. But it'd be really easy to stay on your eating program.

On the other hand, there is something to be said for variety. The difference between this generation and the Israelites is junk food is a phone call away for easy delivery or a quick trip to the *Quick Trip*. Moses didn't make a trip to Costco for *Snickers* bars and bagels in bulk. The Israelites ate what was presented to them and that had to sustain them.

Perhaps we should consider adopting an *"Exodus"* state of mind with regards to meal planning. If you are struggling with too many choices perhaps it's time to limit your choices – for a while anyway. Remember to WRITE EVERYTHING down that you're eating. Consider taking the time to write out a menu for the next day (or the next week) in order to limit your options. Knowing one day ahead of time exactly what you will be eating will help you to stay accountable and on target.

The one thing that can be learned from reading the book of Exodus is regardless of what's on our menu or our plates, it's important to always remember it is God who provides for us. Before each meal why not take a second to thank Jehovah-Jireh our provider.

In order to change we must be sick and tired of being sick and tired.
~ Author Unknown

GOD *spoke to Moses, "I've listened to the complaints of the Israelites. Now tell them: 'At dusk you will eat meat and at dawn you'll eat your fill of bread; and you'll realize that I am GOD, your God.'"* Exodus 16:11-12 (The Message Bible)

PRAYER FOR TODAY: *Thank You, Lord, for the many varieties of food You have provided. Help me to stay strong and committed to my eating plan. Help me not to overindulge and help me to be diligent in writing down all that I'm eating. In Your name I ask all these things, Lord Jesus. Amen.*

JANUARY 31
The Time Difference

If we are in that group of people who suffer from low self-esteem (or no self-esteem) we need to be realistic and accept that losing weight will only solve some of our issues. Losing weight or reaching our desired goal weight may significantly lower blood pressure and cholesterol and help us to climb stairs without huffing and puffing. Honestly, if we achieve both of those goals, we should be ecstatic. If we aren't happy with ourselves and never have been regardless of what our weight is now or has been in the past, weight loss won't magically fix those things. We may have deeper emotional scars that need healing.

Athletes, especially runners, achieve the most success when they look ahead toward the finish line and visualize themselves crossing the line to victory. It's been said, that when a runner has any kind of lead it can be detrimental for them to turn around and look behind them to see who's chasing them.

With this weight loss journey we need to strive to adopt a similar game plan. If we've been at our desired goal weight in the past and been unhappy with ourselves how can we make this time successful? If we hope to achieve weight loss success by the end of the year it's imperative to learn and practice self-acceptance. That means accepting all our flaws and less than perfect body.

We only get one chance at this and we can't turn back time to correct our previous wrongs. We CAN look towards our ultimate goal and imagine success *this year*. We need to imagine crossing the finish line and liking who we are and who we will become once we've made our healthy lifestyle changes – regardless of the number on the scale.

Respect yourself and others will respect you. ~ Confucius

I don't know about you, but I'm running hard for the finish line. I'm giving it everything I've got. No sloppy living for me! I'm staying alert and in top condition. I'm not going to get caught napping, telling everyone else all about it and then missing out myself. 1 Corinthians 9:26-27 (The Message Bible)

PRAYER FOR TODAY: *Lord, help me to run this race with endurance and not look back to my past failures but look toward the future. Help me to see myself as succeeding at my goals; help me to believe I am created in Your image. Help me to see the beauty buried within me and not concentrate on my imperfect outer shell. Thank You for continuing to love me in spite of my weird attitudes and paranoid idiosyncrasies. In Your name I ask all these things, Lord Jesus. Amen.*

FEBRUARY 1
Play 60 – Laugh 60

The NFL partners with several organizations including The American Heart Association to combat childhood obesity with a program they call, NFL *Play* 60. Basically, it's a challenge designed to encourage kids to get active and play for at least one hour a day. With techno-goodies galore the 21st century is raising an obese generation of couch potatoes.

We've likely all been guilty of couch potatoing on occasion which is why the *Play* 60 challenge is a great idea not just for children – but for adults, as well. A well-balanced exercise routine should include a mix of both cardio and weight lifting several times a week. If you're new to exercise, shoot for 2-3 days of strength training/weight lifting and cardio each week.

Without variety, exercise can quickly become bor-ing and many people ditch their programs shortly after starting. (Those are probably the same people that give up on their New Year's resolutions within the first two weeks!) Hiking, running the bleachers at the high school track or stairs at your office building provide a great cardio workout for those that hate the idea of joining a gym. Experts recommend walking 10,000 steps per day. Pedometers that track your steps can be purchased for around $5.00 and are a great tool to keep you on target.

The Play 60 challenge should be expanded to include *Laugh* 60. That's a two-fold challenge that not only benefits your body but your spirit as well. If you're going to exercise (and you should be exercising) why not make it fun? Laugh at your efforts and strive to *Play* 60 today!

A good, real, unrestrained, hearty laugh is a sort of glorified internal massage, performed rapidly and automatically. It manipulates and revitalizes corners and unexplored crannies of the system that are unresponsive to most other exercise methods. ~ Author unknown

Tell God what you need, and thank him for all he has done. Then you will experience God's peace, which exceeds anything we can understand. His peace will guard your hearts and minds as you live in Christ Jesus. Philippians 4:6-7 (NLT)

PRAYER FOR TODAY: I bless You, Lord Jesus for the wonderful gift of laughter. Laughter truly is a good medicine. Please remind me to partake of a dose of laughter every few hours as needed. Help me to remember it's the one medicine I can never overdose on. Thank You for all life's many blessings. In Your name I ask all these things, Lord Jesus. Amen.

FEBRUARY 2
"IT'S NOT FAIR!"

We've done everything right. We've stuck to our meal plan – maybe not 100% to the letter, but fairly close to that. We've been exercising four or five days a week, maybe more. We're giving our self a daily pep talk and loving our self and reversed our negative attitudes. Yet in spite of all our best efforts, in this the beginning of the second month of our New Year's resolution, our weight remains the same as when we started as have most of our body measurements. What now?

When you've given it your all and have little to show for it, how do you keep a positive attitude when it feels like there's absolutely nothing to celebrate? You feel as though you're being punished. If we've been victims of fad diets and years of yo-yo dieting – repeated weight loss and weight gain, your metabolism may be on a permanent hiatus and nothing short of an act of God is going to get it to move and burn fat.

Rather than succumbing to the temptation to eat an entire sleeve of packaged cookies, maybe what's needed is to drop to the floor on our faces before God and pour out our hurts and the emotional pain of dealing with unwanted weight. God sees our hearts and He knows how troubled we are because of these weight/body issues. Be comforted knowing that God hears you.

We cannot give up or give in. Press forward through this trial and trust God to bring you through. Nowhere in the Bible is it written that *life is fair*. God designed us to be unique and individual. Who are we to complain that *"He made me SO unique that what works for everyone else, doesn't work for me."* Some days it is a stretch to remain positive, but stretching our faith muscles will ultimately bring us closer to the heart of God.

Without the burden of afflictions it is impossible to reach the height of grace. The gift of grace increases as the struggles increase. ~ Saint Rose of Lima

Come to me, all you who labor and are heavy laden, and I will give you rest.
Matthew 11:28 (NKJ)

PRAYER FOR TODAY: *Lord, I will not give up or give in to this desire to wallow in self-pity. Help me to stand strong against affliction and temptation. May I grow stronger in grace and character as a result of my adversity and this "thorn in my flesh." Thank You for life's many blessings. In Your name I ask all these things, Lord Jesus. Amen.*

FEBRUARY 3
Weight For It

In the early stages of any weight loss program, it's tempting to want to weigh yourself on a daily basis. For those of us who suffer from a serious addiction to the scale – or PAMMI (Personality Altering, Mood Monitoring Instrument) it's important to find balance when monitoring our weight loss with the scale.

Being out of balance in the opposite direction can be equally destructive. Refusing to get on the scale and opting for total denial can be a foolish oversight on our parts. While it's not healthy to weigh every time we eat, we can't completely ignore the scale and never weigh ourselves. Going from obsessive PAMMI checks and weighing constantly to never stepping on a scale can be equally as detrimental to our emotional balance.

If we're weighing daily, it's not uncommon to have a sudden weight gain overnight. This gain is not necessarily indicative of over-indulgence. There are many reasons that we can have a sudden slight gain that are just temporary increases such as water weight; too much sodium in our diet or constipation. By weighing too frequently a slight weight increase might just become the catalyst that will undo all of our hard work and push us face first into a sudden binge.

Limit your weighing to no more than once a week, or even once a month. Once we reach our healthy weight, the way our clothes fit is a good reference to what's happening with our weight.

Getting healthy and gaining freedom over food addictions should be first and foremost in lifestyle changes, but gaining freedom over an unhealthy addiction to the scale rates a close second. Eventually many of us become sick and tired of being in bondage to food and the scale. Our ultimate goal should be to live free and not let any of our fleshly desires control us.

When the world says, "Give up," Hope whispers, "Try it one more time."
~ Author Unknown

"I have told you all this so that you may have peace in me. Here on earth you will have many trials and sorrows. But take heart, because I have overcome the world." John 16:33 (NLT)

PRAYER FOR TODAY: *Thank You, Lord for whatever weight loss I achieve. I pray I will stand strong against the enemy and defeat any and all discouragement. May my body obey the dictates of a healthy lifestyle and do what You designed it do—get healthy and trim. May I go forward and not look behind, focusing only on the future and my success. In Your name I ask all these things, Lord Jesus. Amen.*

FEBRUARY 4
What's Eating You?

Do you eat to live or live to eat? Believe it or not, there are actually people who possess that natural caveman propensity which means they merely eat for survival and don't eat based solely on their emotions.

For many of us our eating habits, both good and bad, were developed in our childhoods. If we grew up in dysfunctional homes, our eating habits may be considered dysfunctional as well. Eating when we're stressed, depressed, worried or lonely are all emotional responses that could be triggered by hidden underlying emotions tracing back to our childhood. These emotions may be "eating away" at us causing us to stuff our emotions with food.

As we struggle to get to the core of why we use food to assuage our emotions, we need to think of the process like we are peeling back the layers of an onion. Once we conquer one issue, we need to begin peeling back the next layer of our tangled emotions and tackle the next level.

In order to peel back the onion of our emotional eating, eventually we need to start digging a little deeper to see what's at the hidden core of our problems. The first month was a gentle easing into the resolution lifestyle changes. This new month may prove more difficult emotionally, but a necessary evil if we're to conquer the inner beast. The prospect of discovering what's hiding underneath the layers of emotional scars can seem quite frightening, but each day we get a little stronger. Eventually we will be strong enough to tackle the real issue of what's *been eating us*.

I know God will not give me anything I can't handle. I just wish that He didn't trust me so much. ~ Mother Teresa

No, dear brothers and sisters, I have not achieved it, but I focus on this one thing: Forgetting the past and looking forward to what lies ahead, I press on to reach the end of the race and receive the heavenly prize for which God, through Christ Jesus, is calling us. Philippians 3:13-14 (NLT)

PRAYER FOR TODAY: Lord, I'm not sure if I'm ready to start digging into my emotional psyche and see what's at the root cause of all my eating problems. I pray that You'll be with me every step of the way and only reveal as much to me as I can handle. Go easy on me, Father, I'm a mess. In Your name I ask these things, Lord Jesus. Amen.

FEBRUARY 5
I Expect It's Up to You

Successful Hollywood stars are anything but average or normal when it comes to weight. Yet many submit themselves to body sculpting surgeries and procedures to erase even miniscule amounts of body fat because they live their lives under a microscope. *Real women* can't expect to compete with actresses in the media.

Unfortunately society, the media and the enemy work hard trying to convince us "real women" that to be happy we must be a certain size. If you're not a size 0 or a size 2, you're not worthy. Real women have curves, real women are round, real women go through menopause and get midriffs. And yes, real women have body fat!

Pain and disappointment are inevitable if you look for it and expect it. If you expect to be a failure – you will. If you expect to fall back into bad habits and patterns – you will. If you expect your quest to get healthy will be too hard and you won't be able to stick with it … guess what? You're likely to get *exactly* what you're expecting.

Why not expect to succeed this year? Why not expect to be happy regardless of what you weigh. Why not expect that your attitude will be SO positive, everyone you meet will want what you have – an expectant, unshakeable attitude. Why not give it a shot? *I expect it's up to you.*

Cure yourself of the affliction of caring how you appear to others. Concern yourself only with how you appear before God, concern yourself only with the idea that God may have of you. ~ Miguel De Unamuno

If you look for me wholeheartedly, you will find me. Jeremiah 29:13 (NLT)

PRAYER FOR TODAY: *Lord, I pray that You will help me to EXPECT great success this year with ALL of my resolutions. I pray that when I am down, You will remind me that YOU have a great plan for my future. I pray you will bless me with a positive attitude that cannot be shaken, regardless of what's happening around me. In Your name I ask all these things, Lord Jesus. Amen.*

FEBRUARY 6
Welcome to the PGA

You know you're in trouble when you wake up late and breakfast is a banana in the car on the way to work and the day seems to go downhill from there. You race to work, get through piles of paperwork and inhale your lunch without tasting it. After work it feels as though you've a million errands to run: the grocery store, the dry cleaners, the post office and oh yeah – don't forget to pick up the kids (or grandkids) and take them to soccer.

Life is busy and yet somehow, we're still trying to keep a food diary, weigh and measure our food portions, squeeze in a good cardio workout, lift weights AND journal our moods, fears and phobias when we turn to food in times of stress. You may be asking yourself, *"Am I the only one whose life is crazy like this and is having a hard time juggling all these things while sticking to my healthy eating plan?"*

Where do our priorities lie? In order to remain serious about our goal of losing weight and getting healthy, for everything else in our lives to exist in harmony there must be cooperation from your household. Ask for help when needed; delegate chores or errands if at all possible. Try to carve out a certain amount of time each weekend to sit down and write a meal planner for the upcoming week. Consolidate your errands if at all possible.

This IS going to be tough, which is why so many people fail early on with their resolutions. This positive attitude thing could be the missing link to achieving success this time. All these things won't go away because we complain about them, so we might as well figure out how to restructure our priorities and decide how bad we want this. Welcome to the **PGA** of healthy living; **Priorities, Goals** and **Attitude**. You won't succeed without them.

Use what talents you possess; the woods would be very silent if no birds sang except those that sang best. ~ Henry van Dyke

And we know that God causes everything to work together for the good of those who love God and are called according to his purpose for them. Romans 8:23 (NLT)

PRAYER FOR TODAY: *Lord, help me not to be overwhelmed by the day-to-day business of life. I pray I won't look to food to console myself when I'm stressed out or overtaxed with worry or pressed for time. Slow me down and help me to maintain a positive attitude and help me to keep my priorities in order. In Your name I ask all these things, Lord Jesus. Amen.*

FEBRUARY 7
Accentuate the Positive

When you're in the beginning stages of any weight loss program and you've yet to show any substantial weight loss, it's probably not in your best interest to shop for clothes. While it would be desirable to tell ourselves we will do no clothes shopping until we've lost "X" amount of weight, sometimes things come up that require a trip to the mall for something new to wear.

If you're significantly over your goal weight, shopping for clothes is about as much fun as root canal surgery. The combination of the lights and the mirrors in dressing rooms force you to view your body from every conceivable and painful angle, making you privy to places on your body you haven't dared look at in ages – in triplicate.

The many mirrors and lights might prompt you to beat yourself up about how little progress has been made thus far. But don't give into those negative urges. Dressing for your size or dressing for success all amount to the same thing: you've got to do what that old song says. *Accentuate the positive and eliminate the negative.*

Remind yourself that you won't always be this size and that you're making positive steps to lose weight and get healthy. Don't focus on all the things *you hate* about your body, but do your best to choose clothes that make you feel good.

Accentuate what you *do like* about your body. Seek the help of someone who has an eye for color and fabrics and someone who will tell you honestly "don't buy that dress, it makes your butt look huge!" Look towards the future and how you hope to look (realistically) when you've lost the weight. Dream your dreams; envision your success but in the interim – accentuate the positive and above all – eliminate the negative!

Remember that the Devil doesn't sleep, but seeks our ruin in a thousand different ways. ~ Angela Merici

Faith is the confidence that what we hope for will actually happen; it gives us assurance about things we cannot see. Hebrews 11:1 (NLT)

PRAYER FOR TODAY: *Lord, thank You for accepting me just as I am. Thank You for not basing Your love for me on my outward appearance but by what's in my heart. I know You are with me on this difficult journey and I pray that You will give me strength for each new day and each challenge. May I put my faith in You and not give up when it gets too hard. In Your name I ask all these things, Lord Jesus. Amen.*

FEBRUARY 8
Do You See What I See?

A friend emailed me some pictures she snapped of me and my family last weekend when we were together for a going away party. As soon as I got these pictures, my immediate reaction was to hit "delete" because I despise looking at pictures of myself. My eyes are immediately drawn to all the things I hate about my body. I see only flaws.

Two of the most effective (and damaging) tools the enemy uses against us (especially women) are mirrors and photographs. Somehow he distorts our images so we are incapable of seeing our reflections clearly. Any anorexic can attest to that.

Every time we berate ourselves because of our physical appearance, our Heavenly Father is weeping for us. It hurts Him to hear His children speak so negatively about themselves. He came that we might have life to the fullest! (John 10:10) God didn't die for us and save us so we could verbally beat ourselves up every day over our perceived physical imperfections.

Satan is a liar! And it's high time we all get that message and receive the fullness of joy that our Lord has for us. When these negative thoughts come to us, we need to IMMEDIATELY discard them and replace those negative thoughts with something positive. We are made in the image and likeness of God (Genesis 1:27) and nowhere in the Bible does it say that God is fat and ugly so that means WE ARE NOT FAT AND UGLY!

God thinks we're beautiful! It's high time we see what He sees!

Beauty… when you look into a woman's eyes and see what is in her heart.
~ Nate Dircks

"For my thoughts are not your thoughts, neither are your ways my ways," declares the LORD. Isaiah 55:8 (NIV)

PRAYER FOR TODAY: *Thank You, Lord for helping me to cast down all those negative thoughts and images. Thank You for helping me to replace those negative thoughts with positive thoughts. I thank You for seeing the real me — the one on the inside. Thank You for creating me in Your image and seeing me as Your beautiful child. In Your name I ask all these things, Lord Jesus. Amen.*

FEBRUARY 9
Stop and Smell the Barbecue

Weekends can create conflict of a whole new dimension when we're trying really hard to make lifestyle changes to get healthy. Weekends afford more situations for eating out and can also wreak havoc on our clearly defined eating schedules. However, if weekends are the only time you have to enjoy your family, sometimes you have to ditch the schedules, the cardio burn and the heart rate monitoring to stop and enjoy life's journey, or before you know it, your number is up and you've missed important family time. Take the time to truly appreciate all that God has blessed you with, without completely undoing all your hard work. You can relax your rigorous planning and exercise schedules but don't completely "fall off the wagon." Weekends are not an excuse to cut loose and go wild.

Turn your weekends into family fun time and take the kids to the park for a play date. Include your kids in your exercise without letting them know that you're going to exercise. Take a soccer ball to the park and run around with the kids chasing the ball. If soccer's not your game, try basketball or softball. Your kids will love you for taking the time to play with them. Don't let life pass you by because of your busy agenda. Stop and smell the roses ... or most likely if you're at a public park – the barbecue! God himself appreciated the smell of grilled meat. The Old Testament is filled with scriptures referencing what a pleasing aroma the sacrifices were to God. *HEL-LO* ... that sounds like barbecue to me! Follow God's example and be blessed by the aroma of life.

Weekends don't count unless you spend them doing something completely pointless. ~ Bill Watterson

Along with the bread, present seven one-year-old male lambs with no defects, one young bull, and two rams as burnt offerings to the LORD. These burnt offerings, together with the grain offerings and liquid offerings, will be a special gift, a pleasing aroma to the LORD. Leviticus 23:18 (NLT)

PRAYER FOR TODAY: *Thank You, Lord for weekends. Refresh my body, soul and spirit and prepare me for the week ahead. May I give my all in everything I do. Help me to exercise and eat right and have a positive attitude and be recommitted to my resolution to get healthy. May I resist temptation and use wisdom and balance in both my eating and exercise this week. In Your name I ask all these things, Lord Jesus. Amen.*

FEBRUARY 10
Extra Grace Required

It's reasonable to expect that life doesn't stop because we're trying to get healthy. There are bound to be invitations to things like office parties, tailgate sporting events; birthday parties, baby showers, or weddings to name a few. All of these are situations that can be classically defined as an EGR function. *Extra Grace Required*.

There are ways to get around some of these party situations if you plan ahead. When faced with bowls of chips and dip, offer to bring a low-fat option. Your hostess will likely appreciate your offer and you'll be guaranteed of at least one low-fat appetizer. Substitute light sour cream for regular; baked chips instead of the greasy regular chips; or veggies for dipping rather than chips.

If you're grilling meat, ground turkey is a healthy alternative to ground beef or turkey hot dogs rather than Polish dogs or beef hot dogs. Try using a whole wheat bun in place of a sesame seed bun or regular high calorie/high carb bun.

At events that feature cake as a center point of celebration such as a birthday party, baby shower or wedding, again, set limits before you dig in. Have a small piece of cake but opt for a center cut piece that won't have as much frosting. When at all possible scrape off as much frosting as possible. Although realistically if you're a cake freak like me, this may be an impossible task so allow yourself a SMALL piece.

Following a weight loss program doesn't have to mean isolating yourself from friends and family. Enjoy your day. You don't have to skip it and be a party pooper because you're losing weight. With a positive attitude and some careful preparation and planning you can enjoy those *EGR* functions without guilt.

I am thankful for the mess to clean after a party because it means I have been surrounded by friends. ~ Nancie J. Carmody

Let us then approach God's throne of grace with confidence, so that we may receive mercy and find grace to help us in our time of need. Hebrews 4:16 (NIV)

PRAYER FOR TODAY: *Thank You, Lord for opportunities to be with friends and family and to relax and enjoy life, food and laughter. Please help me to set a guard over my mouth and be mindful of what I'm eating and of my portion sizes. Help each day to be about friends and family, not weight loss. In Your name I ask all these things, Lord Jesus. Amen.*

FEBRUARY 11
I've Got a Secret

It's easy to be attracted to charismatic people. People who always have a smile on their face are more appealing to hang around than a sourpuss. Is it any wonder when we encounter someone who's been hugely successful at losing weight, we flock to them like bargain shoppers at a clearance sale? We want to know, *"What's your secret?"* Aren't we all secretly hoping their success will rub off on us? We want them to breathe on us in the hopes we'll catch their thinness like a contagious disease. As lovely as that would be, we can't catch weight loss – not by osmosis or by duplicating someone else's weight loss regime to the letter. We're all different.

Our weight loss journey must be walked out by us, one step at a time. We can enlist the aid of an accountability partner to keep us on target with our food plan. We can find an exercise buddy to work out with, but ultimately our bodies – our DNA belong only to us and we've got to put the work in ourselves. Contrary to what weight loss pill manufacturers want us to believe – there is no magic pill that will melt the weight off. Losing weight is hard work.

The good news is, if we put the work and effort into seriously losing weight, time passes and we eventually become that walking success story giving off that positive vibe. Before you know it, we'll become that person that everyone flocks to and starts badgering, *"Hey, what's the secret to your successful weight loss?"* That's when you tell them the truth, "Hard work and prayer and lots of it!"

I have read in Plato and Cicero sayings that are very wise and very beautiful; but I never read in either of them: "Come unto me all ye that labour and are heavy laden." ~ St Augustine

God is not unjust; he will not forget your work and the love you have shown him as you have helped his people and continue to help them. Hebrews 6:10 (NIV)

PRAYER FOR TODAY: *Thank You, Lord for life's many blessings. Help me to have a positive attitude throughout my entire weight loss journey. May I be a magnet for others who might be negative and struggling with their own weight loss journey. I ask that You would use me to encourage others rather than being a negative naysayer. In Your name I ask all these things, Lord Jesus. Amen.*

FEBRUARY 12
The Shovel that Digs for Faith

Life is rarely perfect and we should expect to have those days that require us to dig down deep and pull strength, faith and attitude all the way up from our toes. Maybe you wake up on the wrong side of the bed, or you simply didn't get the proper amount of sleep. Perhaps your flesh wants chocolate and will get it at any cost! Maybe it's PMS (yes, men have it too!) or maybe it's a rainy day and you want to cuddle up in a blanket, watch old movies and eat all the wrong things and say, *"There's no way I'm exercising today!"*

Whatever is causing you to dig deep, you've got to know where to dig and exactly what kind of shovel you're going to need. The 12-step program refers to this as relying on your Higher Power. I'm not ashamed to admit that my higher power is the Lord Jesus Christ. There are times I have to fall on my face (sometimes figuratively, sometimes literally) and cry out to my Lord and Savior to give me the strength to stay strong and not give up and throw in the towel. Some days when I feel as though I might starve, I have to pray for strength not to eat the towel!

If losing weight were easy we'd all do it without any trouble! When the going gets tough, the tough don't have lunch at an all-you-can-eat buffet. No – the tough tap into that internal strength and call on something bigger than them (what's bigger than God?) and they believe that God cares enough about their struggle to step in and help them.

If you're not sure you believe in God, it's very simple to get to know him personally. Simply admit that you're a sinner in need of a Savior. Ask God to come into your life and be in control of every aspect of it. Trust Him from here on out to help you in your weight loss efforts and with everything in your life. *Bing-bang-boom*, these simple words have just changed your entire future and guaranteed you a place in Heaven. Now, wasn't that simple?

Faith can move mountains, but don't be surprised if God hands you a shovel. ~ Author Unknown

And everyone who calls on the name of the Lord will be saved. Acts 22:21 (NIV)

PRAYER FOR TODAY: *Lord, I thank You that you call me Your own and I can call on You in times of trouble. I know that You hear my prayers and I pray You will give me strength for each day. Multiply my faith and help me to believe that with You nothing is impossible and I can be successful in losing this weight. In Your name I ask all these things, Lord Jesus. Amen.*

FEBRUARY 13
One Big God and Little Old Me

The serving size specifically states 14 pretzels equals one serving. Yet somehow you feel compelled to have two extra pretzels. It's just two small pretzels what could it hurt? When you're pouring out cereal in your bowl, the serving size is one cup, but you conveniently don't count the many pieces that spill over the cup and fall in the bowl during the measuring stage. It's just a few pieces, what could it hurt?

All those BLTs (bites, licks and tastes) that amount to nothing on their own, eventually all join together to become a whole lot of something extra. Before you know it, your weight has reached an immoveable plateau, yet your stymied because *"I've been sticking to my eating program – to the letter. I don't understand why I'm not losing more weight!"*

The combination of not weighing our food and giving into extra BLTs has landed us exactly where we are today: overweight, out of breath, wearing bigger clothes than we ought to and quite simply … out of options.

Because God deals with so many issues around the globe, many people wonder why He would care anything about us and something as insignificant as our weight loss. God is a big God who can do abundantly more than we could ever dare to imagine (Philippians 4:19). Yes, God cares about the big things in life, but He also care about every little detail of our lives – even the number of hairs on our head (Luke 12:6-8). God cares about our weight loss and even our urge to push the envelope with our portion sizes.

We all need to get it through our heads that we're not fooling anybody – especially not God and least of all ourselves. Take this "secret" snacking to God and ask Him for help; ask Him for deliverance, and ask Him for strength to resist these repeated temptations. God *does* care and God *is* listening!

God understands our prayers even when we can't find the words to say them. ~ Author Unknown

I can do everything through him who gives me strength. Philippians 4:13 (NIV)

PRAYER FOR TODAY: *Lord, give me strength to stay true to my eating program. Help me to stop being rebellious and having larger servings than what I'm supposed to. I know You're there and You love me and want me to succeed. I can do this with Your help! In Your name I ask all these things, Lord Jesus. Amen.*

FEBRUARY 14
Be My Valentine

Valentine's Day is here already. Time really does seem to fly. If we're still committed to our New Year's resolution, we may be surprised to know that we're in the minority of people who are STILL committed to those resolutions. The average person has already scrapped their resolutions and traded in their good intentions for old familiar bad habits.

While it may be tempting to invite a few of those comfortable bad habits back into our lives, our resolve must be stronger than ever. Each day we manage to press forward, we become a whole new success statistic. If we've made it this far, we can go farther.

We may go along from day-to-day thinking nothing is changing, but all of a sudden one day – poof – change is in the way our clothes fit. Or changes are occurring on the scale. Success feels wonderful!

Enjoy your Valentine's Day without making it about what goes in your mouth today. Take a day to relax and celebrate with someone you love. If you don't have a special someone, find someone you can do something nice for today. Valentine's Day doesn't have to be a "couples" thing and it doesn't have to be celebrated with romantic dinners and chocolate. It's a great day to love your neighbor as yourself!

A baby is born with a need to be loved – and never outgrows it. ~ Frank A. Clark

For God so loved the world that he gave his one and only Son, that whoever believes in him shall not perish but have eternal life. John 3:16 (NIV)

PRAYER FOR TODAY: *Thank You, my Lord that You loved me so much you sent Your only son to die for me. If I spend the rest of my lifetime trying to give back to You as much as You have given me, it would still not be enough time. Thank You for the love You give so that I might give to others. In Your name I ask all these things, Lord Jesus. Amen.*

FEBRUARY 15
The Flesh Wants What the Flesh Wants

There are times when you need to listen to your body and times when you need to tell it to shut up. Most of us know *the flesh wants what the flesh wants* – but it doesn't always want what's best for us. It's okay to listen to your body as long as you don't let IT tell you what to do.

If your body wants peanut M&Ms or Double Stuff Oreos or chocolate in any form, those are the demands we should quash. Refuse to let the flesh dictate its demands. Our flesh does not need Oreos, Double Stuff or otherwise.

When we're thirsty we need to replenish our body with water, not tea, coffee or soda. Your body may crave caffeine and that's not strictly forbidden, but as with anything – set boundaries. You can't survive on mass quantities of caffeine, regardless of what form you ingest it. Remember moderation in everything.

We control our flesh – our flesh does not control us. Our flesh will rarely agree with us when it comes to exercise. Sometimes we've got to force our body to comply. Our flesh has to do what we tell it to do.

Occasionally your flesh hungers for fulfillment that can't be satisfied with food or drink. Your flesh could be crying out for fulfillment of a different kind – something deeper. Blaise Pascal said that God created each of us with a God-size void that only His spirit can fill. By all means, listen to your flesh when it hungers for that something deeper and let God fill you with all the good things He has planned for you. As for me, when my flesh hungers for God, I choose to give the flesh what the flesh wants!

I bid you conquer in your warfare against your four great enemies, the world, the devil, the flesh, and above all, that obstinate and perverse self-will, unaided by which the other three would be comparatively powerless. ~ Augustus William Hare and Julius Charles Hare, *Guesses at Truth, by Two Brothers*, 1827

Keep watch and pray, so that you will not give in to temptation. For the spirit is willing, but the body is weak! Matthew 26:41 (NLT)

PRAYER FOR TODAY: Lord, help me to listen to what my body really needs and not just what it thinks it wants. I want to put only good things in my body that will be for my nourishment. Help me to resist the temptation to give in to my flesh. Strengthen me in all areas, Lord. Fill me with Your Spirit so my soul may be continually fed. In Your name I ask all these things, Lord Jesus. Amen.

FEBRUARY 16
Control-Alt-Delete Your Guilt

Wouldn't it be nice if God had designed humans like computers so that when we ate something we wished we wouldn't have, we could simply hit *Delete?* To be able to magically *backspace* over our food indiscretions would be a luxury, to be sure. After a great day with our menu and exercise program we could simply *Copy and Paste* so we wouldn't have to go to all the effort of doing the work again tomorrow.

To be designed with a Control-Escape button would certainly prove advantageous when we're embroiled in a difficult life situation or in the middle of a grueling task that we think will be the end of us.

Obviously God didn't design us like computers for a reason. He created us in His image and because of our uniqueness and individuality we can't simply *backspace* to correct our mistakes. God however, did not design us to live in guilt and condemnation. When we do overeat the enemy would like nothing more than for us to wallow in our guilt and feel shame because we have no self-control.

In lieu of a backspace or delete key, God created us as beings who should be laying our guilt at the foot of the cross. Once we lay it down, we can ask for and receive God's forgiveness. None of us are perfect and weight loss programs remind us just how *imperfect* most of us are. Prayer and faith are our "Anti-Virus" protection or our Security Firewall against those "dangerous viruses" (like guilt and condemnation) that seek to infiltrate our spirit.

We are not machines programmed to be perfect. We are sons and daughters of the King of Kings and He delights in the fact that we need to rely on Him *for everything.* Copy and Paste this thought for today: *I'm not perfect, but that's okay because my Heavenly Father loves me anyway!*

Our greatest glory is not in never failing, but in rising up every time we fail. ~ Ralph Waldo Emerson

And because you belong to him, the power of the life-giving Spirit has freed you from the power of sin that leads to death. Romans 8:2 (NLT)

PRAYER FOR TODAY: *Lord, help me not to suffer with guilt when I don't follow my eating or exercise program perfectly. I know You don't expect me to be perfect but to simply do my best. Help me to stand strong against temptation today. In Your name I ask all these things, Lord Jesus. Amen.*

FEBRUARY 17
Failing Forward

Skipping meals whether intentionally or by accident can lead to some disastrous consequences. If we go for long stretches of time with no pre-prepared or readily available healthy snacks our empty stomachs can succumb to the temptation to indulge in some serious binge eating. Binge eating rarely involves a bowl of carrots and celery but more likely a bowl of chips and dip or unhealthy packaged or processed junk food snacks.

Who of us hasn't fallen victim to an occasional binge? We can't however, let one *"off"* day make us feel like we're a total failure. When we veer from our menu plan we cannot let the enemy weigh us down with negative thoughts about *what a pig we are*. It's unlikely we're going to be perfect every day. There will be slip ups; there will be occasional extra servings and there will be *"off"* days.

Exchange any guilt you may be carrying about these "slip-ups" for freedom that can only come from Jesus Christ. Ask God to give you strength to not repeat these "slip-ups." Ask God to strengthen you from the inside out so you can stand strong against the temptations that come. Realize that there WILL be temptations and pray that when they do come you may build up your resistance against them.

Never confuse a single defeat with a final defeat. ~ F. Scott Fitzgerald

Then Jesus explained: "My nourishment comes from doing the will of God, who sent me, and from finishing his work." John 4:34 (NLT)

PRAYER FOR TODAY: *Lord, poor planning on my part caused me to mess up again and I forgot to rely on You for strength when I was weak. Please forgive me. I pray each day will be better than the previous day. Thank You that I haven't given up on myself yet. In Your name I ask all these things, Lord Jesus. Amen.*

FEBRUARY 18
Choose Change

The road to successful weight loss may be paved with good intentions, but unless we back up our good intentions with hard work, our good intentions will only lead us to a dead end. We can WANT to lose weight. We can PRAY about losing weight and we can TALK about losing weight until we're blue in the face, but unless we actually start saying "NO" to bigger food portions, wrong food choices and secret snacking addictions, it will amount to nothing.

We need to say "YES" to burning more calories than we consume. We need to work as hard at losing weight as we do complaining about being overweight. Our over-all numbers may not be radically different at this point, but we should be seeing a difference in other areas. Can we walk a little further than we could seven weeks ago? Is our blood pressure or cholesterol reduced at all? Can we button or zip our jeans and actually breathe now?

Success isn't necessarily measured by the scale. Look for the small victories and congratulate yourself. However small that victory may seem, if we're seeing changes that means what we're doing is working.

Change can only be beneficial if you put it into motion and back it up with hard work. If you're unhappy with where you're at today, CHOOSE today to make changes that propel you forward rather than continuing where you are. Celebrate your victories; change what you don't like and turn your good intentions into concrete plans that will lead you down the road of success.

Some people dream of success… while others wake up and work hard at it. ~ Author Unknown

Consider it pure joy, my brothers, whenever you face trials of many kinds, because you know that the testing of your faith develops perseverance. Perseverance must finish its work so that you may be mature and complete, not lacking anything. James 1:2-4 (NIV)

PRAYER FOR TODAY: Lord, thank You for victories no matter how small they may seem to others. Thank You for perseverance to continue this journey. I pray for strength to work hard. Help me to make changes that will further my success. I pray against a spirit of complacency and boredom. In Your name I ask all these things, Lord Jesus. Amen.

FEBRUARY 19
The Lies that Bind

Just because you believe something to be true, doesn't necessarily make it a fact – it's just what YOU believe, so it becomes truth to YOU. A great example of this is the things we tell ourselves to justify our bad habits:

- *There is no caloric value in the crumbs you eat in the bottom of the chips bag.*
- *If you eat a piece of cake standing up the calories don't count.*
- *There aren't enough calories in the ice cream you scoop off the lid of the container to matter.*
- *A finger full of peanut butter is less than a tablespoon. I don't have to count those calories.*
- *Broken cookies have very few calories in them.*
- *If I wear black and 3" heels, I can camouflage the weight I've gained.*

Most of us have *little white lies* we've been living with for a long time. But if you're squeezing into clothes that used to fit you or if you're buying larger sizes than you used to wear, you know you're not fooling anyone – most of all yourself.

The whole purpose of making a commitment to lose weight and get healthy is because we know that these *little white lies* are catching up to us and we now have to be held accountable for a lifetime of *little white lies*. It's time to set a guard over our mouths (Psalm 141:3) and stop allowing these lies to come out of our mouth. We've got to stop believing these lies to be truth.

It's important to renew our minds DAILY (Romans 12:2) and replace these lies with the truth of God's Word. I challenge you to replace a *little white lie* with a positive word from Scripture every day for the next 30 days and see if you can't change an attitude you've been living with. You've got nothing to lose – except a little extra weight and hopefully you can be set free from telling those *little white lies* and experience what a life of freedom feels like.

We swallow greedily any lie that flatters us, but we sip only little by little at a truth we find bitter. ~ Denis Diderot

The LORD is my strength and my shield; my heart trusts in him, and I am helped. My heart leaps for joy and I will give thanks to him in song. Psalm 28:7 (NIV)

PRAYER FOR TODAY: *Lord, I'm guilty of telling myself these little white lies and I confess them to You. I ask that you would help me to renew my mind and replace these lies with the truth of Your Word. Please help the Bible come alive to me so that I might walk out YOUR truths daily. You are my strength and my shield. In Your name I ask all these things, Lord Jesus. Amen.*

FEBRUARY 20
A Picture is Worth a Thousand Tears

Have you ever come across an old picture of yourself taken many years ago and been saddened by what you saw? My kids were looking at old pictures of me taken some 20 years ago and couldn't believe "what a bone rack" I was back then. It saddened me to see that I had indeed been a skinny girl at one time, but I never realized it, nor enjoyed it while I was in that skinny body. I was decidedly unhappy with myself back then thinking I needed to lose about five more pounds. For me this has been a recurring pattern my whole life. It seems as though I've never been satisfied with the status quo while it was indeed the status quo.

"If only" keeps running through my brain taunting me that I've wasted a good portion of my life wishing for things to be different rather than enjoying the moment. No, I'm not at my desired weight – not even close at this point. But rather than wasting any more precious time wishing I was thinner, I have committed to getting healthy this year and whether I lose another pound or not, I will commit to being a happier, more positive me.

Life is to be lived and enjoyed – today – not 20 or 30 pounds from now. Tomorrow is not a guarantee, so in order to make the most of today, I won't cry over the past, but live in the present and treat it like the precious gift that it is.

What you need to know about the past is that no matter what has happened, it has all worked together to bring you to this very moment. And this is the moment you can choose to make everything new. Right now. ~ Author Unknown

The thief comes only to steal and kill and destroy; I have come that they may have life, and have it to the full. John 10:10 (NIV)

PRAYER FOR TODAY: *Lord, I feel like I'm always asking You for forgiveness for being so stupid – but yet here I am again, asking for the same thing. I don't want to live in the past and live with regrets. I can't change what was, I can only go forward. Help me to have a positive attitude and be happy and enjoy my life to the fullest each and every day. In Your name I ask all these things, Lord Jesus. Amen.*

FEBRUARY 21
The Big Picture

When we are in our teens and 20s, or even 30s, gaining or losing five pounds overnight is rather easy. If we're in our 40s, 50s or older our body metabolism operates at a much slower pace so after eight weeks or so, we may be discouraged if we've only lost five or ten pounds total thus far. If we're averaging a one pound weight loss per week, that isn't a bad thing. Ideally to continue at this pace, a person could boast just over a 50-pound weight loss after one year. While five pounds may seem insignificant today, 50+ pounds by the end of the year is not. That's why when engaged in any weight loss program, it's so important to keep your focus on the big picture and not nit-pick about the day-to-day.

Remember it's not about the numbers – it's about the journey to change our life. Whenever we're tempted to give in to despair because the weight isn't coming off fast enough, we must quiet those thoughts and replace them with positive thoughts. *I can do all things through Christ who strengthens me.* (Philippians 4:13). *With man this is impossible, but with God all things are possible.* (Mark 10:27)

To experience any kind of success, we must not open the door for the enemy and let him dictate our thoughts. We must not give the enemy even the tiniest of footholds. Don't let your thought life and your mind become the devil's playground. Rejoice in even the smallest of victories; replace negative thoughts with positive ones; keep your eyes on the prize and your eyes on the One who saves!

Every day may not be good, but there's something good in every day.
~ Author Unknown

These trials are only to test your faith, to show that it is strong and pure. It is being tested as fire tests and purifies gold - and your faith is far more precious to God than mere gold. So if your faith remains strong after being tried by fiery trials, it will bring you much praise and glory and honor on the day when Jesus Christ is revealed to the whole world. 1 Peter 1:7 (NLT)

PRAYER FOR TODAY: *Thank You, Lord for a victorious week and for the weight loss, no matter how insignificant it might seem. Help me to stand strong against the lies of the enemy and look towards the end goal, never taking my eyes off of You. I love You and I thank You for every step that leads me to success. In Your name I ask all these things, Lord Jesus. Amen.*

FEBRUARY 22
TGIC!

When was the last time you heard anyone say *"Thank God, it's Monday?"* I'm guessing, probably never. Yet the mere mention of Friday typically results in a faraway look or the slightest hint of a smile. Numerous song writers have capitalized on the "Thank God it's Friday" theme elevating the status of Friday's to a smooth segue to the weekend.

However, TGIF is more than just a popular saying or a nationwide restaurant chain. The Friday mentality that consumes people oftentimes seeps into our brains giving us a built in excuse to relax. Many offices and corporations observe "Casual Fridays," but dressing down one day a week at work can affect more than just our wardrobe.

If we're serious about losing weight and getting healthy, we can't afford to let the TGIF state of mind affect our eating choices. We may be approaching a weekend, but that's no excuse to relax our menus and get sloppy with our food choices. When losing weight, Friday should be treated the same as every other day for us and not be an automatic excuse to skip our regular exercise or treat ourselves to dessert, because *"Hey, it's Friday!"* If anything, we should be digging in our heels and standing fast to resist that relaxed attitude.

Many of us know weekends often bring with them extra challenges in the way of barbecues, get-togethers or dining out challenges. We must resist the urge to *relax – it's Friday* because we know weekends are challenging in and of themselves.

So – when someone asks you to ditch your diet and head to the all-you-can-eat pizza buffet because *it's Friday,* put on your armor to resist the temptation and kindly tell them, "TGIF? No thanks, it may be Friday but *TGIC … thank God, I'm committed!"*

The person who really wants to do something finds a way; the other person finds an excuse. ~ Author Unknown

Since we are living by the Spirit, let us follow the Spirit's leading in every part of our lives. Galatians 5:25 (NLT)

PRAYER FOR TODAY: *Lord, I do thank You for Fridays and the start of a weekend and a chance to relax and enjoy my family. Help me however to stand strong against the temptation to relax my attitude and my commitment to get healthy and lose weight. Strengthen my resolve to serve You completely and help me to include You in every aspect of my life. In Your name I ask all these things, Lord Jesus. Amen.*

FEBRUARY 23
Shame Hangovers

Occasionally God will go to great lengths to drill the principles of life into our brains – whether we want to receive them or not. One particularly tough principle to learn is the Godly principle of sowing and reaping.

If we've omitted fatty fried foods from our diet over the last seven or eight weeks and we decide to indulge in the occasional treat of French fries or onion rings, don't be surprised if your body suddenly rejects foods that you once enjoyed with reckless abandon. The basic principle of sowing and reaping is likely to come home to roost in the manifestation of mild to moderate stomach upset.

I had such an opportunity to indulge in said fried foods recently. What followed was a stomach ache of epic proportions and other uncomfortable symptoms too graphic to share. Oh, the horror of learning life's reaping and sowing reminders the *hard way*. The *morning after* resulted in a king-sized shame hangover, the likes of which I haven't experienced in a while. When we make bad food decisions, we are likely to reap stomach upset, intestinal problems and the accompanying guilt and shame that always follow our poor choices. We can't afford to let our guard down, even temporarily. There is a reason French fries and onion rings aren't on the Food Pyramid!

It's time to *Let Go and Let God* have control of our food addictions and food indiscretions. The road to freedom is littered with speed bumps and our shame hangovers are just a slight setback. We need to believe God's Word is true and He will set our feet on the right path if we let Him.

The difficulties of life are intended to make us better, not bitter. ~ Author Unknown

Your word is a lamp to guide my feet and a light for my path. Psalm 119:105 (NLT)

PRAYER FOR TODAY: Lord, some days I want to give up but I know that's what the enemy would have me to do and I won't give in to that feeling. I pray that when temptation comes my way again (as I know it will), help me to remember this experience and learn from it so I won't repeat this mistake. I know You are there and I pray You will help me hear Your voice and make better choices in the future. In Your name I ask all these things, Lord Jesus. Amen.

FEBRUARY 24
The Last Straw

A few years ago I was working for a major international weight loss organization when a lady came in to join the program. As she filled out her paperwork, she blushed all the way to the roots of her hair as she explained she'd been bowling that morning and as she bent over to retrieve her ball, she split her pants. She said, "I knew in that moment that I NEEDED to do something about my weight gain. That was the straw that broke the camel's back!"

Most of us have had those *straw* moments. In fact, many of us have had several of those moments, since so many of us have gained and lost the same weight many times over. And if we're honest we haven't gained and lost weight repeatedly because we're stupid, but more likely because we're lazy.

When we start justifying our reasons for gaining weight it allows us to use our circumstances as a crutch and takes the responsibility and the blame off of us. Rather than seeking our comfort from God, we turn to food which most of us know is a heartless mistress that cares not a whit for us. Food is not your friend, especially in times of crisis.

The one source of strength you can ALWAYS count on in life, be they good times or bad, is the Lord Jesus Christ. He is your shield, your rock, your refuge, your ever present help in times of trouble. When life gets you down, when the last straw that breaks the camel's back feels as though it's going to crush you, don't reach for your fork, reach out for the Savior.

Life's problems wouldn't be called "hurdles" if there wasn't a way to get over them.
~ Author Unknown

O LORD, be gracious to us; we long for you. Be our strength every morning, our salvation in time of distress. Isaiah 33:2 (NIV)

PRAYER FOR TODAY: *Thank You, Lord for opening my eyes to past failures and helping me to see where I've fallen. Help me not to make excuses any longer for my weight issues. Help me to look to You for my strength and comfort to deal with life's adversities. I pray I'll make no more excuses for my failures and I'll stop looking to food for comfort when dealing with difficult situations. In Your name I ask all these things, Lord Jesus. Amen.*

FEBRUARY 25
Mistaken Identity

Driving around the city on any given day you're likely to spot a police cruiser which bears its vehicle I.D. number in gigantic print on the car roof. These numbers and letters are there for easy identification for police helicopters flying overhead or news media helicopters. With a few keystrokes, the helicopter can enter those identifying numbers into a computer and be able to tell you everything about the officers driving that vehicle.

Sometimes I wonder if that's the way our Father in heaven identifies his children. Does he somehow label or number us according to our gifts, our past failures or our sins? Are we branded with invisible scarlet letters that only the Savior can see that instantly identify us as a food addict, a compulsive gambler or habitual liar? It's important for us to know that *we are not our sins or our addictions*. God does not distinguish one believer from another by any particular trait or shortcoming we may have.

If you're struggling to lose weight and battling with a major food addiction, God does not look upon you with anything less than love and adoration. When we admit that we're in bondage to something that is taking the place of God in our hearts, merely by confessing that bondage to God and asking Him to help us overcome it, our release of that burden gives God permission to come in and work on our behalf.

He will not do the work for us by making our excess weight and addiction to food magically disappear – but HE WILL stand beside us and help us through every step of the journey. He knows your name and what you have need of before you ask. He knows you intimately, not by your sins but by your heart. You're not just a number to the Father, but His beloved.

When we put our cares in His hands, He puts His peace in our hearts.
~ Author Unknown

You watched me as I was being formed in utter seclusion, as I was woven together in the dark of the womb. Psalm 139:15 (NLT)

PRAYER FOR TODAY: *Thank You, Lord that You know me intimately and what I have need of before I even ask it. You know that I'm struggling and I need You to help me through this journey. Thank You that You never leave me or forsake me. I am asking for help, guidance and direction to overcome my food addiction, to lose weight and get healthy. In Your name I ask all these things, Lord Jesus. Amen.*

FEBRUARY 26
WIP-It Good

I was talking with a group of people last week and we got on the subject of food. One of them confessed he was a diabetic and even though *he knew* he shouldn't eat sweets, he was going to treat himself that night when he got home to a big bowl of ice cream with chocolate syrup. Someone else confessed even though they were allergic to wheat and white flour, they still managed to become significantly overweight because they simply overcompensated for what they could *not* eat by eating larger portions of the foods they *could* eat.

How many times have you heard someone say (or maybe you have said it yourself), *"I know I shouldn't eat this, but ..."* If we KNOW we shouldn't eat something but yet we eat it anyway, clearly we've got some work to do. The good news is, we are all a **Work In Progress (WIP)**. God sees our hearts and He knows when we're serious about losing weight and sticking to a program and He knows when we are NOT serious about it.

If you fall, don't beat yourself up; none of us are perfect. When you fall, it's important to pick yourself up and get right back on track rather than letting your fall lead you down a slide into a pit of despair. Each time you fall and you pick yourself back up again, you get a little stronger so you're never going back to square one where you began on January 1st. We've come a long way in almost two months, but we're not there yet. We've much to learn, much knowledge to gain and still more weight to lose. We are all WIPs – so do your best to be a good WIP!

From the bitterness of disease man learns the sweetness of health. ~ Catalan Proverb

I want to do what is good, but I don't. I don't want to do what is wrong, but I do it anyway. Romans 7:19 (NLT)

PRAYER FOR TODAY: *Lord, You know in my heart I want to serve You and not obey the desires of my flesh. I pray for strength to resist those urges that move me to eat the things I know I shouldn't. I want to obey and serve only You. Help me to focus on this day only and not worry about tomorrow. In Your name I ask all these things, Lord Jesus. Amen.*

FEBRUARY 27
All-You-Can-Eat = All-You-Can-Pray

We've all faced the challenge of the all-you-can-eat buffet. For a lot of us, all-you-can-eat is an open invitation for a no-holds-barred pig-out. If you're facing a challenge of a buffet style meal, you may need to be all prayed up and enlist the help of anyone willing to cover you in prayer before you set out for a buffet restaurant.

Many would say, *"What's the big deal? Eat up and enjoy yourself."* And while that would be lovely, we're on this journey with God to get healthy, lose weight and hopefully draw closer to God than we've ever been before. We would hate to digress after all this time.

Let's face it; an all-you-can-eat buffet conjures up images of falling face first in a giant vat of potato salad and wading through hip-dip platters of baked goods. I have been guilty on many occasion of "getting my money's worth" at a buffet style restaurant. When you're addicted to food, this scenario is similar to inviting an alcoholic to a wine tasting party. It's a terrible combination.

Whenever we face challenges such as the buffet restaurant, it's best to approach it with a definitive game plan. Start your day with a healthy breakfast at home, if at all possible. Drink lots of water before your meal. Healthy foods can be found at a buffet style spread – but you have to be willing to look past the mounds of potato and macaroni salad – and the dessert bar. Praying for extra strength will be your most repeated prayer for the meal.

All-you-can-eat is doable with careful planning and lots of prayer. All-you-can-eat doesn't have to mean *ALL*-you-can-eat. It's just a suggestion not a commandment!

We have to pray with our eyes on God, not on the difficulties. ~ Oswald Chambers

My child, never forget the things I have taught you. Store my commands in your heart. If you do this, you will live many years, and your life will be satisfying. Proverbs 3:1-2 (NLT)

PRAYER FOR TODAY: *I trust You, Lord with all areas of my life and I ask You to intercede on my behalf and stop me from giving into gluttony whenever I eat out. Thank You for life's many blessings. Help me to focus on the fellowship of meal time rather than the food. In Your name I ask all these things, Lord Jesus. Amen.*

FEBRUARY 28
When the Going Gets Tough – the Tough go to God

Spending too much time watching the *E!* Channel or Bravo TV can be detrimental to a woman's self-esteem and self-confidence. The stigma women live under forced upon us by a society fixated on outer beauty is stealing our precious resources … the spirit of the modern woman. Regardless of the fact we know we're never likely to be a size 2 or 4 we labor under these unrealistic expectations, because billions of dollars in advertising campaigns tell us we must.

IT'S TIME TO STOP and accept ourselves as the beautiful creatures we are. We are real women, not botoxed, air-brushed, surgically enhanced Hollywood wives who have no concept of the weight loss struggles real women face.

Rather than throwing away your hard earned money on a new miracle diet pill or piece of exercise equipment that will blast your belly flab away in *as little as 10 minutes* – DON'T! Keep doing the work we've started by making healthier food choices, keeping sweets and sugar to a minimum, *Play 60* four or five days a week and get your heart pumping. *Let go and let God* have your sadness and depression regarding your immovable metabolism and get up every day thanking God that you CAN get out of bed.

Look in the mirror and thank God you're a real woman and believe you are created in His image and He thinks you're spectacular! Stop wishing to be something you're not. Love yourself for who you are and let God worry about the rest. Don't waste any more precious time or money on the endless pursuit of unrealistic beauty goals, but learn to *love yourself right where you are.* If you can't be happy with yourself at the weight you are today – losing 30 or 40 pounds will not change that. True beauty starts on the inside and as long as YOU think you're beautiful, it matters not what the world thinks.

You can take no credit for beauty at sixteen. But if you are beautiful at sixty, it will be your soul's own doing. ~ Marie Stopes

Don't be afraid, for I am with you. Don't be discouraged, for I am your God. I will strengthen you and help you. I will hold you up with my victorious right hand. Isaiah 41:10 (NLT)

PRAYER FOR TODAY: *Lord, I'm thankful that You've given me this desire to press forward and not give up. I trust in You and believe that my efforts will eventually pay off. I pray for a healthier mind and body. I believe that the changes I am making will help me reap the rewards of a healthier lifestyle. I pray for determination to stay strong. In Your name I ask all these things, Lord Jesus. Amen.*

MARCH 1
Sugar Shocking Blues

When you've spent nearly your entire life satisfying your cravings for sugar, it goes without saying that when you decide to eliminate that addictive substance from your body, there's going to be a certain amount of resistance.

I've heard it takes 12-14 days before your body adequately adjusts to life without sugar. Experts agree it is "normal" to feel a degree of discomfort as your body adjusts to the withdrawal of sugar from your diet. It's not uncommon to expect some unpleasant physiological symptoms resulting from the withdrawal of sugar. Withdrawing from sugar is a very real physical malady which can affect everyone differently. Headaches and irritability are not unusual symptoms, as well as anxiety, depression and mood swings.

The story of King David in 1 Chronicles 21 is a great chapter to read for encouragement when you're eliminating something important from your life. In this chapter, David has committed a great sin against God by having a census taken of all the Israelites. God was displeased with him and offered David three punishments to make restitution – none of which were pleasant. In the end, the option David chose resulted in the immediate death of 70,000 people. Wanting to offer a burnt offering in sacrifice for his sin, David sought to purchase property where he could offer his sacrifice. The owner of the property refused payment wanting to give the property to David. David refused saying that *he wouldn't give a sacrifice to the Lord that cost him nothing.*

Sacrificing our sugar addiction in no way compares to what David suffered as a result of his sin or what Christ sacrificed for us on Calvary. Any sacrifice on our part though can draw us closer to our Lord on a more intimate level. But rather than sacrifice something that would cost us little, giving up something that we've been in bondage to our whole lives will ultimately result not only in our freedom and release from that addiction, but a closer walk with our Lord.

Judge your success by what you had to give up in order to get it. ~ Author Unknown

But King David replied to Araunah, "No, I insist on paying the full price. I will not take for the LORD what is yours, or sacrifice a burnt offering that costs me nothing." 1 Chronicles 21:24 (NIV)

PRAYER FOR TODAY: *Lord, I offer my sacrifice of sugar to You in the hopes to draw closer to You. I pray as You deliver me from this addiction, I can replace my love of sugar for a closer relationship with You. Please help me to cope with the uncomfortable physiological symptoms I'm feeling, and I pray they will serve as a reminder to me of what You sacrificed for me. In Your name I ask all these things, Lord Jesus. Amen.*

MARCH 2
This is Only a Test – Or Not

Reading the book of Job recently, I was perplexed about the fact that Satan and God had a running conversation regarding this man and his life. Job was a blameless man who feared God and stayed away from evil (Job 1:1). Satan approached the Lord and they discussed Job and what a fine man he was. What transpired was a series of tests discussed and debated between Satan and the Lord. These weren't just little tests, but life-changing, catastrophic events that changed the course of Job's life.

If we're struggling to lose weight, there may come a time that we start to feel "tested" wondering if our inability to lose weight in spite of our best efforts is some sort of trial God is putting us through. Or, is this merely the enemy getting involved in our lives *watching everything that's going on* (Job 1:7) and purposely tripping us up? Perhaps the enemy wants us so discouraged, we'll just "curse God and die," which is what Job's friends encouraged him to do during his trials.

Comparing our inability to lose weight to Job and his ordeal is really no comparison at all. We're simply trying to lose weight and get healthy. Job lost all of his live-stock, became disease ridden and saw all of his children struck down and killed in one fell swoop.

If our weight loss issues are simply a test, the only option is for us to press through and endure to the end. If this is more about the enemy trying to ensnare us and goading us into quitting, the alternative is still the same. We must hunker down and find comfort in the fact that God cares enough about us to test us. If this is a test, He wants us ALL IN and totally committed so we can pass with flying colors.

I have heard there are troubles of more than one kind.
Some come from ahead and some come from behind.
But I've bought a big bat. I'm all ready you see.
Now my troubles are going to have troubles with me!
~ Dr. Seuss

When Job prayed for his friends, the LORD restored his fortunes. In fact, the LORD gave him twice as much as before! Job 42:10 (NLT)

PRAYER FOR TODAY: *I thank You that each day, my resolve deepens and my desire to serve You is flourishing. Thank You for all the blessings in my life and for sticking with me through this journey. Continue to give me strength. In Your name I ask all these things, Lord Jesus. Amen.*

MARCH 3
Picture Imperfect

Searching through thousands of photos recently, I was hard pressed to find more than a dozen or so pictures of myself, with the exception of wedding pictures. This of course has been a regular complaint from my children whenever they've needed family photos for anything at school. *"Mom, there are no pictures of you!"*

My picture phobia is a lifelong problem dating back to my chubby childhood which invariably captured my image spotlighting my horrendous overbite, freckled face and pixie haircut. Today isn't much better. Every picture I've ever seen of myself is a constant reminder of the things I dislike about myself. Usually my weight is first and foremost.

While God has been doing a mighty work on me and my attitude, some habits are harder to break than others. I'm uncomfortable having my picture taken. Some day when I die, my children and their children will have few photographs to remember me by. I know I must work hard to change this before it's too late. I KNOW I need help in this area!

Just as excess weight gain is typically a manifestation of some deeper issue, I'm certain this picture paranoia is a manifestation of something much deeper as well. There are days I wonder how it's possible for God to take someone like me who is such an emotional mess and continue to grant me mercy and still love me in spite of all my problems.

It's a good thing I know that Scripture says *"submit yourself to God, resist the devil and he will flee."* (James 4:6-8) Picture this – if you have a picture phobia like mine, in the future each time someone points and shoots for that perfect Kodak moment, smile and say *"no weapon formed against me will prosper"* (Isaiah 54:17). And then remind yourself that you are made in the image and likeness of God. You look like your Father and He thinks you're amazing!

Though we travel the world over to find the beautiful, we must carry it with us or we find it not. ~ Ralph Waldo Emerson

So God created human beings in his own image. In the image of God he created them; male and female he created them. Genesis 1:27 (NLT)

PRAYER FOR TODAY: *Lord, I know that it grieves You each time I find fault with my appearance and my weight. Please forgive me, but unless You send Your Holy Spirit to change me from the inside out, I fear I'll never overcome these issues. Come Holy Spirit and do a mighty work in me so that when I look in the mirror, I see what You see – my beautiful spirit and my loving heart. In Your name I ask all these things, Lord Jesus. Amen.*

MARCH 4
Extra! Extra! Read All About It!

Hormones, emotions and feelings (HEF) are what I call the Trifecta of Trouble when it comes to losing weight. This trinity of trials oftentimes attacks us subtly or separately, but they can all gang up on you at one time too. There must be a scientific reason regarding the Earth's orbit or some such thing that causes women to be overly emotional on some months and not others.

HEF can cause us to be extra tired, extra cranky, extra weepy, extra-extra emotional and over the top extra hungry. The harsh reality of these *extra-extra, read all about it* hormones, emotions and feelings means sticking to our menu plan is harder than ever. Weighing and measuring food portions – and avoiding sweets and sugar – are you kidding me? *I don't think so!*

If we're to survive the HEF days, we'll require a very specific, detailed road map – otherwise we'll lose our way and get so far off track; we'll end up right back where we started. If ever there was a time to stick to the plan – this would be it.

While hiking today, my hiking partner reminded me of the parallels to hiking and our weight loss journey. If we look too far ahead we'll become discouraged when we see the gigantic hill we must climb. If it looks too hard and steep for us, we'll be tempted to turn around and go back the way we came.

The same is true if we look behind us to see who's trying to overtake us. When we're looking behind us – we'll miss the obstacles under our feet and most likely trip and fall. If we must look anywhere – look up to God and envision Him encouraging our progress. Even if you don't "feel" like you're making progress, stick with it. Every day that you say NO to temptation – YOU ARE MAKING PROGRESS! Every day you are one step closer to victory.

Feelings are much like waves, we can't stop them from coming but we can choose which one to surf. ~ Jonatan Mårtensson

For the Kingdom of God is not a matter of what we eat or drink, but of living a life of goodness and peace and joy in the Holy Spirit. Romans 14:17 (NLT)

PRAYER FOR TODAY: *Lord, I pray my hormones, emotions and feelings won't control me and cause me to get off course. Help me to dig deeper and uncover that hidden strength inside of me as You work out all these addictive behaviors in my life. I bend my knee to You, Lord Jesus and ask for Your constant presence and guidance as I walk this difficult path. In Your name I ask all these things, Lord Jesus. Amen.*

MARCH 5
Dying to Self

Sometimes we have to get tough with our eating commitments and lay down our addictions to certain foods – like chips, chocolate or sugar in any form. It turns out there IS NO substitute for sugar when our hormones are all over the map. When we experience sugar withdrawals we may find ourselves as jumpy as a barefoot tourist on hundred degree day at the beach.

To combat the sugar cravings it may become necessary to find a good substitute that will satisfy our cravings for sweet foods that will fill us up. Fresh fruit may be a good alternative. The fiber of an apple or a bowl of berries are both infinitely more filling than a chocolate brownie. Trying to convince the brain to stop thinking about chocolate may prove to be a Herculean task when we are emotionally eating.

Look for healthy alternatives to the chocolate/sweet thing especially if you're a woman who has difficulties with sweets during *that time of the month*. If fruit simply won't get the job done and you need a cookie or a brownie, there are a number of low-calorie sweet treats out there that adequately satisfy your sweet tooth. Look for low-calorie or high-fiber granola bars or pre-measured low-calorie cookie options if you must have a sweet treat.

Sometimes we need to be reminded of what real sacrifice really means. For me, when things get particularly tough and my flesh wants a cookie or a brownie, if I picture my Lord stretched out on the cross and him looking down at me saying, *"Oh really, you're uncomfortable and miserable,"* somehow it helps me to refocus on what's really important.

It brings tears to my eyes that I could compare my discomfort of sugar withdrawals to my Lord's suffering. Some days it's hard to wrap our brain around the fact that Jesus could still love us – especially when we're whiny or complaining. Luckily we don't have to analyze it – just accept it.

It is not the mountain we conquer but ourselves. ~ Edmund Hillary

Look upon my suffering and deliver me, for I have not forgotten your law. Psalm 119:53 (NIV)

PRAYER FOR TODAY: *I know sugar withdrawal is nothing compared to what You suffered, Lord, and I'm sorry for being so focused on myself. The fact remains that my suffering is very real to me and I'm feeling extremely weak and challenged. I'm consumed with fear that I'll be tempted to eat something to alleviate this very real addiction and I don't want to. Please give me strength to get through this day. In Your name I ask all these things, Lord Jesus. Amen.*

MARCH 6
The Winds of Change are not Always Tornadoes

In the past whenever we've received invitations to social events such as a birthday party, a reunion, a family barbecue or even a wedding, our thoughts may have occurred like a conditioned response or Pavlov's dog. We may have always responded with, *"How can I lose 10 or 20 pounds before this event?"* Maybe I'm the only one who is obsessed with body issues or my weight, but this thought occurs regularly whenever I'm invited to any social function. We tend to be so inwardly focused, letting our imaginations run wild with thoughts that everyone is going to be judging us by how much weight we've gained or how we've "let ourselves go."

If you've been guilty of this like I've been, there comes a point when we may need a serious wake-up call. We have to ask ourselves why anybody would really care about our weight because people are usually too busy dealing with their own issues! We need to blow off those fears and realize that not everyone is judging us.

Perhaps you're like me and tend to be a little too self-absorbed when it comes to admitting our weaknesses with regards to our body image. The good news is by admitting these weaknesses to a trusted friend or accountability partner; we are taking responsibility for our issues, which is a real step towards healing.

Change doesn't happen overnight, but occasionally the winds of change begin rustling through our lives prompting us to blow these self-absorbed, addictive behaviors out of the way and get on with what God has in store for our future. When that happens, we have to stop and ask ourselves, *why did we wait so long?*

If nothing ever changed, there'd be no butterflies. ~ Author Unknown

I tell you, you can pray for anything, and if you believe that you've received it, it will be yours. But when you are praying, first forgive anyone you are holding a grudge against, so that your Father in heaven will forgive your sins, too. Mark 11:24 (NLT)

PRAYER FOR TODAY: *Thank You, Lord, for small victories! I see Your hand at work in my life and I'm so immensely grateful. I pray You will continue to guide me and lead me and change anything in my attitude and heart that are displeasing to You. In Your name I ask all these things, Lord Jesus. Amen.*

MARCH 7
Rainy Day Cookies

Just when we think we've uncovered all our hidden food addiction triggers, we wake to discover a brand new trigger. Who knew that weather could trigger powerful eating urges? Lo and behold, it seems as though rainy days, cloudy days and/or snowy days have a power all their own.

Nasty, inclement weather conjures up images of snuggling under warm blankets, sipping hot cocoa by the fireplace and nibbling on fresh baked banana bread or worse … chocolate chip cookies or cupcakes.

In order to avert a weather-borne bingeing disaster, it's important not to let our feelings dictate how we plan a day around unexpected weather changes. If you awake to nasty weather, devise a plan – and there really must be a plan – to get you through the day without allowing your feelings to dictate your responses. Get your brain to focus on something other than food. Half the battle is fighting the thoughts in our head. Replace those thoughts of food cravings with positive alternatives. Use those "go-to" Scriptures. Just like PMS doesn't have to mean chocolate, rainy days don't have to equal baking cookies.

Of course a sure fire cure would be to go upstairs and rummage through our closet and maybe pull out all the clothes we've outgrown in the last couple of years. Maybe trying to squeeze into clothes we used to wear comfortably will provide enough incentive to take our minds off cookies and cupcakes, at least for today.

Conquering this rainy day battle is just that, one rainy day. We're a long way from winning the war on excess weight. But this is a war we must fight one day at a time, one cookie at a time.

Anyone who says sunshine brings happiness has never danced in the rain. ~ Author Unknown

Don't copy the behavior and customs of this world, but let God transform you into a new person by changing the way you think. Then you will learn to know God's will for you, which is good and pleasing and perfect. Romans 12:2 (NLT)

PRAYER FOR TODAY: *Thank You, Lord for the weather changes that make every day new and exciting. I ask for strength to not allow the weather to trigger my desire for junk food. Help me to overcome these urges to eat the wrong foods today. In Your name I ask all these things, Lord Jesus. Amen.*

MARCH 8
Battle Gear

Pat Benatar sang, *Love is a Battlefield*; Joyce Meyer wrote the best-selling book, *The Battlefield of the Mind*. Many of us are *battling depression, battling the bulge* and *battling addictions*. And let's not forget the battle of the sexes. Goodness – life can be war sometimes!

One of the most difficult battles to fight and win is the battle that rages in our mind. The hardest part of eating right and getting healthy has been the constant mental fencing and parry our minds are engaged in on a *daily* basis. Because our moods can change overnight, we shouldn't be surprised if one day we're upbeat and positive and the next day, quite the opposite.

Holy Scripture says in the book of Ephesians 6:10-12 (NLT): *A final word: Be strong in the Lord and in his mighty power. Put on all of God's armor so that you will be able to stand firm against all strategies of the devil. For we are not fighting against flesh-and-blood enemies, but against evil rulers and authorities of the unseen world, against mighty powers in this dark world, and against evil spirits in the heavenly places.*

Dressing for success doesn't just mean designer clothes and fashionable jewelry. A *real power suit* means donning some necessary battle gear. The Word of God tells us we need to be outfitted from head to toe: shoes of peace, the breastplate of righteousness, a shield of faith, the sword of the spirit (the Word of God) and the helmet of salvation.

We must constantly be renewing our mind, thinking positive thoughts even on rainy, gloomy days. We can't focus on the way the climate makes us feel, but must stand on the truth of God's word and be prepared to fight!

Feed your faith and your fears will starve to death. ~ Author Unknown

For though we live in the world, we do not wage war as the world does. 2 Corinthians 10:3 (NIV)

PRAYER FOR TODAY: *Lord, I pray for a sound mind that helps me to take all negative thoughts captive. Help me to don my armor and stand strong fighting this battle and help me never to let my guard down. In Your name I ask all these things, Lord Jesus. Amen.*

MARCH 9
A Weighty Snowball

My husband and I have been working on a "debt snowball" for some time trying to reduce our debt and live without the stranglehold of financial bondage. It's rewarding to look and see how far we've come and the progress we've made with regards to reducing our debt.

That started me thinking about how nice it would be if we could somehow do a "weight loss snowball." While we can't apply weight loss to the same "snowball" principle, we can make it easier on ourselves if we don't focus on the overall number of pounds we wish to lose.

Suppose for example, you weigh 200 pounds to start. If your desired goal weight is somewhere in the neighborhood of 130 pounds (hmm, I'd like to live in that neighborhood), if you start dwelling on the 70 pounds you need to lose, the urge to give up along the way may be overwhelming. It seems unattainable. Seventy pounds is a significant amount of weight to lose. Rather than focusing on the 70, think rather on 10 pounds. Concentrate on getting just below that 190 mark. Then once you've crossed over into the 180s, don't think about the 60 you want to lose – think only about the next 10 pounds.

The same way the debt snowball helps you to knock out your little bills first, concentrating on smaller weight loss goals helps you to stay focused and not become overwhelmed by the much larger goal. Once you've lost 30 or 40 pounds, you will find yourself pushing yourself harder to achieve your goal weight.

Remember, a weight loss journey is not a sprint, it's a marathon. If you jump out ahead and set unrealistic goals without looking at the finish line, you'll wear yourself out and quit long before you reach the finish line. It is possible to achieve lifelong success if you pace yourself and focus on one step – one pound at a time.

All the so-called "secrets of success" will not work unless you do.
~ Author Unknown

Fear of the LORD is the foundation of true knowledge, but fools despise wisdom and discipline. Proverbs 1:7 (NLT)

PRAYER FOR TODAY: Lord, help me not to focus on how far I have to go to lose weight, but focus on the progress I've made so far. My clothes are getting looser and that equals success to me. Give me the tenacity to go the distance and see this journey through to the end. I pray for success regardless of how long it may take me. In Your name I ask all these things, Lord Jesus. Amen.

MARCH 10
Substituting Monotony

One way to avoid "menu monotony" is to take the time to sit down one day a week and plan your menu for the entire week. By taking the time to lay out a solid plan it can become a road map for success. If we know ahead of time what each day will look like, it can help us to avoid repeating meals day after day and eliminate boredom. With careful planning it can also help us to avoid spontaneous eating when we're hungry and don't want to wait to plan a healthy meal.

Spontaneity tends to be our arch enemy when it comes to staying on a healthy eating program. If we stick to a prepared menu plan, we'll know if we've allowed for a little "wiggle room" in the menu, in case we find ourselves facing a snack emergency. Some days we may plan for a full day of eating consuming every available calorie; other days, we may not be as hungry and have leftover calories to spare.

Each day we should have a calorie target and purpose in our minds to stay within that target range. However, if we fail to have a clear-cut eating plan or a pre-arranged menu – we set ourselves up for failure. Success is more likely to occur if we know ahead of time what each day will look like.

It may seem like a huge bother to carve out enough time one day a week to devise a plan for the upcoming week, but it really doesn't take as long as you may think. Plus, the little effort necessary for proper menu planning will pay off in the end. Trying to stick as close to our menu "road map" as possible will help us stay on track, helping us to avoid getting lost on the way to where we are going – healthier, happier minds and bodies!

One moment of patience may ward off great disaster. One moment of impatience may ruin a whole life. ~ Chinese Proverb

If you need wisdom, ask our generous God, and he will give it to you. He will not rebuke you for asking. James 1:5 (NLT)

PRAYER FOR TODAY: *Lord, I ask for the patience I need to take the time to sit down and make a solid plan for my eating. I know that without a plan and clear-cut direction my chances for success are reduced. I want to be obedient in all things, even if it means taking the time to plan ahead and making a menu for the entire week. In Your name I ask all these things, Lord Jesus. Amen.*

MARCH 11
Warning: Objects May Appear Larger

If we're someone who has struggled with weight issues we may not be capable of seeing ourselves clearly in the mirror and therefore cannot be objective. When we look in the mirror we have a tendency to zero in on all the things we think are wrong with our bodies.

Most women whether they are supermodels or "regular women" have a hard time seeing themselves in a favorable light and seeing the positives. We see all of our flaws. While men, on the other hand, seem to always see themselves as better than they really are.

One suggestion to improve this negative outlook regarding our physical appearance might be to put on your favorite outfit – you know, the one that makes you feel really good about yourself. Have someone take your picture and then file it away somewhere you'll be sure to find it 10 years from now. When you see that picture you'll be saying, *"Man, I looked pretty great back then!"*

The harsh reality of life is you're only going to get older and if you don't learn to love yourself the way you look today, chances are things won't improve with age. Don't wait 10 years to appreciate who you are today. Love yourself NOW right where you are and keep telling yourself, *"I'm beautiful, my Father thinks so, and I look just like Him."*

I believe the future is only the past again, entered through another gate.
~ Arthur Wing Pinero, The Second Mrs. Tanqueray, 1893

… but no one can tame the tongue. It is restless and evil, full of deadly poison. James 3:8 (NLT)

PRAYER FOR TODAY: *Lord, I ask that You would help me to tame my tongue and stop speaking negative things about myself. Help me to stop THINKING negative thoughts before they form in my brain! Retrain my mind and my mouth and help all my thoughts and words line up with the Word of God and be positive, helpful and encouraging. In Your name I ask all these things, Lord Jesus. Amen.*

MARCH 12
Dodging Bullets While "Just Looking"

When battling any addiction life becomes about dodging those triggers that might set us off. My addiction – my drug of choice is food. Some days I feel as though I'm making progress while other days feel like "two steps forward – three steps back."

Little problems can feel much larger in the mind of an addict who is waging mental battles. With all these "triggers" it can feel as though we spend all day dodging the bullets life is firing at us. Yesterday, I had some "issues" that sent me to the nearest mini-mart where I perused the aisles for something smothered in chocolate to help me cope. "What's the harm in *just looking?*"

I bought a jumbo Diet Coke and made a slow deliberate trek around the perimeter of the store. I lingered over baked goods momentarily and mentally undressed the foil wrapped Ding Dongs. At that point I felt this noise in my head like the buzzing of a thousand bees and realized I was near to passing out with the lust I was feeling over a display of snack goods.

Grabbing the strap on my shoulder bag in a white-knuckle grip, I made a hasty retreat to my car. I locked myself inside and prayed and pleaded for mercy. *"Please God, stop me now! Take these cravings from me that are so powerful I want to scream until I'm hoarse! I need HELP!"*

With shaking hands, I put the car in reverse and exited the parking lot in a hail of gun-fire – no not real bullets, but the lies the enemy was firing at me: *"You'll never be free from this junk food addiction! You're a weak spineless mess—you'll never change!"* Inside my head there was a battle raging with my thought life. Once safely home, I buried myself in work; I prayed some more and eventually I made it through – slightly worse for the wear and slightly stronger for having survived my near slide back into the pit of addiction. You do what you have to do to make it through. There will be temptations – but there can also be victories.

Chocolate is like medicine - but as with medicine, the key is the proper dose. Don't overdo it. ~ Edward "Grandpa" Jones

The name of the LORD is a strong tower; the righteous run to it and are safe. Proverbs 18:10 (NIV)

PRAYER FOR TODAY: *Thank you, Lord, for helping me through life's difficulties. Give me strength for each day; control my cravings and draw me closer to You daily. In Your name I ask all these things, Lord Jesus. Amen.*

MARCH 13
Deliver Me From Me

I'm not someone who's plagued by frequent migraine headaches but I've had a handful over the course of my lifetime. Each time I've suffered through one, I found myself begging God, "Please don't ever let me get one of *those* again." After my close call with the snack attack that sent me to the mini-mart, I've found myself praying a similar prayer, "Please don't *ever* let me feel that desperate again, Lord!" I'm beginning to understand the phrase a monkey on your back.

I can't seem to shake this feeling, *is it stalking me? Is it waiting to pounce on me in a moment of weakness?* Addiction can have a powerful hold on us making us feel unable to shake the shackled feeling binding our mind. A friend recently admitted similar feelings of uncontrollable fears of giving in to her own food addiction. To hear someone voice the very same fears I'm struggling with seemed somehow comforting. *I'm not the only one.*

Of course, the answer to conquering any addiction should be obvious: none of us can shake our addictions on our own. That's why 12-step programs for addictions have such a great success rate. We need help not only from a support group or whatever program we choose, but we need to have a solid spiritual foundation that we can rely on as well.

The other day when I found myself wandering the aisles of the mini-mart fondling bags of chips and pinching packages of cupcakes, I should have reached out and called my accountability partner, but I was too embarrassed. I did however, immediately remove myself from the situation and prayed for God to deliver me.

If that's the only prayer I ever pray again "Please deliver me, Lord" I'll keep on praying until I AM delivered. As with most addictions, we can't afford to let our guard down and feel like we're cured – especially when it comes to food. Food is legal and easily attainable. It's "the good girl's drug." We must never forget where we started from and how easily it would be to slip back into old habits. "Deliver us from evil, Lord! We cannot do this without You!"

The difficulties of life are intended to make us better, not bitter. ~ Author Unknown

Keep watch and pray, so that you will not give in to temptation. For the spirit is willing, but the body is weak. Mark 14:38 (NLT)

PRAYER FOR TODAY: *That is my prayer, today and every day, Lord – please deliver me from evil. Help me to resist the devil so he will flee. I pray I will not give into temptation because You know how weak my flesh is – but my spirit is willing and wants to defeat this foe. In Your name I ask all these things, Lord Jesus. Amen.*

MARCH 14
Discouraged Not Defeated

At some point in this weight loss journey, a certain amount of boredom or discouragement is bound to kick in. For many that time came sooner rather than later and good intentions turned into yet another failed attempt to shed the pounds. Many have given up already.

If you're struggling and only averaging minimal weight loss you may feel as though you're hanging by a thread. If others around you are experiencing great success and you are not, you may feel as though you've boarded an emotional roller coaster; up and excited one minute, wallowing in self-pity and as low as low can get the next.

At times it may seem as though we have a two-year-old toddler living inside of us on the verge of a major tantrum that needs a time out. *"It's so unfair! What's wrong with me? Am I being punished?"* I've thought all of these things and more. I wish I had answers, but even the best of us feel discouraged at one time or another.

At some point, regardless of our discouragement, we must choose to either quit or continue. It matters little if our results will be slower than the average person. This is not a "diet" but a long-term lifestyle change. After nine or ten weeks, the honeymoon is officially over. As with any commitment the real work is just beginning. Anyone can go on a diet. Not everyone can experience lasting weight-loss success. We can do all we know to do and still not get the results we are after.

Discouragement is to be expected in any tough life challenge. There is no quick fix. There is only one real option for someone battling both a food addiction and excess weight: just keep moving forward!

Motivation is what gets you started. Habit is what keeps you going. ~ Jim Ryun

Though they stumble, they will never fall, for the LORD holds them by the hand. Psalm 37:24 (NLT)

PRAYER FOR TODAY: *I'm feeling a little discouraged today, Lord, and I'm trying hard to stay focused and positive. Please forgive me and help me to change my attitude. Help me to get a good night's rest and awaken refreshed tomorrow with renewed determination. In Your name I ask all these things, Lord Jesus. Amen.*

MARCH 15
Size DOESN'T Matter

Spring is in the air and that means it's a great time to do a little spring cleaning. Because my weight has changed by as much as 50 pounds in the last few years, that translates to an assortment of sizes in my closet. And that means I've got a bunch of clothes that are either too big or too small, so spring cleaning isn't just a good idea – it's necessary.

Like most women who've encountered sudden gains or losses in their weight, it pays to keep an assortment of sizes because *you never know* when you might need those other sizes. We women rationalize holding on to things because we're planning on losing weight and fitting into that size 4 sometime in the near future. Even if we're a size 16 now – *hey, it could happen.*

As with everything, we can justify anything even buying bigger or smaller clothes, when in fact, what we should be doing is keeping our daily food plan, exercising four or five times a week and meeting on a weekly basis with other people who are struggling as we are so we can share our trials, our failures and our victories. We need to concentrate on sticking to our healthy lifestyle and stop making excuses for the sizes in our closet.

The best incentive for losing weight and keeping it off is to bless someone else and give away those clothes that are too big for you now. Once a week, get out that next size smaller and try them on until you can actually wear them comfortably. And then – give away – again.

Before long, you'll be out of your "bigger" clothes; you will have blessed your friends with "recycled" clothes, you'll be at the size of your dreams and the best part – you'll have to go shopping for newer smaller clothes. *Hey, it could happen!*

Shopping is a woman thing. It's a contact sport like football. Women enjoy the scrimmage, the noisy crowds, the danger of being trampled to death, and the ecstasy of the purchase. ~ Erma Bombeck

But the LORD said to Samuel, "Don't judge by his appearance or height, for I have rejected him. The LORD doesn't see things the way you see them. People judge by outward appearance, but the LORD looks at the heart." 1 Samuel 16:7 (NLT)

PRAYER FOR TODAY: *I ask, Lord that You would help me to change my thinking from a fat girl/skinny girl mentality and just think "beautiful me at any size!" You don't judge me by my outward appearance or the sizes I wear and I shouldn't think I'm inferior based on the size of my jeans. Renew my thinking every day, Lord. In Your name I ask all these things, Lord Jesus. Amen.*

MARCH 16
A Desperate Housewife

When we hate the weight we are currently at, it may drive us to do things that aren't exactly smart or safe. I knew a girl who was so desperate to lose weight; she chose illegal drugs to help with her weight loss and ended up nearly killing herself. Sadly, desperation pushes people to do stupid things. I know because I've felt the kind of desperation that led this girl to that option. I've done other stupid things besides drugs to lose weight - none of which I'd recommend to anyone. Desperate situations lead to desperate alternatives.

At some point, regardless of our weight, we must learn to accept and love ourselves at whatever weight we are. In the same way, the size we wear doesn't define us neither does the number on the scale. We are not a number.

We need to keep repeating that statement of fact over and over until we get it down in our soul. Maybe deep down we all secretly hope God will eventually take pity on us and we'll have a "suddenly" moment when our metabolism will miraculously be supercharged into burning calories at a faster-than-humanly-possible fashion.

In the meantime, we need to keep praying for the "suddenly" moment and remember the importance of "loving ourselves" at any weight until it actually resonates in our spirit, in our head and in our soul. There are people out there who have it worse than we do and we'd do best to make "lemonade out of lemons" and stop complaining. Someday when we all get to Heaven and get those new bodies we're promised, this time in our life won't bear thinking about. For now … this is me … this is you!

I had the blues because I had no shoes until upon the street, I met a man who had no feet. ~ Ancient Persian Saying

There are also heavenly bodies and there are earthly bodies; but the splendor of the heavenly bodies is one kind, and the splendor of the earthly bodies is another. 1 Corinthians 15:40 (NIV)

PRAYER FOR TODAY: *Lord, I pray that before I can speak my complaints about my body, You will snatch the words away and help me not to voice them. I pray for self-acceptance and a new love and appreciation for my body that I've never known before. In Your name I ask all these things, Lord Jesus. Amen.*

MARCH 17
Love It – Not Covet

The Ten Commandments were drilled into me from an early age. As I've gotten older it's been a challenge to remind myself that they are in fact commandments (laws of God) and not merely suggestions. Most of the commandments are easy for me to follow.

I do confess to having a problem with the commandment that says thou shalt not covet. The dictionary defines covet as: *to feel inordinate desire for what belongs to another.* I want what my neighbor has in the way of her metabolism. By all outward appearances, she's a tiny little thing that doesn't appear to have any weight struggles and can eat whatever she wants. I know I'm not supposed to be jealous of that – but I'm ashamed to admit it – I AM.

Life is filled with trials and tribulations and living side-by-side with people who can eat all they want without consequence is simply a trial designed to make us stronger and develop our character. As believers in Christ we're to be an example to non-believers by casting all our cares on God rather than giving in to worry, fear AND jealousy. In order to win souls for Christ, we're to model mature behavior and remain peaceful through life's tough situations like battling food addictions and living with a metabolism that moves like sludge.

In addition to remaining peaceful we're to be happy when our neighbors prosper and to celebrate with them rather than giving in to jealousy. So when our other neighbor who is following the same meal plan as we are loses 10 pounds in two weeks and we've lost nothing – we're supposed to rejoice and be glad with her rather than crying and complaining that *"it's not fair!"* Above all, regardless of our weight or our neighbor's weight, we will love the Lord our God with all our heart and rejoice and be glad in Him.

We are not human beings going through a temporary spiritual experience. We are spiritual beings going through a temporary human experience. ~ Author Unknown

You must not covet your neighbor's house. You must not covet your neighbor's wife, male or female servant, ox or donkey, or anything else that belongs to your neighbor. Exodus 20:17 (NLT)

PRAYER FOR TODAY: *Lord, give me strength to follow Your laws and commandments. Help me to be a light to the lost. I pray against feelings of jealousy for those who are enjoying success when I am not. Strengthen me and continue to mold me and make me in Your image. In Your name I ask all these things, Lord Jesus. Amen.*

MARCH 18
Stupid Balance

A common misconception with regards to weight loss is that we can tackle this whole thing on our own. We can do nothing on our own, but with God all things are possible. So why would we ever think we could handle any kind of weight loss program without His help?

Other than not including Jesus in our weight loss journey, one of the worst mistakes we can make is not listening to our own body. If we push ourselves to unrealistic expectations, especially with exercise when we're not getting the results we want, we risk injury and setbacks. Sometimes we justify eating extra calories by working out for longer, more strenuous periods of time in the hopes of erasing those calories.

We need to have balance in all areas of weight loss that include menu planning, prayer and meditation, eating and exercise. I'm guilty of not listening to my own body and now I'm nursing a knee injury. The pain in my knee serves as a constant reminder to me that occasionally in weight loss matters; I tend to throw all common sense out the window.

Desperate times ... sigh. Even the best of us get stupid sometimes. The only way to survive our stupid selves and lack of common sense is to make sure our permanent lifestyle changes are sound, balanced and include God!

Mama always said "Stupid is as stupid does." ~ Forrest Gump

The sayings of Agur son of Jakeh contain this message. I am weary, O God; I am weary and worn out, O God. Proverbs 30:1 (NLT)

PRAYER FOR TODAY: *Lord, please forgive me for my ignorance. I ask for healing of every area of my body that isn't as it should be. I pray that You will pour out wisdom and common sense to me so I won't repeat my mistakes. Thank You for loving me in spite of my stupid self. In Your name I ask all these things, Lord Jesus. Amen.*

MARCH 19
Because I Said So

I grew up in an *"I told you so"* household with a *"because I said so"* mother. Now that I'm a *grown-up*, I frequently find myself getting those same responses and admonitions from my Heavenly Father. After having a few desperate moments this week and feeling discouraged by this whole weight loss thing, I keep asking myself, "Why bother? Why should I continue?"

Oddly enough, my Lord has been telling me very clearly, "Because I said so;" while my body has been reminding me that if I slack off I'll be sure to get plenty of "I told you so" responses from Him if I do quit. It's one thing to get a *"because I said so"* from your mother, but altogether different when you get one from the Creator of the universe.

As feelings of hopelessness have mounted this past week, my Heavenly Father has been a gentleman in the fact that He's not threatening me with corporal punishment if I give up, but rather whispering in my ear, "I love you. I'm pleased with your efforts. Don't give up."

In the end perhaps we all need to be reminded that it's not about the weight – it's about the relationship. And when we doubt, all we have to do is remind ourselves we'll keep doing this *"because HE said so!"*

I believe in the sun even if it isn't shining. I believe in love even when I am alone. I believe in God even when He is silent. ~ Author Unknown

For the LORD disciplines those he loves, and he punishes each one he accepts as his child. Hebrews 12:6 (NLT)

PRAYER FOR TODAY: *Lord, I love You and thank You for saving me and calling me Your own. I pray You will continue to pour Your Spirit into me and guide me and direct me on this journey. In Your name I ask all these things, Lord Jesus. Amen.*

MARCH 20
It's Hard to Be Blue in Yellow

Weather certainly can have some strange side-effects with regards to our eating habits. Rainy days make us long for fresh baked cookies. Warmer climates can make us think of barbecues and all that barbecues imply. Apparently weather-related food triggers are yet another manifestation of serious food addictions.

Beware of those Spring barbecue cravings for grilled meat, corn on the cob and apple pie. On the plus side, the good thing about barbecue is it's easy to keep it healthy and nutritious. Anything grilled is better for you than frying. Grilled vegetables lightly seasoned are full of flavor. Meat grilled on an open flame is both mouth-watering and healthy. Avoid fatty cuts of meat and fattening glazes; remove the skin from chicken and it's easy to keep your meal low-cal.

Barbecue "trouble-foods" are things like potato chips, condiments and buns and salads made with mayo. Pick healthy alternatives to keep your calories down. If your taste buds are craving apple pie, there are ways to bake apples without spending calories on carb-laden pie crusts. Fresh fruits are a healthy alternative to traditional desserts and are chocked full of fiber.

One of the best things about Spring is it's a great time to be outside and burn some calories. Any activity you do that gets you outside and moving is a plus and is better for you than holing up inside watching TV and snacking.

A sure-fire, never-miss Spring suggestion is to go through your closet and find something to wear that's brightly colored and sleeveless. It's hard to be blue when you're wearing yellow! Put on your crop pants, slather on some sun block and enjoy the Spring weather while you can. It'll be temperatures in the hundreds before you know it.

The day the Lord created hope was probably the same day he created Spring. ~ Bern Williams

If you carefully obey all the commands I am giving you today, and if you love the LORD your God and serve him with all your heart and soul, then he will send the rains in their proper seasons—the early and late rains—so you can bring in your harvests of grain, new wine, and olive oil. Deuteronomy 11:13-14 (NLT)

PRAYER FOR TODAY: *Thank You, Lord for the newness of Spring and the sunshine. Drive out all the dark corners and help my spirit to be reborn and refreshed and blossom with the richness of life. In Your name I ask all these things, Lord Jesus. Amen.*

MARCH 21
Free To Be Me

I have this friend who is very self-conscious about her arms. Even though she is probably 60 pounds lighter than I am and is a tiny petite woman, she still worries about her arms. She is seven or eight years older than I am and long past the age of worrying about what people think of her, yet she's so troubled by the appearance of her arms – even in the full heat of summer, she wears long sleeves.

On the opposite end of the spectrum, I have a group of friends who can boldly declare they simply don't care what other people think about them and the way they look on the outside. I admire these women who've decided their main focus is to get all the junk out of their lives so they can go deeper with God without all their baggage.

In order to be set free from our emotional baggage, adopting this attitude and choosing to fast from the negative body images will carry us from defeat to success. Hauling around our emotional baggage is exhausting. It's high time to shed these negative attitudes much the same way a reptile sheds its outer layer of skin and start enjoying our freedom from bondage.

When we choose to go deeper with God it means shaking off the shackles of our emotional bondage, giving us the freedom to *finally* just be ourselves – and that means regardless of our age and weight.

We run away all the time to avoid coming face to face with ourselves.
~ Author Unknown

Then he said to the crowd, "If any of you wants to be my follower, you must turn from your selfish ways, take up your cross daily, and follow me." Luke 9:23 (NLT)

PRAYER FOR TODAY: *Thank You, Lord for helping me to recognize these unhealthy attitudes in myself. I pray You will help me to lay them down and go forward with You. Mold me and make me into a pleasing reflection of You, Father so that I might be fully used by You to further the kingdom of God. In Your name I ask all these things, Lord Jesus. Amen.*

MARCH 22
Faith in a Can

The airwaves are filled with people selling stuff designed to separate us from our hard-earned money. Most of the time, I'm immovable when it comes to *As Seen on TV* ads and rarely give them a second thought. I must confess though to a certain degree of temptation when someone is selling the latest greatest exercise gadgetry or revolutionary miracle pill that melts your fat away.

Even though I'm making progress in my weight loss journey, I fear I'm still vulnerable to the hype of easy weight loss solutions. Realistically I know there are no easy solutions, only hard work with every aspect of the weight loss journey: diet, exercise, journaling, prayer and meditation.

In theory, it sounds foolproof but I still can't help wishing there was a surefire can't-miss product that would guarantee my success. Actually, there is and I stumbled upon it reading my Bible this morning. It's called "Faith" and it comes in a can.

I *can* do all things through Christ who strengthens me. I *can* walk three miles today faster than I walked it yesterday. I *can* write down all my food choices today and stick with them. I *can* call my accountability partner when I'm feeling weak or challenged. I *can* have a positive attitude even when the scale isn't moving the way I think it should. I *can* be successful no matter what the enemy tells me.

There's all kind of faith to be found in a *can* and all it takes is the right kind of *can opener*. We need to open our minds to the possibilities of what we can do rather than what we cannot. Once we've opened up all our cans of faith, we've still got a bunch of other cans we can try. There's a can of hope, a can of love, a can of trust, a can of self-control. Who knew there were so many cans to be found simply by reading the Bible?

I have found that if you love life, life will love you back. ~ Arthur Rubinstein

For I can do everything through Christ who gives me strength. Philippians 4:13 (NLT)

PRAYER FOR TODAY: *Thank You, Lord for Your encouraging words found in Scripture. I know that with You all things are possible. Thank You for standing beside me on this journey and encouraging me when I lose my focus. In Your name I ask all these things, Lord Jesus. Amen.*

MARCH 23
Sleepwalk Away the Pounds

If you're someone who suffers from some sort of sleep disorder that seems to have no real pattern, it's oftentimes difficult to plan too far ahead until you can gauge what your energy level will be each day. When we are able to finally drag our exhausted bodies from bed we're likely to feel lethargic, fuzzy headed and just overall yucky.

Days like this are the hardest to stay on track with our eating plan. We're too tired to weigh or measure our food portions; too tired to cook something healthy when it's just easier to run out for take-out.

It's on days like these that it pays to have a menu plan written out ahead of time. Equally as important is making sure that our pantry and fridge contain healthy, nutritious snacks and our freezer is packed with several days' worth of healthy frozen microwave meals. These meals are premeasured and only require a few minutes in the microwave, taking all the guess work out of their caloric and nutritional value.

When it comes to exercise, we need to remember that even slow or moderate walking is far better than no exercise at all. Remaining sedentary or napping in front of the TV may feed those couch potato desires, but won't do much for our circulation, our blood pressure or our cardio-vascular health. Remember, some activity is better than no activity.

Sleep disorders are yet another tool in the enemy's bag of weapons designed to keep us from being used by God. We become useless when we're exhausted and sleep-deprived. The good thing is to recognize these attacks against our sleep as just that – an attack. We need to attack right back with prayer and go about our regular day as if nothing is amiss.

If a man had as many ideas during the day as he does when he has insomnia, he'd make a fortune. ~ Griff Niblack

In peace I will lie down and sleep, for you alone, O LORD, will keep me safe. Psalm 4:8 (NLT)

PRAYER FOR TODAY: *Thank You, Lord, that I have a comfortable bed to sleep in each night. I pray that You will help me to lie down to sleep in peace and that my dreams would be restful. Thank You for watching over me each night as I rest. I pray the presence of Your Holy Spirit will surround me when my sleep is troubled. In Your name I ask all these things, Lord Jesus. Amen.*

MARCH 24
I Think I Can, I Think I Can

There have been times in the past when I've dragged my sorry self to bed with a stomach so full of food I was beyond miserable. On those nights I prayed to be swallowed up by my king-size pillow top in my sleep so I could hide from my shame and be spared the reflection of my gluttonous self in the mirror the next morning. With each trip down Failure Boulevard, I succeeded in not only stuffing my face and my stomach, but my self-esteem brimmed over with self-hatred and self-loathing.

Since January 1st when I began my resolution to get healthy, I haven't had too many of those uncomfortable shame-filled nights. In fact, I seem to be going to bed with a growling stomach more often of late. That is a discomfort that comes with the satisfaction of knowing I didn't bow down to the food gods. Self-restraint fills me with joy in the way food never could.

Regardless of how much weight we've lost at this point, what's more important is shedding bondages that have held us captive for so long. For some of us, it may be difficult to recall what life without food addictions was like. Most addictions are cloaked in secrecy and fear because that's another way the enemy gains control over us.

Most of us know that as a food addict we are only one Snack-pack away from a full on binge. We must be careful never to declare we are totally free or completely healed of our addiction. When it comes to food versus an addiction to an illegal substance, food is always going to be readily available so we've got to learn to control it rather than letting it control us.

Change begins with saying NO, one snack – one meal - one binge at a time. Change is successful when you control your thought life one negative thought at a time and replace it with a positive thought or Scripture verse. Having done all, we need to stand upon the promises of God.

You and I are not what we eat; we are what we think. ~ Walter Anderson, The Confidence Course, 1997

We demolish arguments and every pretension that sets itself up against the knowledge of God, and we take captive every thought to make it obedient to Christ. 2 Corinthians 10:5 (NIV)

PRAYER FOR TODAY: *Lord, thank You that I am gaining control over my thought life. Help me to continue to walk in Your ways and take every thought captive that does not line up with Your Word. Strengthen me in thought, word and deed. Continue to mold me in Your image, Lord Jesus. In Your name I ask all these things, Lord Jesus. Amen.*

MARCH 25
Can I See Some I.D.?

*S*omeday I'm going finish writing another novel. *Someday* I'm going to vacation in Italy. *Someday* I'm going to see all my children graduate from college. *Someday* I'm going to golf at Pebble Beach. Someday I will have more grandchildren to spoil. *Someday* I'm going to weigh what it says on my driver's license.

It's not that uncommon for most of us to entertain someday dreams. Oddly enough, the one someday dream that may present the biggest challenge is the one about weighing what it says on my driver's license. Surely I'm not the only American who has been less than honest about her driver's license weight. Doesn't everybody fib on that one?

It's doubtful men embellish as frequently as women when it comes to their weight, but certainly there must be a few. I'm not even sure why we go to such lengths to avoid putting our actual weight on that official licensing document. Luckily for most of us they don't make us strip down to our skivvies and weigh at the DMV. That would be ugly and not surprisingly there might actually be fewer licensed drivers if that were the case.

If for some reason I don't manage to lose this weight by the end of the year, then I'll try not to fret since my driver's license doesn't expire until the year 2022. A lot can happen to a girl's body over a decade. Hopefully by the time 2022 rolls around, my weight won't continue to be my major focus.

Whatever we weigh, I pray that *someday* we'll be happy with who we are and can look back over our life and not have everything be about our weight. Eventually we can come to a place where we can say with all confidence, "what a great life we've had! Who cares what we weigh?"

There is one kind of robber whom the law does not strike at, and who steals what is most precious to men: time. ~ Napoleon I, Maxims, 1815

This vision is for a future time. It describes the end, and it will be fulfilled. If it seems slow in coming, wait patiently, for it will surely take place. It will not be delayed. Habakkuk 2:3 (NLT)

PRAYER FOR TODAY: *I pray, Lord, that You will help me to make the most of each day – to work hard, play hard and laugh long and loud. I ask that at the end of each day I have no regrets only satisfaction at having made the most of my time. In Your name I ask all these things, Lord Jesus. Amen.*

MARCH 26
Naked Before God

Sometimes we can't help but wonder what life would have been like for us if Adam and Eve hadn't fallen from God's grace and eaten that forbidden fruit. I for one am grateful to them with regard to the whole nudity thing because I'm profoundly uncomfortable in my own skin. Can you imagine how different life would be if we all walked around in our birthday suits and that was the norm?

For those of us suffering under a full on assault from Mr. Gravity, Father Time and Mr. Menopause, the triple threat of weight gain; we find ourselves somewhat grateful for the camouflage clothes provide. Hiding under yards of fabric can be a good thing.

I'd like to think if we were all on regular display we'd stop treating out bodies like toxic waste dumps and actually revere them as sacred temples of the Holy Spirit. Because our food addictions are tightly bound up with our emotional lives, our childhoods and all matter of accrued dysfunction, would we look at food differently if we knew that eating a dozen donuts was going to show up on our thighs in a few days – where EVERYONE could see it?

The truth is, even though our bodies are covered by clothes not only do WE still see ourselves and what's hiding underneath, but GOD still sees what we're hiding under all those layers. We have no secrets from God. We're all naked before the Father.

We continue to be a *Work in Progress* (WIP). Hopefully though, we're learning something new about ourselves each and every day. It's a good thing that God is merciful and taking His time with us. If He were to reveal everything that is wrong with us in one fell swoop, we'd surely buckle under the load of our own problems. *Oh give thanks unto the Lord for His mercy endures forever.*

Our bodies are apt to be our autobiographies. ~ Frank Gillette Burgess

Now the man and his wife were both naked, but they felt no shame. Genesis 2:25 (NLT)

PRAYER FOR TODAY: *Lord, I ask that You would help me to become comfortable with myself and my body and not hide in shame. Help me to remember I am Your creation designed by Your magnificent workmanship and You created me to be unique. In Your name I ask all these things, Lord Jesus. Amen.*

MARCH 27
It Is Well With My Soul

When we're trying to eat right and get healthy the temptation to weigh daily (or sometimes more frequently) can feel like the pull of the dark side. Weighing daily can be dangerous, especially if we register a weight gain rather than loss. Weight gain can push us into the slippery slope of self-pity and depression. We must not languish in the pity pool as that can lead us right back to emotional eating and/or bingeing. We must repent instantly.

Spending quality time in Scripture can quickly take our minds off our perceived failures. The stories of the trials of the apostle Paul can serve to boost our morale. Paul suffered from some sort of affliction; *his thorn in the flesh* for which there are no real answers. There is much speculation regarding his affliction, but no definitive answers. Paul *begged* God *three times* to remove the "thorn in his flesh" and God refused. God responded with: *"My grace is all you need. My power works best in weakness."* 2 Corinthians 12:9 (NLT)

It's humbling to realize that Paul wrote much of the New Testament while in prison – knee deep in sewage, yet he managed to write : *Not that I was ever in need, for I have learned how to be content with whatever I have.* Philippians 4:10-12 (NLT)

We should ask ourselves, "Who am I that I should complain because I can't lose 40 pounds?" We should ask God to pour out His grace on us; help us to understand that His power works best in our weakness. Most importantly, we need to learn to be content in every situation, whether we are at our goal weight or 40 pounds over that number. *I will be content*.

There's a period of life when we swallow a knowledge of ourselves and it becomes either good or sour inside. ~ Pearl Bailey

Three different times I begged the Lord to take it away. Each time he said, "My grace is all you need. My power works best in weakness." 2 Corinthians 12:8 (NLT)

PRAYER FOR TODAY: *Lord, I pray that Your grace will be sufficient for me and give me the strength to be content in whatever situation I am in. Help the refrain on my lips to always be it is well with my soul. In Your name I ask all these things, Lord Jesus. Amen.*

MARCH 28
Who's Driving the Car?

I heard a message at church recently entitled "Surrender Leads to Freedom." I equate surrender with war, terrorists and hostage situations, imagining innocents being held captive against their will by a hostile enemy. The message however, implied surrender leads to freedom from captivity.

The message posed the question: who's in the driver's seat of your life? The pastor explained three options for this scenario, one being a control freak is more apt to be driving the car and not even let Jesus in the car. Secondly, a divided person might let Jesus sit in the passenger seat but they still wanted to be in control and drive. Or the third option was to let Jesus have total control of your life and let Him drive while we sit in the passenger seat.

I felt convicted knowing that I've allowed Jesus in my car, but I've been doing most of the driving. I'm sure these analogies were meant to challenge the congregation with regards to every area of our lives, but I knew instantly that I was supposed to deal with my food addictions and weight loss issues. In nearly every other area of my life, I've surrendered all to God, but I realize that I've not totally bent my knee to Christ in this area. I've not let God have complete control of my food addictions and weight loss.

Oh my lips may have been saying all along that I was trusting God in this area, but my heart was not in agreement with my mouth. Before I left the service I confessed my rebellious attitude to God and decided that before I put anything in my mouth from here on out – I'm surrendering my stubborn will to God. Is this what's been holding me back?

Am I the only one holding onto my food addictions? God knows us better than we know ourselves. It's time we stopped trying to control what only God can fix. Move over ... it's time to let Jesus drive us toward victory.

If you don't get lost, there's a chance you may never be found. ~Author Unknown

Then Jesus said to his disciples, "If any of you wants to be my follower, you must turn from your selfish ways, take up your cross, and follow me. Matthew 16:24 (NLT)

PRAYER FOR TODAY: *Thank You, Lord Jesus for helping me to see where I've been missing the mark. Forgive me for my ignorance and I pray with this new enlightenment You'll grant me greater wisdom and deeper discernment. Help me to bend my knee and totally surrender EVERY area of my life to You. In Your name I ask all these things, Lord Jesus. Amen.*

MARCH 29
Sweetly Broken

Having decided to fast from sugar for the past 30 days has been more than ample time to break this bad habit; yet somehow, it doesn't feel "broken" after all this time. The possibility of reintroducing sugar into my diet may very well end up being like opening Pandora's Box. Once these taste buds sample sugar again I fear I'll resume my previous lifestyle; or worse, try to make up for lost time and eat myself stupid with cookies and candy.

Perhaps what's needed is to restrict sugar from my life altogether – indefinitely. But somehow a life without sugar feels impossible. Obviously there are individuals disciplined enough to eliminate processed sugary foods from their diets altogether. I fear I am not one of them. For many women chocolate and candy are "go-to" foods when it comes to emotional eating. It feels like an impossible task to exist without sugar.

Digging deeper and trying to root out the underlying issues of the correlation between sugar and emotional eating can be a long drawn-out process. Self-discovery is important if we're ever to walk in total freedom. There's still a lot of self-discovery left as there's still a lot of the year left. Deciding to change is a big part of our self-discovery. Experiencing those changes is another story altogether. One change at a time – one day at a time – one story at a time; that's all we can hope for.

We are made wise not by the recollection of our past, but by the responsibility for our future. ~ George Bernard Shaw

Wisdom is more precious than rubies; nothing you desire can compare with her. Proverbs 3:15 (NLT)

PRAYER FOR TODAY: *Lord, I ask that You would guard my heart and my mind and help me to stay strong and resist temptation. I pray You will take away all desire for sweets and sugar so that I won't even miss it from my diet. Give me wisdom to eat healthy and stay away from the things that I know I can't control. Continue to walk beside me on this journey. In Your name I ask all these things, Lord Jesus. Amen.*

MARCH 30
He Gets Me

God has a unique way of keeping us grounded and helping us to see beyond our little "me bubble." The last few days I've received emails from friends and loved ones asking for specific prayers – situations so unbearably hard to even read about, let alone to try and live personally. A friend of mine lost her husband this weekend after a long, grueling battle with cancer. Two friends lost young loved ones to drug overdoses. Another friend was asking for prayer for a friend of hers whose son was severely wounded in Afghanistan – the only survivor in his platoon. Another friend just received a diagnosis of cancer. Another's husband of 20 years has left her and her children.

The prayer requests are endless and all heartbreaking. In light of the many attacks brothers and sisters in the body of Christ are laboring under at the hands of the enemy, I'm feeling ashamed of myself for even bothering God with my complaints about not being able to lose weight.

Bearing one another's burdens is a heavy responsibility, but one that we should happily volunteer for because we know that God hears our prayers as we seek His mercy on behalf of others. Praying for others serves a dual purpose. Firstly, we are interceding for these troubled friends, but secondly, it takes our mind off our own problems.

God is a BIG God who is the ruler of Heaven and Earth and He is capable of meeting all of these needs and requests – and more. He loves us all in our own uniqueness and He is capable of dealing with a sister suffering with cancer AND meeting my needs to be healed from my food addiction and my slow metabolism. The omnipotence of God is a hard concept to comprehend sometimes.

We don't always understand how God can continue to love us even though we're severely flawed, but thank goodness God always gets us so we must never stop putting our hope and trust in Him.

Let God's promises shine on your problems. ~ Corrie Ten Boom

But when you pray, go away by yourself, shut the door behind you, and pray to your Father in private. Then your Father, who sees everything, will reward you. Matthew 6:6 (NLT)

PRAYER FOR TODAY: *Lord, thank You for hearing my prayers – the spoken ones and the ones buried in my heart. Please help me to take my eyes off myself and help me to be more aware of the problems of others so that I might intercede and pray for them rather than focusing all my attention on myself. In Your name I ask all these things, Lord Jesus. Amen.*

MARCH 31
HE IS RISEN

Easter Sunday is the perfect time to think beyond ourselves and contemplate the brutal death of our Lord and Savior, Jesus Christ and His triumphant resurrection three days later. Being a person of faith it's hard to think on anything else during this particular holy weekend.

In my contemplative state I started thinking that perhaps Easter would be a good time to bury my shortcomings and failures with diet and weight loss – *once and for all*. My pattern has always been to gain victory over my food addictions but then "resurrect" them when life throws me a curve ball.

Jesus died and rose again to bring salvation to mankind. His resurrection is symbolic of burying our old sinful pasts and being born again as joint heirs with Christ. What is past is passed and we don't need to keep digging it up again because we've been reborn – made new with Christ. Because I've refused to keep my past mistakes and failures buried, I've not placed my complete trust in Christ and I'm refusing His sacrifice on my behalf.

I am grateful to God for helping me to see where I've erred.

This holy week I intend to bury my past failures and leave them in the grave this time. I ask once again for forgiveness for my sins which are many. Even as I repent of my sins, I know my repentance and sacrifice will never equal or compare to what my Lord sacrificed for me.

The resurrection gives my life meaning and direction and the opportunity to start over no matter what my circumstances. ~ Robert Flatt

He took the punishment, and that made us whole. Through his bruises we get healed. We're all like sheep who've wandered off and gotten lost. We've all done our own thing, gone our own way. And God has piled all our sins, everything we've done wrong, on him, on him. Isaiah 53:5-6 (The Message)

PRAYER FOR TODAY: *Lord, I am eternally grateful for Your sacrifice so that I could be saved. I pray that people everywhere will come to know You and serve You as Lord and Savior. Forgive me of all my sins and help me to accept Your forgiveness and live each day as a new creation in Christ. In Your name I ask all these things, Lord Jesus. Amen.*

APRIL 1
A Fool's Paradise

Imagine for a moment that you awoke from a dream to discover that the body you've been lugging around for your entire adult life was just the result of a very cruel *April fool's* joke. You climb out of bed to find out that your real body reveals that you have *Buns of Steel, Six-Pack Abs and legs to die for.*

A nice fantasy, to be sure, but one that isn't likely to materialize any time soon. Lasting weight loss and overall wellness takes time; sometimes *lots* of time.

Suppose it takes you five years or ten to finally get the body you've always wanted, would you exchange those five or ten years for the "quick, over-night fix?" Even if it meant sacrificing time with your children, your spouse, your parents, your friends – could you bargain away precious time for something like physical perfection?

None of us knows how much time we have on planet earth, nor do we know how much time we'll have with our loved ones. We would do best to take this health-journey one day at a time; enjoy every day as if it is our last and treasure time spent with loved ones.

It is April fool's day and time wasted in pursuit of vain glory is foolish and won't produce lasting results. Live each day as if it's your last; enjoy the body that you're in and surround yourself with people who love you just as you are, not because you're perfect, but because you are *you.*

Real friends are those who, when you feel you've made a fool of yourself, don't feel you've done a permanent job. ~ Author Unknown

People ruin their lives by their own foolishness and then are angry at the Lord. Proverbs 19:3 (NLT)

PRAYER FOR TODAY: *Lord, help me to be satisfied with who I am and not give in to foolish thinking when it comes to my weight loss and wellness goals. I know this will take time – maybe lots of time. Help me to dig in and do the work and not waste precious time dwelling on all that I am not; but rather all that You've blessed me with. In Your name I ask all these things, Lord Jesus. Amen.*

APRIL 2
Addicted to Guilt

If you've ever lived with anyone whose fallen victim to some sort of addiction, you get to where you can recognize the signs of denial. Yesterday I felt very much like an addict covering her tracks even though my situation was purely innocent. I was cleaning out the pantry and I came across an opened bag of Cheese Puffs that had about 12 cheese doodles left in the bag. My mouth started watering for the fluffy puffs and I gave in and ate the remaining doodles.

Even though I counted my calories I still felt extreme guilt holding the empty Cheese Puff bag. Somehow that binge mentality kicked in and I felt like a common criminal left holding the bag. My mind was accusing me of doing something wrong.

Because those old mindsets are not changed overnight, my behavior was still one of an addict falling off the wagon. I ate the doodles when I was alone. I even went so far as to bury the evidence – the empty bag – at the bottom of the garbage can. I didn't say anything about having finished them when asked, *"What happened to the Cheese Puffs?"*

Regardless of the fact that I'd counted my extra doodle calories I still behaved like I was guilty. The one thing about pilfering Cheese Puffs is the evidence stays with you a long time. That cheesy orange doodle dust clings to your fingers that nothing short of sand blasting can remove. In spite of the fact that I washed my hands a dozen times, that doodle dust residue had stained the tips of my fingers a dull orange color – a constant reminder of my self-imposed guilt.

If you're going to give yourself permission to indulge in a snack, make allowances for your snack by cutting your calories elsewhere. Don't let the enemy steal your joy of enjoying your premeasured snack. An occasional cheese doodle won't throw your entire program off if you practice portion control. Life's too short to sweat the small stuff.

Every survival kit should include a sense of humor. ~ Author Unknown

The thief comes only to steal and kill and destroy; I have come that they may have life, and have it to the full. John 10:10 (NIV)

PRAYER FOR TODAY: *Thank You, Lord that You came so that we could enjoy our lives. Help me to make the most of every day and live it to the fullest for we never know when a day may be our last one. May all that I do bring honor and glory to You. In Your name I ask all these things, Lord Jesus. Amen.*

APRIL 3
Brush Away the Guilt

Because I'm so far from "getting this" whole abstinence from binge eating, I still find myself eating some of the wrong things throughout my week. I am getting better, but still have so far to go. I already confessed to snorfing down Cheese Doodle Puffs earlier this week. Even though 10 or 12 doodles are a long way from a binge, I still indulged.

Preparing my menu ahead of time has truly helped to curb that obsessive compulsive snacker that I once was. Keeping track of the food I'm consuming has given me a certain freedom from that old addict mindset. But yet I still find myself behaving like I'm trying to cover my tracks.

After indulging in something "sinful" my first natural reaction is to head for the bathroom to brush my teeth. As if brushing away the residue of a piece of pizza, will help me to brush away the underlying guilt I feel from eating the pizza. The taste of guilt leaves a residue all its own that cannot be brushed away.

While I did refrain from having a second piece of pizza I continued to find my feelings conflicted – awash with guilt. Somehow the mere idea of pizza makes me feel guilty because it's not exactly a traditional "diet" food.

The further I go into this "healthy" lifestyle, the more I prefer to make healthier food choices and that's a plus. One of the harder things for me to conquer is the notion that I can indulge in "non-diet" foods as long as I count the calories and limit my calories in another area. The winds of change are blowing – doing their best to blow me in the right direction. Why do we resist change even when it's change for the better?

Diseases of the soul are more dangerous and more numerous than those of the body.
~ Cicero

The LORD will fight for you; you need only to be still. Exodus 14:14 (NIV)

PRAYER FOR TODAY: *Lord, how thankful I am that You are risen and how grateful I am for Your sacrifice. May people the world over come to recognize You as Lord and Savior. In Your name I ask all these things, Lord Jesus. Amen.*

APRIL 4
Relax – There's NOTHING Wrong With You!

Occasionally life throws us unexpected curve balls designed to derail our "Weight Loss Train." Being laid off from a well-paying job like a friend of mine or a family crisis or sudden illness can send us to the pantry in search of a sleeve of cookies or a tub of chocolate frosting.

Why can't we get this? Like "trying to see the forest through the trees," we put so much pressure on ourselves and God to help us "figure this out" that it can become all consuming. Many of us hear that never-ending record playing in our head that screams at us, *"What's wrong with me,"* blocking out all else.

Today I felt a shifting inside. I got a one word message in my spirit: relax. In my pursuit to be healed from my many emotional wounds I've been coiled up like a jack-in-the-box waiting for this great revelation to pop up any second.

Just because the answers we seek aren't coming as quickly as we'd like, we shouldn't automatically assume that God isn't listening to us. Whatever is *"eating me"* will reveal itself over time, or maybe it won't. Perhaps whatever "it" is may be so traumatic, we've buried it so deep we'll never uncover it. Or perhaps it's nothing and we've just got an overinflated imagination *because no sane person would be addicted to food if they didn't have a valid reason.*

I've decided to listen to that voice in my spirit and *relax.* I will continue to do my part and pray and seek God for answers and wait upon Him. Some days we just have to be glad He's in control and we are not.

Whatever the case may be, Life is really simple, but we insist on making it complicated. ~ Confucius

He replied, 'Because you have so little faith. I tell you the truth, if you have faith as small as a mustard seed, you can say to this mountain, 'Move from here to there' and it will move. Nothing will be impossible for you.' Matthew 17:20 (NIV)

PRAYER FOR TODAY: *Lord, help me to accept that there is nothing wrong with me; that I am exactly as You made me to be. Help me to relax in this journey and trust that You will peel back the layers of my brokenness as You see fit. Help me get past reaching for food to feed my emotions, but rather reach out for comfort from You, the only real Comforter. In Your name I ask all these things, Lord Jesus. Amen.*

APRIL 5
Pray Without Ceasing

Some days the effort to maintain this healthy lifestyle change is more than we can bear. It becomes increasingly more difficult if we are surrounded by people who seem to be able to eat whatever they want – yet they don't look like they've gained any weight. Even though these same people may be hiding a multitude of bulges under layers of clothes, our auto-response is triggered by that complaint that will not die, *"It's just not fair!"*

Being surrounded by people who either don't care about their diets, people who can eat whatever they want without consequence or people who are comfortable with their excess weight can make us feel very alone.

Isolation is a tool the enemy uses to make us feel just that – trapped and alone … like we're the only one struggling. I got an email from a friend who said she'd been praying for me and I'm somewhat comforted by that notion. While others are praying for me, God has been putting other people on my heart who are struggling as I am.

Even in isolation, God continues to work on our behalf by bringing people to mind that we can be praying for. Sometimes it helps to know that we can serve a vital purpose by praying for others who are fighting the same battles as we are. Without our even being aware of it, God is doing the same for me by prompting others to pray for me.

Contrary to what the enemy would like us to believe, we are never alone.

I have been driven many times to my knees by the overwhelming conviction that I had nowhere else to go. ~ Abraham Lincoln

I pray that God, the source of hope, will fill you completely with joy and peace because you trust in him. Then you will overflow with confident hope through the power of the Holy Spirit. Romans 15:13 (NLT)

PRAYER FOR TODAY: *Lord, thank You that You bring people to my mind that are in need of prayer. I ask that You continue to prompt others to pray for me as well – especially in those times when I feel at my lowest and I can't seem to pray for myself. Thank You that You hear us, Lord. In Your name I ask all these things, Lord Jesus. Amen.*

APRIL 6
Some Days Just Are

Some days are *just … boring* and nothing much is happening in the way of life, except *life*. It's during these *just boring life* days that doing this weight loss thing can seem a bit boring as well. It feels like a major pain to weigh and measure our food portions and guessing just seems easier. But that's a huge mistake and that's how a simple turn in the wrong direction begins.

It's on these *life is boring* days that we don't feel like doing that four mile walk so we settle for three or two – or none. But that would be a mistake.

Some days life is so boring, dull and routine we're tempted to throw out all those good intentions, weight loss resolutions and go and buy the biggest banana split we can find and dive in face first, but we don't. That would be a colossal mistake.

Some days life is just routine and boring and that's simply the way life is. We can't afford to be lazy and veer from our goals. After all that's what got us in this mess of extra weight to begin with.

Rather than dwelling on how boring weight loss resolutions and programs are, we must think of every day as the first day of a diet rather than the last days. If you're like me and not anywhere close to your goal weight, we've got to get up every day and be willing to attack this with a strong mind and immovable positive attitude.

Some days life is just boring – but that's life. We never know when a day may be our last one. We would do best to make the most of the days we do have. We need to buckle down and work a little harder so we can extend our remaining days and squeeze as much out of this life as we can.

If you worry about what might be, and wonder what might have been, you will ignore what is. ~ Author Unknown

Never be lazy, but work hard and serve the Lord enthusiastically. Romans 12:11 (NLT)

PRAYER FOR TODAY: *Lord, thank You for today. This is the day the Lord has made; may I rejoice and be glad in it – all day and every day. In Your name I ask all these things, Lord Jesus. Amen.*

APRIL 7
The Green-Eyed Monster

I know I'm supposed to be above *that sort of thing,* but somehow I still find myself battling with *jealousy.* Last week I heard a woman confess that she'd eaten an entire bag of Easter candy, but somehow she still managed to lose a couple of pounds for the week. I KNOW I shouldn't be jealous, but I AM! I have another friend who hates to work out and isn't following her meal plan exactly and yet she's losing weight every week. I KNOW I shouldn't be jealous, but I AM!

My husband whom I love dearly, can eat whatever he wants and be very sporadic with his exercise, and yet was complaining this week because he's losing too much weight. Seriously? Is there such a thing??? I KNOW I shouldn't be jealous, but by golly, I SO TOTALLY AM!

I know being jealous solves nothing and it only serves to make me look and feel petty. I'm working on my jealousy issues, but still find myself wrapped up by this green eyed monster and wanting to claw someone's eyes out.

Jealousy is a very real emotion that I know I must deal with now, before it festers inside me like some sort of cancer. This morning as a way to combat my jealousy I started the day with exercise and lots of it. Breakfast was weighed and measured to perfection and nary a crumb was added or eaten that wasn't recorded. I've been filling my mind with praise and worship both in music and through television. I'm getting ready to head to my prayer chair and spend time in the Word and a little one-on-one time with God.

What more can a girl do? Not much, other than admitting my jealousy to God and asking His forgiveness. Because we are all so different and God designed us all so uniquely, I know there are multiple opportunities each day to feel jealousy. As long as I don't take up permanent residence in Jealousy Junction ... I know *this too shall pass*.

Jealousy... is a mental cancer. ~ B.C. Forbes

A peaceful heart leads to a healthy body; jealousy is like cancer in the bones. Proverbs 14:30 (NLT)

PRAYER FOR TODAY: Lord, I admit my weakness and my feelings of jealousy. I pray Father for forgiveness and ask that You would help me to conquer these ugly feelings. May I be happy and excited for my friends and their success. I pray You would grant me success of my own, in overcoming my jealousy and in overcoming my trials with my weight loss. In Your name I ask all these things, Lord Jesus. Amen.

APRIL 8
Starved for Success

I recently saw an interview with an Academy Award Nominated actor who is currently filming a movie that has required him to lose a significant amount of weight. In the film he plays a drug addict and it's important that he *look the part* to add credibility to the film. This actor is being paid millions to appear in this movie so his job, his livelihood – his entire career hinges – on him successfully losing this weight. He's literally starving himself for success.

I had to stop and ask myself *if someone was paying me millions of dollars to lose weight, could I actually do it and be successful?* Is money enough of a motivator when it comes to losing weight? Should losing weight for money make any difference and what amount of money would it take?

While losing weight for millions of dollars might make us all believe that we could AND WOULD lose weight, there is no guarantee we would succeed. If success simply means weight loss -- if you nearly kill yourself in the process, what have you *gained?*

Starvation diets can drop weight from our bodies, but can do irreversible damage. If you survive the process, the second you re-introduce food back into your diet, you end up gaining the weight back *and then some*. Starving to lose weight fools your body into believing you're starving indefinitely and any food you eat will automatically be stored as fat.

Our goal to get healthy isn't just about a number on the scale; it's about getting healthy in our body, our mind and our spirit. Success means overall wellness. We only have this one body and if we mess it up by being stupid we don't get another chance. If you're *dying for success*, you're not really succeeding. Trust your *temple* to God and ask Him for help in losing weight. He will never leave you or forsake you. He died for our success.

Wisdom outweighs any wealth. ~ Sophocles

Wisdom is more valuable than gold and crystal. It cannot be purchased with jewels mounted in fine gold. Job 28:17 (NLT)

PRAYER FOR TODAY: *Father God, I ask for wisdom along this journey to get healthy. Help me not give in to stupid practices that might help me lose weight quickly. Help me to remember that true success means overall wellness in my mind, my body and my soul. I want Your will, not mine. In Your name I ask all these things, Lord Jesus. Amen.*

APRIL 9
No Regrets – Have Mercy, Will Travel

During the course of our healthy eating and lifestyle adjustments we're bound to have a few failures along the way. Sometimes they're not even necessarily failures so much as speed bumps. Today I had a speed bump day. I took my daughter to lunch to celebrate her birthday. We had a fabulous afternoon – one of the nicest we've ever spent together, so no regrets.

We did the "all you can eat" soup, salad and breadstick lunch at our favorite restaurant. I was pleased with myself that I managed to hold my breadstick consumption to a mere two. I could have more than doubled that, but managed to restrain my animal instincts. No regrets.

I also had two helpings of salad – but hey – it was salad, so the fact that it was green means it had to be good for me, right? The soup was delicious but I had only one serving. My real speed bump occurred after lunch. Being my daughter's birthday I forced her to pick a dessert so she could be properly serenaded by the wait staff with song, merriment and candles. It was wonderfully embarrassing for her and perfectly delightful for me to watch her blush. No regrets.

She selected a decadent piece of cheesecake that quite simply was to *die for*. Of course I helped her polish it off in record time and it was sinfully satisfying. Again no, regrets.

Days like today come around so seldom. I intend to file this day away in my backpack of happy memories and cherish my day forever. Tomorrow is a new day and I'm resting in the knowledge that even though I may have used up my allotment of mercy today, God's mercies are brand new every day. Tomorrow I can start fresh and expect a fresh load of mercy for tomorrow's challenges.

You gotta love a God that never disappoints and refreshes and restores us DAILY.

I love the sweet smell of dawn - our unique daily opportunity to smell time, to smell opportunity - each morning being, a new beginning. ~ Terri Guillemets

Great is his faithfulness; his mercies begin afresh each morning. Lamentations 3:23 (NLT)

PRAYER FOR TODAY: *Thank You, Lord for a fabulous day of making wonderful memories. I pray to feel no guilt or shame for eating with pleasure today and not weighing my portions. May my blessings outnumber my regrets. In Your name I ask all these things, Lord Jesus. Amen.*

APRIL 10
Let it Out or Talk it Out

A friend of mine was close to zeroing in on her goal weight. She'd had a long battle trying to safely remove 45 pounds from her petite frame. She'd done everything right, but within eight pounds of victory I noticed subtle changes in her. She became anxious; her resolve began crumbling. She started to "cheat" – only a little at first and then a lot.

She confessed to being terrified of reaching her goal weight. After all, she'd been at her goal weight before but never managed to maintain it. She wasn't the only one in her household feeling anxious about her reaching her goal. She admitted that the closer she got to her "magic number" the more treats her husband brought home. He was taking her out for dinner more frequently to her old haunts. She broke down in tears saying she felt like he was deliberately trying to sabotage her.

The combination of her fear of reaching her goal weight and her husband's not-so-subtle attempts to sabotage her were more than she could handle and she felt herself sliding back into old habits. Believe it or not, it's not uncommon for loved ones to feel threatened by a slender more attractive mate and sabotage is not unusual.

As my friend talked things over with her husband they both were able to verbalize their fears. They both relaxed and she was able to get back on target. They prayed together and she's been able to keep her anxiety in check and has reclaimed her focus. Recognizing our fears and talking them over with a loved one, close friend or account-ability partner can help us to keep things in perspective.

Silence may be golden in a library or the middle of a church service, but when something's eating you in the form of worry, fear or anxiety, get it out and talk it out.

Troubles are a lot like people – they grow bigger if you nurse them.
~ Author Unknown

Don't worry about anything; instead, pray about everything. Tell God what you need, and thank him for all he has done. Philippians 4:6 (NLT)

PRAYER FOR TODAY: Lord, please help me to stop worrying about the things I cannot change. Thank you for people who encourage and support me. Help me to offer encouraging words to others who are struggling along this journey. In Your name I ask all these things, Lord Jesus. Amen.

APRIL 11
Did you Have the Bread?

This morning as I ate my breakfast the words of the Lord's Prayer tumbled around in my head. *Give us this day our daily bread and forgive us our trespasses as we forgive those who trespass against us. Lead us not in to temptation, but deliver us from evil.*

As I ate, I started praying that my outlined menu plan for the day would be exactly enough for me today – my daily bread and no more. It is my desire to eat only what is healthy for me to sustain a healthy body. I truly don't understand why my emotions need to be fed more often than my flesh.

Every week I start out with a perfectly outlined menu but it becomes nearly impossible for me to follow the plan exactly. If my lunch calls for two tablespoons of lite dressing, I feel the need to add a little extra because the required amount doesn't get the job done.

If I measure out 12 yogurt covered raisins, I grab a few extra that I don't count and enjoy those as well. It's the same thing with peanut butter. If I measure a perfect tablespoon, I can't resist dipping the knife in the jar and running it around the edges to smooth it out before I close it up and I lap up any extra hanging from the bottom of the spoon.

All of these little extra bites, licks and tastes are definitely detrimental to my weight loss, but yet I feel powerless over my rebellion. Why can't my daily bread be enough for me?

Today – my daily bread. Tomorrow I'll work on *forgive us our trespasses*. That's a whole other can of worms that most likely won't be fixed in a day or two. The Lord's Prayer … who knew it could be used as an appetite suppressant? We've tried everything else, why not this?

The value of consistent prayer is not that He will hear us, but that we will hear Him. ~ William McGill

This, then, is how you should pray: 'Our Father in heaven, hallowed be your name, your kingdom come, your will be done on earth as it is in heaven. Give us today our daily bread.' Matthew 6:9-11 (NIV)

PRAYER FOR TODAY: *Lord, please help my daily bread to satisfy me and be enough for today. My desire is to eat only what I need to sustain life. Take away my cravings and fill me with Your Holy Spirit rather than me wanting to fill my body with food. Strengthen me today, Lord. In Your name I ask all these things, Lord Jesus. Amen.*

APRIL 12
A Fat Yard Sale

Spring is in the air prompting many to do a little spring cleaning. My husband and I've spent some time cleaning out closets in preparation for a much needed yard sale. While my husband was tempted to pitch as many items as we tagged for sale, my mantra became; *"One man's trash is another man's treasure."* You never know what someone will find worthy of yard-sale price negotiating.

All this spring cleaning got me thinking about a friend of mine who has been suffering with some health issues lately. This poor girl can't gain weight no matter how hard she tries – which is in stark contrast to my struggle to lose weight.

How nice it would be to simply *spring clean* some of my excess body weight and give it to my friend. If I could gather up a few handfuls of fat and share it with her she could paste the fat onto her body wherever she needs to fill in her hollow contours. Somehow by sharing the weight with those less fortunate it would bring perfect balance to an out-of-balance society.

As lovely as it would be to *Yard Sale* our unwanted weight most of us know it's not that simple. Implementing all the things we know to do like keeping a food journal; weighing and measuring our food portions; eliminating "empty" calories from our diet; drinking plenty of water; exercising and adjusting our negative thoughts will help us maintain balance in the battle of the bulge. If we wear out these bodies of ours we don't have the luxury of shopping for another at the next neighborhood yard sale. That "You break it you buy it" mentality doesn't apply here, but rather *all sales final – No Refunds!* We need to take care of what we've got today.

The doctor of the future will give no medicines, but will interest his patients in the care of the human frame, in diet, and in the causes and prevention of disease. ~ Thomas Edison

He renews my strength. He guides me along right paths, bringing honor to his name. Psalm 23:3 (NLT)

PRAYER FOR TODAY: *Father, I ask that You would help me maintain balance in my commitment to get healthy. I know I only have this one body and I don't want to waste any more precious time or money on things that destroy my health. Forgive me for my past mistakes and help me to move forward on my wellness journey. In Your name I ask all these things, Lord Jesus. Amen.*

APRIL 13
Seriously, WHAT IS WRONG WITH ME?

I thought I'd be able to move on to part two of praying the Lord's Prayer to help me with my uncontrollable eating. I tried praying *give me this day my daily bread* before I ate, but somehow I still faltered.

Every new day seems to start with a plan and a truck load of objectives. Most days I do fairly well until the "witching hour" strikes. That's the hours between 3:00 p.m. and 5:00 p.m. *Something* seems to happen to me during that two hour window. I have a friend who struggles after 9:00 p.m. every night; another who wakes up at 2:00 a.m. with her own two-hour struggle.

It's almost like having a stranger inhabit our body for that short period of time. We are consumed by an unnatural hunger and want to start eating – even if we're not hungry. Trying to pinpoint the root cause of these meltdown hours can prove to be as challenging as trying to find a non-food related activity to do during those times so we won't *eat ourselves stupid.*

Praying for strength and begging God to *give me this day my daily bread* seems the only way to keep this monster inside whose sole purpose is to eat its way out. Perhaps we're only consuming mass quantities of food during these witching hours because we're trying to fill our body up with food to keep the monster inside and the guilt at bay.

Today's menu should include a few unexpected side dishes: a bowl of patience sprinkled with a dressing of *let go and let God*, followed by a side order of self-control. They are not always the most popular menu items, but they are filling and the flavors stay with you a while. The taste of success tastes ever so much sweeter without a glass of guilt.

A habit is something you can do without thinking – which is why most of us have so many of them. ~ Frank A. Clark

Now faith is being sure of what we hope for and certain of what we do not see. Hebrews 11:1 (NIV)

PRAYER FORT TODAY: *Lord, please increase my faith and determination to be healthy. Give me this day my daily bread and help me to overcome temptation and remain strong and steadfast in my resolve to lose weight and be healthy. In Your name I ask all these things, Lord Jesus. Amen.*

APRIL 14
Beware of Prowlers

GIVE ME MY DAILY BREAD and no more! I AM going to get this! Yesterday was somewhat better than the previous day. I didn't necessarily eat myself stupid with junk food, but I didn't stick to my menu plan perfectly. I know I can't always be perfect in life, but when I'm the one controlling what goes into my mouth, I should be better at this.

As I went for my three-mile walk this morning, that question ruminated in my spirit – again … *What is wrong with me?* Is there some hidden underlying stress in my life that's causing me to reach for the snacks? Am I walking in fear about something that I've not addressed yet?

Perhaps there is nothing wrong with me, but this obsessive doubt to question who I am is yet another strike by that enemy who is constantly prowling about seeking someone to devour. This doubt makes me weak and distracted; someone who is easily susceptible to devouring. On the surface, life is fine. Things are moving along at a nice clip with no real crisis at this time. Yet something MUST be festering in my spirit if I can't stop my uncontrollable anxiety and feeling that I'm missing something. If there's nothing wrong with me, why this urge for random snacking?

There comes a point when we could all drive ourselves crazy trying to figure out everything that is wrong with us or wrong in life. If my mother were alive she'd simply counsel me to "Stop obsessing and just ignore it. This too shall pass." While that's easier said than done, it's still good advice. Today I think I'll take Mom's advice and dive into some house cleaning and vow not to think about food today or worry about what is wrong with me. If I must think on anything it will be *give me this day my daily bread.*

Good for the body is the work of the body, good for the soul the work of the soul, and good for either the work of the other. ~ Henry David Thoreau

You need to persevere so that when you have done the will of God, you will receive what he has promised. Hebrews 10:36 (NIV)

PRAYER FOR TODAY: *Father, I pray for a strong mind and fierce determination to dig in and resist temptation. May I truly acquire the strength, faith and fortitude it takes to overcome my fleshly weaknesses. In Your name I ask all these things, Lord Jesus. Amen.*

APRIL 15
As a Woman Thinketh

When we choose to bombard our minds with tons of positive messages we improve our overall chances of winning the battle of the bulge. The last few weeks I've been feeding my mind in the hopes that I can figure out how to feed my soul with positive messages so I can win the war waging in my mind – the one that has me convinced I'll NEVER lose weight. The common element of all these messages has been the importance of thinking positive thoughts and refusing to let my mind dwell on the negative thoughts.

As my spirit is being saturated in these positive words I've been feeling that perhaps I can conquer these weight issues. Rather than looking in the mirror and seeing myself as fat and cringing as I scrutinize all my flaws – I look in the mirror and thank God that I have a healthy body. My body is the temple of the Holy Spirit and I am blessed to be able to exercise daily.

I heard a story of a woman diagnosed with cancer whose doctor encouraged her to go home every day and tell herself that she was getting better and stronger every day. She did that numerous times every day for many months and wound up beating the cancer. *As a man thinks so he becomes.*

Another man suffering with a terminal illness locked himself in his room and watched comedies one after another every day for a couple of months. He found the funniest movies he could that would cause him to laugh throughout the day – great big belly laughs. He ended up beating his disease. *As a man thinks so he becomes.*

I've known people in the past who were pessimistic and negative people. Trouble seemed to follow these people everywhere. Do we want to be those kind of people? NO. If we look in the mirror and think we're fat, we are going to give off that vibe. Do we think we are fat … absolutely NOT! WE ARE FIT AND FABULOUS! *As a woman thinks, so she becomes.*

A pessimist is one who makes difficulties of his opportunities and an optimist is one who makes opportunities of his difficulties. ~ Harry Truman

What I always feared has happened to me. What I dreaded has come true. Job 3:25 (NLT)

PRAYER FOR TODAY: *Lord, thank You for making me unique. Thank You that I am healthy and I have a sound mind and body. Flush out any negative attitudes from my mind and help me to always have a positive word on my tongue for myself and others. Thank You, Lord, for life's many blessings. In Your name I ask all these things, Lord Jesus. Amen.*

APRIL 16
Fickle Faith

I went to a class last night where the topic of discussion was "specific answers to prayers that could only have been God." We were asked to share a time when we received an answer to a specific prayer. I had a hard time picking just one instance because I have a tendency pray about everything, so I've had many prayers answered. I include God in every area of my life. I talk to Him about the big things and the little things.

After finally settling on one incident and sharing my prayer success story, I had a tough time falling asleep last night as I thought about all of the wonderful answered prayers I've witnessed. What kept me from sleep was thinking about what has been the biggest prayer I've been praying for years but to date remains unanswered.

I've been praying for decades to be able to look in the mirror and like what I see not based on my weight, but just like me as *me*. I want to lose these extra pounds and maintain a normal weight for the rest of my life without fixating on my diet. I want to eliminate this unnatural relationship I have with food and stop using food for comfort, stress and boredom. And I want to let God fill that area of my emotions so I will make Him number one in my life.

When I write it out and read it back, none of these things seem unreasonable. I've seen God do amazing miraculous things in my life, my family's lives, my friends' lives and I'm continually awestruck by the power of God. Somehow though, I feel let down that God is ignoring me on these problems in my life. Am I asking for something unreasonable? I know nothing is impossible for God and when I ask I need to have faith that God hears me. Perhaps I'll ditch all my other prayers and simply pray for more faith and above all else – help me to believe God loves me no matter how broken I may seem.

Faith is taking the first step even when you don't see the whole staircase. ~ Martin Luther King Jr.

I believe in your commands; now teach me good judgment and knowledge. Psalm 119:66 (NLT)

PRAYER FOR TODAY: *Lord, please increase my faith and help me to believe the impossible is possible with Your help and divine intervention. Help me not to compare myself to others and believe that You have a special plan for my life that is different from anyone else. In Your name I ask all these things, Lord Jesus. Amen.*

APRIL 17
Lost and Found Reward

I'm struggling with a "reward mentality" lately. When I have a near perfect day with my exercise and menu plan, I feel the need to "reward" myself with some sort of treat. In a perfect world it would be great if I rewarded myself with a pedicure, a new pair of shoes or even a bubble bath. Sadly, I feel the need to reward myself with food – which is totally counterproductive to the whole weight loss thing.

My "reward" system isn't limited solely to my menu plan or exercise program. Last night I went to my weight loss support group and upon arriving home I felt the need to "reward" myself with a sweet treat. I had a handful of grapes and some yogurt covered raisins. Neither one was particularly detrimental to my meal plan, but the fact that I felt the need to reward myself for attending my meeting disturbs me. After all, the whole point of a support group is to gain some perspective on why we have an unhealthy relationship with food in the first place.

I feel so lost some days – am I the only one?

Going to meetings is expected. Keeping our menu plan is expected. Exercising is expected. Rewarding ourselves for doing what is expected is a clear indicator that perhaps we're not getting at the heart of our real issues especially if we are still relying on food for emotional support.

We must stop and ask ourselves if deep down we're afraid to uncover the root problem holding us prisoner to our food addictions. If we are seeing recurring patterns and issues and we can't seem to let this go perhaps we've not completely learned to trust God with this part of our lives.

We must be willing to "let go and let God." If we can't trust God, who can we trust?

Few delights can equal the mere presence of one whom we trust utterly.
~ George MacDonald

Do not let me be put to shame, nor let my enemies triumph over me. Psalm 25:2 (NIV)

PRAYER FOR TODAY: *Lord, I ask that You would reveal your truths to me and help me to understand my behavior. I continually do what I don't want to do and then end up feeling guilt and shame. Please help me to overcome my flesh and my bad behavior. In Your name I ask all these things, Lord Jesus. Amen.*

APRIL 18
The Weight is Over – Or Not

Well, here it is again – that time of year when all of a sudden TV ads and Internet ads are flooding us with "sure-fire" ways to lose 10 pounds and slim down by summer. Just opening my email inbox there were a dozen ads in my spam folder all hawking books, pills, juices and exercise equipment guaranteeing me a new body by summer. How dumb do they think we are?

I used to be a sucker for these ads and wanted to try anything and everything to blast away my unwanted winter weight. Now that I'm a seasoned cynic and I've accepted the fact that my winter weight is no different from my baby weight, PMS weight, menopause weight, summer, spring and fall weight, I'm immune to the promises of "instant weight loss."

Most of us have learned that these little tricks to quickly banish 10 pounds, is merely just that a "trick" that usually amounts to a quick loss of water weight. Unless you adopt these "tricks" for the rest of your life, the quickly lost 10 pounds comes right back and usually brings a few extra pounds along for the ride. Following ANY program to the letter usually leads to a quick weight loss, but it is weight that quickly returns if no real lasting long-term compromises are made.

Lifestyle changes are just that – changes that must be instituted and maintained for the remainder of your life. If you wish to see any lasting changes to your body you're going to have to work at it. There are no shortcuts to lasting weight loss regardless of what you may read on the Internet. Real lasting weight loss starts one day at a time; saying "no" more often than you say yes and surrendering your will for God's will. You can't lose weight on your will-power unless you tap into God's will and God's power.

People know you for what you've done, not for what you plan to do.
~ Author Unknown

Lazy people want much but get little, but those who work hard will prosper. Proverbs 13:4 (NLT)

PRAYER FOR TODAY: Lord, I ask for the strength of mind and body to be able to do the work that needs to be done to lose this weight. It is my desire to be pleasing to You and have a healthy mind and body. Help me to get rid of any bad attitudes I may have and the slothful spirit that sleeps inside of me. Replace negative thoughts with a positive mindset and a desire to succeed. In Your name I ask all these things, Lord Jesus. Amen.

APRIL 19
Chopstick or Fork?

Most of us know that long-term restriction has a tendency to make us rebel and go off the program. Normally I'd say, "wait, maybe that's just me," but statistics show that only 5% of all successful weight loss lasts for longer than a year. Lifelong lifestyle changes are not only recommended but absolutely necessary to maintain lasting weight loss success.

Years ago after watching the first episode of *Survivor* I decided I was going to try a *Survivor Diet* which basically entailed eating nothing but rice for every meal, three times a day for 40 days. All those castaways lost 30 or 40 pounds on their island adventure, so why not me? Not surprisingly, my *Survivor Diet* lasted one whole day before I got sick of rice. After the second meal I was adding chicken and gravy to my rice thereby negating the basic concept of "rice only."

Because I like to eat brown rice several times a week, I recently resurrected a variation of the *Survivor Diet* and decided I'd adapt it to be the *Chopstick Diet*. This diet requires I eat all my meals with chopsticks rather than a fork thereby forcing myself to eat slower since chopsticks require a certain amount of skill and coordination. So far so good – I'm finding that the chopsticks turn any meal into an adventure.

Today while I was at the grocery store I encountered a gentlemen who had his cart completely jammed full of cases of Diet Coke and cantaloupe – lots and lots of each. I gave him *the look* and asked, "New diet?" He responded, "How'd you guess?" Hey, it takes one to know one.

No, not many shortcuts for a seasoned dieter, but there's nothing wrong with a little creativity once in a while and a little adventure eating! *"Chopstick or fork?"*

What makes resisting temptation difficult for many people is they don't want to discourage it completely. ~ Franklin P. Jones

He will take our weak mortal bodies and change them into glorious bodies like his own, using the same power with which he will bring everything under his control." Philippians 3:21 (NLT)

PRAYER FOR TODAY: *Lord, help me to keep boredom at bay and help me to keep pressing on towards the goal of successful weight loss. I commit my ways to You and ask that You would grant me success in my exercise program, my eating plan and with my attitude. In Your name I ask all these things, Lord Jesus. Amen.*

APRIL 20
Ugh ... It's Still Here

Have you ever gone to bed with a really bad headache or stomach ache and all you want to do is go to sleep and forget about it? Then once you wake in the morning and get your bearings you take an inventory to see if the headache's gone – or the stomach ache. And if it is, you're like *"whew ... thank goodness that's gone!"*

Somehow I think we all secretly wish to lie down to sleep each night praying, *"Lord, I hope when I wake up in the morning all this fat is gone!"* Each morning upon waking we roll and stretch and check the flatness of our stomach or the girth of our thighs and instantly we're filled with disappointment because *the fat is still there!*

Clearly it's unrealistic to expect to lose 30 or 40 pounds overnight in our sleep. There are days when carrying around the extra weight and thinking and planning how to go about losing the weight is just exhausting! It would be so much easier to pop a pill before bedtime and wake in the morning five or 10 pounds lighter.

The harsh reality is we're several months into this weight loss journey and some of us are still chipping away at our excess body fat one miserable pound at a time. We may even have friends who are 20 or 30 pounds lighter now and we feel as though we're barely making any noteworthy progress.

The good news, if there's any to be had, is we haven't thrown in the towel yet. We're still hanging in there doing our best day-after-day to control our food portions. We're choosing to eliminate binge eating and mindless snacking. Above all, we're standing on the promises of God and trusting that through these struggles, God will bless our efforts and use these struggles to develop character and integrity in us. God will find a way to take what the enemy has meant for our harm and destruction to bring glory and edification to the goodness of God.

Nobody trips over mountains. It is the small pebble that causes you to stumble. Pass all the pebbles in your path and you will find you have crossed the mountain. ~ Author Unknown

And we know that God causes everything to work together for the good of those who love God and are called according to his purpose for them. Romans 8:28 (NLT)

PRAYER FOR TODAY: *Lord, thank You for perseverance to continue this journey. Help me not to get discouraged. May I stay strong and focused in my commitment to lose weight and be healthy. I pray You will continue to mold me and make me in your image, Lord. In Your name I ask all these things, Lord Jesus. Amen.*

APRIL 21
Comparatively Speaking

Most of us are great at telling our friends not to compare themselves with others. It's never a good idea to compare ourselves with anyone else – not with their looks, their spouses, their houses or material goods or finances. Yet, it's so much harder to take our own advice and not compare ourselves with others. Why is that?

I've been chatting back and forth with a couple of friends this week and we've been trading quips and compliments. I look at my friends and see these beautiful amazing women with million dollar smiles and great hair, better clothes and figures to match. I find myself getting all caught up and wrestling with jealousy wishing I had their hair or their teeth or their long thin legs.

On the other hand when I look in the mirror I can't seem to focus on one redeeming quality about myself. My friends are singing my praises about what great hair I have or how put together I look and I'm thinking ... duh ... who are they talking about?

Bottom line time – if we listen to the lies of the enemy most of us would never leave our house. The devil wants us to feel inferior by focusing on our extra weight, wrinkles, gray hair and saggy body parts. All of these insecurities are little arrows aimed at our self-esteem designed to make us draw inward and away from our friends. These attacks are meant to make us doubt ourselves and ultimately cause us to draw away from Christ because we don't feel *good enough.*

It would be oh so easy to do just that, which is why it's important to learn to accept compliments when they're given. We need to accept that our worth and value is NOT based on our outside shell, but on our souls, our spirits and our hearts. Once we accept that we have a beautiful Christ-centered heart we need to let that Christ-confidence shine outward to a society trapped in the darkness of superficial outer beauty.

Beauty is not in the face; beauty is a light in the heart. ~ Kahlil Gibran

But the Lord said to Samuel, "Don't judge by his appearance or height, for I have rejected him. The Lord doesn't see things the way you see them. People judge by outward appearance, but the Lord looks at the heart." 1 Samuel 16:7 (NLT)

PRAYER FOR TODAY: Lord, thank You for true natural beauty. Help me to see myself as You see me; to focus on the things I like about myself and not fixate on all the things I don't like about myself. Thank You for all the beautiful friends in my life. In Your name I ask all these things, Lord Jesus. Amen.

APRIL 22
If You Can't Stand the Heat …

Just like it makes good sense not to ride your bicycle into the wind with your mouth open, it makes good sense not to make extra trips to the kitchen without a reason. Because there are so many tantalizing goodies available in the kitchen, it's best to limit your trips to the kitchen whenever possible.

On days when I'm bored or anxious or feeling particularly unmotivated I find myself wearing a path in the carpet with repeated trips to the kitchen. Like a prize Guernsey nibbling in a field of clover, I graze back and forth between the pantry and the fridge … *just looking.*

The kitchen is a multi-purpose room that acts as the hub for family gatherings, but it's also the room where any health conscious individual can expect to be ambushed by baked goods and packaged snacks.

It's a good idea to develop a habit of eating your meals and snacks in one location – whether that's your kitchen or dining room, that's up to you. Once you form a bad habit of eating in bed or in front of the TV or at your desk, those habits quickly become hard to break and then you've got brand new issues to confront.

It's best to have a preplanned menu. When you're in the kitchen, get in and get out without sampling the wares. The preplanned menu keeps you from wandering aimlessly without a destination in mind. It's not foolproof but it's still best to write it out and post it on the fridge or a cabinet door so you can't ignore it. I paste shiny stars on my menu on the days I've had a good day. It's silly, but when I see those stars lined up it really motivates me.

When we eat based on circumstances or emotions our only chance for success means we may have to avoid the kitchen at all costs. Yeah it seems a little radical, but hopefully once we get a handle on this, we won't have to boycott the kitchen indefinitely. For the time being, if we're weak and we know it, the less time spent in the kitchen – the better.

He that eats till he is sick must fast till he is well. ~ English Proverb

A person without self-control is like a city with broken-down walls. Proverbs 25:28 (NLT)

PRAYER FOR TODAY: *Lord, I ask that You would help me to stay strong, stick to my meal plan and stay out of the kitchen as long as I'm unable to resist the foods that tempt me. Give me confidence to succeed. In Your name I ask all these things, Lord Jesus. Amen.*

APRIL 23
HALT! God's not in there!

When we're in the habit of emotional eating and grazing in the kitchen because we're bored or anxious, oftentimes we're ignoring the root problem of "why" we're grazing or emotionally eating. There is no denial with me – I KNOW I'm guilty of emotional eating and grazing during times of stress and anxiety.

When I'm frustrated, anxious, worried or stressed – *my spirit should know* that I need to stop what I'm doing and invite God to come in and inhabit all those dark areas of my spirit that are troubled and conflicted. What do I do instead? Somehow my flesh thinks that I can get over those anxious feelings by eating my weight in Oreos. In reality this only creates more stress, tension and anxiety now coupled with tons of guilt because I know I'm gaining weight because I turn to Oreos rather than God.

Last night a woman in my support group shared that she frequently turns to food and finds herself grazing in the pantry. Recognizing that she was eating not out of actual hunger but emotional issues, she had enough sense and restraint to stop by telling herself, *"God's not in here!"* I absolutely love that and told the group maybe we should all think about putting a sign on our pantry door or our cupboards that reads, "GOD'S NOT IN HERE!" The sign on the refrigerator should read, "GOD'S NOT IN HERE EITHER!"

Success means sacrifice, but it also means recognizing why we're eating when we eat. Is it because we are really HALT: hungry, angry, lonely or tired or has it been six hours since lunch? Next time the urge to graze hits – *before* we dive face first into a vat of ice cream it would behoove us to take an inventory … HALT, *before* we eat ourselves stupid.

I bid you conquer in your warfare against your four great enemies, the world, the devil, the flesh, and above all, that obstinate and perverse self-will, unaided by which the other three would be comparatively powerless. ~ Augustus William Hare and Julius Charles Hare, Guesses at Truth, by Two Brothers, 1827

Christ has set us free to live a free life. So take your stand! Never again let anyone put a harness of slavery on you. Galatians 5:1 (The Message Bible)

PRAYER FOR TODAY: *Lord, I humbly ask that You would help me to defeat my flesh by not feeding it every time it demands attention. Help me to submit myself to God and resist the devil so he will flee from me. In Your name I ask all these things, Lord Jesus. Amen.*

APRIL 24
Fear of Falling

When unexpected opportunities arise for a spontaneous long weekend or an out-of-town business trip, we must not let the fear of *falling off the weight watching wagon* keep us from enjoying ourselves. Everything we've done thus far has been for the purpose of re-educating ourselves so we can live a healthier lifestyle. We shouldn't be planning our entire life around our next meal, but it is possible to enjoy the unexpected without fearing the food.

It is conceivable to travel and eat out at every meal without sampling everything at the free continental breakfast or getting our money's worth at the all-you-can-eat buffet. *What happens in Vegas* won't necessarily stay in Vegas if we're "doubling down" at the buffet table. You can expect to bring home a few extra pounds if you don't arm yourself with a plan. As with anything regarding our food selections, there must be planning and balance.

If at all possible, make your unexpected, spontaneous weekend about activities rather than your next meal. Keeping busy and incorporating lots of walking into your trip will help to balance an over-indulgence of food. If you know that your trip will involve visiting a number of restaurants, drink lots of water with your meal; share a meal if at all possible and stay away from the bread basket and the dessert menu!

If you do end up over-indulging, don't beat yourself up. As long as you get right back on track with healthy eating, menu planning and exercise the minute your trip is over you can correct any unexpected indiscretions. *Stuff happens*.

God never intended us to live in bondage to anything – not alcohol, drugs, shopping or food or even OCD excessive meal planning and restrictive diets. There is freedom in saying "no" and victory in saying "yes" to moderation and balance.

Your body is a temple, but only if you treat it as one. ~ Astrid Alauda

The temptations in your life are no different from what others experience. And God is faithful. He will not allow the temptation to be more than you can stand. When you are tempted, he will show you a way out so that you can endure. 1 Corinthians 10:13 (NLT)

PRAYER FOR TODAY: *Thank You, Lord, for balance and moderation in life. May I learn to take better care of myself; count my blessings and be grateful for all You've bestowed upon me every single day. In Your name I ask all these things, Lord Jesus. Amen.*

APRIL 25
Journey Pitfalls or Black Holes

Because life frequently gets in the way of our weight loss journey – unexpected parties, funerals, illnesses, injuries, etc. we need to learn to be flexible. And of course we need to be knowledgeable about basic nutrition and calories.

Hopefully most of us have been at this weight loss journey long enough that we've acquired a modicum of knowledge about caloric values, fat grams, carbohydrates and so forth. When life throws us unexpected curve balls and we're suddenly forced to juggle our plans and veer from our prearranged menu plan it's important to know how to best juggle our calories so we aren't being pushed off the weight watcher wagon entirely.

Statistically speaking, the average dieter who is forced off their program because of an unexpected pitfall or crisis rarely returns to their program; oftentimes regaining lost weight at an alarmingly quick rate. We don't want to be one of those people.

For example, I've been plagued with a recurring knee injury for more than a week now. I've been unable to get in any kind of cardio workout, which I've come to depend on for burning those extra calories I like to consume. Because I'm basically sidelined and only able to lift weights right now, I've had to do some creative juggling with my meal plan.

Many experts agree that about 70% of all weight loss comes from what you eat, not exercise. That's good news for someone like me who simply can't make my body cooperate right now. Life is predictably unpredictable and this knee injury will hopefully only be a temporary setback – but there are sure to be other pitfalls, because let's face it – that's life.

It's important not to let the pitfalls turn into black holes for which we can never escape. Injuries and pitfalls may slow us down some, but we must not let them be our undoing.

People are like stained-glass windows. They sparkle and shine when the sun is out, but when the darkness sets in their true beauty is revealed only if there is light from within. ~ Elisabeth Kübler-Ross

"I have told you all this so that you may have peace in me. Here on earth you will have many trials and sorrows. But take heart, because I have overcome the world." John 16:33 (NLT)

PRAYER FOR TODAY: *Lord, help me overcome these obstacles without becoming discouraged or depressed while I am adjusting to the unexpected. Help me to maintain a positive attitude and believe that all things are possible with You. In Your name I ask all these things, Lord Jesus. Amen.*

APRIL 26
Balancing Unbreakable Rules

Most of us have heard that there are three unbreakable rules when it comes to selling real estate. Those rules are: *location, location, location*. Believe it or not, there are three unbreakable rules when it comes to weight loss and achieving a healthy lifestyle. No, it's not about *location* but rather, *balance*. If we hope to lose weight successfully and maintain a healthy lifestyle that will improve our overall quality of life we must do everything with *balance, balance, balance*.

We must have a healthy balance of eating; balance in our menu planning and journaling; balance in our activity and exercise and a balance of positive mental attitudes. My personal favorite and my mission to the misinformed is learning to balance our intake of calories versus exercise.

I suffered from exercise bulimia for nearly 30 years. I was so far out of balance in this area *normal* was unidentifiable. My out-of-balance days consisted of eating myself stupid with all of the wrong foods and then exercising for several hours in the hopes of eliminating those excess calories. After 30 years of being *out-of-balance* in this area, my body is now paying the price with repeated lower back problems and arthritis in my feet, knees and hips that has resulted in constant pain while performing the simplest of tasks.

When we are out of balance, we may not see the effects of our poor choices immediately, but eventually we WILL pay the price. Let the words *balance, Balance, BALANCE* resonate in your brain, your body and your soul and ask God to give you wisdom and balance in every area of your life.

If I ever get out of balance again I pray it's not with exercise or food, but I hope it's with too much God because even with *too much* God I still find myself wanting more.

The trouble with using experience as a guide is that the final exam often comes first and then the lesson. ~ Author Unknown

You say, "I am allowed to do anything"—but not everything is good for you. You say, "I am allowed to do anything"—but not everything is beneficial. 1 Corinthians 10:23 (NLT)

PRAYER FOR TODAY: *Lord, I ask that You would help me learn from these life lessons to help others who are struggling as I have. Help me to find a healthy balance in all things so that I can live the rest of my life serving You and making the most of all the opportunities in my life. In Your name I ask all these things, Lord Jesus. Amen.*

APRIL 27
Thirsting for Sustenance

You just finished a big lunch an hour ago but suddenly you *feel hungry* and your stomach begins that noisy rumble. How can this be when you filled up on salad, protein and fiber a mere hour ago? When your stomach starts demanding to have its way, we have to stop and ask ourselves, are we really hungry or *something else?*

A growling stomach can have a *Pavlov's dog* response. Our stomach growls and we automatically assume we must be hungry so we feed it. We think we need sustenance when in reality our body may simply need to be hydrated. If we are in the habit of drinking beverages other than water, our body has a way of letting us know when it simply needs plain, old H_2O.

A healthy lifestyle should include plenty of water. Some experts agree that we should be drinking half our body weight in ounces of water per day. Meaning if you weigh 150 pounds, you should be drinking 75 ounces of water every day. That may seem like a lot but many of us consume at least that much in soda, coffee or tea combined daily.

Drinking a glass of water before mealtime can actually curb your appetite and decrease the amount of calories consumed at each meal. When our stomach starts to rumble and growl and we think we're starving, oftentimes by drinking a glass of water, the hunger pains will cease.

Consuming water in the colder months of the year can be particularly challenging so you may want to try one of the many flavored waters available at your local supermarket. Consuming the necessary amount of water in the warmer months of the year is doubly important. When engaging in strenuous activity in the heat, if you experience a sudden thirst it's likely you're already dehydrated and in need of some quick rehydration.

Remember, your stomach is not the boss of you, but if it starts growling at you, maybe you just need to take it out for a drink. A drink of water, that is. Life is short – drink up!

Pure water is the world's first and foremost medicine. ~ Slovakian Proverb

As the deer longs for streams of water, so I long for you, O God. Psalm 42:1 (NLT)

PRAYER FOR TODAY: *Lord, as the deer longs for water, so I long for You and Your presence in my life. Help me to understand the signals my body sends me without bowing down to the dictates of my flesh when it demands food. Thank You for this body that is wonderfully made. In Your name I ask all these things, Lord Jesus. Amen.*

APRIL 28
Craving the Good Life

Most people, if they are honest, will tell you that they crave certain foods from time-to-time. What woman hasn't felt that unholy pull of chocolate that coincides with PMS? My husband craves ice cream nightly after dinner. One of my children has an insatiable lust for pumpkin pie months prior to Thanksgiving.

Just because we crave something doesn't mean we have to give in to those cravings. When we experience cravings it's important to identify what has triggered a craving. Cravings can be triggered by memories, smells and circumstances or by something as innocent as reading or watching TV. Whenever I watch *Cupcake Wars* on the food network I get that sudden urge for Betty Crocker and yellow cake with chocolate icing. You don't have to be a brain surgeon to figure that one out. Censor your TV viewing if you're easily triggered by images – subliminal or otherwise.

There are times though when you might be craving a particular food and that is a signal from your body that you are suffering from some sort of vitamin deficiency. As with anything concerning our health, it makes good sense to check with a health care provider to get answers to our questions. A sudden craving for chocolate might simply mean that your body is deficient in either Vitamin B or magnesium. There are no silly questions to ask your doctor when it comes to our health as oftentimes the body knows what it needs and cravings might be signals.

Be diligent and do your research before you give in to your cravings. Sometimes we simply need to *wait it out*. Remove yourself from a situation if you're having a sudden unnatural urge to eat because of your circumstances. Try drinking a large glass of water to stave off what you might be mistaking for hunger. Do the "legwork" before you let your stomach tell you what to do. Repeat after me: *My stomach is not the boss of me*. Above all, before you succumb to your cravings – investigate before you masticate and ask yourself, *what's eating me?*

The more you eat, the less flavor; the less you eat, the more flavor.
~ Chinese Proverb

Jesus said to them, "My food is to do the will of Him who sent Me and to accomplish His work." John 4:34 (NASB)

PRAYER FOR TODAY: *Lord, I ask that the only thing I would crave on a regular basis is You. Help me not give in to the lusts of my stomach, but to be ever mindful of the signals my body might be sending me. I want more of You and less of me. In Your name I ask all these things, Lord Jesus. Amen.*

APRIL 29
Missteps

Sometimes when we least expect it life, the Universe and/or God have a unique way of getting our attention and slowing us down. Yesterday I had such a day. One wrong misstep, a loud pop and the next thing I know pain off the charts sent me to me to the floor in uncontrollable sobbing, which resulted in a lengthy visit to Urgent Care.

I've actually been complaining of hip and knee pain for several months – a direct result from being out of balance with my exercise regime. I've been avoiding going to the doctor but yesterday's "pop" moved it to the top of my To-Do list – *the hard way*. Four hours of Urgent Care pain can bring life around full circle.

I'm convinced that yesterday's misstep was my Lord and Savior subtly telling me what He's been trying to tell me for months; that I've got to take this weight loss thing more seriously but I haven't been paying attention. Yesterday's pop reverberated not only through my knee ligaments, but I heard it loud and clear in my spirit. "Girl, you're carrying around 40 extra pounds!"

That's 40 pounds more pressure on my hip joints, my knee joints and my ankles which multiplies exponentially when you factor in simple gravity. Even though I've been exercising, I am continually reminded of how much easier exercise would be if I didn't have this extra weight on my body.

Has God been trying to get your attention with regards to your health? Could it be that your achy joints, shortness of breath, heart palpitations or just the fact that your underwear is suddenly too tight are all subliminal messages from God designed to be your wake-up call?

Okay, God. You've got my attention. It's time to go back to basics. It's time to get super serious about every morsel of food that goes in my mouth. It's time to see the bigger picture. Yesterday it was a possible torn ligament. Tomorrow it could be a heart attack. That's not a price I'm willing to pay. Thank you, Lord – I HEAR YOU!

The only real mistake is the one from which we learn nothing. ~ John Powell

In the same way, wisdom is sweet to your soul. If you find it, you will have a bright future, and your hopes will not be cut short. Proverbs 24:14 (NLT)

PRAYER FOR TODAY: *Lord, thank You for wisdom and for getting my attention. I pray for a healthy body. I pray I can take all these lessons You are teaching me and learn from them so I can serve You with my whole heart and become the person You would have me to be. In Your name I ask all these things, Lord Jesus. Amen.*

APRIL 30
Growing Pains

Day three of my "Recliner restriction" (as in Lazy-Boy) and lessons are being learned all over the place. I'm hobbling around and becoming quite resourceful at using crutches for things other than what they were intended. I am learning a whole new way of life and have a much greater appreciation for two working legs at this point. I vow never to complain about my legs again. My legs may not be as thin as I would like them to be, but up until a couple of days ago, they worked pretty well and got me from point A to point B without me breaking out in a cold sweat.

I've developed a whole new exercise regime based on my current invalid status. I've probably burned hundreds of calories with my crutches aerobics. Going upstairs or downstairs has now been limited to one trip each way per day, simply because the effort is pretty exhausting. Burning extra calories is never a bad thing.

Only recently I was *complaining* that I didn't have enough hours in the day to spend "quality time" with God. God DOES answer prayers, but clearly not in the way I had hoped for. Now that I'm very limited in my activities, I have little else to do except talk to God and read the Word. Perhaps God knew it would take "an act of God," to get me off my feet with my only focus being on Him. Hmm ... who knew?

The good news is I know *this too shall pass* and this little setback is merely a trial I need to endure. I'm sure when it's all over God will have fine-tuned my attitude and taught me a thing or two to store in my backpack of life. Life's challenges always serve a purpose.

If you're battling through a painful trial, let God use this time to teach you, mold you and remake you into what He wants you to be. It is possible to grow through the pain, but only if you're willing to invite Jesus into the middle of the pain. God doesn't cause the pain but certainly can use the pain if there's wisdom and growth to be had.

Some stand on tiptoe trying to reach God to talk to him – you try too hard, friend – drop to your knees and listen to him, he'll hear you better that way. ~ Terri Guillemets

How do you know what your life will be like tomorrow? Your life is like the morning fog—it's here a little while, then it's gone. James 4:14 (NLT)

PRAYER FOR TODAY: *Lord, I thank You for helping me to slow down. May the trials of life cause me to turn to You and draw into a deeper relationship with You. Increase my faith as You heal my body and may I continually rejoice in the Lord always. In Your name I ask all these things, Lord Jesus. Amen.*

MAY 1
Check Point

When life hands us lemons we'd do well to suck it up and learn to make lemonade rather than complain. Looking on the bright side of my recent injury I've noticed a generous outpouring of support from my friends and offers for food and housecleaning. I'm profoundly grateful for my friends and this injury could be God's way of reminding me of how blessed I am. *Check – lesson number one.*

I'm burning more calories without an actual workout program simply by hobbling on crutches, hoisting myself up and down the stairs and in and out of the shower. I'm not obsessing about exercise but rather, I'm forced to concentrate on simple survival which has caused my metabolism to work a little harder than normal. *Check – lesson number two.*

Many of my friends struggling with weight issues (even minor ones) and/or food addictions are realizing through my struggles that any extra body weight results in a slower and more difficult recovery from injury. Excess weight leads to physical hardships and problems and impedes healing; which makes this lesson one of the most difficult to learn. *Check – lesson number three.*

Through this trial God has been reminding me that I've had my focus on food, exercise, losing weight and all manner of "idols" in my life for far too long. Mistreating my "temple" has taken my eyes off God and because of it, God needed to bring me back to a place of total repentance and dependence on HIM – *check, check and check.*

We shouldn't wait for an injury or other catastrophe to slow us down and redirect our focus to the only thing that really matters in life: loving God with our whole heart, mind, soul, body and strength. Messages received. Thank you Lord!

We turn to God for help when our foundations are shaking, only to learn that it is God who is shaking them. ~ Charles C. West

But by means of their suffering, he rescues those who suffer. For he gets their attention through adversity. Job 36:15 (NLT)

PRAYER FOR TODAY: *Lord, I continue to be amazed at all You wish to teach me. I know I've so much to learn and so far to go. I pray You will continue to be patient with me as I grow in Your wisdom each day. In Your name I ask all these things, Lord Jesus. Amen.*

MAY 2
Fleshy Machinery

The human body is a magnificent creation. I marvel each day at the things the human body can do and yet so many are blind to the Creator of such an amazing piece of fleshy machinery. God has entrusted us with these amazing houses of flesh that are truly remarkable yet many of us take them for granted.

With so much time to sit and think while I recuperate, I've had opportunity to reflect on how I've treated my body over the years. It shames me to realize I've not taken the best care of my fleshy machine. Years (more like decades), of yo-yo dieting and gaining and losing the same 30 or 40 pounds has practically crippled my fat-burning system. My metabolism isn't slow, it's in a coma.

There is a certain amount of fear circling around in my head that if I don't get this weight off, what's to keep this from happening again? I didn't sustain this knee injury performing any unusual stunts. I was simply walking. I plan to do a lot of walking over the remaining years of my life so how can I guarantee I won't walk right into another serious injury?

We all need to pray and ask God to protect our minds from fear. We must refuse to live in fear and worry and let the enemy keep us from living normal lives. It's important to rebuke any and all thoughts that try to penetrate our mind and drag us into a worried state of panic. No good will come of that. *Get thee behind me Satan!*

Many of us would do well to take better care of these "temples" and honor God by denying our flesh and treating our bodies like the amazing machines that they are. If we're not already taking positive steps to get healthy, today is the day – it's never too late! Whatever we can do to make a positive influence in our health may feel like baby steps, but at least they are steps in the right direction.

What good is having someone who can walk on water if you don't follow in his footsteps? ~ Author Unknown

But if we confess our sins to him, he is faithful and just to forgive us our sins and to cleanse us from all wickedness. 1 John 1:9 (NLT)

PRAYER FOR TODAY: *Lord, thank You for the creation of the human body and all that it can do at Your design. I praise You for healing and I thank You for forgiving me of my sins. Strengthen me and give me balance and commitment in all things, Lord. In Your name I ask all these things, Lord Jesus. Amen.*

MAY 3
How Alarming

Because I've learned to expect the unexpected in life, I wasn't at all surprised when my smoke alarm went off at 4:30 this morning. No worries, there was no fire, but the system which operates on electricity also has a precautionary 9-volt battery back-up. When the batteries need changing, the alarm goes off triggering the remaining alarms throughout the house – upstairs and downstairs. We have nine alarms all total.

I'd been sleeping fitfully when the chirping of the alarm bellowed forth rising to full volume. If you've never been awakened in the middle of the night by an alarm, it's an ear-piercing screech which is oftentimes indistinguishable over the pounding of your own terrified heartbeat.

I have a way of seeing the little God clues in everything – including nighttime alarms. My first reaction was to leap from bed. The second I put my foot on the floor, I was instantly reminded of my injury. I hobbled to the stairs with my daughter and husband and all I could think was, *"What if this is a real emergency? How fast can I make it down the stairs on my bum leg?"*

Of course, those thoughts were followed by *"See ... this is EXACTLY why you need to get this weight off!"* How is it even dead batteries in smoke alarms remind me that I'm carrying too much weight?

A middle of the night emergency exodus is no laughing matter and could happen to any one of us at any time. What if you had to help your spouse or one of your children from the house in the middle of the night? Would you be useless in your present condition or a hero? Excess weight is no laughing matter. God's goodness and grace reminds us He cares enough to send us gentle, sometimes "alarming" nudges to get our attention. Are you listening?

The patient should be made to understand that he or she must take charge of his own life. Don't take your body to the doctor as if he were a repair shop. ~ Quentin Regestein

In the end you will groan in anguish when disease consumes your body. You will say, "How I hated discipline! If only I had not ignored all the warnings!" Proverbs 5:11-12 (NLT)

PRAYER FOR TODAY: *Lord, thank You that You care enough for me to gently remind me I need to take better care of myself. I pray I will fully heed Your warnings. I ask Your help in making my body respond to a healthier diet and exercise. Thank You for opening my eyes, Lord. In Your name I ask all these things, Lord Jesus. Amen.*

MAY 4
The New Normal

Through the miraculous power of prayer, a good deal of rest and Ibuprofen as needed, my injury is healing quite nicely. I've ditched the cumbersome knee brace and the crutches and have adopted a new rather quirky gait to my walk. I've got a little hitch in my giddyap, but it gives me character.

I must confess it's great to be able to return to near normal. Thinking about what is supposed to be "normal" though got me wondering: what is normal?

Typically the majority of dieters who reach their weight loss goals have a tendency to slowly start slipping back into old bad habits. Before long and with little or no effort, all the weight that was so hard to lose starts coming right back, usually bringing some friends along with it. Statistically 95% of successful dieters go back to their "old normal" way of life within one year of reaching their goal weight.

In order to keep that from happening, once we start successfully losing weight, we need to adjust not only our attitudes and the way we eat, but our perception of "normal." This healthier lifestyle needs to become our "new normal" and that old unhealthy life needs to become a bad dream from our past.

Normal must mean we embrace a healthier lifestyle and opt for balanced meals, smaller portions and saying "no" more than we say "yes." *Normal* should be making it a habit to "Play 60" three or four times a week and getting our heart rate up and sweating. Normal must mean only *occasional* desserts, not every day. *Normal* should be reaching out and calling a friend when we're tempted to eat unhealthy foods or zip in to a fast-food drive-through line when we're craving French fries.

If we don't adjust our perception of "normal" the chances of us ending up in the 95 percentile failure group is a very real possibility. I for one, intend to be one of the 5% success stories. I hope I have some friends willing to go the distance with me.

Some people dream of success… while others wake up and work hard at it. ~ Author Unknown

Foolishness brings joy to those with no sense; a sensible person stays on the right path. Proverbs 15:21 (NLT)

PRAYER FOR TODAY: *Lord, thank You for all of the blessings You've bestowed upon me. Thank You for the successes I'm enjoying. I pray that I won't become complacent and lose interest in my task. Help me to adapt my thinking to a healthier way of life and let that be my normal way of thinking from now on. In Your name I ask all these things, Lord Jesus. Amen.*

MAY 5
What Would Jesus Do?

Okay we've established that "normal" now means we don't get to eat everything we want, when we want. Normal does not mean we NEVER get to partake of sweet treats again. It does however, mean that we need to limit our sugar consumption and learn to truly enjoy and savor those occasional treats.

There will be times though that we may need to use common sense and sound judgment when faced with a tempting situation. A friend brought me brownies to taste and enjoy today. This is someone who never bakes but needed to take something to a potluck event. She went to a lot of trouble. Baking is as foreign to her as changing the oil in my car is to me. The fact that this person thought enough of me to share in her milestone baking extravaganza was huge.

How does one refuse such a generous effort when someone has clearly put a lot of love and thought into bringing something to you? I had to stop and ask myself: *What would Jesus do?* It sounds cliché but it applies in this situation. I didn't want to refuse this kind offer and hurt this person's feelings, but yet brownies aren't on my daily menu plan. What to do?

Jesus was kind to strangers and rarely rebuffed people. The story of the little boy's lunch of fish and bread would have been totally different if Jesus would have said, *"No, thanks, I'm on a special diet – can't eat the carbs and I don't like fish."* Feeding the multitudes on this boy's generosity would never have been recorded.

We need to employ common sense. There are ways to appease someone without being rude and hurting their feelings. With careful forethought and planning we can enjoy treats as long as we're willing to cut back somewhere else. Saying yes to an occasional treat will help you stay on track and satisfy your flesh so you can go the distance. We don't have to say "Yes" to everything, but as always we need to remember that "B" word: *balance, balance, balance!*

Strength is the capacity to break a chocolate bar into four pieces with your bare hands – and then eat just one of the pieces. ~ Judith Viorst

He gave his life to free us from every kind of sin, to cleanse us, and to make us his very own people, totally committed to doing good deeds. Titus 2:14 (NLT)

PRAYER FOR TODAY: *Lord, thank You for the generosity of friends. May I always have a gracious heart and never let any unwholesome talk come from my mouth so as to hurt others. Thank You for restraint and common sense. May I employ both on a regular daily basis. In Your name I ask all these things, Lord Jesus. Amen.*

MAY 6
Eating Rainbows

I love this time of year as the temperatures heat up. Not because of the hot weather but because eating and shopping takes on a whole new meaning for me. Eating is so much more interesting during the summer months because of the availability of fresh fruits and veggies.

Today I was faced with a choice of snorfing down leftover brownies or pigging out on a jumbo fruit salad. Because I have PMS, the brownie was hard to resist so I indulged in a small brownie.

If it weren't for the PMS I probably would have chosen the fruit salad as fruit is infinitely more filling. Fruit salads can be so aesthetically appealing to the eyes as well as delicious to the taste buds. There are berries of all kinds, red and green grapes, pineapple, melons and kiwi; so many fabulous flavors and so many beautiful colors. God's color palette is magnificent!

Watching your weight doesn't always have to consist of the same old thing. Take advantage of the summer produce and start eating a rainbow of colors while the rainbows are available. Before the rainbows are gone for the summer, stock up while the prices are low and freeze them and save them to use in fruit smoothies.

Summer is a great time to get healthy, eat healthy and make your menu colorful. Before you reach for the packaged snack goods think on this: the caloric value of a two-inch brownie is about the same as eating 4 cups of strawberries or a whole cantaloupe. You don't have to be a genius to figure out that a whole melon or a bushel of strawberries will fill you up and satisfy your hunger a lot faster than a two-inch brownie.

Rather than eating empty calories fill your plate with a rainbow of colors and watch the weight come off.

Did you ever stop to taste a carrot? Not just eat it, but taste it? You can't taste the beauty and energy of the earth in a Twinkie. ~ Astrid Alauda

And if God cares so wonderfully for flowers that are here today and thrown into the fire tomorrow, he will certainly care for you. Why do you have so little faith? Luke 12:28 (NLT)

PRAYER FOR TODAY: *Lord, thank You for the amazing varieties of fresh fruits and vegetables that are grown at Your command. May I eat and be satisfied as I feed my body with such colorful varieties. Continue to provide for my needs daily and nourish my body as well as my spirit. In Your name I ask all these things, Lord Jesus. Amen.*

MAY 7
Feeding the Grief

I spent yesterday afternoon with a friend who was going through a crisis. We sat together crying over her grief (yes, I cried right along with her) for a good solid hour. She was so grief-stricken, she couldn't even think of eating for the rest of the day. On the other hand, because I'd so completely embraced her problem, I wanted to do nothing but EAT.

Eating through a crisis is entirely normal for me. *That's what I do.* That's what I've always done. Part of me was dumbfounded that my friend couldn't possibly think about eating. How is that normal? *Not* eating during a crisis is an entirely foreign concept to me. I'm sure that would explain why my friend weighs 118 pounds and why *I don't* weigh 118 pounds. She starves her problems. I feed my problems. Somewhere in between those two scenarios there must be a practical solution.

Stuff happens so it's important to learn to deal with each crisis by not eating ourselves into a coma. Stuffing our face in the wake of every trial will derail our weight loss goals quicker than Superman can do a speeding bullet flyover.

Note to self: in the event of future crises stock up on rice cakes, apples and sugar-free snacks. Life happens and it will be filled with trials and tribulations. If we're emotional eaters, if we *don't* stock up on low-cal snacks, we're heading down a road that will be our ruin *again*.

There are things that we don't want to happen but have to accept, things we don't want to know but have to learn, and people we can't live without but have to let go. ~ Author Unknown

Laughter can conceal a heavy heart, but when the laughter ends, the grief remains. Proverbs 14:13 (NIV)

PRAYER FOR TODAY: *Lord, I ask that You would bless my friends that might be hurting. I pray You will help me to work through trials without resorting to emotional eating. In the future help me turn to You rather than food when dealing with disappointment or grief. In Your name I ask all these things, Lord Jesus. Amen.*

MAY 8
The Speed of Me

For the first time in two weeks I was able to get some real exercise besides just weight lifting. My knee injury is recovering nicely and I was able to go for a long bike ride today. At first it seemed like a great idea and I felt no residual pain whatsoever. That was the first half of my ride.

My return trip should have been the same but once I turned around and headed home I was pedaling full force into the wind. I was so excited to be getting some real exercise I didn't stop to check the weather prior to leaving the house. When I left the sun was shining, the birds were singing, the temperature was perfect and the breeze was blowing – *slightly.* However when I turned around to head back the way I came, the slight breeze turned into gale force winds which required super human strength to pedal through.

I got a great cardio workout in today as my bike is a Schwinn cruiser bike, which translates to one speed, not three, not five, not ten – just one and that's *the speed of me.* Once I finally made it home (my face and shirt sufficiently covered with the tiny carcasses of flying insects) I felt like I needed a nap as that's the most exercise I've had in nearly two weeks.

Experts suggest that 70% of our weight loss comes solely from what we eat. It's important not to rely completely on our daily menu when it comes to our weight loss, but to take advantage of that 30% benefit we get from exercise. Life's too short to waste away in front of the TV.

Get up and move today if you're able. If you're housebound, bed-ridden or confined to a wheel-chair, move the parts of your body that you can move. Every little bit helps. Do what you *can* do and let God take care of what you *can't.*

Those who think they have not time for bodily exercise will sooner or later have to find time for illness. ~ Edward Stanley

What I am saying, dear brothers and sisters, is that our physical bodies cannot inherit the Kingdom of God. These dying bodies cannot inherit what will last forever. 1 Corinthians 15:50 (NLT)

PRAYER FOR TODAY: *Lord, I rejoice in Your goodness and thank You for physical exercise. Please let the combination of physical exercise, healthy eating and time spent with You transform my mind and body to be the best they can be this side of heaven. In Your name I ask all these things, Lord Jesus. Amen.*

MAY 9
Fake and Bake

With summer just around the corner and the need to bare more flesh and dress for the hotter temperatures, now is when we find out just how successful we've been on our weight loss journey. For me, my days of donning shorts in public are a thing of the past. I do wear Capri pants and sleeveless blouses though so I'm still planning on baring a fair amount of flesh this summer. This is the time of year when I stock up on "tube tan" aka "fake-and-bake" and "tan-in-a-can." My philosophy is: *"fat looks better tan."*

I saw a friend of mine recently whom I'd not seen in several weeks. The first thing I noticed about her was her golden brown tan. When I asked how she'd gotten such a lovely color in such a short amount of time she laughed and told me it was "tube tan." I chortled when my philosophy came out of her mouth, *"Fat looks better tan."* (Alas, we poor women are so persecuted by the lies of the enemy.)

While I avoid using the "F" word (as in "fat") there is a good bit of accuracy in that philosophy about looking better with a tan. At my age sunbathing is not high on my list of "things I love to do." Sunbathing also does cause wrinkles and there's that whole skin cancer worry, which is why sunblock with a high SPF is a must have. Once I've slathered on the sunblock I apply the fake tan stuff liberally. Even though I know my skin is not really that tan, the golden tan really makes me *feel* thinner.

Whether we've lost all of our winter weight or not, summer is coming and the time to reveal how well we're doing with our weight loss is now. As for me – from mid-calf to my ankles and my neck and arms – look *fab-u-lous!* I've got the whole summer to swim away, walk away and bike away the remainder of my winter weight. And the good news is, if I don't lose the weight as quickly as I'd like, I'm well stocked with tube tan!

Gluttony is an emotional escape, a sign something is eating us. ~ Peter De Vries

Delight yourself in the LORD and he will give you the desires of your heart. Psalm 37:4 (NIV)

PRAYER FOR TODAY: *Lord, I pray that You would give me the desires of my heart to lose this excess weight. Help me to work harder and press forward with strength and determination. Thank You for the changes in the seasons and the changes I'm seeing in myself. May I continue to press in and become more like You each and every day. In Your name I ask all these things, Lord Jesus. Amen.*

MAY 10
Left Brain Right Body

Some days we may start to feel that we're getting sick and tired of his whole food thing. We get tired of thinking about what we should or should not be eating. We're tired of menu planning, calorie counting, weighing and measuring and recording our food options. We're sick of the whole concept of eating in general. It seems like such a bother. But we know we have to eat because we need to properly nourish our bodies.

When I start to feel this way I opt to do something really crazy and I listen to my body by waiting to eat until I am really hungry. You know, *the grumbling stomach, light-headed and if I don't put something in my stomach soon, I'm going to faint* feeling. This morning I awoke around six a.m. and didn't even begin to feel hungry until five hours later.

Ideally we should take advantage of these days and really try not to feed our body just for the sake of nutrition. There is nothing wrong with listening to our body when it decides it just doesn't need as much food one day as compared to a "normal" day. Of course listening to our bodies is exactly what has led most of us to battle excess weight in the first place so we can't always bow down to the whims and demands of our body's food cravings.

As with everything we need wisdom and balance when listening to our bodies. Take advantage of those days when you don't feel like eating as much and be very minimal with your calories. The whole point of changing our lifestyles is to stop taking orders from our fickle flesh and learn to eat and exercise with balance and wisdom rather than simply feeding our emotions and our cravings. Listen to your body but don't let it boss you around. Make sure you listen to your brain and not just your body.

Our own physical body possesses a wisdom which we who inhabit the body lack. We give it orders which make no sense. ~ Henry Miller

But true wisdom and power are found in God; counsel and understanding are his. Job 12:13 (NLT)

PRAYER FOR TODAY: *Lord, I ask that You would help me to listen to my body without bowing down to unrealistic or unhealthy demands. I praise You for wisdom and common sense. May I continually employ both while I'm actively working on changing my life to live as healthy a lifestyle as possible. In Your name I ask all these things, Lord Jesus. Amen.*

MAY 11
A Fat Eraser

A friend of mine recently offered some follow-up advice on how to get the best "tube tan." My friend reminded me of the importance of preparing our body before we "tan" with a generous buffing prior to applying self-tanning lotion. This is excellent advice you might want to consider if you're going to be "tanning" anytime soon.

I punish my skin with a coarse loofah sponge before I apply my self-tanning lotion. There's something therapeutic about a good scrubbing of my outer layer and part of me is secretly hoping I can magically erase some of that annoying cellulite stuff that's multiplying on the backs of my thighs. Depending on my mood, the intensity with which I scrub varies.

I'm still so raw and reeling from having spent a weepy afternoon with another friend and her personal crisis, that today I felt the need to "scrub the pain away" from my own emotions. In my mind I thought that if perhaps I could rub off the outer layer of my skin, somehow I might lessen the pain I was feeling in my heart.

How lovely it would be to simply rub out the pain of heartache, but most of us know we simply have to "go through" until the pain subsides. For someone like me who has been overweight and dealing with negative body images most of my life, I've often wished I could scrub away the excess fat. I've tried on more than one occasion to do just that with my trusty loofah so I know from personal experience you can't erase the fat.

We are smart enough to know excess weight cannot be scrubbed away. We must do the work through diet and exercise not with pills, creams or loofah sponges. But oh how nice it would be if cellulite creams worked as instantly as spray-on tans?

With it being Mother's Day weekend; if I could have one wish for this day, I'd wish to have my mother back. My heart still aches for her after all these years. There's not a loofah big enough to scrub away the pain of losing your mother. Sadly, it's not the kind of pain one can scrub away – we just endure.

Mothers hold their children's hands for a short while, but their hearts forever. ~ Author Unknown

The wise woman builds her house, but with her own hands the foolish one tears hers down. Proverbs 14:1 (NIV)

PRAYER FOR TODAY: *Thank you, Lord, for family and for mothers. May I come to accept myself as I am but may I always be striving to improve those things I'm unhappy with regarding myself. In Your name I ask all these things, Lord Jesus. Amen.*

MAY 12
Baby Step, Step, Stepping

I for one am thankful that each week has a Monday. There's something about getting up and starting fresh at the beginning of a new week. Sometimes we need a Monday fresh start. For me starting fresh means getting out my food journal, writing things down – and that means *everything* that I eat today. It also means getting out my food scale and measuring tools and doing the dirty work of weighing all my food rather than merely guessing about my food portions.

Starting over isn't meant to be a punishment so much as a clean slate. While it may feel like punishment to a certain degree when we begin anew, it really is meant to recharge our enthusiasm and reignite our passion for success.

I've definitely felt a waning of my passion for this whole weight loss thing lately. When you have little to show for your efforts and exercising has been nearly impossible for a couple of weeks, it's hard to maintain a positive attitude. The *honeymoon* is definitely over and now it's just about the hard work.

In the same way I was hoping I could scrub the excess fat away with a loofah, I find myself wishing I could get on my bike and ride away from this excess weight. Weight loss lifestyle changes do get boring from time to time and in order to keep from succumbing to the boredom we all need a fresh start.

A fresh start equals baby steps. We have to learn to walk before we can run so for now we simply must baby step … step … step away this weight. Eventually we'll be able to run again – and maybe someday – we can dance.

Though no one can go back and make a brand new start, anyone can start from now and make a brand new ending. ~ Author Unknown

May we shout for joy when we hear of your victory and raise a victory banner in the name of our God. May the LORD answer all your prayers. Psalm 20:5 (NLT)

PRAYER FOR TODAY: Lord, thank You for fresh starts. Help me to make the most of this new day by renewing my mind and my strength. Give me a desire to succeed and help me not get bogged down in boredom or defeat. Help me to commit my plans to You so I may succeed. In Your name I ask all these things, Lord Jesus. Amen.

MAY 13
Want To or Will Do

I was reading Romans 12 this morning and was overcome with sadness as I realized my body has not been a living sacrifice that is holy and pleasing to God. The Apostle Paul wasn't talking about us having a body that's perfect in the way it appears on the outside, but suggests we're to be *wholly committed* to serving God with our entire being: physically, mentally and spiritually.

We're not to abuse our bodies with unclean sexual practices, nor are we to eat or ingest wrong things or unhealthy things. We're not to fill our minds and thoughts with impure, evil or unholy thoughts or images.

For years I've put unhealthy, processed junk food in my body and now I'm paying the price and expecting God to *miraculously* deliver me from my own stupidity. I'm aware I've failed in this though and I am truly repentant. I *want to* offer my body as a living sacrifice and be holy and pleasing to God. But as most of us know, it takes more than "want to" to combat the flesh.

I'm also guilty of *conforming to the pattern of this world* as it states in verse two. I compare myself to others; I constantly berate myself because I don't look like someone else. I am guilty of being angry at the One who created me because He cursed me with this weird body type.

I'm guilty of conforming to the world. But, I've also recognized my flaws and I'm diligently praying *my mind will be transformed* so I can break this debilitating habit. Regardless of how much "want to" or "willpower" we have, the act of offering our bodies as a living sacrifice to God will require our total surrender to God, allowing Him to have "all of us." The question is: *Do we want to?*

Most people are more comfortable with old problems than with new solutions. ~ Author Unknown

Do not conform any longer to the pattern of this world, but be transformed by the renewing of your mind. Then you will be able to test and approve what God's will is—his good, pleasing and perfect will. Romans 12:2 (NLT)

PRAYER FOR TODAY: *Lord, I feel as though I'm constantly asking Your forgiveness. Help me to focus on the future and move beyond my mistakes of the past. Each day is a gift and with Your help, an opportunity for success. Thank You for healing words of Scripture that redirect my path. In Your name I ask all these things, Lord Jesus. Amen.*

MAY 14
It's a Dry Heat

I have a few friends and family members who despise the upcoming summer months. I happen to be in the minority of people who actually look forward to the next few months because I love to swim for exercise.

Because summer is so hot, the daily heat index is a constant reminder that it's not the best time of year to carry excess body weight. Excess weight means excess sweating. I don't mind sweating if I'm working out; but there's nothing worse than sweat pooling under your clothes when you're on your way to an appointment or walking to and from the car. Summer helps me to work a little harder to keep my midriff roll to a minimum.

Sweat serves a purpose though as it's a great way to keep us in line with our eating and exercise programs. The more we eat, the more we weigh and the more we sweat. Compare that to less food, equals less body fat, equals less sweating. Hey, that's math even I can do.

Sure, the summer is long and unbelievably hot and yes we do have to walk faster on the asphalt for fear of our rubber flip flops disintegrating off our feet. And maybe we run the risk of suffering from the Wizard of Oz Wicked Witch syndrome in the fact that we all scurry through parking lots yelling, "I'm melting, I'm melting!" But hey – at least *it's a dry heat.*

If you need a really good reason to appreciate summer, think on this: the heat is a reminder to pray for lost souls and be a better witness for Christ. Hell is most likely much hotter than Arizona in August, and how sad for those that will be thrown into the lake of fire for all eternity.

People don't notice whether it's winter or summer when they're happy.
~ Anton Chekhov

You can enter God's Kingdom only through the narrow gate. The highway to hell is broad, and its gate is wide for the many who choose that way. Matthew 7:13 (NLT)

PRAYER FOR TODAY: *Thank you, Lord for warmer weather and options for getting healthy during the summer months. Help me not to complain about the heat. Help me to enjoy each and every day that You bless me with and maintain a cool composure and pray for those that are lost. In Your name I ask all these things, Lord Jesus. Amen.*

MAY 15
Hollywood Hungry

I recently found myself waiting for an appointment, surrounded by outdated *People* magazines. I perused the pages and got lost in the lifestyles of Hollywood's hottest celebrities. The common denominator I noticed in all the women ages 16 – 60 was how unbelievably thin they all were. Some of them – painfully thin.

I read an article outlining specific diets a few of the stars maintain when preparing for an upcoming role. One young woman ate only fresh spinach leaves for lunch every day and nothing else! One male star ate a mere 500 calories for his entire day. Anyone could lose weight eating that way! But is that the smartest way to lose weight?

These magazines also had their fair share of pictures of close-ups of celebs at their worst: sans make-up, coming out of the gym or frolicking on the beach in bikini-clad bodies highlighting the minimal pockets of saddle-bag cellulite.

The media hounds these celebrities and prints air-brushed pictures of their "perfect" bodies putting pressure on "real women" to emulate these stars when that's impossible. But yet, when they print photos of these celebrities *au natural* they ridicule them because they look like *normal* people. Talk about mixed messages.

None of us should compare ourselves to anyone else. Unfortunately many of the young women who read these magazines are *dying to be thin* because of the media pressure. We "mature women" should focus on setting an example for our daughters by being the best we can be and make the most of what God has given to us. I don't want to pay the price these celebrities must pay to look that thin. I don't want to be *Hollywood hungry* or unrealistically thin and I certainly don't want that for my daughters.

It is possible to eat healthy balanced meals without starving ourselves. It is possible to be beautiful at any age and any size. We must learn to love the size we're in!

I prefer to be true to myself, even at the hazard of incurring the ridicule of others, rather than to be false, and to incur my own abhorrence. ~ Frederick Douglass

You watched me as I was being formed in utter seclusion, as I was woven together in the dark of the womb. Psalm 139:15 (NLT)

PRAYER FOR TODAY: *Lord, please help me to love and appreciate myself at all times, regardless of my age or weight. I pray I can maintain a healthy balanced lifestyle and focus on being the best I can be one day at a time. In Your name I ask all these things, Lord Jesus. Amen.*

MAY 16
Reality 101

At the end of last summer I bought a *Speedo* tank suit for lap swimming. Tank suits aren't exactly the most flattering of styles in swimwear to begin with. Factor in tank suits are designed to fit extremely tight to make a swimmer more streamlined while racing. These tight-fitting suits are designed to smash most of your protruding body parts. The overall picture is decidedly unflattering.

In a delusional state this morning, I decided to try on my *Speedo*. My secret wish was that the combination of my loofah fat eraser, thousands of sit-ups, walking hundreds of miles, biking thousands more and eating healthier over the last few months would have magically changed my body. Hey a girl can wish can't she?

While my tank suit still fits after a long hiatus, my droopy body parts are still glaringly obvious and haven't miraculously shifted defying gravity and the laws of the universe. I may have shed some pounds since last summer, but clearly they weren't the right pounds when it comes to swimwear.

If you're struggling with your eating or exercise program, try donning a swimsuit to get an accurate gauge of how well you've been doing on your program. If you don't like what you see reflected back at you, keep that mental picture of you in your swimsuit as a daily reminder that you need to be working that much harder.

Reality checks can be brutally painful. However, reality checks can sometimes be necessary to get us motivated to kick it in to high gear with our commitment to weight loss. Denial over reality may be gentler to your ego – but denial won't give you buns of steel, but rather buns of cellulite.

Man is the sole animal whose nudity offends his own companions, and the only one who, in his natural actions, withdraws and hides himself from his own kind. ~ Montaigne

You saw me before I was born. Every day of my life was recorded in your book. Every moment was laid out before a single day had passed. Psalm 139:16 (NLT)

PRAYER FOR TODAY: Lord, help me to be realistic in my expectations and what my body can and cannot do. Help me to continue to eat healthy, exercise safely and with balance. Help me to work a little harder each and every day to achieve my goals. Help me treat my body like Your holy temple. In Your name I ask all these things, Lord Jesus. Amen.

MAY 17
Simple Made Easy

I've been researching arthritis, the causes and the cures and one of the key suggestions in most of what I've read recommends losing excess weight for managing this disease. That should be obvious to even the most uneducated. However what I didn't realize was that even a little extra weight puts a tremendous amount of pressure on our joints.

Supposedly your weight bearing joints such as your knees and ankles carry loads up to 10 times a person's weight. That's quite literally a ton of pressure on my joints which explains why my hips, knees and ankles hurt all the time.

Many of us may know we need to lose weight because life in general is more difficult being overweight, but how many of us are in denial about the many levels of damage we're doing to our body. If we've been so focused on healing the emotional part of our food addiction, we may have overlooked the physiological damage.

We have to take an inventory. Is there anything more we can be doing? We're watching what we eat; we're exercising as much as our body will allow; we've seen a medical doctor for all of our health issues and taking necessary medication where needed. We're attending a weight loss support group and filling our brain with positive material and affirmations. Plus we're including God in every aspect of our journey and praying for strength and direction.

Seriously – what more can we be doing? Some days when it feels like we're doing everything right but still not seeing the results we'd like, the only thing to do is *stand on the promises of God*. Have faith and trust God.

He who has faith has... an inward reservoir of courage, hope, confidence, calmness, and assuring trust that all will come out well – even though to the world it may appear to come out most badly. ~ B.C. Forbes

Put on all of God's armor so that you will be able to stand firm against all strategies of the devil. Ephesians 6:11 (NLT)

PRAYER FOR TODAY: *Lord, I ask for strength to continue on this path even though there is ample reason to want to give up. Increase my faith and help me to stand on the promises of Your Word so I may complete this journey and achieve ultimate success. In Your name I ask all these things, Lord Jesus. Amen.*

MAY 18
And Suddenly

To some it would seem that if you have a weight problem the simple answer for losing weight is "stop eating the wrong things." If you have a spending problem the *simple answer* is "stop shopping and spending." If you have a drinking problem the *simple answer* is "stop drinking."

To most of us who've struggled with any type of addiction, be it food, drink, drugs, spending, etc., the *simple answer* clearly is not always the *easiest answer* to our problems. If like me you're doing everything right with little to show for it, my advice is keep on doing the right thing. I exist on faith alone sometimes and faith tells me that *suddenly* good will overpower evil and I will get a *suddenly* breakthrough.

When I did a word search in the New Living Translation for the word *suddenly* there were 101 references combined in both the Old and New Testament. God made sure that we have enough *suddenly* stories throughout His Word to properly encourage us. After reading many of those references, I was greatly encouraged – so much so that I believe if I remain faithful to God, continue praying and including God in the healthy lifestyle path I've chosen, I believe I will definitely get my *suddenly* breakthrough.

Whether our suffering is the result of God's testing us or an enemy attack, we must remain faithful. We never know if we're simply under attack from the enemy, but we must believe God is always in control. *Suddenly* at any moment I might step on the scale and find that my metabolism is *suddenly* working in harmony with my food plan and my exercise plan and I could start dropping weight!

Hey, it could happen. Never doubt God, as when we least expect it, He might *suddenly* perform a miracle in our lives. I for one, hope to be ready and anxious and not whining and complaining!

When I understand that everything happening to me is to make me more Christ like, it resolves a great deal of anxiety. ~ AW Tozer

Suddenly, the glory of the God of Israel appeared from the east. The sound of his coming was like the roar of rushing waters, and the whole landscape shone with his glory. Ezekiel 43:2 (NLT)

PRAYER FOR TODAY: *Lord, thank You for I know You hear my prayers. I pray You will never forsake me and stand by me in this journey. Increase my faith so that I might be a better witness for You. In Your name I ask all these things, Lord Jesus. Amen.*

MAY 19
Killing Me Softly With Triscuits

There's no defining or explaining food cravings. My inane desire to sink my teeth in to something salty and/or crunchy seemed to appear as if from nowhere. My body needs the salt, my teeth want the crunch. While I could have celery to satisfy the crunch or yogurt to fill my stomach, neither offers me the appeal I'm looking for. My taste buds have their sights set on Triscuits and there's no logic to be found – only craving.

I called a friend of mine who is a psychology geek and asked her if she had any explanation for why the body craves such weird things at different times of the month. She explained that it's all about our CHE; or at least that's what I call it. What it really means is it is all about the chemicals, hormones and emotions rushing through our bodies at any given time.

Her first question to me was what was I thinking about when my Triscuit craving hit? Where were my emotions? Before I succumbed to the craving and fell face first into a box of the crisscross crackers, I stopped to examine my motives.

My inventory showed me I was anxious, stressed and tired; the trifecta of trouble when it comes to emotional eating. Before I gave in to my craving I stopped to refuel with diet soda and Excedrin, both considered to be perfectly legal stimulants. Okay, some may say that I'm still relying on a crutch to get me through my stress and anxiety, and perhaps that's true. But with a busy day scheduled, I was running on empty so the body and the brain NEEDED the caffeine.

The bigger picture is simply, before I gave in to my craving I stopped and called a friend for help. I also looked for a lower calorie option and I didn't let the craving beat me this time, rather I beat the craving. That's pretty big to someone like me battling a food addiction. If I were keeping score, today would be ME—ONE … TRISCUITS—ZERO. That's good enough for me.

Most folks are about as happy as they make up their minds to be. ~ Abraham Lincoln

Then Hannah prayed: "My heart rejoices in the LORD! The LORD has made me strong. Now I have an answer for my enemies; I rejoice because you rescued me." 1 Samuel 2:1 (NLT)

PRAYER FOR TODAY: Lord, thank You for victories, no matter how small they may seem. I praise You for standing by me and giving me the strength I need on a day-by-day basis. I pray You will continue to partner with me in this challenge. In Your name I ask all these things, Lord Jesus. Amen.

MAY 20
Accessorizing for Success

The enemy truly dislikes it when believers of Christ achieve any type of victory. He feels the need to challenge the Body of Christ when he feels threatened by Godly advancement or success. I woke this morning feeling as though the enemy had set his personal sights on me and simply unloaded his magazine of emotional bullets straight at me and filled me full of lead.

My CHE (chemicals, hormones and emotions) were so far out of whack I felt the need to log on to Google Maps and do some kind of search giving me directions from where I was emotionally a few days ago, to where I am today. I'm definitely out of synch today and I don't even have a good explanation for it.

The devil wants us paralyzed with fear, locked up in our own heads listening to the lies he feeds us about how fat, ugly, useless and stupid we are. He knows we can't be used by God when we feel this way. Not only are we incapable of helping ourselves but we can't reach out and help others when we're listening to the lies of the devil. We must not live by our feelings or emotions. If we feed those negative thoughts and emotions they will grow and morph into absolute chaos in our minds.

I feel fat and ugly today, but I must not give in to those feelings and believe those lies of the enemy. It's time for a wardrobe change because clearly I forgot to dress for success today. We need to dress for success daily and accessorize with the armor of God. Tomorrow's a new day and it would behoove us to lay our clothes out tonight so we won't risk being naked and exposed to the enemy tomorrow.

Let's not forget that the little emotions are the great captains of our lives and we obey them without realizing it. ~ Vincent Van Gogh, 1889

Put on the full armor of God so that you can take your stand against the devil's schemes. Ephesians 6:11 (NLT)

PRAYER FOR TODAY: *Lord, help me not to live by my emotions but by wisdom that comes from the Word of God. Help me to resist the slings and arrows of the enemy and outfit against his attacks. May these trials make me stronger. In Your name I ask all these things, Lord Jesus. Amen.*

MAY 21
Stand Up and Pedal

Today was a glorious morning for a long bike ride. The trail I chose for my ride has four major hills. I avoid this trail most days for the simple reason I don't want to be one of those people who doesn't have enough power to ride back up the hills. The idea of having to push my bike uphill is more than my fragile ego can bear so I've been riding an alternate trail sans hills.

Feeling particularly energetic today, I threw caution to the wind and tried my luck at the hilly trail. Naturally the downward slopes were easy and quite invigorating. As the rule of gravity goes, what goes down eventually makes a turnaround trip. I had to pump my short legs for all they were worth to make it back up the hills. I did it, although on the last hill with my energy spent I had to stand up in the seat to turn the pedals.

Somewhere mid-ride I started thinking about how losing weight and bike riding have a lot of parallels. In the beginning of any weight loss program the average person does fairly well because a new program is exciting and the weight comes off easily. Just like gliding downhill on a bike, those pounds fly off easily with little or no effort.

Once the body figures out what's going on with our diets and we've lost some weight, the body's natural tendencies take over and it stops dropping that easy weight. That's when the serious dieter has to *stand up and start pedaling* for all they're worth if they're going to make it up the hill of lifelong weight loss success. We need to stand on the Word of God and proclaim that *I can do all things through Christ who strengthens me*.

There are no shortcuts to lifelong weight loss – only hard work. And yes – there are going to be hills, some may only be speed bumps, but some may feel like Mt. Everest. If you've got to stand up to pedal harder it's okay; it's better than falling off altogether. Rather than telling yourself I think I can, I think I can start believing in I KNOW I CAN!

Whether you think you can or think you can't – you are right. ~ Henry Ford

Be on guard. Stand firm in the faith. Be courageous. Be strong. 1 Corinthians 16:13 (NLT)

PRAYER FOR TODAY: *Lord, thank You for life affirming promises. Increase my faith and make me stronger. Help me to believe that You are with me and will never leave me. Help me to have confidence in myself to complete this journey. In Your name I ask all these things, Lord Jesus. Amen.*

MAY 22
Beauty Bites

I went to a "girl" party recently for a popular brand of makeup and skin care products. I had a wonderful time surrounded by beautiful woman of varying ages. It didn't take long for this group of lovely women to start bandying about negative comments about themselves and their various skin complaints.

I find it amusing that women are quick to point out their own flaws but so readily complimentary to other women – be they friend or perfect stranger. Clearly there must be a hidden clause in our birth certificates that requires us to belittle ourselves while at the same time encouraging another female. Seriously, why *do* we do that?

As the morning progressed we ran the gamut listing our many flaws: weight, skin, age and personality defects. I'm sure the enemy was secretly delighted to have played such a huge part in our verbal lambasting of ourselves. It wasn't until one of the women spoke up by saying, "Shame on us! We're all beautiful women of God and we should not be speaking this way about ourselves!" Amen Sister!

I started meditating on how grieved our heavenly Father must be when He hears His precious children bemoaning their perceived physical imperfections. Tearing ourselves down seems to come so much more naturally than building ourselves up as we worry about crossing over into conceit. Somewhere out there, there must be a healthy balance.

As children of God we must be willing to embrace the idea that true beauty comes from within. The Holy Spirit lives inside us. It's not about what we weigh, what size we wear, what our age is or what kind of skin care products we use. I know – easier said than done. How about if I go first and pledge to get up and look myself in the mirror every morning and tell myself that I'm a beautiful woman of God AND I promise to do this every day for as long as it takes until I can say it without wanting to gag. It might take a while, but I'm game if you are!

Beauty comes as much from the mind as from the eye. ~ Grey Livingston

Charm is deceptive, and beauty does not last; but a woman who fears the LORD will be greatly praised. Proverbs 31:30 (NLT)

PRAYER FOR TODAY: *Lord, thank You that beauty comes in all shapes and sizes and I delight in the work of Your hand. May I always appreciate the effort You put into creating me. Help me to be comfortable in my own skin. In Your name I ask all these things, Lord Jesus. Amen.*

MAY 23
Pandora's Box

It's amazing how you can be trucking along with God, minding your own business and then SUDDENLY God decides it's time to peel back another layer of your dysfunctional past. I've been praying for healing regarding some major personality issues for decades without seeing a lot of change. But *suddenly* there comes a time when we've got to stop riding the denial roller coaster and disembark to reality. There comes a time to open up *Pandora's Box*.

One of the things I've been forced to deal with has been my particular issue with my snacking "witching hour." For as long as I can remember, the hours between 3:00 and 5:00 in the afternoon have been my trigger times. During this two-hour window my behavior mimics a trained lab animal causing a Pavlov's dog reaction and I MUST eat between those times. Once 3:00 p.m. rolls around I start frothing at the mouth, feeling as though there are a hive of bees buzzing around in my brain.

I started seeking God and praying for why this trigger time was so physical and what was at the core of this anomaly. After a lot of self-examination and prayer God revealed to me that this behavior started in my early teen years; a direct result of my dysfunctional home life and some very inappropriate behavior of a male figure living in our home.

Once God revealed to me the root cause of that specific trigger time of day, I shared my revelation and my pain with a trusted friend who prayed for me. Since my revelation – my witching hour has diminished, nearly vanishing altogether.

When we shine a light on those dark places of pain, the enemy no longer has the power to haunt us. At some point if we ever expect to enjoy true freedom, we all need to let God dig around in our dysfunction and get His hands dirty in our *Pandora's Box* by bringing the pain into the light. Settle for baby steps if that's all you can do for now, but take it from me, freedom is liberating.

All men should strive to learn before they die what they are running from, and to, and why. ~ James Thurber

Come to me, all you who are weary and burdened, and I will give you rest." Matthew 28:28 (NIV)

PRAYER FOR TODAY: *Lord, I thank You for taking my burdens and carrying them. Thank You for rest from these troublesome emotional burdens. Give me the courage and the strength to face whatever remaining issues You wish to uncover from my past. In Your name I ask all these things, Lord Jesus. Amen.*

MAY 24
Blasted Fat and Oral Hygiene

I went to the dentist for my six month cleaning and check-up today. I take my oral hygiene VERY seriously. During my 45-minute visit I felt the need to let my mind wander so I wouldn't fixate on the sharp metal hooks digging at my tender gum tissue. During my mental lollygagging I started thinking about how nice it would be if someone invented a tool similar to that of the Water-Pik that blasted away fat the way a Water-Pik blasts away plaque hiding between your teeth; like an at-home liposuction fat blaster. You could aim the tool at those deposits of excess fat hanging over the waistline of your jeans or that back-fat sneaking out the back of your bra.

While there are various types of exercise equipment and apparatus designed to target problem areas like your hips and buttocks, most of them mainly lighten your wallet as opposed to your glutes. Those machines may tighten your fat but rarely eliminate it.

Isometric exercise has been proven to be very ineffective. Do not confuse isometric exercise with weight lifting exercises. Using weight resistance to target body parts – arms, legs, abs and glutes, absolutely does work. The key to reshaping or sculpting your body is a combination of healthy, balanced eating with a program that does not exceed a certain amount of calories.

There are no easy fixes, no at-home Water-Pik liposuction fat blasters – just good old fashioned hard work. The principle is no different than maintaining good oral hygiene. Regular cleanings and check-ups aren't fun, but they'll keep your teeth and gums healthy for as long as you have them.

Lack of activity destroys the good condition of every human being, while movement and methodical physical exercise save it and preserve it. ~ Plato

And if the Spirit of him who raised Jesus from the dead is living in you, he who raised Christ from the dead will also give life to your mortal bodies through his Spirit, who lives in you. Romans 8:11 (NIV)

PRAYER FOR TODAY: *Lord, help me to be willing to do the work necessary to reshape my body. Help me to be consistent and strengthen me when I am weak or feeling too lazy to do the work. Help me to focus on what I hope to look like once I've lost the weight and may that image constantly encourage me. In Your name I ask all these things, Lord Jesus. Amen.*

MAY 25
Guard Your Mouth

For us to be successful on our weight loss journey it is extremely important to maintain good oral hygiene with regards to what we're putting into our mouths. Obviously that means we need to take care with what kinds of foods we are eating.

But, equally important when it comes to our oral hygiene – we need to be careful with what comes OUT of our mouths, as well. Basically this means we need to guard the words that we speak in relation to our food program and when talking about ourselves.

If we are constantly spewing forth negative comments about how fat we are or how it's impossible to lose weight, we're practically paving the road for Satan to come in and have a free-for-all with our lives. The book of Job says it better than I can: *What I feared has come upon me; what I dreaded has happened to me.* Job 3:25 (NIV)

We need to face every day of our journey to better health with optimism and excitement, not discouragement and dread. It wouldn't hurt to get a mental picture in your mind of what you're hoping to look like once you've successfully lost your desired weight. (Be realistic according to your age, body type and height.) Carry that image in your brain especially at meal time and repeat Psalm 141:3 before you dive into your meal.

Ask God to help you to resist temptation not merely one time, but each and every time you're ready to sit down for a meal. Most importantly, EXPECT God to come through for you and give you the strength you need to be successful.

The best way to lose weight: LOSE the bad attitude and negative talk and clean up your thoughts and your mouth. Practice good oral hygiene!

Being an optimist after you've got everything you want doesn't count. ~ Kin Hubbard

Set a guard over my mouth, O LORD; keep watch over the door of my lips. Psalm 141:3 (NIV)

PRAYER FOR TODAY: *Lord, I ask that You would set a guard over my mouth and my mind. Help my thoughts to be positive and focused on success. Help my mouth to be positive and speak only good things rather than negative words. In Your name I ask all these things, Lord Jesus. Amen.*

MAY 26
Midnight Attacks

I awoke in the middle of the night a few nights ago and for whatever reason was ravenously hungry. My stomach was so empty and grumbled so loudly, I couldn't fall back asleep. Even though I've been battling food addictions for a couple of decades, I've got certain hard and fast food rules that I strictly adhere to regardless of the circumstances. The one rule I never break is I NEVER eat in the middle of the night. The main reason for my thinking is if I eat in the middle of the night and then go back to sleep, I've got all this food just sitting in my stomach and I'm convinced midnight calories morph into excess body fat at a quicker than normal rate of return than food eaten during daylight hours. I've heard it said: *Eat it late – it makes weight!*

What is one to do when they wake up and the grumbling tummy is so loud and obnoxious that sleep is impossible? For me, the solution was trial and error. I got up went to the bathroom, checked on the sleeping kids, had a drink of water and then another. Eventually, the tummy quieted enough for me to be able to return to bed.

Somehow it seems like cruel and unusual punishment for our bodies to have a mind of their own and haunt us with hunger when we're sleeping. I mean, isn't it bad enough that we have to face hunger or cravings during our waking hours? Does the enemy have to attack us while we're sound asleep too?

Clearly there are some things we cannot control. My advice is the same for all uncontrollable situations. **Pray.** If that doesn't produce immediate results reword your prayers and ask God for peace and strength. Midnight cravings don't seem fair, but even when we're practically unconscious, it doesn't hurt to go to bed in our "armor jammies." Have some Scriptures committed to memory so even when you're sleepy, you can dwell on the Word of God to get you through those midnight cravings.

And if tonight my soul may find her peace in sleep, and sink in good oblivion, and in the morning wake like a new-opened flower then I have been dipped again in God, and new-created. ~ D.H. Lawrence

David also said to Solomon his son, "Be strong and courageous, and do the work. Do not be afraid or discouraged, for the LORD God, my God, is with you. 1 Chronicles 28:20 (NIV)

PRAYER FOR TODAY: *Lord, thank You for the Scriptures I've buried in my heart so when I wake disturbed in the middle of the night I can seek Your comfort. Help me to remain strong and steadfast. In Your name I ask all these things, Lord Jesus. Amen.*

MAY 27
Problem Solved

In my quiet time with God this morning I camped out in the first chapter of 2 Chronicles. In this passage of Scripture, God visited Solomon in a dream and told him he could ask Him for anything. Solomon asked God for wisdom. God was so impressed that Solomon didn't ask for riches, long life or even the death of his enemies that He gave Solomon what he asked for and *what he didn't ask for.*

As I sat silent before the Lord, I prayed for wisdom to understand why I turn to food in times of stress rather than God. I didn't exactly receive a vision in a dream, but the first thing I read after my quiet time was I am fearfully and wonderfully made. Then I read that God predestined me (Ephesians 1) for a great life and that He knew me before I was even born (Psalm 139).

All that was comforting and I started feeling as though God impressed upon me that as much as I write about "it's not what's on the outside – but what's on the inside," I don't fully believe that for myself yet. I believe God wants me to learn to love myself *at this weight* and see myself as He sees me and believe that I'm important to Him no matter what I weigh.

While I can believe these truths for all of my beautiful sisters around me – I can't believe it for myself because I'm cloaked in a garment of fear. I'm afraid to let go of this excess layer of body fat because I'm safe under this protective layer. Without even realizing it, my excess weight makes me feel like a failure. I've failed God by not taking care of the "temple" He's entrusted to me. And because I'm a failure and I know it, He won't expect much from me and therein lays the root of my problem.

Quite simply – I'm afraid to be used by God because I'm afraid He'll ask something too hard of me and I will fail Him on an even grander scale. Once we pinpoint our problems, how do we fix them? Clearly, WE cannot. Lucky for us we have a Savior who's still in the "fixing business." *Let go and let God …*

You block your dream when you allow your fear to grow bigger than your faith. ~ Mary Manin Morrissey

"Fear not; you will no longer live in shame. Don't be afraid; there is no more disgrace for you. You will no longer remember the shame of your youth and the sorrows of widowhood. Isaiah 54:4 (NLT)

PRAYER FOR TODAY: *Lord, I know that You have not given to me a spirit of fear but of power, love, and self-discipline. Help me to live this Scripture and believe it in my soul. In Your name I ask all these things, Lord Jesus. Amen.*

MAY 28
The Smell of Victory

Self-realization can be a bit overwhelming. To unburden your heart and share your innermost hurts doesn't exactly register high on the fun-o-meter, but in order to be healed, it's sometimes necessary. Finding someone you trust and can confide in is oftentimes the catalyst that brings healing. Purging our soul with friends who understand the struggle of addiction can be very therapeutic. Confession is always good for the soul, whether we share with a trusted friend or a trusted therapist, it's important that we don't keep our fears hidden.

Identifying the root of our weight issues and/or eating addictions; and confessing our fears and pain are part of the healing process. But we can't let the knowledge of what may be a root cause for these addictions give us a license to sit idle stewing in our pain while we figure out what to do with this new found enlightenment.

Sure it'd be nice to wait around for God to continue chipping away at our outer shell, but quite frankly there comes a point where it starts to feel old and worn out. Honestly, I'm sick and tired of me and my issues. I'm sick and tired of trying to clear all this junk out.

How many more months, years or decades do we want to waste on our stupid issues? It's time to be about the business of healing. It's time to be about the business of moving on. And it's time to be about God's business. There's work to be done and the time for the devil to have his way with us – is over.

Do you smell that? It smells like progress and success are simmering on the back burner. Don't you think it's time to move them to the front?

The man who views the world at fifty the same as he did at twenty has wasted thirty years of his life. ~ Muhammad Ali

So we say with confidence, "The Lord is my helper; I will not be afraid. What can man do to me?" Hebrews 13:6 (NIV)

PRAYER FOR TODAY: *Lord, I know You have a good plan for my life. I thank You for spiritual enlightenment. May I continue to grow and mature as You chip away at my fears and pain. I will trust in You always. In Your name I ask all these things, Lord Jesus. Amen.*

MAY 29
I Hate to Complain

As the mother of three college-age children, I'm tickled pink when they have a summer break from school. My kids have jobs they return to once they're out of school. When they are working they're spending their own money rather than mine, so I hate to complain about their jobs. However, this summer I find myself doing an extraordinary amount of whining and/or complaining.

My son has been working a bread route with a friend and while it's a long shift for him, as a 21-one-year-old young man he's thrilled with the perks of a bread route. Before he restocks the shelves with fresh bread products, he's required to remove any bread from the shelves nearing its expiration. He's invited to help himself to whatever castaways he wants.

This young man thinks he's hit the mother lode of carbohydrates – and of course he's bringing it all home. How is a girl with a passion for all things bread supposed to handle this type of cruel and inhuman punishment when it's delivered right to her home?

For the most part, I've done pretty well not eating most of the goodies. The one item that's giving me the most grief though, is the Old-Fashioned Donuts. Oh my goodness, even a small bite of the golden orbs of ecstasy taste like little drops of heaven.

I'm suddenly counting the days until my son returns to college and the breads and donuts magically disappear. There was a time when he first left for college three years ago that I would have been so depressed at his leaving I could have eaten my weight in Old-Fashioned Donuts until the depression subsided. Luckily, I've matured since then and that's no longer an issue. Maturity is a real bummer some days and right now it smells like donuts.

Oh, wouldn't the world seem dull and flat with nothing whatever to grumble at? ~ W.S. Gilbert

Soon the people began to complain about their hardship, and the Lord heard everything they said. Then the Lord's anger blazed against them, and he sent a fire to rage among them, and he destroyed some of the people in the outskirts of the camp. Numbers 11:1 (NLT)

PRAYER FOR TODAY: *Lord, please help me to curb my complaining and focus on the benefits of steady employment for my family. Help me to appreciate time spent with my family and not give in to whining. In Your name I ask all these things, Lord Jesus. Amen.*

MAY 30
Roll the Dice

I keep a large dice on the corner of my desk in my home office where I work every day. It's not an ordinary dice like you'd find in a board game, but a dice imprinted with words on each of the six sides of it. The words are: LOVE, BLESSED, BELIEVE, LIVE, PRAY and LAUGH. These simple words remind me throughout my day how important it is to focus on the little things in life.

Everyday life presents us with challenges – especially those of us on this journey to get healthy and shed a few pounds this year. We've just celebrated a three-day Memorial Day weekend and summer looms long and hot with the promise of barbecues, pool parties, camping trips, vacations and all sorts of summer activities.

It's a sad fact that in America much of our summertime fun revolves around food. If we hope to survive our summer fun time activities, we need to arm ourselves with a survival plan. That's where the simple sentiment of my office desk dice comes in handy.

We need to appreciate how *blessed* we are and *live* life to the fullest. We need to *believe* that we can conquer these weight loss challenges and *pray* that God will see us through until we find success. We need to *love* ourselves where we are (no matter what we weigh) and above all, *laugh* all throughout our journey because life's too short for us to take ourselves so seriously that we miss the simple fun of summer.

We need to include God in all of our summer fun and keep our eye on the goal of getting healthy. Some days this task – this journey may feel insurmountable, but it's important to remember that what is impossible for us on our own – is entirely possible with God!

It is wise to keep in mind that no success or failure is necessarily final. ~ Author Unknown

Jesus looked at them and said, "With man this is impossible, but not with God; all things are possible with God." Mark 10:27 (NIV)

PRAYER FOR TODAY: *Lord, help me to focus on the simple things like all of life's blessings and my ability for loving, living, believing, laughter and prayer. I serve a mighty God and I am thankful that nothing is impossible for You. Keep me grounded, Lord. In Your name I ask all these things, Lord Jesus. Amen.*

MAY 31
I Am

This time of year, the television airwaves are filled with commercials for weight loss programs and products encouraging us to shed our winter weight so we can wear our shorts, sun dresses and even those bikinis. (Yeah right!) Summertime can be a good news/bad news time of year for many of us.

The good news is that with the warmer weather we're faced with the challenge of wearing fewer layers of clothes – more exposed skin. The bad news is we're faced with the challenge of wearing fewer layers of clothes – more exposed skin. With all that exposed skin we need to love the skin we're in regardless if we've actually lost all the weight we want to lose or not. Sometimes that's easier said than done as we tend to be our own worst critics.

Finding our self-confidence when we're unhappy with our weight can sometimes be harder than trying to find an address in an unfamiliar neighborhood without the benefit of MapQuest.

Today in my daily Scripture reading I was reading the book of Exodus, the third chapter. Throughout the exodus of Moses and the Israelites, God continually reminded Moses exactly who He was and what He was capable of doing for His people. God was the inventor of self-confidence. God instructed Moses to tell the people *I AM WHO I AM*. God had a way of saying so much with very few words.

Life would be ever so much simpler if we would adopt those simple words for ourselves: *I AM WHO I AM*. When we don our summer shorts, capris or sun dresses and look in the mirror and simply tell ourselves, "I look great and I AM WHO I AM," we'd likely find ourselves much happier with life in general.

Summer is here and we need to embrace who we are whether we're full-figured and round, short and squatty or tall and fluffy. God created us in His image and He is the great I AM and we are His beautiful children. HE IS and WE ARE.

I just hope God does not get bored of dreaming of me. ~ Author Unknown

God replied to Moses, "I AM WHO I AM. Say this to the people of Israel: I AM has sent me to you." Exodus 3:14 (NLT)

PRAYER FOR TODAY: *Lord, I am grateful that You are who you say You are and that You have called me Your own. Help me to look in the mirror and love myself just as You created me. You have called me blessed. Help me each day to walk in those many blessings. In Your name I ask all these things, Lord Jesus. Amen.*

JUNE 1
Success is NOT a Number

In the blink of an eye it's suddenly June! Five full months have come and gone since our New Year's resolution began. Some days it may feel as though the food is still mastering us. But some days we feel as though we're making real progress.

Whether we've lost a bunch of weight in the last five months or no weight at all, God is sending us messages about learning to love ourselves at ANY weight. Throughout this entire journey, we must remember it's not about the numbers; it's about loving ourselves regardless of the number on the scale. When it comes to numbers, we should take a lesson from King David.

In Second Samuel, the 24th chapter, David conducted a census to count the number of his people causing God's anger to burn against David. This always bothered me. Perhaps David was too concerned about the actual number because he would become proud about the army he had built. God didn't want David to fixate on the number of men in his army but rather, wanted David to focus on God's provision.

As with King David, we should not fixate on *our number*. If we are still doing the work and haven't quit yet – that is progress. Part of the reason so many "diets" fail is because the average person sets their sights on reaching a particular number by a certain date. If they fail to reach their goal by the set time, they have a tendency to quit altogether.

We need to redefine success. Success should mean we need to *ditch the dates and throw out the numbers*. If by year's end we're still hanging in there and eating healthy and exercising, what we weigh shouldn't be as important as the fact that we're still working on our plan to get healthy. Success looks different to everyone. For now, this is our success because we're not quitters!

The two hardest things to handle in life are failure and success. ~ Author Unknown

But after he had taken the census, David's conscience began to bother him. And he said to the LORD, "I have sinned greatly by taking this census. Please forgive my guilt, LORD, for doing this foolish thing." 2 Samuel 24:10 (NLT)

PRAYER FOR TODAY: *Lord, thank You for continuing this journey with me. I pray You will help me to love myself a little more each day. Help me to focus on Your provisions and how far I've come, not on how far I still need to go. In Your name I ask all these things, Lord Jesus. Amen.*

JUNE 2
If it's Free – It's for Me

When we're watching our calories, temptations come at us from every conceivable angle. Some of the temptations are downright unfair. It's easy to understand temptations like the free sample stations at Costco or Sam's Club.

Today I was at The Dollar Store and they were giving out free samples of chocolate bars. Nothing in the store costs over a dollar so why do they need to give things away for free? Not just any chocolate, mind you, but Tobblerone chocolate, which should be in a category of deliciousness all by itself. It's quite simply *melt in your mouth delicious*.

The bite-sized chocolate was displayed on a plate. I felt like I deserved a medal for limiting my sample to one measly bite. While waiting in line to pay, I couldn't help noticing those that sampled and those *that didn't*. Some even had "extra" samples.

The differences between those that passed and those that over-indulged was startling. Perhaps those that indulged did so because it was chocolate and that's hard to ignore in any situation. Or quite possibly the mere idea of the notion "free" was the bigger draw. "Free" by the very nature of the word makes us feel as though we're cheating the powers that be by getting something for nothing.

This *if it's free – it's for me* way of thinking can lead to much bigger problems. Mainly because free food is rarely calorie free and all of those bite-size samples added together equal a whole lot of unscheduled calories.

When counting calories, it's best to shy away from the sample ladies and eat a balanced meal – one that you can record and keep track of. What may be *free* today could end up costing you more than you want to pay in the future.

Research tells us fourteen out of any ten individuals likes chocolate.
~ Sandra Boynton

Therefore, prepare your minds for action; be self-controlled; set your hope fully on the grace to be given you when Jesus Christ is revealed. 1 Peter 1:13 (NIV)

PRAYER FOR TODAY: Lord, thank You for the restraint and self-control You've bestowed on me. Continue to refine me, mold me and make me into the best person that I can be – free from judging others and always striving to be a better example of You. In Your name I ask all these things, Lord Jesus. Amen.

JUNE 3
Hormonal Power Surges

There are going to be days during this weight loss journey when our emotions and feelings defy all "normal" human logic and we feel and act *persnickety* and *discombobulated*. Which are just fancy words for saying we feel crabby, cranky and/or confused. The catalyst usually reveals it to be nothing more than those nasty hormones that stir us up once a month.

Our mothers lovingly referred to this as *that special time of the month and a wonderful journey into womanhood on a road that all women must travel*. This *special* time of the month usually brings with it bloating so acute we don't need a bathroom scale to tell us we're clearly over the legal limit for hauling poorly distributed fat cells. Who needs a bathroom scale to confirm our lack of progress when our favorite pair of pants will do?

Our natural inclination may be to hole up in the house with the drapes shut and hibernate like nocturnal rodents for the next two or three days. But because of these hormonal power surges, hibernation may not be the best idea. Isolation can lead to random acts of snacking.

Don't let your emotions hold you prisoner. Stay away from making too many decisions when you're bubbling over with hormones. Exercise is often the best medicine and even though it's the last thing you may feel like doing, an evening walk around the block may be the thing needed to clear your head and balance your mood swings.

Remember to keep your sense of humor when your husband asks you if that cookie is on your diet plan. Those hormonal cravings for chocolate may be curbed by a Magnesium vitamin supplement during these emotional days. Bear in mind, this too shall pass in three to seven days. Your hormones and emotions will be regular visitors for a good part of your adult life but you can control them without them controlling you.

Humor is... despair refusing to take itself seriously. ~ Arland Ussher

God blesses you who are hungry now, for you will be satisfied. God blesses you who weep now, for in due time you will laugh. Luke 6:21 (NLT)

PRAYER FOR TODAY: *Lord, thank You that laughter is good like a medicine. May my sense of humor and imagination buoy me during emotionally hormonal days. I thank You for life's many blessings. In Your name I ask all these things, Lord Jesus. Amen.*

JUNE 4
Mrs. Toad's Wild Ride

During our journey these past months to get healthy and shed a few pounds, God's been busy digging around in our emotional dysfunction uncovering all manner of denial, guilt and shame. We may feel as if we've been dirtying our hands in painful childhood memories and longstanding issues. It can be a bit scary and overwhelming at times. We may start to feel as if we're dangling on the edge of precipice not sure if we want to dive in or jump over it like some sort of spiritual Evel Knievel.

It's time to get this junk out of our lives – out of our heads – out of our hearts and move on to the next chapter of life. At some point we need to take the jump and hope we don't do an Evel Knievel crash and burn.

If you're like me and suffer from self-loathing and self-hatred, we need to take that daredevil leap and conquer these issues. We need to move on rather than continuing to spin our wheels remaining in denial over these unsettled emotional issues.

I look in the mirror and see this ugly toad staring back at me. Some days I can fix it up and make it look nice, but the toad image haunts me and goes with me everywhere. I know this isn't "normal" behavior but a lifelong ongoing issue I feel powerless to control. I'm not sure what the root cause is but clearly somewhere in my past someone must have given me reason to believe I'm an ugly person. I am having trouble moving past this.

These issues run deep. God is teaching me that each day requires me to get up, look in the mirror and give myself a pep talk. You know the one – "God made me in His image and He thinks I'm fabulous. My husband adores me and my children love me and think I'm a great mom."

If you suffer like I do, we need to tell ourselves, "toad or not, this is as good as it gets so get up and make the most of each day and be the best looking toad you can be."

Beauty comes as much from the mind as from the eye. ~ Grey Livingston

Thank you for making me so wonderfully complex! Your workmanship is marvelous—how well I know it. Psalm 139:14 (NIV)

PRAYER FOR TODAY: Lord, I know that the image I see reflected back at me is distorted by lies from the enemy. I pray that You would help me to look at myself and see myself the way You see me. Help me to redefine what beauty means to me and to know that You don't judge any of us by our outward appearance, but by our hearts. In Your name I ask all these things, Lord Jesus. Amen.

JUNE 5
Loving the Lumps

Being part of a weight loss support group is so rewarding and inspirational. My gal pals are great for listening, sharing, observing and above all – they're always willing to pray for me and the rest of the group. I would be lost without them.

One of the benefits of group support is we girls continually exchange ideas and tips for long-lasting weight loss and emotional healing. Recently one of the ladies shared a tip about a varicose vein product. I don't struggle with that particular issue but rather, my problem is cellulite. I told her if she knew of anything for eliminating my ample supply of fat cells – let me know.

One woman shared something she'd seen on a talk show about mixing up a concoction with coffee grounds, brown sugar and vinegar that was supposed to work wonders as a cellulite exfoliate.

I'm ashamed to admit that if someone told me they had a surefire recipe for eliminating cellulite but it was made of eye of newt, crushed bat wings, garlic paste and lizard eggs – I'd slather it on my hips, thighs and knees in a New York minute.

Even as I contemplate this "miracle salve" for eliminating cellulite I'm feeling that voice of reason arguing with me, *"Seriously – you're going to waste more money on more stuff that probably won't work? Why can't you love yourself the way you are?"* My standard answer is always: *"But what IF IT DOES work this time?"* Of course I know the voice of reason is the Holy Spirit trying to impart wisdom to me; reminding me to use good old fashioned common sense rather than chasing after empty promises and pipe dreams.

My HOPE is YOU, Lord Jesus. I surrender ALL to You – and I'm going to learn to love myself, lumps and all.

Some see a hopeless end, while others see an endless hope. ~ Author Unknown

Lead me by your truth and teach me, for you are the God who saves me. All day long I put my hope in you. Psalm 25:5 (NLT)

PRAYER FOR TODAY: *Lord, I put my hope and trust in You alone. I pray You will continually guide me and give me the wisdom I need to overcome temptations. I pray for a healthy dose of common sense so I won't give in to the desire to spend money foolishly on weight loss gimmicks. Give me strength for each day. In Your name I ask all these things, Lord Jesus. Amen.*

JUNE 6
Inside Out

If grown-ups were allowed an occasional "spirit week" like kids have in school, I'd vote for the "inside-out" day. I'm not talking about turning my clothes inside out, mind you. I'd love one whole day where we could literally turn our whole bodies inside out and not have to worry about what we look like on the outside – but rather focus on the inside.

I wouldn't be thrilled to see internal organs, muscles or veins and what not. But it would be interesting to be able to see the kindness, compassion and love people carry around on the inside. By the same token, I suppose that would mean if you had a particularly ugly heart and foul mind with no sense of right and wrong you wouldn't be able to hide that.

The movie Shallow Hal is probably one of the most creative films to ever come out of Hollywood. Self-help guru, Tony Robbins slaps Jack Black's character, Hal, on the head and commands the demon to come out of him because Hal is so shallow he won't talk to women who aren't attractive. After his Tony Robbins encounter, Hal can only see people for what they represent; not what they look like on the outside. He dates an obese woman but he sees her as thin and beautiful because he knows the real her – inside, not what the world sees outside.

Wouldn't it be lovely if we could see people for what they truly are on the inside? Truthfully, we CAN see people for what they really are if we look hard enough. Outer beauty is fleeting, but true inner beauty radiates out from the heart and changes a person's exterior.

It's a hard thing to look in the mirror and not see what we despise most about ourselves. God didn't create the world overnight and clearly our emotional issues will not be cured instantly. We are forever a work in progress; trusting God to give us grace one day at a time.

We are so accustomed to disguise ourselves to others that in the end we become disguised to ourselves. ~ François Duc de La Rochefoucauld

For your royal husband delights in your beauty; honor him, for he is your lord. Psalm 45:11 (NLT)

PRAYER FOR TODAY: *Lord, help me not to judge others by their physical appearance and grant me the same grace for myself. May I see my true inner beauty and may I have such confidence in my beautiful heart that the beauty of my Lord Jesus will shine forth and change my appearance. Make me a reflection of Your beauty. In Your name I ask all these things, Lord Jesus. Amen.*

JUNE 7
Chewing on Shame

I like food! I like to eat! We hear people confess these simple statements daily. There's nothing wrong with enjoying good food. What would be the point in eating if food didn't taste good? A problem arises when food becomes a substitute for friendship, comfort, grief, depression and a host of other emotions. When our relationship with food becomes a love/hate struggle and we feel powerless over the control food has on us, we've got a problem.

Overeaters Anonymous is a support group that operates on a 12-step recovery program. The first three steps of the program are: I know I'm powerless over food; I believe that God can restore me to sanity; and I've made the decision to turn my will and my life over to God. Step four requires a moral inventory.

Many people get stuck on this step for the simple reason it's very difficult to itemize all of our wrongs. Even harder still is believing that if we've confessed everything to God, God has forgiven us. Many of us continue carrying around shame and guilt for the things we've done and refuse to accept God's forgiveness.

God has set us free from shame. He's given us the gift of forgiveness but by continuing to wear our shame we've rejected God's free gift to us. Because we don't "feel" forgiven we continue to live with our shame. When will we learn not to trust our feelings?

Forgiveness IS NOT A FEELING! To "let go and let God" sounds simple in theory, but clearly not as easy as one would imagine. If it truly were that simple, God's children wouldn't continue to live in bondage – but many of us still do. We are slaves to our feelings held prisoner by these bondages and only God can set us free.

What you need to know about the past is that no matter what has happened, it has all worked together to bring you to this very moment. And this is the moment you can choose to make everything new. Right now. ~ Author Unknown

But if we confess our sins to him, he is faithful and just to forgive us our sins and to cleanse us from all wickedness. 1 John 1:9 (NLT)

PRAYER FOR TODAY: *Lord, I confess that I have sinned and I ask Your forgiveness for sins past and present. As You shower me with Your love, mercy and* FORGIVENESS, *I humbly ask that I could know in my heart that I am forgiven because Your Word tells me it is so. Even though I may not feel forgiven help me not to rely on my feelings. In Your name I ask all these things, Lord Jesus. Amen.*

JUNE 8
Emotional Detox

As part of the emotional recovery process for any type of addiction it's important to come to grips with our past, the people we've hurt and the people that have hurt us. This inventory requires us to uncover old hurts and sins that we've worked so hard to keep buried.

The skeletons in our closet continue to have power over us as long as we keep them in the dark. Once we're able to shine the light of Christ upon them, they lose their power over us and we can begin to walk in freedom from these painful memories.

This personal inventory is like an *emotional detox*. We need to flush out all of the toxic attitudes and poisonous memories that continue to pollute our emotional and spiritual well-being. These hidden toxins suck the life out of us like an emotional cancer, slowly seeping into every area of our life if we don't deal with them.

God already knows all of our secrets, yet for whatever reason, many of us remain in denial or are victims of selective amnesia, completely blocking out the grisly details of abuse or the details of our silent suffering. Some may ask, "What's the point of reopening old wounds? Why can't I just let it go and forget my past?"

Wouldn't it be lovely if we could detox our souls and hearts in the same fashion as we detox our colons for a colonoscopy? I would gladly drink a gallon of nasty juice if it would induce the spewing of all the harmful memories *once and for all*.

If we've buried lies and secrets in our minds and hearts it's time to spew the toxins and get healthy from the inside out rather than letting the poisons of our past steal our healing and keeping us sick indefinitely.

The man with a clear conscience probably has a poor memory. ~ Author Unknown

To all who mourn in Israel, he will give a crown of beauty for ashes, a joyous blessing instead of mourning, festive praise instead of despair. Isaiah 61:3 (NLT)

PRAYER FOR TODAY: *Lord, prepare my mind and my heart to deal with old wounds and memories. I pray that once I shine the light of Christ upon my past You will cast the painful memories into the sea of forgetfulness. Stand beside me with love and support as I walk this difficult road. In Your name I ask all these things, Lord Jesus. Amen.*

JUNE 9
Time Out

The heaviness of dealing with all of these old wounds and detoxifying our spirit can leave us feeling emotionally retarded and spiritually exhausted. The urge is strong to stay in our jammies for one whole day, hide from the world behind closed drapes, watch Doris Day movies and pretend that we're normal and healthy.

Denial is an easy pill to swallow when you've been choking it down as long as many of us have. The enemy loves to make us feel as though we're worse off than everyone else and nobody could possibly have as many issues as we have. And of course, he loves to convince us that God couldn't possibly love someone like us. When we start to feel like this and the temptation to pull away from family and friends and isolate ourselves tugs at us, we need to dig in our heels and do exactly opposite of what we "feel" like doing.

Emotional and spiritual exhaustion can have some dangerous consequences because we have a tendency to follow our feelings when we're depleted. Most of us know those fickle feelings make us believe things we wouldn't ordinarily believe because feelings usually aren't rational.

There comes a point in any recovery program where you need to give yourself permission to take a time-out from the emotional probing and let your mind and spirit rest. Recharge your spirit by reading a good book or the Word of God. Go ahead and watch a good movie. Go to church or enjoy some praise and worship; maybe take a leisurely drive somewhere and simply relax.

The best advice for getting your mind off yourself and your problems is always to go and help someone else. There are always people out there who have it worse than we do. Time-out or Help-out – both are great alternatives to a "pig-out."

Let's not forget that the little emotions are the great captains of our lives and we obey them without realizing it. ~ Vincent Van Gogh, 1889

Even if we feel guilty, God is greater than our feelings, and he knows everything. 1 John 3:20 (NLT)

PRAYER FOR TODAY: *Lord, I pray for a time of recharging in my spirit and my heart. Help me to reach out to help someone else who may need an emotional lift. I pray You will give me a heart for others who are hurting so that I may be an encouragement to those who have it worse than I do. Give me compassion and discernment. In Your name I ask all these things, Lord Jesus. Amen.*

JUNE 10
Lord, Bless this Mess

If there is anything "good" to say about suffering it's that God never wastes pain. God does not inflict pain on us, but He can allow situations into our lives for the purpose of growing us and maturing us. The Bible tells us that we will all have trials and tribulations in this lifetime.

Some of the trials from our past may be directly responsible for our food addictions. Some of the things we've suffered have brought us closer to the Lord thereby forcing us to rely totally on Christ for deliverance. Many of life's trials help us to develop into the followers of God that we are today. Trials are great for building character and unfortunately there's rarely an easy way to do that without pain.

Sadly the most severe emotional damage inflicted on many of us occurs during those early formative years from birth to puberty. The devil cleverly plans his attacks on the minds of youth because children are emotionally immature, vulnerable and completely ill-equipped to deal with life's heartaches and pain.

Eventually we need to stop using the tragedies of our dysfunctional childhood as a reason to remain in our pain and dysfunction. The past must be learned from but eventually laid to rest. It's important however, that once healing comes in order to keep from slipping back in to old destructive patterns, we've got to make the most of our healing. Our success and testimony needs to bless others around us; to offer hope rather than continually rehashing past abuse and drawing attention to how bad our life was.

Some days you just have to wake up and say, "Enough already! It's time to stop fretting over the past and look to the future." You've got to ask God, "Who can I help today that has it worse than I had it?" And then, you take action.

Bring the past only if you are going to build from it. ~Doménico Cieri Estrada

So the Lord must wait for you to come to him so he can show you his love and compassion For the Lord is a faithful God. Blessed are those who wait for his help. Isaiah 30:18 (NLT)

PRAYER FOR TODAY: *Lord, I pray that You will help me to use my trials as opportunities to minister to others in need. Bring people across my path that I can have compassion on – people who I can bless with my testimony. May I cease to wallow in my own pain but use it as a springboard for opportunities to share the goodness of God. In Your name I ask all these things, Lord Jesus. Amen.*

JUNE 11
Forward Progress

There will be times on this journey when you wake up and think "I'm not making any progress so I may as well quit!" Of course, if you're still able to get out of bed every day and worried about progress or the lack thereof, that should prove you're at least still making an attempt at this weight loss thing, otherwise you wouldn't care if you weren't making progress.

I for one haven't had much time to think about forward progress this week. I spent most of my week volunteering at church. For several days, I didn't fixate on my menu plan, my issues or my exercise program. I was totally committed to my service at church and it felt great not to be the center of my universe. That's progress.

Some may see my total disregard for anything related to my weight loss plan as complete surrender; but it wasn't. Even though my schedule was not my own, I still managed to make reasonably healthy eating choices and that is progress.

For every day that you can wake up and not hate yourself or the way you look – that my friend is most definitely progress. Success isn't just about losing weight. This journey isn't just about changing the way our body looks; it's about being comfortable in our own skin regardless of how much we weigh. It's about being productive and happy in whatever situations come our way; and it's about getting up every day with the knowledge that we're the best we can be regardless of what size our jeans are today.

Progress – it looks different to each of us. Recognize and celebrate your progress today, whatever size it may be.

A truly happy person is one who can enjoy the scenery while on a detour. ~ Author Unknown

But we must hold on to the progress we have already made. Philippians 3:16 (NLT)

PRAYER FOR TODAY: *Lord, thank You that I am learning how to be comfortable with myself. Thank you for helping me to see beyond me and my own needs and for opening doors of opportunity for me to give back to others. Help me continue to make progress and not measure my success to that of anyone else. In Your name I ask all these things, Lord Jesus. Amen.*

JUNE 12
Laughter is the Best Medicine

The other day I was getting my hair done and during my appointment I found myself at the center of what can only be described as something straight out of a hidden camera show *"cat fight"* involving my trusted stylist of 10 years and another stylist in the salon.

I'm as blind as a bat without my glasses which I remove during my appointment. While I was lost in my own little sightless world, my stylist tried a new color product on my hair guaranteeing me shinier, healthier hair. Unbeknownst to me the product turned my hair an interesting shade of green, which elicited comments from the stylist working next to us. The stylist, her client and a friend of theirs who was waiting for her to finish all started laughing at me telling each other I looked like a troll.

My stylist (who is the owner of the salon) calmly walked over to the stylist, tapped her on the shoulder and nicely asked her to keep her comments to herself telling her it was unprofessional to talk about the clients in the salon. From that point on, the events unfolded like an episode of *The Jerry Springer Show* stopping just short of the eye gouging and hair pulling. The police were called ending with the other stylist and her friends being escorted from the salon with their belongings by the armed police officers.

If this incident would have occurred 10 years ago, I probably would have come home and eaten my weight in Oreos. The mere idea that a gaggle of girls were poking fun at me would've reduced me to a sniveling pile of self-loathing. I wasn't even tempted to feel sorry for myself, but rather relished in the retelling of the story with great laughter. Once I'd made sure my stylist was unharmed, I asked her the most important question, "Is my hair going to be okay?"

I am the daughter of the Most High, the King of Kings and I don't care if a couple of girls I don't know feel the need to poke fun at me because I know who I am. I am loved and so are you!

They cannot take away our self-respect if we do not give it to them.
~ Mahatma Gandhi

Make allowance for each other's faults, and forgive anyone who offends you. Remember, the Lord forgave you, so you must forgive others. Colossians 3:13 (NLT)

PRAYER FOR TODAY: *Lord, thank You for allowing me to grow in maturity and self-respect. Help me to continue to grow in my walk on this journey and to grow more comfortable with myself each and every day regardless of the circumstances. In Your name I ask all these things, Lord Jesus. Amen.*

JUNE 13
She'll Be Coming Around the Mountain … Again

There's no denying that weight loss has been my central-most focus for the better part of the last four decades. I'm not sure whether I should feel shame over that or utter disbelief that I've given something like my weight this much attention for so long.

One of my daily devotionals today recalled an account of the Israelites exodus from Egypt. This massive group of people spent 40 years wandering in the desert on a trip that should realistically have taken only 11 days. Because they spent so much time whining and complaining, God let them wander for 40 years around the same dang mountain until most of them were dead. It was only their descendants that made it to the Promised Land.

By comparison my own journey has taken me nearly as long as the Israelites exodus. I started wondering if perhaps it's been my whining and complaining that has kept me from entering the Promised Land of good health and normal body weight.

In retrospect, a normal weight loss journey should only take a few months, maybe even a year – but four decades? While I've had a certain measure of success over those four decades – I've reached my goal weight and maintained it several times, but always wandered back into weight gain.

In a perfect world, one should lose the weight and hopefully maintain that weight loss for the rest of their lives. The sad reality is only about 5% of people successfully maintain their weight loss for more than five years. What are we missing? *What am I missing?*

The answer is obvious – as a whole we're lazy and don't like to work that hard at anything. What are our choices though? Continue *wandering in the desert and circle the same mountain* for these last 40 years of life … or do the job right this time, lose the weight once and for all; get healthy and then stay healthy. How hard can that be?

Being in a good frame of mind helps keep one in the picture of health.
~ Author Unknown

So letting your sinful nature control your mind leads to death. But letting the Spirit control your mind leads to life and peace. Romans 8:6 (NLT)

PRAYER FOR TODAY: Lord, thank You that I have the mind of Christ. I believe it is Your will for me to be healthy and take care of my body. Help me not give in to my sinful nature or obey the lusts of my flesh. I pray with all my heart that You will help me to stick to my eating and exercise program and help me to resist temptation. Give me strength for each day. In Your name I ask all these things, Lord Jesus. Amen.

JUNE 14
Know Your Limits or No Limits?

The summer months bring with them the promise of vacation for many people. Regardless of whether we have a real vacation getaway or just a day trip, both scenarios present opportunities to let our menu and exercise programs slip into a *vacation state of mind*.

Veering from the plan doesn't have to be detrimental to our overall health and waistline. There are ways to make a getaway both fun and healthy at the same time. Unless of course you have a spouse who gives you the standard vacation warning: "While we're on vacation I'm eating anything I want *because I'm on vacation*."

The eating thing is where a lot of us tend to struggle with vacations. Remember, vacations should be "know your limits" not *"no limits."*

When I worked for a weight loss company many years ago, I'll never forget the woman who'd worked for one whole year to lose 100 pounds. She was within seven pounds of her goal weight and booked a cruise. This woman bragged to our group that she was going on vacation and was going to have a good time without worrying about her diet. Long story short – she didn't worry about it and ended up gaining 20 pounds while on her cruise which was her slow slide back to regaining every single pound she'd lost.

A vacation shouldn't mean giving yourself permission to binge, pig-out, go hog-wild and eat yourself stupid. Make your vacation more about the destination and your family or friends. Don't undo all the hard work you've put into getting healthy just for a few moments of caloric pleasure.

That old saying still rings true: *"A moment on the lips – forever on the hips!"*

I travel not to go anywhere, but to go. I travel for travel's sake. The great affair is to move. ~ Robert Louis Stevenson

You see me when I travel and when I rest at home. You know everything I do. Psalm 139:3 (NLT)

PRAYER FOR TODAY: *Lord, thank You for opportunities to get away and relax. Help me not to relax my attitude about losing weight, my exercise and getting healthy. Help me to be diligent at all times and make my health a priority. Give me the strength I need for each and every day and each and every situation I find myself in. In Your name I ask all these things, Lord Jesus. Amen.*

JUNE 15
Between the Waking and the Sleeping

Do you ever wonder what happens to your thought processes, your feelings and your sanity between your waking and sleeping hours? Some mornings I wake to find that my rationale has staged a mutiny while I was unconscious and supposedly dreaming a peaceful sleep.

Upon waking I simply can't understand my moods and emotions ... and those blasted *feelings* that propel me to action and conviction one day and total despair the next. Managing these fickle feelings is downright exhausting some days.

During my time in prayer this morning I was asking God to give me that "want to succeed attitude" even when my flesh (and emotions) rebel. I pray that God sees my heart and realizes that in my heart *I want to* succeed and *I want to* beat this food addiction – contrary to what my abnormal reasoning thinks when it's trying to talk me into pigging out on chips. *I want to* be better, but some days my flesh trumps all my want to.

Today, let's all pray and ask in the name of Jesus (because there's power in the name of Jesus) that our *want to* attitude will be enough to succeed. We pray our feelings will mind their own business and stop getting in the way of our success. Lord Jesus, *we want* to serve You and not our stomach, our emotions or our flesh. We want to – we really, really *want to*.

I have found that if you love life, life will love you back. ~ Arthur Rubinstein

I tell you, you can pray for anything, and if you believe that you've received it, it will be yours. Mark 11:24 (NLT)

PRAYER FOR TODAY: *Lord, I pray that You see my heart and that You know that my desire is to serve You and to please You. I want to succeed at my weight loss program and I want to treat my body like the precious temple that it is. May I not give in to the desires of my selfish flesh or fickle feelings but operate on faith, mercy and God's grace. In Your name I ask all these things, Lord Jesus. Amen.*

JUNE 16
What Was I Thinking?

I went on a bike ride this morning grateful my body was cooperating and I was able to get some much needed exercise. One minute I was thinking about how happy I was that my knee was feeling better and enjoying my ride and the next minute, my thoughts completely wandered somewhere I didn't want them.

I started thinking about how just a few months ago I was walking four and five miles a day, and today … I can barely get out of bed and walk to the bathroom. Within a matter of seconds I started worrying about where my activity level would be a year from now. In the blink of an eye I could see myself wheelchair bound taking advantage of my Handicapped parking status. How did I get from happily enjoying my bike ride one minute to a cripple in a wheelchair in the span of a few seconds?

We can't afford to let our minds wander aimlessly dwelling on whatever pops into our head. It's so easy to let our thoughts lead us into depression by thinking about negative things. We need to keep our minds sharp by filling our empty heads with positive images, reaffirming Scriptures, praise songs and hopeful thoughts.

A great part of success on any weight loss program is to be able to envision ourselves as we hope to be once we've lost weight. In order to keep those positive images at the forefront, find an old picture of yourself of when you were happiest and hang it on the fridge or your mirror. If you've got a pair of jeans or a special dress you can't wait to fit into again, hang it somewhere obvious so you'll see it every day to remind you of where you're hoping this journey takes you.

Keep the positive images right there in your face so you won't be tempted to dwell on the negative. We CAN control our thought life. It's up to us to dwell on good things like our eventual success. If you think it, you can be it.

If you don't like something change it; if you can't change it, change the way you think about it. ~ Mary Engelbreit

Instead, let the Spirit renew your thoughts and attitudes. Ephesians 4:23 (NLT)

PRAYER FOR TODAY: *Lord, help me keep a positive attitude and to think on what is pure and lovely. I pray when darkness tries to intrude in my thoughts I will replace the lies from the enemy with the light of Your Word. Help me to see the good things in life and to maintain a positive attitude regardless of the circumstances around me. In Your name I ask all these things, Lord Jesus. Amen.*

JUNE 17
Let Them Eat Rice Cake

Sometimes I have to ask myself why I *volunteer* to do things I know will cost me dearly. And I'm not talking about monetary expense, but rather the price of emotional sacrifice. My husband and I host a marriage group at our home and I volunteered to bake a cake for someone celebrating a birthday in the group.

Halfway through the mixing I felt the first stirring of panic settle in. The temptation to eat cake batter was tangible. I saw on a talk show recently that an addiction to carbs and sugar has the same chemical reaction in the brain as heroin has to a drug addict. In my cake baking moment, I became an instant believer.

At one point the temptation to lick the beaters was so strong I felt myself near to swooning. I had to stop and ask myself why I *volunteered* to bake this cake. Was this mission of kindness merely a smokescreen to justify giving in to my temptation to lick the beaters and eat the batter from the bowl? Were my *volunteer* intentions misplaced intentions designed to give myself a reason to cheat?

Are we food addicts really self-sabotaging our efforts by justifying our actions, whether they seem well-meaning missions of mercy or otherwise? I *do* seem to volunteer for a lot of food related projects. I don't want to let my food addictions conflict with my genetic predisposition for hospitality; but somewhere in the midst of all these hospitable actions I – WE– need to do that "B" thing again: *balance*. We must balance our volunteer commitments and for me, perhaps consider volunteering to read to orphans rather than baking for shut-ins … at least until I conquer these food addictions.

Before tackling the frosting part of my *volunteer* birthday cake, I helped myself to a full serving of rice cakes with some low-fat cheese and fruit. It's not exactly my cake of choice, but cake that works in a time of crisis nonetheless. The next time anyone suggests, *let them eat cake*, play it safe and make it *rice cake*.

If you mess up, 'fess up. ~ Author Unknown

Then Jesus explained: "My nourishment comes from doing the will of God, who sent me, and from finishing his work." John 4:34 (NLT)

PRAYER FOR TODAY: *Lord, thank you for revelation – no matter how twisted it may sound in my head. Thank you for giving me the strength to battle through temptations and providing suitable alternatives in my weakened state. Please continue to give me strength for each new day. In Your name I ask all these things, Lord Jesus. Amen.*

JUNE 18
Make a Choice

Some days it may feel as though you're simply being pushed and pulled along with the normal ebb and flow of life's tide. You bob along minding your own business riding the waves not wanting to rock the boat. After all there are so many things in life that are beyond our control; the economy, the price of gas, the rising and setting of the sun, rampant evil, taxes, pestilence, yaddah, yaddah, yaddah.

It's enough to make you want to take your little boat and pull it in to a nice quiet cove and hide from the rest of the world. Oh, if only life were that simple.

Many of the things about our own personal lives are beyond our control; our DNA, our height, our race, our parents and family of origin, our age. Not much we can do on most of those issues. Many of us, myself included, have a tendency to complain about some of these things which are totally out of our control.

Regardless of our DNA, God instilled one characteristic in all of us that we can capitalize on – our free will. Every day we can CHOOSE to forgive those that have hurt us. We can CHOOSE to make healthy choices about our diet, our exercise – our bodies. We can CHOOSE to be positive or negative about everything that comes our way over the course of each and every day.

There may come a time when choice may be taken away from us because of age or illness. We can pray that won't be the case, but there are no guarantees in life – just another one of those things that are beyond our control.

While the choice remains mine – I CHOOSE to cast my cares on God. I CHOOSE to learn from my past and forgive. I CHOOSE to trust God for my future rather than worry. I CHOOSE joy – for the joy of the Lord is my strength. What will YOU choose?

Human life is purely a matter of deciding what's important to you. ~ Anonymous

"Today I have given you the choice between life and death, between blessings and curses. Now I call on heaven and earth to witness the choice you make. Oh, that you would choose life, so that you and your descendants might live!" Deuteronomy 30:19 (NLT)

PRAYER FOR TODAY: *Lord, thank You for the gift of free will and choice. Help me to choose a good attitude every day rather than choosing to walk in despair or worry. In Your name I ask all these things, Lord Jesus. Amen.*

JUNE 19
Time Machine Epiphany

I had to go for an MRI this morning on my knee – at long last. Never having an MRI before, I must admit to a certain pre-procedural trepidation. I was a little worried that I'd be too heavy (okay, I'll say it – *fat*) to fit in the machine. My fears were unfounded – I fit fine, not too fat, and nary a hint of judgment from the technician about my size.

As I was lying there in the tube that to me looked like a high-tech time machine, it was easy to let my mind wander during the painless procedure. Through the miracle of music being piped through the over-sized headphones I contemplated the fantasy of time travel. The 1980s music filling my head transported me to decades past. My memories zeroed in on 1975 – the year most likely to be my pick of the decade I'd return to.

That year I was at my "ideal" weight, right around the 120 pound mark. That was a good year. I didn't like myself any more than I do today at that weight but I had more self-confidence back then. Even though I knew I looked pretty good, I was terribly unhappy with myself.

Inner peace and contentment isn't based on what the number on our bathroom scale reads. How many times do we have to hear this? Surprisingly though, we sometimes attempt to convince ourselves that *if I only weighed 40 pounds less I'd be happier with myself.*

Somehow the gamma rays – or whatever the heck radiates through the MRI machine must have zapped my brain, because I had an epiphany mid-MRI. If I didn't like myself at my ideal weight, then reaching my projected goal weight years later won't fix my self-worth.

We must believe *it's not about the number.* If we can learn to love ourselves at our current weight then the possibilities are endless. It really is sad that there are no time machines. If we could know *then,* what we know *now.* We can't get younger, but we still have *time* to get smarter!

Resolve to be thyself; and know that he who finds himself, loses his misery. ~ Matthew Arnold, "Self-Dependence," Empedocles on Etna, and Other Poems, 1852

The man answered, "'You must love the LORD your God with all your heart, all your soul, all your strength, and all your mind.' And, 'Love your neighbor as yourself.'" Luke 10:27 (NLT)

PRAYER FOR TODAY: *Lord, thank You for the progress I've made with my past issues. Continue to work on my behalf revealing Your plan for me. Set my feet upon the path you wish me to take and grant me strength and courage for each new day. In Your name, Lord. Amen.*

JUNE 20
Diet Mulligan

A few days ago I had one of those rare days where I did pretty much nothing. I spent the better part of my day test driving the Lazy-Boy, watching golf on TV; and even as I type those words I find myself thinking "Good Lord, I can't believe I spent A WHOLE DAY watching golf!"

Because I have a tendency to think metaphorically about so many things, I started thinking about the similarities between golf and dieting. Some days the eating/exercise thing can be rolling along "right on par," and then we find ourselves succumbing to an unexpected temptation that throws us off course.

If we succumb to a binging meltdown, we start thinking "okay, time for a mulligan," or a "do-over." We tell ourselves, "from here on out, we'll get things back on course." If we're lucky, we hit a few good shots, or we have a couple of really good diet days and we think "we've got a real chance at beating this."

Professional golfers obviously don't get "Mulligans" during tournament play – but diets are not like golf in the fact that at any point in our program we can start fresh. We can get a "do-over" at any point on our diet. If we slip up at one meal, we can correct at the next meal.

Tomorrow is a brand new day. If we had a "bad round" today, get up tomorrow "tee it up" and "go for the green." Don't "fudge on the score" and stick to the plan. We need to play our best game and refuse to be intimated by how well the other players are doing. At the end of the day, if we know we did our best, didn't cheat, recorded everything accurately, we're way ahead of the game and can be happy if we played par or better.

Golf is a game that is played on a five-inch course - the distance between your ears. ~ Bobby Jones

The thief comes only in order to steal and kill and destroy. I came that they may have and enjoy life, and have it in abundance (to the full, till it overflows). John 10:10 (The Amplified Bible)

PRAYER FOR TODAY: *Lord, thank You for relaxing days. I pray You will help me to keep my diet on par and eat healthy; make time for exercise and do the very best I can each and every day. In Your name I ask all these things, Lord Jesus. Amen.*

JUNE 21
Cause You've Got to Have Friends

I spent yesterday with a friend, whom we'll call "Lisa" for arguments sake. Lisa has been on her own weight loss journey for several months and was near to a bingeing breakdown yesterday. Lisa's weight gain has been slow, but rather substantial over the course of the last ten years. Since the birth of her first child she's gained 100 pounds.

Lisa has been doing really well the last few months, but her weight loss is going much slower than she'd like. (Isn't that the way it is for most of us?) She's been very faithful with her exercise program and belongs to an exclusive gym that's addressing not only her weight issues, but some minor underlying health issues as well.

The problem is yesterday she was having a severe PMS attack and all she wanted was junk food. The program she's been on is very restrictive and she's had minimal carbs and zero bread for the last couple of months.

Yesterday all she could think about was French bread and chocolate. The one thing Lisa had going for her was she came by my house and alerted me to her cravings, allowing me to shut her down before she could do any serious damage.

When we find ourselves teetering on the brink of self-destruction, it's important to have a good friend, family member, relative or accountability partner who can come to our immediate rescue. It you have no one you can rely on at home, make sure you keep a phone number handy of someone trustworthy who can bail you out in a moment's notice.

If you slip and fall off the wagon, don't just lay there and let it back up and mow you over two or three times. GET UP, dust off and climb right back on the wagon IMMEDIATELY! And remember, help needs only be a phone call away. We'll all get by with a little help from our friends!

Friendship isn't a big thing - it's a million little things. ~ Author Unknown

A friend is always loyal, and a brother is born to help in time of need. Proverbs 17:17 (NLT)

PRAYER FOR TODAY: *Lord, I'm so thankful for the blessing of friends and grateful that I could lift my friend when she was down. I pray when I'm the one struggling You'll send me a friend to lift me up. I thank You for all of life's blessings. In Your name I ask all these things, Lord Jesus. Amen.*

JUNE 22
Numbing the Snack Attacks

I think I've stumbled upon a great appetite suppressant – quite by accident. I had a tiny filling for a small cavity at the dentist office today. It's been years since I've had a cavity so I'd forgotten how uncomfortable Novocain can be.

Five and a half hours after my procedure, the effects of the Novocain finally wore off. It was the longest, most uncomfortable feeling for that entire time. What made things worse, it was nearly impossible to eat anything during that time as I couldn't feel my teeth, tongue, cheek or gums. Of course, that made chewing nearly impossible. When I did try to drink or chew, the dribble down my numb chin made the whole effort frustrating.

I started thinking that it'd be nice to have an at-home Novocain kit so I could inject my mouth every time the urge to snack hit me. Not being able to chew would certainly eliminate sudden binges. Although I doubt I'd have the nerve to inject myself in the mouth with a needle on a daily basis. Because temptation hits me at regular intervals – nearly every single day, I'd need the maximum injections possible.

Practical solutions are necessary to curb the appetite. It's important to think ahead in order to beat the snack attacks. Pre-measured snacks in zippered sandwich bags in the cupboard or pantry go a long way to keeping us out of trouble. It's smart to keep plenty of fresh fruits and chopped veggies in the fridge so when we feel those urges we can quickly grab something healthy rather than succumbing to mindless grazing.

Snack attacks happen frequently and can be triggered by simple things like sudden smells, TV commercials, even reading a book or magazine can trigger you if you see a picture of food or read about a tantalizing treat.

Injecting ourselves with Novocain isn't a realistic option when we're assaulted by frequent snack cravings, but snack attacks don't have to be our undoing if we're prepared. Plan ahead to avoid disaster and we can overcome these cravings and addictions … all without resorting to numbing pain.

The belly rules the mind. ~ Spanish Proverb

For life is more than food, and your body more than clothing. Luke 12:23 (NLT)

PRAYER FOR TODAY: *Thank you, Lord that You continually provide for my needs. I pray You will grant me self-control so I won't give in to my urges to binge eat or eat things not on my program. Give me restraint and strength for each day. In Your name I ask all these things, Lord Jesus. Amen.*

JUNE 23
Nighttime Vigil

Yesterday was one of those days that would be best never repeated. Too many attacks on me personally and assaults against members of my family as well. As bed time rolled around last night, an all-over fear gripped my mind refusing to release its hold, making sleep nearly impossible. When sleep did come, it was fraught with troubling nightmares.

At one point during the night I awoke with a start certain there were three people stationed at the end of my bed. Not normal people, but apparitions that *glowed*. Rubbing my eyes against what I was certain was my mind playing tricks on me – I relaxed feeling a certain peace. More noticeably was the absence of the fear that gripped me earlier. For whatever reason, my foggy awareness convinced me that the three forms at the end of my bed were none other than the Father, the Son and the Holy Spirit. I finally slept peacefully, wrapped in the knowledge I was protected.

I spent the next morning in prayer and time in the Word. I kept hearing that still small voice telling me everything will be fine. I hope that's more than just wishful thinking and actually the voice of the Holy Spirit sent to encourage me as depression and fear are paralyzing and not the way I want to spend my day.

Whether we're recovering from an injury, dealing with a crisis in our life or that of a loved one, or just working hard to lose excess body weight and keep our temple healthy for God – HE IS WITH US. We are never alone. He will NEVER forsake us.

Every evening I turn my worries over to God. He's going to be up all night anyway. ~ Mary C. Crowley

For I am convinced that neither death nor life, neither angels nor demons, neither the present nor the future, nor any powers, neither height nor depth, nor anything else in all creation, will be able to separate us from the love of God that is in Christ Jesus our Lord. Romans 8:38-39 (NIV)

PRAYER FOR TODAY: *Lord, I am comforted by Your holy presence. Knowing that You watch over me and protect me as I sleep, fills me with peace. May You continue to make Your presence known to me throughout each and every day. Please continue to stay close in my life. In Your name I ask all these things, Lord Jesus. Amen.*

JUNE 24
Cleaning House

This has been a week where the repeated messages God seems to be sending me are centered on "obedience." At first, I thought all these related messages were merely a coincidence, but as the week's progressed, there's no denying God wants to get my attention.

I've just finished reading a great book by a Christian author. The combination of this book and the many obedience messages God's been slapping me in the face with – and I have to ask myself *"Where am I being the most disobedient, God?"*

Recently I was reading the book of Nehemiah in the Old Testament and there were several references to the people of God not taking care of God's temple. When I read the account of their disobedience, conviction pierced my spirit like a flaming arrow. I'm guilty Lord, of misusing the temple you've entrusted to me: my body, your holy temple.

By submitting to my food cravings and allowing myself to regain weight previously lost, I've basically allowed squatters to move into my temple and misuse the premises. First Corinthians 3:16-17 (NIV) says it far better than I ever could: *Don't you know that you yourselves are God's temple and that God's Spirit lives in you? If anyone destroys God's temple, God will destroy him; for God's temple is sacred, and you are that temple.*

We all need to sweep out the garbage we've let pile up in the corners of our neglected temple. Some serious remodeling is in order to get *our house – God's house –* in order. Perhaps during this critical remodeling phase we can evict the previous tenants of fear and insecurity. They've been terrible tenants and we've allowed their raucous behavior to have free reign of the property. Well no more! Today we're serving up an eviction notice and a new land-LORD is taking over the property. It's about time!

Health is a state of complete physical, mental and social well-being, and not merely the absence of disease or infirmity. ~ World Health Organization, 1948

Praise the LORD. Blessed is the man who fears the LORD, who finds great delight in his commands. Psalm 112:1 (NIV)

PRAYER FOR TODAY: *Thank you, Lord for wisdom and knowledge. May I use both to the fullest each and every day. Help me to sweep out the corners of my neglected temple and rebuild and remodel it to be healthy and full of joy. Thank You for the blessings in my life. I pray I can be an encourager to those who struggle. In Your name I ask all these things, Lord Jesus. Amen.*

JUNE 25
Paved With Thanks

You're out in public and someone tells you "You look nice. Is that a new outfit?" or "You look pretty today." All that's required on your part is a simple, *"Thank you."*

Somehow what's simple for some, sticks in your throat like you're gagging on a fiber filled throw pillow. You can't bring yourself to utter those simple words because inside your head you're hearing, "Yuck I look like a giant wart hog," or perhaps something similar but less flattering.

When you've grown up cloaked in shame, self-loathing and self-hatred it doesn't matter the sincerity of the compliment or who offers it up, you immediately reject statements which you perceive as sugar-coated bold face lies.

The road to recovery of a lifetime spent under this mantle of self-doubt will be paved with positive affirmations and encouragement along the way and we need to respond with simple trust not doubt.

Part of the recovery process is to stop listening to the negative voice of the enemy whispering in our ear regarding all that *we are not*. Healing from our wounded past means we must start agreeing with that still small voice of our Savior who's trying to tell us, *"He accepts us just as we are."*

The next time someone says: "Gee, you look really pretty today!" You say: "Thank You!" From here on out the road to recovery should be paved with compliments, thanks and gratitude.

God gave you a gift of 86,400 seconds today. Have you used one to say "thank you?"
~ William A. Ward

And let the peace that comes from Christ rule in your hearts. For as members of one body you are called to live in peace. And always be thankful. Colossians 3:15 (NLT)

PRAYER FOR TODAY: Lord, thank You for the healing from the inside out. May You continue to heal my past wounds and scars. Help me to grow in maturity and wisdom daily. I am thankful for all that You have blessed me with. May I never forget to be thankful and have an attitude of gratitude. In Your name I ask all these things, Lord Jesus. Amen.

JUNE 26
A Special Kind of Stupid

Sometimes I can't help but think I must be a special kind of *stupid*. Case in point: I volunteered to get up at the crack of dawn and be at church at 6:00 a.m. this morning to help cater a breakfast seminar. The operative word here is volunteered.

I didn't mind the early morning hour or the six hours I put in setting up food tables or cleaning up afterwards. I didn't even mind all the dishes I washed and dried. The *stupid* came in to play when the volunteer staff was invited to help themselves to the breakfast goodies being served: namely, at least 12 different types of cheese Danish, iced pastries, muffins, bagels, croissants and oh yeah, some fruit and yogurt.

As we were cleaning up and packing up the leftovers, the *stupid* reared its ugly head. Several bags of goodies were packaged up and shoved in my arms to take home … *for the kids*. Oh the lies we tell ourselves.

I worked really hard this morning; gave unselfishly of my Saturday free time to serve the church, the community and God. I was tempted to "reward" myself by eating the goodies, but there's a reason I don't eat this stuff anymore. I know it's not good for me. And even though the enemy was whispering in my ear about how I *deserved* to treat myself by indulging in these baked goodies, the voice of the Lord was louder.

He tells me "You are forgiven and You are the daughter of the King of Kings." He knows my struggles and my weaknesses and He loves me in spite of them. He created me for more.

Learning to say "NO" when all you want to do is say, "YES, YES, YES!" will take practice. We have to dig down deep in our souls and trust God will give us the strength we need when we need it most. The more we get in the habit of saying NO, the easier it will become. Following God means we have to practice denying our flesh; which isn't as easy as it sounds when our flesh is stupid.

Common sense is not so common. ~ Voltaire

I turned away from God, but then I was sorry. I kicked myself for my stupidity! I was thoroughly ashamed of all I did in my younger days. Jeremiah 31:19 (NLT)

PRAYER FOR TODAY: *Lord, thank You for opportunities to give my time in service to You. I know that You hear my prayers and Your forgiveness is immediate, total and unconditional when we fall into temptation. I know I'm not perfect and You don't expect me to be. I ask that while I'm not perfect, I would simply be the best that I can be each day. In Your name I ask all these things, Lord Jesus. Amen.*

JUNE 27
Once a Cheater Always a Cheater

There's a line from an old *Friends* episode I can't get out of my head. Ross and Rachel were thinking about getting back together again after Ross had cheated during their previous relationship. A skeptical Rachel shared with Ross her mother's opinion of *"Once a cheater always a cheater."* I wonder if that theory applies to diets as well?

If anyone knows how to cheat on a diet, it's me. After working for a weight loss organization for several years, I learned a few new tricks from some very creative members. I discovered that cheating on a diet is a universal problem. Most dieters cheat. Clearly there are exceptions, but the "average" dieter is likely to give in to temptation at some point.

In the Bible there's a verse of Scripture that says simply looking at a woman with lust is every bit as bad as actually committing a lustful act. Does lusting after a Whopper make me as guilty as if I'd actually eaten one? Yes and no.

If our thoughts are focused on sinful foods we'd like to eat then that opens our mind up for the enemy to come in and have a field day. The more we focus on something the more likely we're apt to give in to those thoughts and possibly act on them.

If we continually have a cheater's mindset, it's likely we'll give in to those desires at some point. It's highly advisable that we learn to restructure our thoughts on less destructive desires. Thinking about sugar-free Jell-O is a lot safer than dwelling on burgers and fries.

Whoever said that watching your weight was easy clearly has never successfully lost weight and kept it off. Not only does watching our weight require will-power to resist temptation, but we've got to put our thought life on a strict diet as well.

Sometimes the littlest things in life are the hardest to take. You can sit on a mountain more comfortably than on a tack. ~ Author Unknown

For out of the heart come evil thoughts, murder, adultery, sexual immorality, theft, false testimony, slander. Matthew 15:19 (NIV)

PRAYER FOR TODAY: *Lord, please help to retrain my thoughts, my mind and my heart so I would not harbor lust for the things I know are not good for me. Help me to eliminate all destructive thoughts and retrain my mind to dwell only on what is pleasing to You. In Your name, Lord Jesus. Amen.*

JUNE 28
We're Not Animals

Our relationship with food can be a scary thing. So many of us have a love/hate relationship with food and we find ourselves out of control or out of balance with regards to the foods we eat. Healthy foods can control us every bit as much as the junk foods.

This control was evident to me last night while I was enjoying a small cup of raspberry sherbet. I'd made allowances for my treat and measured out a half-cup serving. What bothered me was that I stood up at the kitchen sink and shoveled sherbet in like it was my last meal before being sealed in a sleep tube for a space mission rather than taking the time to sit down and enjoy my treat. Am I eating standing up because I need to be prepared for a fight or flight encounter should someone come and try to take my sherbet from me? My behavior when enjoying a planned healthy snack was *no different* than my binge eating.

After examining my behavior I questioned when this caveman attitude towards food must have surfaced. This urge I have to rush through every meal protecting my plate, has roots that go back to my childhood. I grew up in a house with a single-working mother and our food budget was a bleak thing. Treats were rare and there was always a sibling who would eat their treat quickly and beg for what was left of mine. I would hide my treats to savor for later and eat in secret without interference.

Childhood habits clearly define some of our poor eating habits today. We need to make a menu plan, stick with it and then sit down and enjoy each planned meal. Make mealtime a dining experience and share it with loved ones – not in secret. Savor the flavors (even if it's only broiled chicken and brown rice). Slow down and smell the rosemary. We're not animals for goodness sake!

Nothing would be more tiresome than eating and drinking if God had not made them a pleasure as well as a necessity. ~ Voltaire

When I was a child, I talked like a child, I thought like a child, I reasoned like a child. When I became a man, I put childish ways behind me. 1 Corinthians 13:11 (NIV)

PRAYER FOR TODAY: *Lord, thank You for enlightening me with new revelations regarding my character and my habits. Please help me to savor the gift of mealtime and not hurry through it like it's something to be conquered. I pray You will continue to work in me and change the things that aren't pleasing to You. In Your name I ask all these things, Lord Jesus. Amen.*

JUNE 29
Sweatpants Mentality

It begins like any other day. You get up, shower, breakfast and read the morning news. You head to the closet to pick out something comfy to wear for weekend loafing. The first red flag should be that you reject the tight denim Capri pants for the over-sized Capri sweat pants with the long draw string. The sub-conscious mind has decided it's to be *one of those days*.

There's nothing wrong with relaxing and taking an occasional break. We all need those kinds of days once in a while. It's important at this point that we don't let our sweatpants attire dictate a sweatpants mentality when it comes to food. Just because we're relaxed and dressed for comfort and left alone with no witnesses, it's not an open invitation to a secret raid on the pantry.

I found myself battling a sloppy attitude this afternoon simply because of my sloppy clothing. That's when it hit me that I had subconsciously opted for the uniform of the depressed today. I'm not depressed, just feeling a little under the weather and battling some physical challenges.

Even though I wasn't depressed, with my sweatpants attitude I felt like I should be digging in a container of Rocky Road ice cream like a miner digging for buried treasure. And I very nearly did succumb until I caught myself and stopped to ask *who is that girl? I thought I'd buried the old me*.

For most of us, "the old me" may never completely leave us. The secret is we can't allow those old alter-egos to rule our lives, our diet, our thoughts or even our wardrobe. The quickest way to stop a snack attack is to immediately change out of your depression uniform and squeeze into your swimming suit. A few minutes in front of the full length mirror and any and all snacking urges may be instantly erased.

I think I may be on to the greatest appetite suppressant yet – just wear your swimming suit every time you're tempted to eat and that ought to do the trick! It doesn't have to be *one of those days* if we don't let it.

The greatest discovery of my generation is that a human being can alter his life by altering his attitudes. ~ William James

I do not understand what I do. For what I want to do I do not do, but what I hate I do. Romans 7:15 (NIV)

PRAYER FOR TODAY: *Lord, create a clean heart in me and renew a right spirit within me. Cast me not away from your presence and please continue to teach me Your ways. In Your name I ask all these things, Lord Jesus. Amen.*

JUNE 30
Snap Out of It!

I was watching an old movie the other day called *Moonstruck*. I cracked up laughing at the part where Nicholas Cage's character tells Cher's character that he loves her. She's engaged to his brother so clearly it's a poor idea for him to be in love with her. She looks at him and then slaps young Nick across the face and tells him to *"Snap out of it!"*

My point in sharing this is some days I wish God would do the same thing to us. Just slap us in the face and say *"Snap out of it,"* with regards to our bad attitudes, challenges and excuses with this weight loss journey.

If we're constantly worried about our next meal and always playing *"Let's Make a Deal"* figuring out what we can give up in order to eat what we really want rather than exercising, we've got to ask ourselves: *is this program really working?* Are we simply manipulating the program to make it *look like* it's working?

Perhaps a good slap upside the head could act as a "Reset" move. Maybe a good slap would zap us into the right mindset the same way those electric paddles shock a person's heart back into rhythm. It could be like internal exercise.

Recognizing our problem doesn't go far in solving our problem. Whether we exercise regularly or rarely exercise due to physical limitations it goes without saying that we have to rely on healthy eating rather than exercise to help in our weight loss efforts. Experts agree that most weight loss is directly related to what we eat, not in how much we exercise. It's unlikely we'll simply *"Snap out of it"* when we get off track with our weight loss journey, so the next best thing is to *snap to it* and just do the work.

I have sometimes been wildly, despairingly, acutely miserable, but through it all I still know quite certainly that just to be alive is a grand thing. ~ Agatha Christie

I have told you these things, so that in me you may have peace. In this world you will have trouble. But take heart! I have overcome the world." John 16:33 (NIV)

PRAYER FOR TODAY: *Lord, please help me to snap out of this funk that I'm in. Give me a new appreciation for life and all that You've blessed me with. May I dwell on all the good things in life rather than fixating on all the things that I think are wrong with my life. Heal my mind, heal my spirit and above all, please heal my body. In Your name I ask all these things, Lord Jesus. Amen.*

JULY 1
An Unquenchable Thirst

I spent an hour in the pool today swimming laps and doing some simple water aerobics. When I was finished I couldn't believe how thirsty I was. I'd spent so much time in the pool all my digits were sufficiently pruney. I had water in my ears and my eyes stung from the chlorine, but yet I was really thirsty. That doesn't make sense to me.

Oddly enough I was watching a program on TV this morning on nutrition. The host mentioned that 70% of our bodies are made up of water, which is why it's so important to stay properly hydrated and to drink plenty of water throughout our day.

The benefits of drinking at least 64 ounces of water each day are endless. Drinking a large glass of water before mealtime helps fill your stomach and keeps you from overeating. Obviously because we're eliminating our water supply throughout the day through sweating or urination, it's important to put the water back into our bodies.

Drinking the recommended amount of water each day is far easier in the summer than it is in the winter. If you're like me and you find drinking plain old water a challenge, you may need to get creative. You may want to try flavored water as an alternative.

Drinking tea is a healthier alternative to drinking soda, but because tea is a diuretic you're eliminating as quickly as you take it in. There are benefits to drinking tea because many teas contain antioxidants; but as with anything too much of anything isn't healthy.

We get water from many of the food sources we eat such as fresh fruits. However, there's no substitute for simply drinking water throughout the day, as the fruit contains natural sugars and carbs and of course they do have calories as well.

Don't wait until you're thirsty to drink a glass of water. By that time, it may be too late and you may be on the verge of dehydration. Don't underestimate the benefits of water … it does a body good. Don't leave home without it.

We never know the worth of water till the well is dry. ~ Thomas Fuller, Gnomologia, 1732

I thirst for God, the living God. When can I go and stand before him? Psalm 42:2 (NLT)

PRAYER FOR TODAY: *Lord, I thirst after You and I seek Your favor. Thank You for providing for my needs. May I be filled with Your love, Your Spirit, Your wisdom and Your knowledge. May I continue to grow and mature in the things of the Lord each and every day. In Your name I ask all these things, Lord Jesus. Amen.*

JULY 2
One Hot Mama

During these dog days of summer, living in the desert southwest is something akin to taking a trip to the surface of the sun. It's hot. How hot is it? Every trip to and from the car makes me think of the Wicked Witch in The Wizard of Oz and her famous last words, *"I'M MELTING! I'M MELTING!"*

I had a support group meeting last night and I wanted to dress in something that wouldn't stick to me and make me feel all sweaty. I opted for a lightweight summer skirt and layered tank tops with a kicky belt. I thought I looked okay – not great but comfortable, temperature wise at least.

It's the sleeveless thing that's a major issue for me and tends to dictate my wardrobe. I'm uncomfortable with my "bingo arms." The fact that it's 197° outside (give or take) cannot be ignored. Comfort takes precedence over flabby arms.

For me the challenge was not to look in a mirror for the entire evening. Denial goes a long way as salve for my bruised ego, which had convinced me I looked completely awful in my summer ensemble. Oh the lies *he* tells us, are never ending.

While denial might be the multi-purpose dysfunction that works in so many situations, if we're ever to experience true soul healing, we must stop the denial. Perhaps it's just the heat that makes us crazy, but we need to learn to look in the mirror and accept our arms – flabby or otherwise. While we're at it, we need to love our butts and make peace with our thighs – whatever their size.

Healing comes when we can look in the mirror and see ourselves as "one hot mama!" Its' not about what size we wear it's about loving the size we're in.

Heat, ma'am! It was so dreadful here, that I found there was nothing left for it but to take off my flesh and sit in my bones. ~ Sydney Smith, Lady Holland's Memoir

For the LORD has told me this: "I will watch quietly from my dwelling place—as quietly as the heat rises on a summer day, or as the morning dew forms during the harvest." Isaiah 18:4 (NLT)

PRAYER FOR TODAY: *Lord, thank You for life's blessings, even the heat of a summer day which reminds me that You are in control. Help me not give in to whining and complaining and help me keep my cool even in the midst of this long hot summer. I love You and thank You for the pleasure of serving You. Continue to watch over me and direct my steps. In Your name I ask all these things, Lord Jesus. Amen.*

JULY 3
The WHOLE Week

L ast night a challenge was presented to my support group for the upcoming week. The challenge was to resist thinking OR saying anything negative about ourselves for the upcoming week. One girl in the class said it best: *"The WHOLE WEEK???!!!!"*

If that girl's reaction is any indication, clearly I'm not the only woman who struggles with taming her self-deprecating thoughts. It is somewhat easier to tame the tongue in comparison to our thoughts. Those seem to have a mind of their own. How do we go from zipping our lip to not even letting those negative put downs into our brains in the first place?

For me it comes down to practicing what I preach. I'm the first one to tell others when you start dwelling on a negative thought, you must instantly replace it with a positive affirmation about what God says in His Word. That's why it's so important that we read the Word on a regular basis. We need to study the Word; we need to memorize the Word and we need to KNOW the Word.

When we think, "I'm so fat and disgusting in my swimsuit;" we need to replace that instantly with "I am made in the image and likeness of God." We need to write 1 Peter 3:4 on an index card and post it on our mirror so we can remind ourselves every day: *You should clothe yourselves instead with the beauty that comes from within, the unfading beauty of a gentle and quiet spirit, which is so precious to God.*

It's not easy to retrain our thoughts and words. It starts with one thought at a time. If we practice replacing those negative thoughts and words for the next week, perhaps we'll do it the week after that ... and the week after that ... and just maybe it'll become a habit to look in the mirror and see the beautiful souls God created us to be.

Cure yourself of the affliction of caring how you appear to others. Concern yourself only with how you appear before God, concern yourself only with the idea that God may have of you. ~ Miguel De Unamuno

Do not let any unwholesome talk come out of your mouths, but only what is help-ful for building others up according to their needs, that it may benefit those who listen. Ephesians 4:29 (NLT)

PRAYER FOR TODAY: *Lord, I ask that You would guard the words of my mouth and the thoughts that I think. May I refuse all negative thoughts that pop into my mind and replace them with affirming and uplifting thoughts. Help me to dwell on what is pure and lovely and refuse to give voice to those negative thoughts about myself. In Your name I ask all these things, Lord Jesus. Amen.*

JULY 4
Declaring Independence

It seems only fitting that on this Independence Day that those of us who struggle with food addictions or weight problems should declare this our "Independence Day" from bondage. It may feel as though the skinny girl inside of us is being suffocated by a not-so-skinny girl and protective layer of body fat. We would like nothing more than to secede from the union of the fat girl and be released. Our inner skinny girl wants to be set free from the captivity of fat.

Since it's impossible to completely declare overnight independence from fat, the next best thing is to declare we are set free from the bondage of food and our addiction of always worrying about what we weigh – at least for today. Ideally we'd like to be free from this addiction the rest of our lives, but we all know that's easier said than done.

Today we declare our independence from our addiction to food and do hereby set forth from this day forward we shall be free and refuse to bow down to the whims of our flesh. Grant us liberty or grant us thin thighs –whichever comes first.

May this be our Independence Day!

We must be free not because we claim freedom, but because we practice it. ~ William Faulkner

So if the Son sets you free, you are truly free. John 8:36 (NLT)

PRAYER FOR TODAY: *Lord, thank You for the freedoms we enjoy in this country. I pray for all the people who have fought and served for the privilege of freedom. I pray that starting today I can be free from my addictive behaviors to food and free from always worrying about my weight. Help today be the first day of my freedom from bondage and may I enjoy freedom every day from here on out. In Your name I ask all these things, Lord Jesus. Amen.*

JULY 5
When In Doubt Throw It Out – Or Just Donate

Any woman who has ever worried about her weight is likely to have a smorgasbord of sizes in her closet. My walk-in closet has sizes ranging from sizes 6 to a 16 and small to double XXL. That's a pretty big span and range of weight gains and losses.

I reached my reality check point last week when I was looking for a pair of shoes in my closet. During my search I found a hidden stash of forgotten clothes. I'd conveniently forgotten them because they were mostly shorts, all sizes 6 or 8.

Reality can be a bitter pill to swallow when you finally choke it down and face the fact that your size 6 and 8 days are long behind you because the *behind* you currently have simply can no longer fit into a 6 or an 8.

When I look at the bigger picture, at the start of this New Year I was barely squeezing into a size 16, but rather than focusing on my progress the enemy would have me wallow in self-pity because I'm no longer a size 8. He's good that way.

It can be tough to face facts and discard or donate old clothes. As a rule when cleaning out your closet, regardless of your assorted sizes, if you come across something you haven't worn in two or more years – discard it!

Why do we insist on hanging onto clothes that are out of style? In all reality, even if we lost a significant amount of weight most of us want to shop for newer, more fashionable clothes. Isn't shopping for smaller sizes one of the perks of losing weight in the first place?

If it's out of style and you haven't worn it in a while, gut it out and pitch it out. Buy brand new when you are through. Words to live by, my friends! Words to live by.

Reality bites… and doesn't let go. ~ Author Unknown

Brothers, I do not consider myself yet to have taken hold of it. But one thing I do: Forgetting what is behind and straining toward what is ahead … Philippians 3:13 (NIV)

PRAYER FOR TODAY: *Thank You Lord, for opportunities to organize my life. Help me to forget what size I was in the past and help me not to waste my life wishing for things than can never be. Help me to remember my weight doesn't define me or make me happy or a success – but the power to be happy lies within me. I can be happy at any weight. In Your name I ask all these things, Lord Jesus. Amen.*

JULY 6
Chew On This

I was watching National Geographic *Taboo* on TV last night. The program high-lighted two different cultures; one here in America and our obesity crisis. The second part of the show outlined the culture in the African nation of Mauritania where fat women are idolized and sought after.

The first part of the show chronicled one obese man who weighed 750 pounds and was confined to his bed. He had to be removed from his house with a special winch. It took six very large men to remove him from his bed.

In the country of Mauritania in western Africa, women are encouraged to be heavy and many are severely obese. A woman who is heavy is said to be much loved by her husband. Mothers start force-feeding their young daughters at ages five or six to fatten them up to make them more appealing for marriage. They even resort to torture when a girl refuses to eat and it's perfectly legal and accepted in their society. They bind their little feet between wooden stakes and squeeze them until the child finishes her meal, which in that culture consists mainly of cow's milk fortified with millet and butter.

The program pointed out that obesity is becoming a global problem (even calling "it *"globesity"*) because more fast food restaurants are popping up internationally in countries that previously had no problems, like China.

We don't live in a perfect world and thousands of children go to bed hungry while others gorge themselves and grow up to be unhealthy adults. What is wrong with this picture? There's a lot of imbalance in this imperfect world. We should do our part and eat healthy and pass along proper nutritional balance to our children and grandchildren. It won't fix the world's problems, but it's a start. We must never forget that "B" word: *BALANCE* … again.

We shall require a substantially new manner of thinking if mankind is to survive.
~ Albert Einstein

Nehemiah said, "Go and enjoy choice food and sweet drinks, and send some to those who have nothing prepared. This day is sacred to our Lord. Do not grieve, for the joy of the LORD is your strength." Nehemiah 8:10 (NIV)

PRAYER FOR TODAY: *Lord, I pray You will grant me compassion for brothers and sisters who struggle with obesity and for those that suffer from malnutrition. Open my eyes to serve where You lead me; help me not to judge others, lest I be judged. May I always be grateful for all that You've provided for me and my family and never give in to complaining. In Your name I ask all these things, Lord Jesus. Amen.*

JULY 7
Half-Way Half-Done

Flipping through my calendar recently I noticed that not only is summer half over, but the calendar year is officially half over. With more of the year gone than is left, perhaps this might be a good week for a resolution inventory. If we started our New Year's resolution on January 1st and six full months have come and gone, it's time to take stock of any success we may be enjoying.

Many of us know that if we don't see some sort of immediate progress when it comes to losing weight we tend to ditch the program and revert back to old ways. Perhaps like me, your success is measured very slowly and you're not seeing the results you'd like, but you're still following a program. That's huge! Don't give up because you haven't lost as much weight as someone who started the same time as you. Hang in there!

Success isn't necessarily measured by total pounds lost. If you've only lost a few pounds but you're blood pressure or cholesterol is improving – that's progress. If you've kicked some bad eating habits and eliminated unhealthy sodas or fried foods from your diet – that's progress. If you've only lost a few pounds but you're exercising three or more days a weeks and making better food choices – that is progress.

If you can look back to where you were six months ago and see positive changes in your attitude, what you are eating, your exercise program or the way your clothes are fitting – that's all good and that's all progress.

Ideally it'd be great if six months from now we were at our goal weight. Hopefully six months from now it will be more about laying down our obsessions or our addictive behavior towards food. Success isn't about the number on the scale but what's going on inside our head. Success is about maintaining a healthy attitude about food. Success means drawing closer to God than ever before because we've submitted our unhealthy attitude about food over to Him. In six months from now hopefully we can declare unequivocally that we eat to live rather than live to eat.

If we're not willing to settle for junk living, we certainly shouldn't settle for junk food. ~ Sally Edwards

So if we have enough food and clothing, let us be content. 1 Timothy 6:8 (NLT)

PRAYER FOR TODAY: *Lord, thank You that I'm past comparing my progress with that of others. Even though I may not be where I want to be as far as my weight goes, I thank You that I have made progress. Please help me continue to make wise choices. I pray You bless me with wisdom and common sense regarding food and weight. Give me the strength to finish this journey with excellence. In Your name I ask all these things, Lord Jesus. Amen.*

JULY 8
Thank You, Thank You

Recently at a gathering with friends the topic of discussion moved around to how we ought to be praying. One man felt led by the Lord to present his requests to God and immediately offer thanks to God for hearing him and answering his prayers. Rather than dwelling on repetitive prayer, God impressed him to spend his prayer time thanking God for the answers. Even though my friend has no way of knowing how God will answer his prayers he felt it was important to be thankful in advance.

We know that God hears us when we pray because Scripture is filled with reassurances that God hears us. There are Scriptures that tell us that Jesus Christ is interceding on our behalf to Father God so we know that whatever we pray in His name, God has heard us.

Starting today, when I prayed about my day and asked God to help me to be in control of my food, rather than letting my food control me, as soon as I spoke my request, I thanked God for hearing me. I also started thanking and praising God for the victory I know I will have in successfully losing weight.

Rather than praying, *"I wish You would take away these food cravings TODAY, God,"* I prayed, *"Thank You, Lord Jesus for helping me to overcome these food temptations today."*

Attitude is everything. Isn't it better to carry around an attitude of faith that we will be successful rather than a half-baked attitude that we *hope* we'll succeed and lose weight *someday?*

There's always something to chew on. Rather than chew on something that is unhealthy and filled with empty calories, let's chew on a heart full of thanks.

Who does not thank for little will not thank for much. ~ Estonian Proverb

Give thanks to the Lord, for he is good! His faithful love endures forever.
1 Chronicles 16:34 (NLT)

PRAYER FOR TODAY: *Thank You, Lord for all that You have blessed me with in this lifetime. Thank You for hearing my prayers. Search my heart and see if there be any wicked ways in me. Forgive me of my sins and may I harbor no unforgiveness against anyone. As You hear my requests, grant them according to Your will and not mine. Your will be done on earth as it is Heaven. In Your name I ask all these things, Lord Jesus. Amen.*

JULY 9
Me, Myself and I

If you're like me chances are you have a few personality quirks or idiosyncrasies that you're uncomfortable with – maybe even downright unhappy about. My list of quirks is too long, but at the top of that list is my propensity for isolation. I wish I was more of a social butterfly, but that gene bypassed me and went right to my kids.

Don't get me wrong, I like people – *most of the time* – and I enjoy being sociable – *some of the time*. Some days though, I'd rather while away the hours in front of the computer or the TV *by myself*.

When we suffer from any type of addiction, spending too much time isolating ourselves can be a sign that we need help. I have a friend who is a recovering alcoholic who has a hard time being with people. He's even taken to watching church online because he hates crowds. Too much isolation is unhealthy. He's also terribly lonely – *you think?*

As with everything we need to have balance in our social life. (There's that "B" word again!) Spending quiet time by ourselves and with God is important for our own peace of mind and developing a closer relationship with Christ. However, God created diversity in mankind for a reason, because we complement one another and *we need one another.*

One of the enemy's most successful tools is isolation. If he can keep us separate and alone, he can chip away at our confidence and our self-esteem. Isolating ourselves actually makes it easier for him. DANGER! DANGER! Red flags waving all over the place!

The road to recovery means reintroducing ourselves to society occasionally. We all have the potential to be beautiful social butterflies but we've got to be willing to leave the isolation and safety of the cocoon.

A good friend is cheaper than therapy. ~ Author Unknown

They worshiped together at the Temple each day, met in homes for the Lord's Supper, and shared their meals with great joy and generosity ... Acts 2:46 (NLT)

PRAYER FOR TODAY: *Lord, I pray You will motivate me to interact with others when all I want is to hide from the world. Help me to come out of my shell and open up to others and become more involved in the lives of those around me. I pray You will continue to mold me and make me and help me to become all that You have planned for me. In Your name I ask all these things, Lord Jesus. Amen.*

JULY 10
Hide and Seek

If ever there was a legitimate reason for wanting to isolate myself from the world – today would be that day. I got a haircut recently that's *less* than what I was hoping for. It's *short*; so short that I'm worried I'll be mistaken for a boy. Hence the need to isolate myself from the rest of the world at least until it grows out.

It's really quite comical though as for decades it was my hairstyle that I chose to cower behind. In the 80s I sported really big hair (*TV evangelist wife* big) coupled with glasses as large as satellite dishes. Thinking to camouflage my body flaws, I chose extreme hair and glasses to hide behind. My central goal was to be invisible.

After the turn of the century I opted for brand new super short hair for a brand new century thinking a new attitude and a "new me" would follow. Having short hair has challenged me and my self-esteem mainly because what I feared most has come to pass – there's nothing to hide behind and I'm no longer invisible.

When we struggle with food addictions and weight problems, we seek ways in which to hide ourselves. We hide behind our kids or our spouses. We can hide from the world behind hair, clothes or addictions, but we cannot hide from God. He already knows everything about us; including the ugliness we work so hard to keep buried. The good news is – He loves us any way. Regardless of how ugly our past may be, God doesn't look at the ugliness of abuse, addiction or sin; God sees our hearts.

If we have confessed our sins to Him, he is faithful and just to cleanse us from all unrighteousness and He has forgiven us. (1 John 1:9) In order for us to be truly free – *free enough to stop hiding*, we need to accept God's forgiveness AND most importantly, we need to *forgive ourselves* and those that have hurt us.

Forgiveness does not change the past, but it does enlarge the future. ~ Paul Boese

"For everything that is hidden will eventually be brought into the open, and every secret will be brought to light." Mark 4:22 (NLT)

PRAYER FOR TODAY: Lord, I know I cannot hide anything from You. Help me overcome any low self-esteem issues I wrestle with and help me to conquer that need I feel to hide myself from the rest of the word. Help me to operate in the gifts of the spirit. Fill me with the confidence that I am loved by the Savior so that I may reach out in love to others who struggle with insecurity and low self-esteem. In Your name I ask all these things, Lord Jesus. Amen.

JULY 11
Escape From Neverland

Without warning you wake up and there it is that *I'm NEVER going to beat this weight problem* state of mind. No matter how hard you wish it away, pray without ceasing or even try to shop, read, or nap it away, those negative thoughts have implemented themselves in your brain and refuse to be shaken.

We ALL have days like that when despite our best efforts those NEVER thoughts pound at your brain like an annoying drippy faucet ... *you'll NEVER get this* ... *you'll NEVER lose weight* ... *you'll NEVER overcome your food addictions.*

Rather than thinking I will NEVER get this weight off, we need to remind ourselves that we are eating healthy balanced meals. Think of all the positive steps we're making to get healthy and lose weight.

How can we believe we'll NEVER achieve our goals when we're going to weekly support groups, journaling our trials and our victories or calling a friend when we stumble or fall? If we take the time to list all of the positive steps we are making to get healthy and lose weight, they far outweigh the NEVER thoughts that try to control us.

Even if we're not dropping weight as fast as we'd like or even as fast as our friends, getting healthy should not be a competition because then it becomes about something other than getting healthy.

Don't let yourself board the bus to NEVERland. That's a dead end trip that ends up costing you more than you're willing to pay. Get on board the, *At least I'm making progress* bus that's bound for success – no matter how long the journey takes or how many stops we make along the way, at least we're moving forward!

Success consists of going from failure to failure without loss of enthusiasm. ~ Winston Churchill

Common sense and success belong to me. Insight and strength are mine. Proverbs 8:14 (NLT)

PRAYER FOR TODAY: *Lord, help me to banish those thoughts that tell me I'll never succeed and beat these weight issues. I pray for success and ask that You would control my negative thoughts and give me control over my mouth so I will not speak negative words. May each day have a measure of success so I will not become discouraged and be tempted to quit altogether. In Your name I ask all these things, Lord Jesus. Amen.*

JULY 12
Junk Free Help

Struggling with food addictions, weight problems and low self-esteem issues often-times make it hard to admit when we actually need help from anyone. Somehow the shame of our addiction brings with it the stigma of failure and weakness so that when we need to ask for help it seems to only magnify our weaknesses and failures. Or so the enemy would have us believe.

A couple of weeks ago I heard a sermon on discouragement. At the end of the sermon the pastor gave an invitation to those struggling with discouragement to stand and receive prayer. Even though I knew that the message was tailored for me I froze in my seat. I could not make myself stand up to receive prayer.

I argued internally that I was simply too discouraged to even bother standing up, but God knew that I was standing up on the inside. For me the second I made a choice not to stand up and publically admit I was struggling with discouragement opened my eyes to an even bigger problem. I was filled with pride.

Part of my problem is publically admitting that I'm weak and ashamed. God helped me see that by refusing help I'm too full of pride to admit that I have a problem. He also reassured me there is no shame in asking for help. When we refuse offered help is it because we can't get past our shame or is it because we think *I can do this on my own?*

If we're feeling shame, we need to lay that down and get past it. If we think we can complete this journey without help from *anyone*, we're kidding ourselves.

This journey is hard enough and not a quick, easy process. We need to learn that it's okay to ask for help. Recognizing our pride issue is just one of the stops along this journey. If we take it one day at a time, eventually God will help us to overcome all of this junk. Eventually, *with God's help*, we can hope to become "junk free."

God has not called us to see through each other, but to see each other through. ~ Author Unknown

First pride, then the crash — the bigger the ego, the harder the fall. Proverbs 16:18 (The Message Bible)

PRAYER FOR TODAY: *Lord, help me to overcome any shame I continue to carry inside me. Forgive me for this need I have to keep my problems to myself, never admitting my weaknesses and my faults. Please be patient with me as I learn to trust others and lift me up when I am down. In Your name I ask all these things, Lord Jesus. Amen.*

JULY 13
No Created Equals Here

A couple of friends of mine are getting ready to leave on a two-week vacation. In preparation for their trip they've been "dieting" hoping to lose a few pounds so they can enjoy their vacation without guilt. Translated that means they intend to eat anything and everything they want while on vacation. In order to be able to do that, they both set out to lose 10-20 pounds *before* their vacation starts.

The female half of this couple is a woman five years older than me, has gone through the joys of menopause and has had surgery on her non-working thyroid. She accepts that she's about 30 pounds heavier than she needs to be. She watches what she eats and I suspect she will practice *some* restraint while on vacation.

Her husband on the other hand has seen his weight yo-yo up and down every year as he prepares for vacation. He eats his weight in fried foods and cakes and pies throughout the duration of whatever vacation he's enjoying. Upon his return home, he cuts back slightly and manages to lose the 15 or 20 pounds of vacation weight. I've seen him do this pre-vacation starvation diet and watched him lose 20 pounds in a two-week time frame year-after-year, and then resume "normal" eating and regain all his weight.

It's no secret that men and women lose weight differently. Life isn't fair and when it comes to metabolism, body types, DNA, etc., we are NOT all created equal. Yes, *it's not fair*, but the fact that God created us all to be *individuals* should be a great reminder that we are loved by our Creator *because* He took the time to make us all different. In the end, God is still good and He is in control!

Everyone is kneaded out of the same dough but not baked in the same oven. ~ Yiddish Proverb

Yet God has made everything beautiful for its own time. He has planted eternity in the human heart, but even so, people cannot see the whole scope of God's work from beginning to end. Ecclesiastes 3:11 (NLT)

PRAYER FOR TODAY: *Lord, I admit my feelings of jealousy over my friend's weight loss and I ask that You would forgive me for feeling this way. Wipe away my sin and replace these jealous feelings with kindness, compassion, joy and love for my friend. May I exhibit grace to all and share in the success of others. In Your name I ask all these things, Lord Jesus. Amen.*

JULY 14
A Pain in the ... Ask Me Later

For anyone who lives with daily pain – be it physical, mental or emotional, you know how debilitating it can be and how exhausting it is. I've been living with physical pain for about six months now and some days I think I've more than had enough. Trying to maintain a positive attitude in light of the chronic pain has presented certain challenges. One of the benefits to all this pain: it's made me more compassionate towards people who are battling chronic illness. I'm beginning to better understand how easily people can become addicted to drugs or alcohol. Anything that dulls the pain – even for a little while, is a temptation.

I've never had a drug or alcohol addiction, but during the last few months I've reached for prescription pain pills on several occasions to dull the pain. This need I've had to reach for synthetic pain relief has opened my eyes to addiction.

For those of us that battle food addictions, when we've felt the need to dull the pain of rejection, abandonment, abuse, etc., we've used food to anesthetize our emotions. I understand the need to numb emotions. I'm not proud of the fact that I wasn't a strong enough person to push through my pain and tough it out without the need of stuffing my face with food.

In the long run stuffing our face only numbs the pain for a very short while. Once the bingeing is over the residual side-effects kick in and we are filled with shame and guilt. Addiction is a vicious life-sucking cycle that robs us of self-worth, self-esteem and our dignity. Not surprisingly, that's right where the enemy wants us!

I understand the need to dull physical pain with pain killers, but as with anything we must have balance. (There's that "B" word again!) It's important to closely monitor our dosage so it doesn't end up controlling us. What controls us becomes an idol in our lives that eventually crowds out the Savior – and that's a pain we can't afford to succumb to.

From the bitterness of disease man learns the sweetness of health. ~ Catalan Proverb

Seventy years are given to us! Some even live to eighty. But even the best years are filled with pain and trouble; soon they disappear, and we fly away. Psalm 90:10 (NLT)

PRAYER FOR TODAY: *Lord, I know that even in the midst of pain You are with me and watching over me. I pray Father God for those that suffer daily with any type of pain. I know You are the healer of the sick and the comforter of those who mourn. Give me compassion for those who suffer daily. In Your name I ask all these things, Lord Jesus. Amen.*

JULY 15
Do You Think She Saw Me?

Not long ago I was shopping at Walmart with my husband. While he waited in a long check-out line he sent me off to McDonald's for a cheeseburger for him for the ride home. After I placed my burger order, cold beads of sweat gathered on my top lip as I spotted someone I used to work with in a weight loss class. Oops! What to do?

I'd already ordered my hubby's burger and was waiting off to the side. I did my best to stare off into space. I tried to hide behind the giant Happy Meal cut-out sign. I really was hoping she wouldn't notice me.

Somehow the fact that we knew each other from a weight loss class and we were both ordering food at McDonald's filled me with instant guilt. On top of that, I know I'm not in that weight loss class anymore because I'm over my goal weight. One quick dart in her direction and I sized her up as being way beyond her goal weight as well.

After this woman placed her order, she grabbed her drink glasses and disappeared around a corner to the soda fountain. Relief flooded through me as my number was called. I grabbed my burger bag and made a beeline for my waiting husband. Score! The woman never spotted me! *Or had she?* Perhaps like me she was too embarrassed to say hello?

Somehow my radical attempts to remain invisible got me thinking on the drive home. Obviously I've not come as far in repairing my damaged self-esteem as I'd hoped. I had one little burger in my bag and it wasn't even for me, yet I was acting guilty, guilty, guilty.

The fact that I was able to face up to my insecurity so quickly makes me realize I am experiencing success, but there is still work to be done. We are all destined to be a *Work In Progress*, because we will never achieve perfection this side of Heaven. But it's nice to have something to look forward to, isn't it?

Every one of us has in him a continent of undiscovered character. Blessed is he who acts the Columbus to his own soul. ~ Author Unknown

So we can say with confidence, "The LORD is my helper, so I will have no fear. What can mere people do to me?" Hebrews 13:6 (NLT)

- -
PRAYER FOR TODAY: *Lord, I pray that You would continue to do a work in me and mold me and make me into Your image. Help me not to hide and cower behind my insecurities. Fill me with Your Holy Spirit and help me to see beyond my fears so that I might be able to reach out and offer a kind word to others. In Your name I ask all these things, Lord Jesus. Amen.*
- -

JULY 16
Praying One Bite at a Time

I have a friend who shared with our support group that when she feels like eating something she's not supposed to, she stops and asks God if it's okay for her to indulge. If He says "yes" she feels free to indulge without guilt. If He says "no" she won't eat it. Of course she said there are *those* days when she forges ahead and doesn't even bother to ask God's permission and she eats what she wants and usually suffers the guilt afterwards.

If it were simply that easy to stop and ask God's permission before we eat, believers in the body of Christ would never struggle with their weight. Because there are so many of us who are battling food addictions and weight issues, it's slightly more complicated than simply asking God for help.

My family usually prays before meals, but I've never stopped to pray over my premeasured pretzels or my afternoon apple. On those occasions when I've succumbed to a minor fall from grace and given in to a binge, I've barely had enough forethought to tear the wrapper off my *Fiber One* Brownie.

Perhaps, the restraint would be there if we took the time to get in the habit of praying before we ate *anything* – no matter how large or small. Taking time out for prayer might actually keep us from eating that handful of gummy bears we know we're not supposed to eat. Praying about the food would suddenly make us accountable for the food.

Bless us oh Lord and these thy gifts for which we are about to receive…

You never know, this might be an undiscovered diet secret that ensures absolute success. Rather than waiting until it's too late and we're wracked with guilt over what we've eaten, how about a *preemptive strike*. Pray without ceasing and pray without eating.

**The value of consistent prayer is not that He will hear us, but that we will hear Him.
~ William McGill**

"Keep watch and pray, so that you will not give in to temptation. For the spirit is willing, but the body is weak!" Matthew 26:41 (NLT)

PRAYER FOR TODAY: *Lord, I ask that You would help me remember to stop and take the time to pray BEFORE I eat ANYTHING, no matter how small. Make me cognizant of the mindless eating I tend to do and help me to stick to my menu plan without giving in to temptation. I want to gain control over my food addictions, but unless You step in and help me Lord Jesus, I am doomed to failure because I know I cannot do this without Your help. In Your name I ask all these things, Lord Jesus. Amen.*

JULY 17
Feel the Pinch – Pinch the Fat

I've been having trouble sleeping lately because of pain in my knee resulting from an injury sustained several months ago. The pain wakes me frequently throughout the night. Obviously most of us know carrying even 10 or 20 pounds beyond what is comfortable for our frame can lead to serious illnesses, like Type II Diabetes, heart problems, circulation problems, KNEE AND JOINT PAIN and many, many others putting us at risk for things like high blood pressure, cancer, heart attack and strokes.

In addition to the chronic pain in my knee an incident occurred a few weeks ago that brought the message home to me with a very real, very painful reminder. I had an MRI on my knee and when the technician was fitting the specially designed shell over my knee that tells the machine which body part to focus on, it got … (oh the embarrassment) sort of *stuck* on my leg.

Actually what it really did was pinch the heck out of my knee because I have a pocket of excess fat surrounding my knee. As the tech was lowering the device it pinched a fat pocket between the edges of the device just as he was getting ready to click and lock it in place. I started wincing and yelling, *"Ouch!!! Release! Release! You've got my fat!"*

Now as I'm staring down my options of either painful injections or surgery to repair the damage, I keep hearing that still small voice reminding me it is now imperative that I get rid of some of this extra weight.

Because like so many who have walked this road with me, we are learning weight gain, food addictions, excessive dieting and exercise are about much deeper issues. I am finally at a place of acceptance of who I am AT THIS WEIGHT. Just when I was getting used to the idea that I may have to remain at this weight for a while, the cold hard facts of life remind me once again: *it's not about the number* – emotionally anyway. Though once you've had your fat pinched by an MRI machine, there's no denying it starts to be about the number, at least a little bit.

If we only have the will to walk, then God is pleased with our stumbles. ~ C. S. Lewis

"Therefore, this is what the Sovereign LORD says: I will surely judge between the fat sheep and the scrawny sheep." Ezekiel 34:20 (NLT)

PRAYER FOR TODAY: *Lord, thank You for reminders that weight loss is necessary for health reasons. If I'm messing up and missing something, please point it out to me so I can complete this journey and have true success. Please continue to walk this road with me and be my guide. In Your name I ask all these things, Lord Jesus. Amen.*

JULY 18
A Day Off or an Off Day

I've had a pretty good week. I've kept my food journal and not gone over my allot-ted daily calories. For some reason though, I felt the need to *give myself permission* to take a day off. I started the day well, and then poof – out of the clear blue sky my mind seemed to lose all sound logic and reasoning. Suddenly I found myself smoothing out the top layer of a tub of ice cream straight from the carton with a big giant spoon.

You know how it goes – you open up a carton of ice cream and one side has ice cream piled higher than the other. Like an expert brick layer, you start smoothing off the rough edges like you're brandishing a cement trowel. Before you know it, you've smoothed away a couple of servings of ice cream and you stand there wondering what in the heck just happened to you?

When we suffer from an addiction – *any kind of addiction* – taking a "day off" should basically be right on the top of our *Stupid List*. If your drug of choice was crystal meth or alcohol and you took a day off from your sobriety, you'd be opening a can of worms that would quickly lead you down a quick road to self-destruction.

Why should food be any different? Yes we need food for our basic survival, but food isn't the same as other addictions. Lord knows food is every bit as controlling as alcohol or drugs, however, we can never completely abstain from eating.

We HAVE to eat every day, but we don't have to binge eat every day. We don't have to eat unhealthy foods or wrong foods to fill up the empty places in us.

A food addict cannot afford the luxury of a casual day off. As most of us know once you open the cookie jar or the bag of chips, you can't stop at just one. We must not give in to the little voice that tells you it's okay to take a break. Once we slip it's a short fall off the wagon altogether, making it that much easier to stay down indefinitely.

The best way to succeed in life is to act on the advice we give to others. ~ Author Unknown

A person without self-control is like a city with broken-down walls. Proverbs 25:28 (NLT)

PRAYER FOR TODAY: *Lord, I know self-control is a gift of the Spirit and I KNOW I am born again so that means I have self-control in me. Help me learn to use it! I clearly can't conquer these demons on my own and unless You step in and help me, I fear I will never beat this. Please walk beside me and convict me before I put anything in my mouth. In Your name I ask all these things, Lord Jesus. Amen.*

JULY 19
Inside and Out

Maybe it's a karma thing, or perhaps the moon is aligned with Jupiter and Mars, but I woke up feeling fabulous today! I had some great time with God, got in some exercise and thanks to a very timely cortisone injection in my knee last week; I was relatively pain free today for the first time in months.

I was feeling the need to strip myself bare and get naked before God. Sort of like an inventory of all my vital parts. After my shower I took the time to thank God for all of me – inside and out – yes even the parts I'm unhappy with like my thighs and my love handles.

I used to schedule this sort of inventory on a weekly basis, but must confess once I started tipping the scale to the dangerous red zone, I backed off. Not to mention having to face yourself in front of wall-to-wall mirrors in your birthday suit can be hazardous to your eyesight and your ego. I am a middle-age woman and *this is my body*. This may be the best I can hope for at this point. Who knows? But *this is me*.

I have a friend who recently confessed that she's been doing a little naked time before God lately and its working wonders for her. We all need to get naked before God occasionally to get a good dose of reality. God obviously already knows us inside and out, but once in a while it's a good idea to truly see ourselves just as we are as well.

We know the number on the scale does not validate us, but it does help us to keep track of our progress. Once you reach a certain age and all the pressure is relieved about comparing yourself with firm, fit bodies, there's a certain freedom in simply enjoying who you are. It's sad for us that we wait until we're older to enjoy who we are without comparing ourselves to others. Let this be a lesson to all of you who are younger. Stop the comparisons NOW.

I can look in the mirror and appreciate who I am now. I may have slipped a little yesterday, but today is a brand new day; the possibilities are endless and some days you just have to say "thank you, Lord, life is very, very good!"

The best vitamin to be a happy person is B1. ~ Author Unknown

A glad heart makes a happy face; a broken heart crushes the spirit. Proverbs 15:13 (NLT)

PRAYER FOR TODAY: *Thank you, Lord for the good days. I know every day can be a good day if I set my mind to it. Help me to always see things in a positive light and trust You for daily blessings like good health and a life free of the pressures of comparisons. In Your name I ask all these things, Lord Jesus. Amen.*

JULY 20
BUT Stupid

How many times have you heard someone say any of the following? "I know I shouldn't drink this **but** I'm going to anyway." "I know I probably shouldn't share this gossip, **but** I will anyway." "I know I shouldn't buy this because I'm broke, **but** I'm going to anyway." "I know I should go and visit my sick neighbor in the hospital, **but** I don't feel like it because I'm too busy." "*Everybody* says stuff they don't mean. God will understand because He knows how busy my life is."

I was hanging out with a friend and I ordered a mega ice tea chocked full of caffeine. I was enjoying wonderful "girl talk" fellowship so I had the strong iced tea anyway. I paid the price for it with insomnia and repeated treks back and forth to the bathroom. Sometimes I have to simply stop and ask myself, "Just how stupid am I?" I knew better, **but** ….

Whenever any statement we make is prefaced with, *"I know I probably shouldn't but,"* that should be a lightning bolt from God's mouth to our ears that tells us – "Hey, if you KNOW you shouldn't – then don't!"

When will we wake up and learn that the words of our mouth are digging our own grave? We need to stand firm on God's promises, say no to our flesh and tough it out and be the master over our feelings and become the strong, confident people God created us to be.

By taking everything one step at a time, taking every thought captive one thought at a time and praying for help and direction one prayer at a time, God will help us to be victorious.

The road to success is dotted with many tempting parking places. ~ Author Unknown

Because you have obeyed my command to persevere, I will protect you from the great time of testing that will come upon the whole world to test those who belong to this world. Revelation 3:10 (NLT)

PRAYER FOR TODAY: *Lord, I humbly ask that You would protect me from my own stupidity. Help me not to bow down to my feelings or my fickle, unpredictable, selfish flesh. May I walk uprightly in all Your ways. Give me lasting peace, wisdom, common sense and a genuine sense of joy and contentment each and every day. In Your name I ask all these things, Lord Jesus. Amen.*

JULY 21
Pain Versus Pleasure

I have a friend, Lucinda, (not her real name), who's recently been undergoing testing for stomach pain. The doctors ruled out an ulcer and are now doing further testing for gallbladder problems. She's doing fairly well and eating healthy and managing her pain with diet and medication.

A few days ago, someone at her work brought something in to share that was over-the-top in deliciousness, presentation, calories and temptation. Poor Lucinda wanted to taste the tempting treat so badly, even telling herself the intense pain she knew she would suffer would be worth it just to taste this treat. Luckily her moment of insanity passed and she declined to indulge, saving herself hours of severe pain and most likely an unscheduled trip to urgent care.

Many of us like to push the envelope and see how far we can go before we get ourselves in trouble so deep there's no return. I can no longer eat the same things I used to. I'm learning which foods to say "no" to in order to avoid those *Pepto* chasers and a life filled with physical pain.

As I compile my list of "danger foods" I know I've made definite progress as there are certain foods I absolutely can turn down without a second thought because of the "after burn" pain involved.

Like Lucinda, I still want to push the envelope from time to time. The good news is as my list of things to stay away from grows longer, the things I'm willing to eat once in a while in spite of the pain is growing shorter. Any way you spin it that spells progress to me. And forward progress of any kind is a win-win situation.

The more you eat, the less flavor; the less you eat, the more flavor. ~ Chinese Proverb

Those who worship the Lord on a special day do it to honor him. Those who eat any kind of food do so to honor the Lord, since they give thanks to God before eating. And those who refuse to eat certain foods also want to please the Lord and give thanks to God. Romans 14:6 (NLT)

PRAYER FOR TODAY: *Lord, I ask forgiveness for my stubborn will that makes me want to do things I know aren't good for me. Help me to practice restraint and not feel cheated because there are certain foods I know I should stay away from. Continue to guide and direct me. In Your name I ask all these things, Lord Jesus. Amen.*

JULY 22
What's in a Name?

I'm a very vivid dreamer and I don't just mean day dreams. Last night I did battle in my sleep with enemies of doom bent on my personal destruction. In spite of the heaviness in my spirit from the dark dream, I immediately sensed God's presence with me. In fact, I knew even in my dream-like state that God was with me. In the middle of my nightmare I kept crying out to God by simply saying His name over and over and over again.

As soon as I was conscious I felt God impressing upon me that the name of Jesus is so powerful and a mighty battle weapon that we fail to use to its fullest potential.

The example God gave me was if you were given a brand new car free and clear but you let it sit in your garage and opted to take the bus or rely on friends for rides, then your new car is useless and nothing more than a very expensive dust catcher. The car gives you the freedom to get where you want to go, but because you don't use it, it's as good as worthless.

The name of Jesus Christ operates on the same principle. When we find ourselves tempted to give in to our food addiction and sneak away to bury our faces in a carton of ice cream, we've got the power on the inside of us to stop the binge *before* it happens, but if we choose not to use it, it's worthless.

The next time we feel the urge to attack a stack of Oreos, if the only thing we know to do is walk away chanting, "Jesus, Jesus, Jesus!" then we've got to trust the power of the name alone will change our circumstances and help us to walk away from the Oreos. We've all got that same power available to us. The question is – are we using it to its maximum potential? Call on the name and find out the next time you find yourself facing temptation.

How sweet the name of Jesus sounds in a believer's ear; it soothes his sorrows, heals his wounds, and drives away his fear. ~ John Newton

That at the name of Jesus every knee should bow, in heaven and on earth and under the earth and every tongue confess that Jesus Christ is Lord, to the glory of God the Father. Philippians 2:10-11 (NLT)

PRAYER FOR TODAY: *Lord, thank You that I can call on the name of Jesus at any time, night or day. May I take advantage of the power available to me through the name of Jesus so that I can stand fast in my convictions to eat healthy and conquer my food addictions. In Your name I ask all these things, Lord Jesus. Amen.*

JULY 23
Sweeping out the Basement

They say confession is good for the soul. I'm not sure who they are but, it turns out *they* know what they're talking about. Last night I attended my support group and was invited to share a brief part of my testimony – the part that directly related to my relationship with food and the addictive strangle hold it has on my emotions.

Initially I was terrified to open up and spill my hidden secrets. Once I started though, it was like releasing the valve on a pressure cooker and the ugliness I'd buried in the basement of my dark past spewed forth.

I was in denial for so long about my food/exercise addiction making it easier to explain away my obsessive behavior due to stress or anxiety. *I only eat when I'm depressed, sad, angry, happy, hurt, scared,* etc. Turns out I was not only eating all the time, but on many occasions doing most of this eating in secret, hiding the evidence of my binges. Then of course, those secret binges were followed up with hours of strenuous exercise to burn off all those extra calories.

Since I shared my testimonial, I feel as though a huge burden has been lifted from me. I feel 10 pounds lighter today. It goes without saying that once I'd unburdened my soul the enemy did his best to make me feel foolish for sharing so much. I've learned to recognize when negative thoughts about my character come into my mind it is never from God, but from the enemy. The enemy's lies cannot hurt me.

Confession is truly healing for the soul. Anything we keep hidden in the darkness can no longer hurt us once we bring it up into the light and expose it. Today I feel as though I've turned the lights on in the basement of my soul and I've swept the space clean. Now that my hidden secrets have been exposed they no longer have power over me. Maybe it's time to ask yourself, "What's hiding in my basement?"

We must be free not because we claim freedom, but because we practice it. ~ William Faulkner

Sin is no longer your master, for you no longer live under the requirements of the law. Instead, you live under the freedom of God's grace. Romans 6:14 (NLT)

PRAYER FOR TODAY: *Lord Jesus, thank You that You have set me free from hiding the pain of my past. Help me to walk confidently in this freedom now that I've been released from my emotional prison, refusing to be held captive by hurtful memories, shame or guilt. In Your name I ask all these things, Lord Jesus. Amen.*

JULY 24
Weighing Success

The subject of how we measure success on our weight loss journey is a highly debated topic. Because not all weight loss programs are created equal and not all who begin a program are losing weight for the same reasons, we may all measure success differently.

For me the ultimate goal is to lose weight, but I am also focused on the need to lower my blood pressure and eliminate the need for blood pressure medicine altogether. In addition, I'd like to relieve some of the pressure from my overburdened knees and joints. I don't measure my success solely on what my scale registers.

Many of us know how to *work the system* and manipulate our eating plans so we can have those occasional extras bites and calories. We have to stop and ask ourselves if we've been manipulating our food plan overly much lately and sabotaging our efforts. Once we get lazy or sloppy, it's just a hop, skip and a jump to a total backslide.

We can't afford to get sloppy when keeping track of what we're eating. If we've gotten lazy and we're giving in to guessing about what we're eating we might as well accept that we are headed down a familiar road. We must stick to the plan without extra bites, licks and tastes and keep track by writing things down.

If you're like me and the weight isn't coming off as quickly as you'd like or if you've reached a plateau, go back to basics. Take the guesswork out of what you're eating and measure out one serving at a time. Keep track and journal what goes in your mouth. Add more protein, reduce the amount of carbs and eat fresh veggies and fruits. Our bodies can get lazy as well when it's being forced to submit to the same plan week after week. Try new recipes; mix up your exercise plan and do something different. We can't afford to get lazy or bored. If we do there won't be any success to measure – *again*.

I'm not overweight. I'm just nine inches too short. ~ Shelley Winters

The Lord is my strength and shield. I trust him with all my heart. He helps me, and my heart is filled with joy. I burst out in songs of thanksgiving. Psalm 28:7 (NLT)

PRAYER FOR TODAY: *Lord, thank You that I am finally able to surrender to Your Will for my life. I thank You for success and pray that I won't be tempted to fall back into old ways because I'm enjoying a little success. Help me to remain steadfast and strong in my commitment to get healthy. In Your name I ask all these things, Lord Jesus. Amen.*

JULY 25
The Wonder Diet

Like many people, I've been on just about every diet program over the course of my dieting career. There's no denying there are some great programs that work well when the right amount of effort is applied. Weight Watchers®, Jenny Craig® and Nutri-System® are all excellent programs with great success stories.

I've been on a few other weight loss programs which you may or may not recognize as well, such as the *Seefood* diet. This program literally translated means if you see food – you eat it. Another popular program is the *No Holds Barred* program, which is code for *get out of my way before I stab you with my fork* program that is a license to do bodily harm to anyone daring to cut in front of you in an all-you-can-eat buffet line.

One of my favorite programs was the *Amelia Earhart* Diet, which basically was me committing to a program and then getting lost along the way, never to be heard from again. As you can imagine, this is not a great program because too many people were constantly bugging me about *"Whatever happened to that diet you were on?"*

Without a doubt the most popular diet program available may be one that I've been on repeatedly throughout my life. I call it the *"Wonder Diet."* This is EVERY program rolled into one, which has us crying out to God and hoping … I *wonder* if this will be the program that *finally* works for me?"

We should put our faith in the Lord Jesus Christ rather than putting all our hope in a program. We must believe that Jesus can make our program work if we remember to include Him in all aspects of our program. Putting our faith in God will go a long way to seeing us through to a happily ever after success story and hopefully will keep people from asking us, *"So … whatever happened to that diet you were on?"*

There is a charm about the forbidden that makes it unspeakably desirable. ~ Mark Twain

And it is good for people to submit at an early age to the yoke of his discipline. Lamentations 3:27 (NLT)

PRAYER FOR TODAY: *Lord, help me to submit to Your will and live in balance and moderation. Help me to mix things up so I won't get bored eating the same things all the time. Help me to accept that for this season I must abstain to gain control over my flesh. In Your name I ask all these things, Lord Jesus. Amen.*

JULY 26
Too Thin or Too Rich

I'm sure most of us have heard the statement, *"there's no such thing as being too thin or too rich!"* I've never had an issue with either one, but somehow I can't imagine that I'd mind being thinner or having more money, but those are two separate fantasies to be sure.

Of the two though, I can speak to the too thin issue as I watched my mother struggle with hyper-thyroid problems. I, on the other hand battle hypo-thyroid issues. For those of you who don't know the difference: *hypo* thyroid is your metabolism is in a coma and barely works; *hyper* thyroid is like the Energizer bunny on crack.

My mother couldn't gain weight no matter what she ate. She never topped the scale higher than 135 pounds throughout her entire life. The last few years of her life she averaged about 110 pounds and hugging her was like hugging a bag of bones. My daughter has a co-worker struggling with the same over-active thyroid problems. At 107 pounds this woman cannot gain weight despite her record breaking eating binges.

While those of us carrying too much weight wish we could trade places with these people, not being able to gain weight is every bit as serious a health risk as obesity. Just hearing about the things this little tiny woman eats hoping to gain weight makes me cringe, as she's filling up on giant burritos, onion rings and French fries. Simply because someone is very thin is no guarantee they are healthy.

Clearly there must be balance whether we're too heavy or too thin. If you're not sure what your thyroid is doing, a simple blood test can give you a better idea. Malfunctioning thyroid problems are responsible for a host of problems in our bodies. If you're past due for a check-up or physical, make an appointment soon. You can't fight the battle if you don't even know there's a war going on. Be informed and take control over your own health.

The greatest wealth is health. ~ Virgil

And it is a good thing to receive wealth from God and the good health to enjoy it. To enjoy your work and accept your lot in life—this is indeed a gift from God. Ecclesiastes 5:19 (NLT)

PRAYER FOR TODAY: *Lord, thank You for preventative medicine that allows us to track health issues and deal with them as they arise. Help to make me a good steward of this body You have entrusted me with. Help me to always do my best to care for it and be a living example of the grace of God in my life. In Your name I ask all these things, Lord Jesus. Amen.*

JULY 27
Butterball Reminders

As a little girl my father's favorite term of endearment for me was "Butterball." (Yes, I was a chubby little thing.) I was too young to realize that being compared to a fat, round, name brand turkey was more insult than compliment.

I don't think my dad called me that to be intentionally cruel. His was a different generation that parented with humiliation because *that which doesn't kill us makes us stronger.* As a shy insecure girl, even negative attention from my dad was better than no attention. There are days I wake up and still feel like Daddy's little Butterball girl.

Those old insecurities resurface, I feel shy and indecisive. Perhaps the mass of freckles dotting my face; the direct result of my daily swim in the sun has propelled me back in time. Each time I look in the mirror I'm reminded of the 12-year-old girl I've tried so hard to forget.

I suspect the real culprit for my Butterball mood is simply my body's way of reacting to what was a very positive upbeat weekend. I spent the whole weekend being "up" because I'm feeling good and making weight loss progress. The enemy would have us believe that after days of being "up" the only place for us to go is back down again.

There's nothing wrong with being pleased with our accomplishments and celebrating our victories. For me, my Butterball feeling reminds me of how far GOD has brought me. We work hard to exorcise the negative images of our past, but perhaps occasionally it is okay to revisit those forgotten images to remind ourselves of who we are now and how far we've come.

We are continual works in progress and God's not done with us yet. We're forever being molded into the image and likeness of Christ and I, for one, am enormously grateful that He loves me, Butterball and all.

What you need to know about the past is that no matter what has happened, it has all worked together to bring you to this very moment. And this is the moment you can choose to make everything new. Right now. ~ Author Unknown

No, dear brothers and sisters, I have not achieved it, but I focus on this one thing: Forgetting the past and looking forward to what lies ahead. Philippians 3:13 (NLT)

PRAYER FOR TODAY: *Lord, thank You for keeping me grounded and on firm footing in Your Word. I thank You for occasional reminders from the past, but help me not to dwell in the past and focus on painful reminders. Thank You that You are continually at work in my life. In Your name I ask all these things, Lord Jesus. Amen.*

JULY 28
Surrender Leads to Freedom

Back in January when I started my weight loss journey I'm convinced I didn't go into it with my eyes wide open. I thought I'd hop right back on the weight watcher wagon and reach my goal weight by the time spring rolled around.

Spring rolled into summer and now summer is at its pinnacle with fall not too far around the corner and I'm still a long way from being at my goal weight. I may not be where I thought I'd be at this point, but in some ways I've far surpassed my expectations.

While I expected I'd lose weight, I never expected to become mentally strong enough to deal with what was at the core of my eating issues. That saying, "it's not what you're eating, but what's eating you" now has a brand new meaning.

After decades of being in denial about my food addictions, I've finally uncovered what was eating me. For so long I'd convinced myself that I didn't have an eating disorder but merely enjoyed eating food – lots of food and a great variety of foods.

The fact that I was eating in secret, hiding the remains of my binges, spending hours exercising to counteract the foods I ate and then lying about the quantity of foods consumed, never struck me as addictive behavior.

Surrendering to God and facing our problems will lift the burden of secrets from our shoulders and our hearts. God doesn't intend for us to live in bondage. He sacrificed His Son on the cross so that we might have and enjoy our life.

We can't get back all those years wasted in denial but we can look forward to the future with a new attitude, freedom from the past and enjoying every day we have left. Surrender does lead to freedom, and being willing to admit we need help is a positive step towards healing.

In the truest sense, freedom cannot be bestowed; it must be achieved.
~ Franklin D. Roosevelt

The thief comes only to steal and kill and destroy; I have come that they may have life, and have it to the full. John 10:10 (NIV)

PRAYER FOR TODAY: *Lord, help me to surrender my issues, my worries, my fears and anything else in my past that might be hindering me from living in total and absolute freedom. Thank You, Lord for loving me enough to stand beside me and walk this difficult journey with me. Thank You for never leaving me or forsaking me. In Your name I ask all these things, Lord Jesus. Amen.*

JULY 29
Sitting at His Feet

My good friend, Linda, began her weight loss journey around the same time I did earlier in the year. Her starting weight was much higher than mine, but while I've lost little weight, Linda has lost 80 pounds at this point. Her success has been remarkable; so much so that she is being dogged by desperate women, anxious for a similar experience. Linda is asked on a daily basis, "What's your secret?"

When we see someone who has had a weight loss success we want to learn their secrets. We want to copy their methods. We want to buy the same products. We want… oh, who are we kidding? We want to rub up against them and hope that their weight loss is catching much like an airborne flu virus.

To her credit, Linda is very candid about her success. Because she's walked the weight loss road repeatedly throughout her life, she decided this would be the last time she would attempt another weight loss program. Her 80 pound weight loss is the result of doing all the things we know to do: keeping a food journal and measuring her food portions; partnering with an accountability partner; joining a support group, and exercise.

The one key factor to her true success has been her daily time spent with God. When Linda gets hungry, she retreats to her bedroom and her "prayer chair" and she sits at the feet of Jesus and talks to God. She refuses to leave her prayer chair until she finds peace and the strength needed to overcome her food temptations. She confesses to spending "a lot" of time in her prayer chair as she finds immense peace sitting at *His feet*.

Perhaps my friend has unlocked the hidden component to lasting weight loss. Regardless of whether her prayer chair retreat is a hidden secret or not – is there really anything wrong with spending extra time sitting at the feet of Jesus?

We can't put all our hope in a diet plan or program and hope to experience true, lasting success without including Jesus. When temptation or discouragement strikes, don't fret – just sit.

No man can follow Christ and go astray. ~ William H.P. Faunce

Suddenly Jesus met them. "Greetings," he said. They came to him, clasped his feet and worshiped him. Matthew 28:9 (NIV)

PRAYER FOR TODAY: *Lord, thank You that there is comfort to be found sitting at the feet of Jesus. I thank You that You let me spill my hurts until I am spent. Help me to retreat from life's challenges and find peace when I seek You with all my heart. In Your name I ask all these things, Lord Jesus. Amen.*

JULY 30
When Chocolate Doesn't Work

Have you ever had a day when the stresses of life push you so far that you're ready to eat your weight in anything covered in chocolate? If we're women and we have hormones, we're going to have those cravings.

Hopefully we've learned some lessons along our journey so far and we KNOW chocolate won't help. Do we really want to undo all of the hard work that we've put into our efforts at this point? Rather than succumbing to our craving for chocolate we should spend some time in prayer. A chocolate craving might be the best time to try out our prayer chair (or couch, or bed or corner) and see if sitting at the feet of Jesus might actually de-stress us and eliminate those cravings.

We should remove ourselves from the environment that is making us crazy and engage in an activity that will distract us from the temptations of our flesh. My solution was an unplanned, long drive downtown and back today. If an afternoon drive in crazy downtown and freeway traffic doesn't cure you of wanting to eat then there is no help. I felt more like throwing up by the time I arrived at my destination.

By the time I arrived home, I had a moment of panic when the feelings inside of me created that familiar beehive buzzing that stimulates my emotions. I felt the need for an outlet but for once I really didn't want it to be food. Hallelujah! I settled for a diet soda and a chick flick and thankfully, that was the right recipe to avoid a foray to the M&M section of the quick-mart.

Any way we slice it, if food is no longer our automatic response, that is progress. When we can de-stress without a digression into chocolate – that means *something* is clearly working. Can I get an *Amen!*

You can't run away from trouble. There ain't no place that far. ~ Uncle Remus

But by means of their suffering, he rescues those who suffer. For he gets their attention through adversity. Job 36:15

PRAYER FOR TODAY: *Lord, I believe everything happens for a reason and I believe You will help me with all these unexpected stresses. I ask for strength and an extra portion of faith and grace to deal with everything as it happens without resorting to food when I feel defeated or anxious. In Your name I ask all these things, Lord Jesus. Amen.*

JULY 31
Triggering the Triggers

Food triggers are everywhere. These triggers have the potential to propel us into our next binge or cause us to fall back into self-destructive eating patterns. Triggers can come at us in many forms and assault all of our five senses.

There are days when we find ourselves in a very vulnerable state of mind. A TV commercial, magazine ad or even spotting someone who vaguely resembles someone from our past can trigger us without warning and suddenly, WE NEED FOOD!

When we are in that weakened state those triggers to our emotions are so explosive we feel as if we've been shot from point blank range and we need to quickly fill the deep hole. For many of us we fill that hole with food.

Unlike someone who turns to alcohol or illegal drugs, we will never be able to do completely without food in our life. We can say with all certainty – food will always be an issue for us. Food will always be in our life, **BUT** food is not a sedative. Food is not our friend. Food will not provide us comfort, nor will food ever fill those voids in life. Each day is a new challenge and we must learn to set boundaries with food and respect those boundaries. We must not let food run our lives or control us.

Food is not our friend – but food is not the enemy. The emotions that drive us to eat are the real culprit; Satan is usually the puppeteer manipulating the strings of tangled emotions. Managing our emotions is a tall order, but as with everything else in life, with God all things are possible.

It's unlikely we will ever *completely* manage our emotions; this side of heaven, anyway. We are human – we are women, after all. We are women – hear us roar! Nothing much left to say, except … *Grrrr* …

Let's not forget that the little emotions are the great captains of our lives and we obey them without realizing it. ~ Vincent Van Gogh, 1889

Even if we feel guilty, God is greater than our feelings, and he knows everything.
1 John 3:20 (NLT)

PRAYER FOR TODAY: *Lord, I am glad You designed me the way You did and that You're never surprised by my breakdowns, setbacks or emotional tantrums. I thank You that You continue to love me unconditionally in spite of the fact that I am so flawed. I thank You for choosing me as Your own and for continued patience with me as I grow and mature on this journey. Give me strength! In Your name I ask all these things, Lord Jesus. Amen.*

AUGUST 1
A *Fast Solution*

I've been reading a book recently on spiritual discipline written to help believers develop a deeper spiritual walk with God. One of the disciplines which I find most interesting is the discipline of fasting.

If we look to the Bible, many of the spiritual giants of both the Old and New Testament frequently engaged in regular periods of fasting. This book outlines healthy guidelines for preparing for a spiritual fast as well as recommendations for short-term fasting and extended fasts.

I recently felt God prompting me to employ the discipline of fasting for a short period of time in order to gain some perspective regarding some spiritual challenges I'm facing. I followed the outlines in the book and decided upon a three day fast. I am a food addict and deep down, I really wanted to see if I could actually go that long without food. Somewhere in all of my reasoning, I needed to know that I really love God more than I love food.

My three day fast was difficult but rewarding. Every time my stomach growled, I pressed through the discomfort using the time to seek God. My constant prayer was, "I am hungry Lord, but I love You more than I love food and I am hungry for more of You." While I didn't get specific direction on some of the problems I was praying about, I did have a wonderful encounter with the Holy Spirit and God did in fact show me, that the desires of my heart were genuine.

We each have to find our way through life's difficulties in our own way. If you find yourself struggling with managing your food intake or you're struggling with spiritual peace, perhaps a spiritual fast might move you to reconciliation. Obviously, a fast isn't for everyone and I would never suggest that you fast for the simple sake of weight loss. I'm all about eating – but every once in a while we need to take a bite out of something other than food; something that will fill our souls as well as our stomachs.

Discipline weighs ounces, regret weighs tons. ~ Author Unknown

So we fasted and earnestly prayed that our God would take care of us, and he heard our prayer. Ezra 8:23 (NLT)

PRAYER FOR TODAY: Lord, thank You for hearing my prayers. Continue to move me forward so that I can be all that You desire for me to be. In Your name I ask all these things, Lord Jesus. Amen.

AUGUST 2
Hiccups

Occasionally without provocation the human brain suffers some sort of misfiring in normal brain waves resulting in a strange anomaly known as brain hiccup or brain fart. Oh wait, maybe that's just me, but I seem to have these occasional brain hiccups or brain farts on a regular monthly basis. Perhaps these hiccups are directly related to PMS, or menstrual cramps and the female uterus are somehow connected to our brain transmitters and the onset of menstrual cramps is choreographed to brain cramps.

For some bizarre reason I woke up with anxiety today for no apparent reason. The best way to combat anxiety is to empty our head of all negative thoughts (not an easy task for a woman) and remove ourselves (if at all possible) from those outside negative influences. Get alone somewhere and spend some quiet time with God. Pray, read your Bible and meditate on Scripture. Let the Son fill you with peace.

During my swim today it occurred to me that I'd been dwelling on negative events and letting my mind wander to "what if" scenarios regarding some upcoming events. I'd let my mind wander over into the negative and started thinking on the worst case scenario. Once I recognized that negative mindset I quickly set about casting my cares on God and rebuking those evil mindsets. As soon as those negative thoughts try to burrow into our brains we've got to immediately sweep them out.

Life comes at you fast and if we don't gird up our minds and properly outfit ourselves to fight the battles against our mind, life will mow us down and keep us down. Rather than sitting around waiting for the next brain hiccup, we can't let our mind feed on wrong thoughts. The Word of God taken in regular doses will not only eliminate brain hiccups but it will fill your head and your heart so full of God's promises those brain hiccups can no longer cramp your style.

No matter where you go or what you do, you live your entire life within the confines of your head. ~ Terry Josephson

Finally, brothers, whatever is true, whatever is noble, whatever is right, whatever is pure, whatever is lovely, whatever is admirable—if anything is excellent or praiseworthy—think about such things. Philippians 4:8 (NIV)

PRAYER FOR TODAY: *Lord, help me to dwell on what is pure and lovely and refuse to give in to doubt, worry and fear. I will not be held prisoner by the thoughts of my past or worry for an uncertain future. Give me peace of mind and strength for each new day. In Your name I ask all these things, Lord Jesus. Amen.*

AUGUST 3
Road Tripping Snack Happy

Not wanting to risk life and limb with a hormonally-challenged, anxiety-ridden crazy woman, my husband suggested a road trip for the day and a respite from the desert heat. You've got to love a guy who understands a woman's need for an occasional change of scenery.

Seeing as how I'm doing so well on my program and continuing to lose weight, I can hardly justify a full day off with the promise of unlimited junk food and of course the requisite stop for lunch at some sort of greasy classic burger joint along Route 66 (where we're guaranteed to get not just our kicks but a good case of heartburn). Can a road trip be successful with Nurtri-grain bars, rice cakes and a can of chocolate Slim-Fast? YES, if you want it to be.

No road trip would be complete without a mandatory stop at a few tourists' shops along the way for souvenirs for the kids and of course – homemade fudge for the hubby. My treat was the beautiful red rocks of Sedona so I required nothing edible to appease me as God and Mother Nature filled my cup full to overflowing with the breathtaking scenery. (Sedona, Arizona should go on everyone's bucket list as a must-see.)

Road trips don't have to equal M&Ms and beef jerky. If you absolutely must indulge in a road trip goody, limit yourself to a *minimal* sampling (the operative word being "minimal"). Offset your extra calories with some tourist walking, hiking, spelunking or power shopping. When confined in a car for long periods of time, it's important to circulate the blood after extended sedentary periods of rest. Even on a road trip, we have to always be thinking of ways to maintain healthy habits and keep our eyes on the destination to good health and weight loss.

I travel not to go anywhere, but to go. I travel for travel's sake. The great affair is to move. ~ Robert Louis Stevenson

You see me when I travel and when I rest at home. You know everything I do. Psalm 139:3 (NLT)

PRAYER FOR TODAY: *Lord, nature's beauty abounds reminding us of what a masterful artist You are! Thank You for time spent with family in beautiful surroundings. I thank You for helping me to enjoy a day without letting my addiction for food crowd in and steal my joy. In Your name I ask all these things, Lord Jesus. Amen.*

AUGUST 4
Technology or Friends?

There's something to be said for today's advances in modern medicine and surgical procedures. I had my knee surgery recently and it went fabulous – better than expected. Anesthesia is a wonder drug. I got the best 55 minute nap I've had in a really long while. We are lucky to have advances in modern technology to help with every area of our lives.

For those of us battling addictions there is help available to us at our fingertips. The telephone is another one of those modern inventions, as well as computers, email text messaging and instant messaging so that if we feel ourselves on the verge of a relapse or meltdown we can instantly reach out to a trusted friend.

A lot of us try to convince ourselves that we can kick our addictions on our own; especially when it comes to food addictions. Most of us know that nothing could be further from the truth. We need to stay accountable to someone about what we're eating until we learn some self-control.

The only way to kick a food addiction *is get to the core issues of why we turn to food in the first place*. We need counseling or a group support system where we can learn from others, garner support and encouragement from trusted friends who will stand beside us as we uncover painful truths. We need people who can be there to pick us up when we struggle or are down.

Modern science may be great for a lot of things, but nothing beats a friend to give you a hug and tell you, "You're going to get through this. You can do it!" Medicine may be great, but nothing beats a friend that can pull you back from the brink of insanity when all you want to do is eat something that you're not supposed to eat. Reach out and find out.

If you're alone, I'll be your shadow. If you want to cry, I'll be your shoulder. If you want a hug, I'll be your pillow. If you need to be happy, I'll be your smile. But anytime you need a friend, I'll just be me. ~ Author Unknown

The godly give good advice to their friends; the wicked lead them astray. Proverbs 12:26 (NLT)

PRAYER FOR TODAY: *Lord, thank You for modern medicine and advances with surgery, medicine and technology. Thank You for the many friends I have. You have blessed me abundantly and I am ever aware that everything in life is so much easier when I've got friends to help me through. I pray for opportunities to return friendship to those in need. In Your name I ask all these things, Lord Jesus. Amen.*

AUGUST 5
Panic Attacks

This has been a tough week for me because of my surgery I've been unable to exercise. It's likely to be a couple of weeks before I can resume even light exercise. Add to that I've got amazing friends who've been bringing my family dinner, snacks and desserts every day this week while I recuperate. The combination of delicious foods and no exercise and I'm a little panicked that all the weight I've lost will quickly return.

Somehow it doesn't seem fair that what has taken me eight months to get rid of could reappear in a fraction of the time. But such is the nature of the beast and what most of us know to be true. Losing weight is hard work and takes a long time – gaining weight ... poof ... happens practically overnight! There's definitely something wrong with the math and physics of that equation.

What really has me concerned is this unnatural fear I'm feeling at the very thought of regaining the weight. I know that God doesn't want us to live in fear and He expects us to cast all our cares on Him.

The good news is God knows all our worries, our fears and our temptations and we KNOW that He will help us through trials. Perhaps God allows these times in our lives so we can reconnect with Him on a deeper level. I know I've enjoyed my quiet times with God this week.

In the grand scheme of life, the bigger picture is telling me this is a short season and as long as I take precautions with my food, I don't have to live in fear. We can't trade one addiction – *food* – for another – *fear*. God is so awesome that a few extra pounds are nothing to freak out about. It will all balance out in the end.

Readjusting is a painful process, but most of us need it at one time or another. ~ Arthur Christopher Benson

Lead me by your truth and teach me, for you are the God who saves me. All day long I put my hope in you. Psalm 25:5 (NLT)

PRAYER FOR TODAY: *Lord, thank You for life's many blessings. I praise You for quiet times and a chance to dive into Your Word and hear that still small voice that reminds me how much You love me. Continue to help me to cast all my fears and worries upon You, Lord Jesus. In Your name I ask all these things, Lord Jesus. Amen.*

AUGUST 6
The Rock Bottom "O" Group

There is a major food group that's often overlooked by the FDA but it's a food group known intimately by anyone with a major food addiction. This food group is directly responsible for my personal downfall and most of my weight gain.

I'm not talking about the meat and protein group; fruits, veggies, dairy or even the teeny tiny group at the top of the pyramid that comprises your carbs and sugars. The food group I'm referring to is the "O" food group. Once you're seduced by the dark side of the "O" group it's a fight for your life to be freed from the tentacles of the strangle hold these foods have on you.

The following is a list of "O" group staples: Frosted Cheerios, Chicken Noodle-Os, Burritos (from Filiberto's), Nachos, Doritos, Cheetos, Fritos, Dominos, Jeno's, Ho Ho's, Rolo's, Mentos and of course my personal all-time favorite – Oreos.

I medicated my emotions for years eating my weight in Oreos and many of these other food items on a regular basis. Ignoring my internal pain and stuffing my emotions seemed easier – at first. You can only stuff your emotions for so long before you either implode or explode.

The good news about stuffing our emotions is that for the average person there eventually comes a point when you reach rock bottom and you tell yourself "enough is enough" and you seek outside help.

The funny thing is, "rock bottom" looks different to everyone so we can only reach it and look up for help when it feels like rock bottom to us. God can meet us where we are and He knows where rock bottom is for each and every one of us. I am so blessed He reached down and saved me before the "O" group got the best of me. I'd say that's worthy of a standing "O!"

If ignorance is bliss, why aren't there more happy people? ~ Author Unknown

Trust in him at all times, O people; pour out your hearts to him, for God is our refuge.
Psalm 62:8 (NIV)

PRAYER FOR TODAY: *Lord, thank You for rescuing me from myself. Thank You for giving me the strength and courage to reach up and grab on to help before I self-destructed. I pray You will continue to walk beside me and be my fortress and my refuge during this journey. In Your name I ask all these things, Lord Jesus. Amen.*

AUGUST 7
A Big Bucket of Sin

Movie popcorn is a flavor that cannot be duplicated at home. If this weren't so they wouldn't be able to dupe ordinary people of average intelligence into purchasing a vat as big as an oil drum and charge you a price nearly equal to that of a barrel of oil.

My friend, Belinda, has a standing date at the movies with her sister every Thursday evening. Each week she takes her refillable souvenir drink cup with her and wears her "free popcorn shirt." She's got a thing for the butter and salt so she gets a generously soaked LARGE bag. She says she can't help it; it's her only indulgence of the week. Belinda is slowly gaining weight and she can't understand why.

As a neutral observer, I would caution Belinda against the weekly popcorn indulgence. While I agree, movie popcorn can be quite addictive, if the popcorn is the only indulgence you're allowing yourself and you're seeing a weight gain, wouldn't it make sense to start limiting that weekly bucket of popcorn?

Belinda has worked hard to lose weight and maintain it. Because Belinda is over 50, with a slower working metabolism and only exercises for 30 minutes, three times a week, her body isn't going to burn those popcorn calories off as quickly as a 20-year-old. Plus, Belinda is indulging in this high-carb, high-calorie snack in the evening so after her movie she's going home and going to bed. Those calories are just sitting there looking for something to grab onto – which seems to be her muffin top and thighs.

Like so many of us, Belinda suffers from that attitude that she's finally "arrived" at freedom because she's successfully lost weight. None of us can ever afford to get complacent and think "I've arrived and I'm cured," when it comes to our weight and our food. We are never "cured" and that's precisely why we need a Savior. We need to be saved from our own ignorance. Most of us know we are only one bucket away from a total relapse. If that bucket is filled with popcorn and smothered in butter and salt, it may as well be a bucket of sin.

Common sense is not so common. ~ Voltaire

Getting wisdom is the wisest thing you can do! And whatever else you do, develop good judgment. Proverbs 4:7 (NLT)

PRAYER FOR TODAY: *Lord, fill me with wisdom and common sense so I can make informed decisions. Help me to overcome my weaknesses and to make healthy snacking choices whenever possible. Don't ever let me think I can do this on my own. In Your name I ask all these things, Lord Jesus. Amen.*

AUGUST 8
Let Freedom Sing

Looking around my kitchen this morning I'm reminded of what great friends I have. My countertops are littered with pies, cakes and breads – all tokens of compassion while I've been recuperating this week. Kind-hearted friends have made sure that my family would not go hungry while I was recovering from surgery.

I'm filled with love and appreciation for all of my wonderful friends. Part of me is looking at all these yummy goodies and I'm filled with shame. There was a time I would have been forking out bites of every one of these goodies until I'd single-handedly finished nearly everything.

I'm cognizant of the fact that I'm not even tempted to sample most of these goodies. The appeal that carbs once had for me is quite simply – non-existent. If that's not a hugundus achievement (my grandson's favorite word) then I don't know what is.

I am delighted the food is here for my husband and kids to enjoy, but I don't feel the pull that these foods once had over me. The guilt and shame have been replaced with such an overwhelming sense of peace and … yes – freedom.

I know that the very thin tightrope of my resolve could break at any time pulling me right back into a serious food addiction – but for today – I am living in freedom. I knew this day would come – eventually, but I've had my doubts; not doubt for my eating program or doubt that God could heal me – but doubt that I would ever be able to fully surrender and LET God heal me.

If you're not there yet, don't despair. God wants us all to experience real freedom from bondage. Perhaps you're getting closer but can't understand why you're "stuck," unable to experience true freedom. Take an inventory and ask God to search your heart and see if there's anything you haven't surrendered to Him yet. God came to set the captives free and if you're still being held prisoner, remember it's God who holds the key. He wants you to be free.

Freedom is the oxygen of the soul. ~ Moshe Dayan

Sin is no longer your master, for you no longer live under the requirements of the law. Instead, you live under the freedom of God's grace. Romans 6:14 (NLT)

PRAYER FOR TODAY: *Lord, thank You that I can practice restraint and I'm not driven to eat based on my feelings or emotions. Thank You for the gift of friends. I praise You for all life's victories. Continue to walk beside me and give me victory – no matter how small – each and every day. In Your name I ask all these things, Lord Jesus. Amen.*

AUGUST 9
Hunger Earthquakes

The U.S. Geological survey has been reporting some unusual seismic activity in my area lately. No wait it's just me and it's the rumblings of my empty stomach as I try and sleep every night!

Because I've been extra strict with my caloric intake I find myself going to bed hungry nearly every night, waking in the middle of the night because my stomach is empty. Not only is it noisy but it's downright uncomfortable. On top of that I wake nearly every morning feeling ravenous and I can't wait for breakfast.

In the grand scheme of life the emptiness is far better than the way I lived for years. I used to go to bed sick to my stomach and hating myself because I'd eaten so much food during the day. It was impossible to sleep comfortably – not to mention I was wracked with guilt for being such a glutton.

Both scenarios remind me that my help comes from the Lord. When I was stuffed to the gills I'd pray at night for forgiveness and strength to resist the next day's temptations. Now I find myself praying that God will help me to feel satisfied with my limited calories and make me thankful for all that I am eating.

Because we must always have balance in our lives, we must make the most of our calories and eat fruits, veggies and high fiber foods so we can curb the hunger pains. Sometimes despite our best efforts, our stomach is ruled apart from our brain and doesn't know the meaning of the word satisfied. Retraining our bodies is exhausting. Maintaining a healthy lifestyle is so much work. No wonder so many people give up so easily.

Remember, we are not quitters! Regardless of the seismic activity in our stomach we will prevail, because our help DOES come from the Lord!

Being good is commendable, but only when it is combined with doing good is it useful. ~ Author Unknown

I lift up my eyes to the hills—where does my help come from? My help comes from the LORD, the Maker of heaven and earth. Psalm 121:1-2 (NIV)

PRAYER FOR TODAY: Lord, help me to rest in the shadow of Your presence and sleep peacefully at night. Satisfy the cravings of my flesh; fill my stomach so I may not be in want. Continue to give me strength for each new day and help me to remain strong and steadfast in my commitment to get healthy. In Your name I ask all these things, Lord Jesus. Amen.

AUGUST 10
Patient Endurance

It's hard to sit and do absolutely nothing. I mean really nothing. Convalescing can be exhausting if you're someone used to lots of activity. Let's face it; one can only watch so much HGTV without suffering some sort of decorating brain seizure.

I know it's been less than two weeks since I had surgery and my body needs time to sufficiently heal, but patiently waiting for *anything* has never been my strong suit – especially when it comes to important things in life.

Most of us don't like to wait for things. When we started this weight loss journey on New Year's Day we would have preferred instant results. Whether we've lost a lot of weight by now or only a little, somewhere deep in our brain we have to believe that eventually everything will fall into place and we'll finally make healthy eating a way of life. We have to believe that positive thinking and dwelling on success rather than failure will eventually come naturally to us.

At some point change occurs while we impatiently wait for it. The time frame is secondary at this point. Failure is not an option – or at least it shouldn't be. Somewhere along the way we have to stop obsessing about things and really practice everything we've learned in the last eight months. Hopefully we've learned a few things and gained some confidence and self-control and are seeing ourselves in a more positive light.

If you had a plan to complete this journey according to your terms on your time frame and you've not met those goals yet trust that God is watching and is in control. As long as we end up at our destination it shouldn't really matter how long the journey takes, as long as we eventually get there.

Patience and perseverance have a magical effect before which difficulties disappear and obstacles vanish. ~ John Quincy Adams

Therefore, as God's chosen people, holy and dearly loved, clothe yourselves with compassion, kindness, humility, gentleness and patience. Colossians 3:12 (NIV)

PRAYER FOR TODAY: *Lord, thank You that You are patient with me and are teaching me patience. I know I'm a long way from where I planned on being at this point, but I thank You that I have come a long way. Continue to teach me in spite of the fact that I continually get in Your way. In Your name I ask all these things, Lord Jesus. Amen.*

AUGUST 11
The Loser's Breakfast

Many experts agree that breakfast is the most important meal of the day. Skipping breakfast is never a good idea. You've been fasting all night and in order to have energy for your day, you need to add fuel to your body. To do breakfast justice it's smart to include high fiber and plenty of protein in your morning meal.

My plan usually consists of a healthy *loser's* breakfast with low carbs and some sort of egg substitute omelet with low fat cheese and veggies. This morning though my oldest daughter unexpectedly invited me out for breakfast. I love my daughter and I love to go out for breakfast which is why I rarely go out for breakfast. I'm sure it's the idea of pancakes or waffles for breakfast that makes it feel like eating dessert for breakfast.

I did my best to pick wisely and chose multi-grain pancakes. Plus those multi-grain pancakes were chocked full of fiber and extremely filling.

Restraint, control and balance are always wise on any weight loss program. Each day, each meal and each opportunity should be handled with simple common sense. Opportunities to dine with a cherished friend or family member should be cause for joy not one that makes us stress over how to tweak our menu.

When it comes right down to it, family and friends are priceless. For me to enjoy a meal this morning may mean cutting back the rest of the day – but in the grand scheme of life, it's worth it to me. Getting healthy is a priority for me, but cultivating relationships along the way takes precedence and makes me a winner today. I'll worry about being a *loser* tomorrow.

You can give without loving, but you can never love without giving.
~ Author Unknown

Be very careful, then, how you live—not as unwise but as wise, making the most of every opportunity, because the days are evil. Ephesians 5:15-16(NIV)

PRAYER FOR TODAY: *Lord, thank You for the opportunity to share a meal with a loved one. Help me to use common sense and cut back when I need to. Help me to cherish people and opportunities rather than making everything about the food. In Your name, Lord Jesus. Amen.*

AUGUST 12
One True Thing

I was reading a book lately with a quirky character who was on a new diet she called *The One Diet*. As long she ate only one of something it was legal; like one pea, one asparagus, one bucket of chicken or one dozen donuts. Oh, if only!

I think I've been on a *One Diet* lately too, only my *one diet* is far different from the characters in the book. For me the *one* most important part of my program is remembering *I'm not on a diet*, but I'm making lifelong lifestyle changes.

The other important part of my program is I know without the help of the *One* and only true God; I'd be up the proverbial creek without a paddle. I know I cannot have success without including God in every aspect of my program. He is the *One* I turn to when I doubt myself and when I fear failure. He is the *One* who answers my prayers and grants me success. He is the *One* who stands with me and will never leave me nor forsake me.

One other important element of my program is when I am tempted by cookies (or chips or crackers or whatever) if I can eat just *one*, it's alright to allow myself to have *one*. However, if I can tell it's *one of those days* chances are limiting myself to one of anything is slim to none so it's best to not even have *one*.

Most importantly I KNOW that *one* day I will achieve success and lose this excess weight, but it may not happen in *one* day, *one* week or even *one* year. I will be successful because I trust in my plan, myself and my Lord Jesus to help me *one* day at a time.

Something in human nature causes us to start slacking off at our moment of greatest accomplishment. As you become successful, you will need a great deal of self-discipline not to lose your sense of balance, humility, and commitment. ~ Ross Perot

Common sense and success belong to me. Insight and strength are mine. Proverbs 8:14 (NLT)

PRAYER FOR TODAY: *Lord, thank You that You are the ONE I turn to and the ONE I rely on constantly for strength, wisdom and common sense. Help me to stand strong on the promises of Your Word and help me to continue to include You in every aspect of my weight loss journey. I ask all these things in Your name, Lord Jesus. Amen.*

AUGUST 13
Hungry for the Wrong Things

I went to my food addiction support group meeting last night and was significantly refreshed. During praise and worship we sang a song with the lyrics, "I'm hungry for more of You," which is a reference to being hungry for God's Holy Spirit.

I've noticed an unusual *hunger* in my spirit this week, but I've been trying to fill it with the wrong things. My insatiable hunger comes from the fact that my kids are leaving to return to college – leaving me and my husband official empty nesters. While I'm excited for all my kids and their upcoming school year, I'm feeling a sense of abandonment.

I've tried feeding these negative feelings with food – although on a much smaller scale than I did last year at this time. I've had enough restraint to know that it isn't food that I want.

I've even tried rearranging furniture which is what my mother used to do when she was unhappy – but I never got that. Suddenly, I get it now. Because I know the house will be significantly quieter and emptier without all my kids and their assorted friends traipsing in and out, I'm attempting to rearrange furniture to give the house a different flow so I won't notice the emptiness. No surprise – furniture rearranging isn't helping either.

It wasn't until I sang that song last night that I felt in my spirit God trying to get my attention. As I poured out my heart singing about being hungry and thirsty – it finally started making sense. I'm hungry for relationship. Yes I will miss my kids and nothing will fill that void, especially not food. What I need, what we all need is to be filled with the love of God and nurturing our relationship with the Savior will fill and satisfy in a way that's incomparable with every other relationship.

I'm so *hungry*, God – please fill me up.

God understands our prayers even when we can't find the words to say them. ~ Author Unknown

So the LORD must wait for you to come to him so he can show you his love and compassion. For the LORD is a faithful God. Blessed are those who wait for his help. Isaiah 30:18 (NLT)

PRAYER FOR TODAY: *Lord, help me to release my children and their future to Your care. I pray You will fill me with Your love and Your Spirit so I may not be in want. Help me to trust that You have a perfect plan for my life and help me stop trying to feed my emotions with the wrong things. In Your name I ask all these things, Lord Jesus. Amen.*

AUGUST 14
Diving In

After nearly two weeks of no exercise I finally got to dive right in today – literally and figuratively – as I went for a long swim this afternoon. Two weeks of sutures and wrapping my leg up in layers of plastic wrap just to shower and I was anxious to observe normal showering routines today as well as a relaxing swim.

I got a clean bill of health from the doctor with a note of caution. Since I never knew what caused my injury it's unlikely that I can keep from doing the same thing again in the future.

Perhaps a paranoid person would be tempted to slack off altogether and simply eliminate exercise from their life for fear of re-injury. After all there's no guarantee another injury won't occur. Whenever we suffer injury we can't afford to become paranoid and withdraw from anything that *might* cause injury. Life's too short and if we are still many pounds from our goal weight we can't afford to slack off altogether. If we've been given an okay and a release from a doctor to exercise, *as long as we use wisdom and common sense* there's no reason to eliminate exercise entirely.

There are other benefits of regular exercise besides losing weight. Exercise is great for our circulation and cardio vascular health and provides us with those endorphins we need for our mental health.

My doctor has recommended starting slowly and trying short walks and short bike rides before I jump into anything more strenuous. I'll start where I can, do what I can and move when I can.

None of us have any guarantees about what tomorrow may bring. We can all sit around on our duffs playing it safe waiting for our lives to be over because we're afraid – or we can get back in the game; jump back on the horse; or dive right in and take a chance. As for me … no surprise – I'm diving in!

The door to safety swings on the hinges of common sense. ~ Author Unknown

And we know that God causes everything to work together for the good of those who love God and are called according to his purpose for them. Romans 8:28 (NLT)

PRAYER FOR TODAY: *Lord, thank You for medical advances, surgery and doctors who can repair damaged bodies. Help me to take excellent care of this body You've entrusted to me. Help me to eat balanced meals, get plenty of restful sleep and use wisdom, common sense and balance when exercising. Help me to always include You in every aspect of my life. In Your name I ask all these things, Lord Jesus. Amen.*

AUGUST 15
Doodle Diving

I'm ashamed to admit it, but yesterday I did something I'm not proud of. I took more than just a dive in the pool; I took a *doodle dive* – as in Cheez Doodles. I'm not going to lie to you; it wasn't pretty. The telltale orange doodle dust clung to my fingers like it had been applied with spray glue. No amount of hand washing could remove the evidence or my shame.

My sudden nose dive into a medium size bag of Cheez Doodles was triggered by the sight of my youngest daughter driving away yesterday – her car packed full to over-flowing, heading off to college and her new life 120 miles away from Mom and Dad. I felt such a hollow void in my gut watching her drive away.

Many of us know from past personal experience, when your heart is aching you'll pretty much throw anything at it to stop the pain. Apparently yesterday's pain needed Cheez Doodles. Staring down at my day-glow orange fingers encrusted with a good half-inch layer of doodle dust was like watching myself from some sort of bizarre out-of-body experience.

Good Lord! Who is that crazy woman foaming orange at the mouth?

I've had enough experience in bingeing bonanzas to know proper protocol. You get up, dust the crumbs and carnage from your chest, locate a good cleaning solvent to sand-blast the evidence from your fingers, you brush your teeth banishing the taste of your debauchery from your mouth and you move forward.

If doodle diving were an Olympic sport, I'd be a gold medal champion by now. Life has proven time and time again that we must always look on the bright side of things and trust that for every trial there is always a triumph and ultimately, *God is in control.*

We have no right to ask when sorrow comes, "Why did this happen to me?" unless we ask the same question for every moment of happiness that comes our way. ~ Author Unknown

For I know the plans I have for you," says the LORD. *"They are plans for good and not for disaster, to give you a future and a hope.* Jeremiah 29:11 (NLT)

PRAYER FOR TODAY: *Lord, help me to look towards the future with excitement for the next phase in my life. Help me to focus on getting healthy, meeting my goals and developing a closer walk with You. In Your name I ask all these things, Lord Jesus. Amen.*

AUGUST 16
Praise Him in the Storms

After my shameful Doodle Dive, I needed a chance to clear my head and gain some perspective on my empty nest meltdown. I visited my kids up north at college, helping my youngest decorate her apartment and get organized before school starts. I gained more than perspective; I found peace. Seeing my daughter adapting to her new surroundings with barely contained excitement, my worries for her were laid to rest.

Driving home I was forced to navigate my way through a scary thunderstorm. Gale force winds buffeted my car; thunder rocked; lightning rolled while the rain pounded. I was forced to pull over on the freeway shoulder with a few hundred other people as visibility was nil due to heavy rainfall. I was terrified to my very core. In my fear, I remembered a line from a song that reminded me, I will praise Him in the storms, so I did just that at the top of my lungs.

We all have storms of life that we must navigate our way through. Maybe not an actual weather storm like mine, but difficult personal trials. As a young child growing up under a constant mantle of fear, I hid my fears by stuffing them down with food. For many of those years I didn't have a close relationship with the Savior so I went to my "go to" comforter – food, rather than Christ.

As we've journeyed these last many months to bring about change in our lifestyles and shed our unwanted weight, we've been in the process of changing many things about ourselves. Many of us fear change for the simple reason that it is "different."

If we are still reaching for the cookies rather than Christ we've obviously got some work to do. The storms eventually pass, but we know from past experience there's always another looming in the future. We need to stay strong and reach for the Comforter and praise Him in the storms.

One may understand the cosmos, but never the ego; the self is more distant than any star. ~ G.K. Chesterton, "The Logic of Elfland," *Orthodoxy,* **1908**

All praise to God, the Father of our Lord Jesus Christ. God is our merciful Father and the source of all comfort. 2 Corinthians 1:3 (NLT)

PRAYER FOR TODAY: *Father, even in the storms I will praise You. Thank You for bringing me safely through and for opening my eyes to areas of struggle. Put my feet back on solid ground. In Your name I ask all these things, Lord Jesus. Amen.*

AUGUST 17
Thumbs Up

I don't have a *bucket list* per se, but I've still got a few things left to accomplish this side of heaven. For the longest time achieving that *perfect weight* seemed to head that list. I can't help but shake my head at my own vanity. So many years wasted in vain pursuit of the wrong things. That's what I thought most about yesterday as I sat contemplating my life in the middle of a terrifying thunderstorm.

For many of us, our weight loss trials have defined us for so long we've lost sight of who we are. When we carry self-destructive thoughts in our head about ourselves they form us into something opposite of what God intends for us. God accepts us as we are based on our hearts not our weight.

Driving out of yesterday's storm, dark rain clouds blocked out the sun's rays. As I passed an odd shaped peak that resembled a giant thumb pointing skyward; a geological "thumbs up" gesture if you will; the sun broke through and shone like a spotlight on that giant thumb.

I wanted to stop and take a picture but I was in the high speed lane. I was certain no one would believe me if I told them that God cares so much about me that He took the time to send a rainstorm to talk to me and give me His own personal thumbs up.

That is a word for all of us. We need to trust God to walk us through this journey and we need not worry about tomorrow. We will not obsess and give any more attention in vain pursuit of the wrong things.

We can maintain a healthy lifestyle and IF weight loss occurs that's great, but it doesn't need to occur on a certain schedule for us to be happy. God loves us. We are created in His image and He desires relationship with us not obsession and worry and fear. I should know He gave me His thumbs up yesterday – so this must be the right path.

Success is blocked by concentrating on it and planning for it.... Success is shy – it won't come out while you're watching. ~ Tennessee Williams

When he speaks in the thunder, the heavens roar with rain. He causes the clouds to rise over the earth. He sends the lightning with the rain and releases the wind from his storehouses. Jeremiah 10:13 (NLT)

PRAYER FOR TODAY: *Lord, thank You for the storms of life that cause me to reflect. Help me to grow and mature and become more of the person You want me to be; help me to stop chasing after the wrong things. In Your name I ask all these things, Lord Jesus. Amen.*

AUGUST 18
Farewell to Fat

Gaining and losing weight is kind of a bizarre phenomenon if you think about it. Not so much the gaining part perhaps, but definitely the losing part. When we gain weight that is something tangible, right there for us to feel and see. Even though we don't gain 20 or 30 pounds overnight, there comes a point when we wake up and realize that all of our clothes are "suddenly" tighter.

Naturally we blame, the dryer that shrunk our clothes or the new medication we've started taking. There is ALWAYS blame. For every pound gained there is an equally legitimate excuse.

Our bodies are created to rid itself of excess fluids and food through the normal "elimination process" specifically designed by the great Master Himself. But when you go to bed and wake up the next morning and suddenly you're down five pounds – where did *that* five pounds go overnight? Did it somehow slide off our body and we've left traces of it in our jammies?

One of the reasons for limiting our obsession to step on the scale too frequently is because we can experience "a false gain." If we are retaining water because we've consumed too much soda or if we are constipated, our weight can jump up a few pounds overnight. When we limit weighing ourselves to once a week or once a month we are likely to get a more accurate reading than if we weigh every day.

Rather than driving ourselves crazy wondering how we can lose or gain weight seemingly overnight, it's best to focus on even the smallest of victories. A half pound lost this week or half a pound last week – eventually those halves combine to make a whole lot of success. Take time to enjoy this journey without obsessing over the number on the scale!

Finish each day and be done with it. You have done what you could; some blunders and absurdities have crept in; forget them as soon as you can. Tomorrow is a new day; you shall begin it serenely and with too high a spirit to be encumbered with your old nonsense. ~ Ralph Waldo Emerson

For we are God's masterpiece. He has created us anew in Christ Jesus, so we can do the good things he planned for us long ago. Ephesians 2:10 (NLT)

PRAYER FOR TODAY: Lord, thank You for designing us to be well-oiled machines that respond to exercise and changes in our diets. I pray the weight I lose will be a permanent loss. I pray with each pound lost, I'll discover more of my true self and I'll draw closer to You. In Your name I ask all these things, Lord Jesus. Amen.

AUGUST 19
When Crazy Calls

August can be a tough month for many women because it's typically a back to school month. While that can be cause for celebration for many stay-at-home mothers, it can also be a time of sadness. If you've got a child who is transitioning to a new phase it can be quite an emotional time for you. Your "baby" is heading to preschool or kindergarten or junior high or high school, or college. All this can mean big changes as much for mom as for the child.

If we are struggling food addicts, when life brings a lot of change we may be tempted to assuage our emotions with our "go to" drug of choice – food. Food is "the good girl's" drug and we can do a lot of damage with a box of snack cakes. Perhaps not as much damage as alcohol or prescription painkillers, but damage, just the same.

If we've been experiencing a lot of recent successes with our healthy eating and weight loss, we may think we'll be "safe" to take a few laps around the pity-pool. That is how the enemy seduces us into failure. We must not listen to those quiet whispers in our ear. *"You deserve a day off; you're sad. You've been so good and taking one day off won't matter. You'll feel better if you eat."*

We've all heard the lies before and we know where one bite, one cookie, one bag of French fries will lead us. At any given time we are only one bite away from a full on binge. When you factor in emotions all over the map because of changes happening in our life and we've got a recipe for disaster.

When those crazy lies of your former life beckon you; inviting you to take one more trip around Failure Mountain, that's the time to run. We're eight months into our healthier lifestyle and we've come too far to backslide now.

Remember that when crazy starts dialing our number, we need to be strong; we need to be smart and we need to make a choice: don't pick up the phone!

A man who is "of sound mind" is one who keeps the inner madman under lock and key. ~ Paul Valéry, *Mauvaises pensées et autres*, 1942

Temptation comes from our own desires, which entice us and drag us away. James 1:14 (NLT)

PRAYER FOR TODAY: *Lord, thank You for new beginnings. Help me to push past the craziness that calls my name when I am sad or conflicted by change. I want to serve You and refuse to listen to the lies of the enemy. Yours is the only voice I want to hear in my head. In Your name I ask all these things, Lord Jesus. Amen.*

AUGUST 20
Surrender Leads to Freedom

If you've ever had a bout of nasty stomach flu you find yourself for a couple of days after approaching any and all foods with much trepidation. You tread lightly picking out your next meal and you eat EVERYTHING with extreme caution. The stomach flu equals yuck and uncomfortable side-effects and once it's gone you spend time praying, "Please Lord, don't let this come back any time soon."

Because I've lived most of my life being in bondage to food and letting this addiction control every aspect of my life, now that my addiction is more controlled, I find myself questioning every day *is it really gone? If I eat one cookie will that trigger a full-fledged binge? Do I really have control of this addiction or is it an illusion?*

Nearly every day I wake up and marvel at the fact that my entire attitude towards food has so completely changed. Most of my life was spent in pursuit of my next secret snacking binge or obsessing over how many miles I'd have to walk/run to burn off the calories of my last binge. EVERYTHING in my life revolved around the bathroom scale and pursuit of the ideal weight.

Because we are unique and loved individually by God for who WE are – God has a different plan for each of our lives. Our addictions may mirror one another but the effects of those addictions look and feel differently to each of us. Victory and liberation will look and feel differently as well. We don't need to be jealous over someone else's success. Rather, we need to surrender completely to God and allow Him to change us according to the plan He has for OUR life.

Surrender leads to freedom. Getting to the point where we're completely ready to surrender is as individual as we are. "Let go and let God" may sound cliché, but it works. Once we finally reach a point of surrender, we have to stop and ask ourselves, "Yeesh, why did it take so long to get a clue?"

We must be free not because we claim freedom, but because we practice it. ~ William Faulkner

The Spirit of the Sovereign Lord is upon me, for the Lord has anointed me to bring good news to the poor. He has sent me to comfort the brokenhearted and to proclaim that captives will be released and prisoners will be freed. Isaiah 61:1 (NLT)

PRAYER FOR TODAY: *Lord, thank You for the freedom I'm enjoying; may I never take it for granted. I know I've come a long way, but still have so far to go. Continue to bless me with wisdom, maturity and insight and may I be used by You to encourage others as I learn and grow. Help me to maintain a positive attitude always. In Your name I ask all these things, Lord Jesus. Amen.*

AUGUST 21
Waste Not – Waist Not!

My husband and I went to a MLB game last night. We were given tickets behind home plate where the *rich and famous* hang out. The game overall was pretty boring. I did however, have a fabulous time people watching as the view from that perspective was quite different from the seats we normally get in the nose bleed section.

My first reaction was that I was surprised by how much money people are willing to spend on food and beverages for the simple pleasure of not having to leave their seat.

One family sitting in front of us brought their two young children with them. They spent a small fortune on meals for everyone after they were seated. Dad consumed a foot long hot dog in record time while mom consumed the uneaten remains of both her children's meals. The portions were too large for the little ones, and like any good mother, she didn't want the food to go to waste so she polished off the leftovers.

About an hour later my husband and I trekked up hundreds of stairs to get frozen yogurt and trekked back down hundreds of steps to enjoy our relatively low-fat/low calorie dessert. The kids in front of us saw our frozen concoctions and put in their order for a treat to mom and dad, whereupon daddy quickly swiped his credit card again to have their treats brought right to their seats.

Their expensive ice cream treats arrived looking as if they'd been stored in a deep freezer for decades. The kids took one look at our fluffy soft-serve yogurt piled high and rejected their own frozen treats. Naturally, no self-respecting mother who'd just spent about $12.00 plus tip on dessert was going to let the ice cream go to waste, so she did what I would have done (and frequently DID do); she ate both the ice cream desserts.

Boy, if I had a dollar for every time I employed that *I don't want to let it go to waste* logic! We mothers need to concentrate on the pounds gathering on our waist line rather than wasting food! We're only hurting ourselves. Ask yourself: should I choose to *waste* food or do I want *waist* food? It's our choice.

I think in terms of the day's resolutions, not the years. ~ Henry Moore

It is better to be godly and have little than to be evil and rich. Psalm 37:16 (NLT)

PRAYER FOR TODAY: *Lord, help me to find joy in all that I do. Help me not to dwell on past mistakes, but to learn from them and move on, gaining wisdom and insight with each opportunity. Help me not to become bitter – but always better. In Your name I ask all these things, Lord Jesus. Amen.*

AUGUST 22
Infectious Affection

Maria has worked hard to lose 50 pounds. She's maintained a healthy balance of meal planning, journaling and exercise. She looks fabulous. Maria's good friend, Shelby isn't quite as excited about Maria's weight loss as she should be. In fact, Shelby is a little bit jealous of Maria's weight loss.

Whenever these two friends get together, Shelby suggests activities that involve a lot of unhealthy food options. Shelby wants to go out for lunch or dinner or stop for coffee and pie. Maria does well to resist these food temptations, but she fears she's nearing a breaking point. Maria is considering limiting time spent with her friend in order to keep from sabotaging her successful weight loss efforts.

What are we to do when we have "well-meaning" friends and relatives who might be trying to undermine our weight loss efforts? We should always have the attitude that we want to "affect" those around us with a positive attitude and example rather than letting others "infect" us with their negative, counter-productive attitudes and gestures.

We need to stay strong and keep our goals before us and keep our eye on the finish line. If we need to put some distance between us and well-meaning friends for a season in order to succeed, then so be it. Obviously if the saboteur in our life is a spouse, that's not as easy. Set aside a time when you can share openly with your spouse or friend and tell them plainly what you're trying to achieve. Stand up for yourself and let people know that you are on a path to succeed and you would love their help and support.

Oftentimes just by opening a door for discussion you may be able to gain insight as to why your friend is trying to sabotage your efforts. Don't be afraid to affect others in a positive why. As long as you're not infected with failure your chances for success are much more likely. We should strive to affect, not infect and we will be more effective in our efforts.

Never miss an opportunity to make others happy, even if you have to leave them alone in order to do it. ~ Author Unknown

No, your sins affect only people like yourself, and your good deeds also affect only humans. Job 35:8 (NLT)

PRAYER FOR TODAY: *Lord, help me to be a positive influence on others so that I might affect people in an encouraging way. I pray I will be strong enough to pull away from those who seek to inflict harm or those wishing to sabotage my efforts. May I continue to grow in strength and maturity every day. In Your name I ask all these things, Lord Jesus. Amen.*

AUGUST 23
The Sky is Not Falling

Life these days can be extremely stressful and my life is no exceptioin. Today was one of *those* days when for no apparent reason, I awoke with anxiety. I'm not even sure how it happens but even when all my ducks are in a row and life is good externally – I still have this internal sense of doom and gloom and a general *the sky is falling* state of mind. I hate it when that happens!

In the past, many of us have always chosen to combat anxiety with assorted junk foods. If we're suddenly finding success on our weight loss program, we may find ourselves in unfamiliar territory as we try to combat anxiety without the aid of food. When we are attacked with anxiety, it's best to take an inventory of what may be the root cause of our sudden angst.

Identifying the problem doesn't fix the problem, but once you've identified the problem you can figure out how to attack it. Without my "go-to" binge foods available to me, I open my Bible and look for answers. I've been reading the Psalms in the Old Testament and 1 Corinthians in the New Testament for the last couple of weeks.

Many skeptics' discount the idea of the Word of God as being practical or relevant to today's issues and often accuse Christians of using their religion as a crutch. Frankly I don't care what the skeptics say. Not only do I use the Word of God and my relationship with Jesus Christ as a crutch - meaning my faith supports me – BUT I use my faith as the whole darn hospital and not just a crutch. I KNOW from personal experience that the Word of God is very practical and relevant to MY life.

In the future, when I feel that *sky is falling* anxiety creeping up on me, I've decided I can find relief by speaking scripture six to eight times daily taken as needed for pain and relief from stress. I want to ingest healing words from Scripture rather than inhale destructive junk food that hurts me.

Good for the body is the work of the body, and good for the soul is the work of the soul, and good for either is the work of the other. ~ Henry David Thoreau

Give thanks to the LORD, for he is good! His faithful love endures forever. Psalm 118:1 (NLT)

PRAYER FOR TODAY: *Lord, thank You for the promises in Your Word. I thank You that when I feel anxious, stressed or defeated I can turn to You and Your Word. Your Spirit lifts me and gives me hope. Help me to always remember to pray first before I give into worry or fear. In Your name I ask all these things, Lord Jesus. Amen.*

AUGUST 24
The Ugly Duckling Swan Song

I used to do this thing where I'd walk into a room – it didn't matter where – and automatically scan the room to determine if I was the fattest or ugliest girl there. Even at my thinnest, I saw my reflection as morbidly obese.

Most of us don't see ourselves as others see us. I can spend an hour primping on my hair and makeup and look in the mirror and think I look pretty good. All it takes to unravel those good feelings is to have one person look at you the wrong way and instantly you become the ugly duckling in the blink of an eye.

I can trace this ugly little fat girl image all the way back to the time I was 15 and someone wanted to set me up on a disastrous blind date. My ego suffered a severe blow after some unkind comments were made about my looks.

It's been nearly 40 years since that occurred, and I'm hard-pressed to understand how my mind fixates on something so insignificant that happened so long ago. Why is the human brain more willing to hold on to the negative things rather than replaying those positive life-affirming moments?

As part of my healing process in the 12-step program, I confronted my *friend* from decades past as we still maintain contact. The sad thing is – she didn't remember ever saying those things to me and barely remembered the blind date incident.

Buried anger and hurt eats away at us like a cancer, poisoning our minds and robbing us of joy. I spent nearly 40 years of my life letting one careless incident define me as an ugly duckling. I was the only one that suffered as the person responsible had no memory of it at all, so she wasn't hurt by it, only me.

We must refuse to waste one more minute letting the words of others hurt us. *Sticks and stones* and all that … We KNOW who we are and we KNOW we are chosen by God. It doesn't matter what ANYONE else thinks of us, because God thinks we are fabulous.

Everything has beauty, but not everyone sees it. ~ Confucius

You should clothe yourselves instead with the beauty that comes from within, the unfading beauty of a gentle and quiet spirit, which is so precious to God. 1 Peter 3:4 (NLT)

PRAYER FOR TODAY: *Lord, thank You that You see my heart and don't judge me by my outward appearance. Help me to see others in the same fashion You see us. May I continue to mature and grow in wisdom and knowledge daily. In Your name I ask all these things, Lord Jesus. Amen.*

AUGUST 25
Chewing on Idols

A woman visited my support group recently who shared with the group that she was past the age of caring what people thought of her regarding her weight. She was actually happy with her body. The only reason she wanted to lose weight was simply because she'd realized as of late, her food addiction had become an idol in her life. Food was crowding out Jesus in her daily walk with Christ. She said, "It's getting so I can't hear Jesus over all my chewing."

Getting to the point where we can accept ourselves just as we are is a sign of spiritual maturity. That doesn't mean we don't want or need change; it simply means that our happiness or contentment has absolutely NOTHING to do with what we weigh. Yet many of us have listened to those lies for years or DECADES – letting the devil convince us the opposite was true.

Spending time in God's Word will help us discover peace unlike anything we ever found in a bag of chips or a tub of ice cream. Like this woman, I chose to crowd out Jesus with my obsession over food and my weight, but no more. The more this food addiction wants to control me, the more I realize I need a Savior.

What a shame we have to wait until we're "older" to appreciate the concept of time – for it's when we are younger that we have more of it, but spend it carelessly. When we are older and time is in short supply, we take advantage of every spare minute to fill that time with things that really matter – like loving our neighbor as we love ourselves; accepting the things we can't change; changing the things we are capable of changing and developing our walk with Christ.

If you're still crowding out Jesus with diet OCD, stop the madness before it's too late. We all have an expiration date so why not make a date with Jesus to figure out the key to your freedom.

Men talk of killing time, while time quietly kills them. ~ Dion Boucicault

"LORD, remind me how brief my time on earth will be. Remind me that my days are numbered-how fleeting my life is" Psalm 39:4 (NLT)

PRAYER FOR TODAY: Lord, help me to spend my time wisely and to enjoy even the little things. May I operate in the gifts of the Spirit each day and help me to make the most of opportunities afforded me. May I never become complacent and may I always have a desire to learn, grow and improve myself during whatever time I have left here on Earth. In Your name I ask all these things, Lord Jesus. Amen.

AUGUST 26
One Cookie at a Time

For most of my early childhood years I was raised predominately by a single working mother. My mother was also full-blooded Sicilian. I think Sicilians are raised from birth with the words "eat – eat … you're so thin" tattooed on their dominant hands used for wielding eating utensils.

I have an acquaintance who is a young single mother raising her daughter with the help of her Italian mother. It's difficult to sit back and watch this young mother who is battling her own weight issues use food as comfort and for soothing her two-year-old child.

When the little girl is angry, their response is "Give her a cookie so she'll quit screaming!" When she falls and hurts herself, their response is: "Here's a piece of cake to make it better." When she's cranky and needs a nap, rather than encouraging her to lie down, their response is to give her food to settle her.

It's easy to cast aspersions when we see others doing things we don't agree with. I've done many of those same things with my children and my grandson. I used food to comfort and soothe because that's what I was taught as I'm sure my parents were taught from their parents. This woman is responding to her child the way she was raised. We're stuck in these vicious generational cycles that are so unhealthy but we continue in them because it's what we know.

Because this young mother is really only a casual acquaintance I'm not comfortable sticking my nose in her business. I can't fix everyone, but I can do something about me. I still fight that urge to use food to fix my kids' problems. Old habits die hard.

How do we change the world … one cookie at a time! Anything you stop feeding eventually dies, including our fleshly desires so we've got to stop feeding our emotions!

It is not the strongest of the species that survive, nor the most intelligent, but the one most responsive to change. ~ Author unknown

Let the wicked change their ways and banish the very thought of doing wrong. Let them turn to the Lord that he may have mercy on them. Yes, turn to our God, for he will forgive generously. Isaiah 55:7 (NLT)

PRAYER FOR TODAY: *Lord, help me to never use food as an idol and only use food as nourishment. Help me to mind my own business when I need to, but help me be open to being used as an example if I can be of help to someone who is struggling. In Your name I ask all these things, Lord Jesus. Amen.*

AUGUST 27
VGR – Vacation Grace Required

It used to be that a vacation equaled pig-out. Not so much anymore. I'm on a short mini vacation the rest of this week and it's been extremely challenging for me to eat healthy and keep those calories in line.

Because I have changed my diet so radically over the last few months, eating a lot of junk food is no longer as much fun as it used to be. I'm inhaling Tums like they were Tic Tacs followed up by *Pepto* shooters. I'm not overly concerned that I will fall back into old habits because the stomach aches simply are no longer worth it.

Over the past many months we've made some big changes and some very subtle changes. We may not realize just exactly how much progress we've made until we're put in a situation that used to spell disaster for us with calorie overload. Whereas vacations used to mean French fries and dessert at least once daily, now I'm discovering that my body can no longer tolerate what once used to be standard vacation fare.

Over time our bodies naturally adapt to our environment. If our environment used to be filled with junk food and we suddenly try and re-introduce greasy foods, our stomach may stage a revolt. Quite honestly, that kind of revolt is the exact reminder that we need to open our eyes to the fact that God has brought us so far.

If you've got a vacation coming up, don't panic. Don't let a vacation be centered on what restaurants you visit. Step outside the box and engage in activities that will keep you moving. Even if your trip is for the purpose of relaxing, relaxing doesn't have to mean eating all the time. There is more to fun than food!

A vacation is like love – anticipated with pleasure, experienced with discomfort, and remembered with nostalgia. ~ Author Unknown

On the seventh day God had finished his work of creation, so he rested from all his work. Genesis 2:2 (NLT)

PRAYER FOR TODAY: *Lord, thank You for opportunities to get away and take a break from the stresses of life. May I employ common sense and wisdom when eating out. May I focus on relaxing with friends and family rather than on my next meal. Remind me daily that I don't need food to make me feel better. May I never forget time off doesn't mean a vacation from eating healthy. In Your name I ask all these things, Lord Jesus. Amen.*

AUGUST 28
The Lesson of Lions

Someone pointed out to me recently that humans are the only species that uses food for anything other than nourishment. We humans eat when we're stressed, tired, lonely, bored, happy and for just about everything else related to our emotions.

Lions don't pounce on a wildebeest because they are stressed. They pounce because they're hungry. When a bird lands on your bird feeder, it's hungry, not bored. Animals eat when they're hungry. If food isn't available to them, they'll hunt for it. Animals don't congregate for the purpose of sharing a meal. If a lion kills a Wildebeest, he fights to protect his kill; he doesn't invite a hyena over to share.

I often wonder if my obsession and addiction to food was birthed with Adam and Eve's disobedience and fall from grace. The lure of that forbidden fruit was their undoing and subsequently ours as well. Human nature wants what we can't have; which is precisely why diets have such a high failure rate.

If you're a bread freak like I am, every time I've tried diets that restrict my carbo-hydrates, I end up going a little crazy and ultimately succumb to a bread binge. Rather than eliminating carbs from my diet altogether, I look for hi-fiber, low-carb substitutions. There are many healthy options available for low-carb English muffins, breads, bagels and even tortillas. Always look for whole grains as opposed to white flour options. Substitute brown rice for white rice and try whole wheat pasta rather than what you're used to eating.

Don't settle for boring and mundane. Try new things that mix up your program while adding flavor, fiber and variety. Most of us don't have to kill to eat, but it doesn't hurt to do a little hunting when it comes to seeking diversity in our meals. As long as we are not living to eat, we can eat to live without being bored by our choices.

I like pigs. Dogs look up to us. Cats look down on us. Pigs treat us as equals. ~ Winston Churchill

Look at the birds. They don't plant or harvest or store food in barns, for your heavenly Father feeds them. And aren't you far more valuable to him than they are? Matthew 6:26 (NLT)

PRAYER FOR TODAY: Thank You, Lord, for reminders that You are ALWAYS in control. I continually ask that You would help me eat to live rather than living to eat. Help me to keep food in its place and not make it the center of my universe. In Your name I ask all these things, Lord Jesus. Amen.

AUGUST 29
Anniversary Reminders

As part of my mini vacation, my husband and I found time to celebrate our wedding anniversary. I've been blessed to be married to a man who has loved me for the last quarter of a century, in spite of the fact that I'm a very moody and emotional woman.

During the 26 years we have known one another; my husband has seen my weight fluctuate from an all-time low on our wedding day of 128 pounds up to 200 pounds during pregnancy and menopause. In all that time he's NEVER been unkind or unloving towards me with regards to my weight. In fact he's insisted that he's more in love with me today than when we married all those years ago when I was at my thinnest.

For him love is not based on the external. The fact that my husband saw beyond the physical and could love me when I had zero self-esteem, no self-confidence and was so completely introverted is a testament to what a faithful man of God he is.

If you're someone who doesn't have the love of a supportive spouse or family member, you need not despair. You can succeed on this journey to wellness without that support, but most of us know that unconditional love and support are a key factor to success. If you call Jesus Christ your Lord, you do have the unconditional support of a loving Savior. Jesus can be that supportive husband; He can be your entire support system. Let God show you what true unconditional love is like through the love of His Son, Jesus Christ.

God can restore to you what the enemy has stolen from you and bring you fullness of joy and a reassurance that you are loved beyond measure. A support system is great, but nothing compares to the unconditional love of Christ.

A happy marriage is the union of two good forgivers. ~ Ruth Bell Graham

The Spirit of the Sovereign LORD is upon me, for the LORD has anointed me to bring good news to the poor. He has sent me to comfort the brokenhearted and to proclaim that captives will be released and prisoners will be freed. Isaiah 61:1 (NLT)

PRAYER FOR TODAY: *Lord, thank You for the gift of a supportive partner and friends. Help me to love unconditionally as I have been loved. May I always strive to never judge others by outward appearances. May I continue to keep You at the center of all my relationships. In Your name I ask all these things, Lord Jesus. Amen.*

AUGUST 30
Born Again, Again

In the last many months God has been doing a tremendous *housecleaning* job with many of our hearts and attitudes. God wants to leave nothing untouched. He wants to meticulously open every hidden closet in our heart and mind and sweep everything clean. He wants to throw open every window and door and flood our house with light; exposing everything we've worked years to keep hidden in the dark.

Hopefully we've had a giant emotional yard sale and eliminated a lot of the useless clutter stockpiling in our heads and hearts and now we're ready to set up house in a brand new space and start fresh. Once our heads and hearts have been de-cluttered we need to start redecorating at some point. We need to make sure that we're filling the spaces with only things that are pure, honorable and lovely and true (Philippians 4:8).

For all of the years that we've felt unloved and unworthy, God has loved us faithfully even though we were too unaware to grasp that concept. Once we grasp this freedom, it's like being born-again *again*. Even though many of us read the Bible and know the Scriptures, we've somehow let the enemy convince us that the healing words are for everyone else, not us.

We are the Father's chosen; loved and precious in His sight. Those parts of our personality that we despise are characteristics that He specifically gave to us to make us unique. If we are believers in Christ we are the offspring of God (Acts 17:28). We've got parts of His DNA. He gives to each of us a little part of Himself so that all of us together make up the Body of Christ. He purposely created us to be individuals, yet so many of us try to be like somebody else because we don't like who we are.

Trying to dress like someone else, cut our hair like someone else, emulating someone's mannerisms or any of the other things we do to be like someone we wish we were is a waste of time. We need to dare to be ourselves. If we are doing something that is displeasing to God; trust that He will let us know about it and then give us the grace to change. Otherwise, we need to be who God created us to be – simply, uniquely us.

He who trims himself to suit everyone will soon whittle himself away. ~ Raymond Hull

Point out anything in me that offends you, and lead me along the path of everlasting life. Psalm 139:24 (NLT)

PRAYER FOR TODAY: *Lord, thank You that I'm free to be me. Stretch me and mold me and help me to walk in confidence rather than living in fear. Thank you for knitting me together just as I am and for loving me as I am. Continue to guide me along this journey. In Your name I ask all these things, Lord Jesus. Amen.*

AUGUST 31
"V" is for Victory

While I was on vacation this past week we stayed at a hotel that offered free continental breakfast every morning. Being married to a man who is the embodiment of the *"If it's free it's for me,"* philosophy of life, you can bet your bottom dollar that we take full advantage of free anything – especially meals.

Breakfast is my favorite meal of the day and one of the toughest meals of the day to keep low calorie and healthy, especially when dining out. And when it's free and continental that usually implies pastries, muffins and bread of every variety; all of which are my very own special Achilles heel foods.

While my travelling companions loaded their plates with piles of eggs, bacon, biscuits and gravy, I contemplated filling the extra compartments of my purse with blueberry muffins. I know free and continental implies you eat it there – but I'm given to the notion that a body can only eat so much in one sitting and those muffins will come in handy later in the morning. It's that kind of logic that has derailed my past weight loss attempts.

This trip showed me that I can go on vacation without making everything about food. I selected healthier choices and split everything I ate with someone else. I balanced my exercise and kept snacking to a minimum.

Progress is progress no matter how small. As long as we are moving forward rather than backwards, any vacation that gets us home without the average 7 – 10 pound weight gain is a huge victory. Maintaining our weight loss with no gain during a vacation puts us in the minority, but that's a statistic we can live with. Ahh, don't you love the taste of victory?

Vacation used to be a luxury, but in today's world it has become a necessity. ~ Author Unknown

For we know that when this earthly tent we live in is taken down (that is, when we die and leave this earthly body), we will have a house in heaven, an eternal body made for us by God himself and not by human hands. 2 Corinthians 5:1 (NLT)

PRAYER FOR TODAY: *Lord, thank You for the opportunity to get away to rest my mind, my body and my spirit. Thank You for all that I've learned about myself in the last few months. Help me continue to move forward and make progress and put into practice all that You are teaching me. In Your name I ask all these things, Lord Jesus. Amen.*

SEPTEMBER 1
I'm Ready for my Close-Up

For most of life I would never have considered leaving my house without fixing my hair or applying makeup. As of late, I've gotten so comfortable with the woman I am I've gotten in the habit of leaving the house with little or no makeup.

Today I had to run a few errands and pick my grandson up from school. I knew I'd be coming home and swimming later so I barely fixed my hair and settled for a quick swipe of mascara across my lashes.

I arrived at school early and I'd no sooner turned the engine off when I kid you not – a television reporter from a local station knocked on my window asking permission to interview me for the evening news broadcast. The story had to do with the excessive heat and kids on the playground. Honestly the topic barely registered.

All I could think of was "of all days to be out without my hair and makeup done!" I quickly declined the reporter's request explaining that I was just a grandma filling in and I wasn't a proper authority on the comings and goings of the students at the school.

Being comfortable with ourselves is great but we also need to remember that these vessels that God has entrusted to us are precious. We have a responsibility to maintain them to the best of our ability. That means not making them a dumping ground for junk food. It means taking care of our bodies by balancing work, play and exercise and being presentable so we are a light that draws people to us and thereby Christ. That doesn't mean we have to wear designer clothes or buy expensive makeup or hair care products. It simply means that we do the best we can with what we've been given.

Today's lesson for me was I'd drifted slightly too far over in the opposite direction and upset that delicate balance. We must have balance in everything! In the future I will make sure that I am camera ready should the need arise. For me that means an extra swipe of mascara, a little blush on my cheek bones and voilà … I'm ready for my close up Mr. DeMille!

Learn to… be what you are, and learn to resign with a good grace all that you are not. ~ Henri Frederic Amiel

For we are God's masterpiece. He has created us anew in Christ Jesus, so we can do the good things he planned for us long ago. Ephesians 2:10 (NLT)

PRAYER FOR TODAY: *Lord, thank You for the freedom to by myself. As I enjoy this new freedom, help me to continually live in balance in every area of my life and do my best to be Your ambassador so I will never bring shame to the name of the Lord Jesus Christ. In Your name I ask all these things, Lord Jesus. Amen.*

SEPTEMBER 2
Shortcuts and Shortchange

I talked by phone with an old friend of mine yesterday. We live a couple of states apart and we rarely see one another. She's kind of a spacey girl who's always got a get rich quick scheme in the works. She's all about shortcuts – especially when it comes to dieting and weight loss.

For as long as I've known her she's called me regularly to gush about her latest sure-fire plan to lose weight. This month she's into some sort of diet pill that she got from a very expensive weight loss clinic, protein drinks and working out in the gym *again*.

I want to be supportive of her weight loss efforts, but she's never experienced any long lasting weight loss success. Like so many of us, she loses 20 or 30 pounds but quickly regains all the weight once she "resumes normal eating."

As much as I love my friend, she's one of those people who consider herself to be very spiritual but she doesn't have a relationship with Jesus Christ. She tends to turn to God only in times of crisis, when she's in desperate need.

I've tried to share with her the difference Christ has made in my weight loss journey, but she files me in the category of *Bible thumper* and mentally shuts down when I insist on sharing. I've filed her in my *friends who are difficult to witness to* category, but I continually pray for her and trust that at some point God will get a hold of her and she'll come around.

Having a relationship with Jesus Christ is no guarantee that you will be successful at losing weight, but having Him along to help when we are weak, to lift us when we are down and to rejoice with when we have success, means we've got a friend on this journey who *gets us* and who supports us when no one else does.

Success is more permanent when you achieve it without destroying your principles. ~ Walter Cronkite

Study this Book of Instruction continually. Meditate on it day and night so you will be sure to obey everything written in it. Only then will you prosper and succeed in all you do. Joshua 1:8 (NLT)

PRAYER FOR TODAY: Lord, thank You for the gift of friendship. Grant me wisdom and patience when sharing the love of Christ with friends. Give me a boldness to tell of the goodness in my life when I share the Gospel. In Your name I ask all these things, Lord Jesus. Amen.

SEPTEMBER 3
Beware the Kryptonite

We all need to be reminded from time to time that we are not superhuman or able to leap tall buildings in a single bound, see through steel walls with x-ray vision, or run faster than speeding bullets. We all have our own special kind of kryptonite that renders us as weak as new born babes. It's not some kind of mystery meteorite flung from the outer reaches of deep space. No, if you're a serious food addict, your energy and strength can be zapped from something as simple as *food*. My kryptonite is any type of baked goods.

Last night my small group reconvened after a brief summer hiatus. We celebrated with a smorgasbord of snacks, 95% of which contained massive amounts of sugar in the form of frosting, fillings, icings, chocolate and general overall *dessert kryptonite*. As the meeting closed and I was cleaning up, things got a bit hazy. In fact, it got downright ugly for me.

I will spare you the gory details. Bottom line, even the strongest, most reformed, hard core food addict succumbs to temptation once in a while. When faced with our own special brand of kryptonite, it can feel like being bowled over by a runaway train.

When faced with temptation I sampled but I wasn't completely felled. But still, I sampled. Today I got up looked myself in the mirror and rather than giving in to the urge to hurl insults at my reflection … I simply stopped and thanked God. With the amount of food left at my house last night, it could have been so much worse.

Even though we may occasionally slip up, there is no fall so far that we can never get back up again. We will prevail. We may not be superhuman, but we serve a mighty God who is better than any fictional superhero. God can restore us and forgive us. With that kind of grace and strength, it should be obvious that Jesus is the real superhero.

All men are tempted. There is no man that lives that can't be broken down, provided it is the right temptation, put in the right spot. ~ Henry Ward Beecher, Proverbs from Plymouth Pulpit, 1887

For we are not fighting against flesh-and-blood enemies, but against evil rulers and authorities of the unseen world, against mighty powers in this dark world, and against evil spirits in the heavenly places. Ephesians 6:12 (NLT)

PRAYER FOR TODAY: *Lord, once I again I've seen firsthand that I cannot fight this battle under my own strength. I confess that I've stumbled and ask forgiveness and pray for mercy and strength to pick myself up and start all over again. Help me not to dwell on where I may have failed, but help me receive Your grace and strength to learn from this misstep and do my best to move forward. In Your name I ask all these things, Lord Jesus. Amen.*

SEPTEMBER 4
Temptation Island

I went to my group support meeting last night after having missed last week because of vacation. Once I heard what the topic of discussion for the evening lesson was to be, I started to get a little hot under the collar. I felt like someone must have ratted me out about my slight fall from grace the previous night. The theme for the class was *"Temptation."* Uh oh – busted!

Once I settled my racing heartbeat and opened my mind and my spirit to receive the teaching, it became abundantly clear – I'm not the only person who's ever given in to temptation. Regardless of whether we are food addicts, drug addicts, alcohol, shopping, sex or gossip addicts – we all are tempted with our own special brand of *kryptonite*.

I suppose if I were an eternal optimist I would be rejoicing in the fact that at least I'm normal. Somehow though, that news doesn't excite me. Few of us ever *arrive* at being cured from addiction. Temptations will likely always be difficult; reminding us we will *always* need Jesus.

Many say that "once an addict, always an addict." We must never forget that we are only one cookie away from falling off the wagon. We must never get to that point that we can convince ourselves otherwise. If we think we are above that sort of logic or if we buy into that notion that we are *cured* and can never fall, we may need to address some pride issues. None of us are perfect regardless of how strong we think we may be.

With each shameful fall comes the knowledge that we are never in complete control. We must continually turn our will over to the Lord Jesus Christ. Apart from Him we can do nothing – especially resist temptation, and certainly we cannot lose weight successfully and keep it off indefinitely without His constant help and presence in our lives.

Failure doesn't mean you are a failure... it just means you haven't succeeded yet. ~ Robert Schuller

I am the vine; you are the branches. If a man remains in me and I in him, he will bear much fruit; apart from me you can do nothing. John 15:5 (NIV)

PRAYER FOR TODAY: Lord, thank You for the constant reminder that under my own strength I can do nothing. Thank You for getting my attention and opening my eyes and for helping me to understand that none of us are immune to temptation. Help me to learn from this experience; grow stronger and always keep You the focus of all my efforts. In Your name I ask all these things, Lord Jesus. Amen.

SEPTEMBER 5
Kindergarten Repeat

Do you ever get the idea that we are a race of mindless eating machines? Everywhere we go we're inundated with free samples, complimentary candy dishes, domed Plexiglas plates of the *cookie of the day* at the grocery store and free mints when we leave the restaurant. There's no end. And what's worse, we all seem to want to help ourselves.

When we first begin any weight loss program it's natural that we weigh and measure everything we eat. We record our calories in our food journal and we can tell you to within a few calories how much we've eaten for any particular day.

Once the *honeymoon* is over though, we tend to get a little more relaxed and slack off on our diligence and our commitment to tracking our calories; which is exactly how I got myself into so much trouble earlier this week.

It's such an unhealthy feeling to go to bed feeling stuffed the way we used to; especially if we kicked all those bad habits months ago. Many of us know once you fall it's surprisingly easy to roll around in our failures – if even for a short while. Those self-induced pity parties – *table for one*, somehow seem justified.

If we slip or fall, the healthy thing to do is drag our sorry self away from the pity party and begin anew. Go back to basics. Force yourself to weigh and measure food portions again. Record everything you eat and keep careful records of exactly what you're eating and make a conscious effort to bypass any and all BLTs (bites, licks and tastes).

We may think we've graduated and are above the elementary steps necessary for weight loss, but occasionally we need to go back to kindergarten and start fresh.

Life is really simple, but we insist on making it complicated. ~ Confucius

For the waywardness of the simple will kill them, and the complacency of fools will destroy them. Proverbs 1:32 (NIV)

PRAYER FOR TODAY: *Lord, thank You for the simple reminders that I'm oftentimes lazy and I need to think before I act. Help me to get back on track by doing the basic things I know that work when it comes to weight loss. Help me, Lord because I am frequently so weak willed. In Your name I ask all these things, Lord Jesus. Amen.*

SEPTEMBER 6
A Little Dab Will Totally Undo You

Have you ever had a friend or relative whose only way to express their feelings for you was through food? I've had several friends and relatives who've done exactly that. Because of my natural affinity for these people I found it nearly impossible to say "no" to their caloric "love offerings."

My grandmother was a bit surly on the surface but a total marshmallow underneath. More aptly, she had a marshmallow center with a graham cracker crust covered in melted chocolate – as describes *Moon Pies*, her love offering of choice. It was hard for her to say "I love you," so she substituted Moon Pies for what she could not say with words.

Thinking back now, I didn't particularly care for Moon Pies, but I didn't want to hurt poor Grandma's feelings. I choked down my fair share of the dessert treats just to keep the peace. Now that I'm older and more able to express my true feelings, I've learned to sugar-coat my refusals when well-meaning loved ones try to foist food off on me.

We cannot be personally responsible for filling someone else's love tank, especially if we've spent a lifetime filling our own love tank with food. Many of us have mistakenly equated love with food.

It's okay to enjoy food with people we love, but beware of those that try to force feed us fattening foods by making us feel guilty if we refuse. Perhaps further investigation might indicate these people are pushing their own hidden agenda that has nothing to do with love – or perhaps they have unresolved food issues of their own or a fear of intimacy.

Wake up and smell the Moon Pies – a little dab will hurt us. If we have people in our lives that insist on showing their love for us with food, we need to come up with some creative ways to give and receive love in a healthier fashion – one that is lower in calories and won't undo us.

Grandmas never run out of hugs or cookies. ~ Author Unknown

Therefore I tell you, do not worry about your life, what you will eat or drink; or about your body, what you will wear. Is not life more important than food, and the body more important than clothes?" Matthew 6:25 (NIV)

PRAYER FOR TODAY: *Lord, thank You for all the people in my life who give and receive love so generously. Help me to be able to communicate healthier ways to give and receive love other than through the sharing of food. Open my eyes and help me recognize all the times I've been guilty of using food to give or receive love and affection. Continue to do a mighty work in me. In Your name I ask all these things, Lord Jesus. Amen.*

SEPTEMBER 7
Holy Crap Girlfriend!

I saw a friend of mine last week that I hadn't seen in a month or so. Since I had last seen Ricki (not her real name), she'd lost a noticeable amount of weight. Like most people, my first reaction was, "Wow, what have you been doing?" She was quick to volunteer that she'd jumped on the HCG bandwagon. I've got quite a few friends that have tried the HCG diet and some have experienced great success, while others – not so much.

HCG is a hormone women secrete during pregnancy. I'm not a medical expert, but from what I understand, this hormone is harvested and women are voluntarily being injected with this hormone to aid in weight loss. The hormone injections (or drops) work together in conjunction with a very strict diet and help people to lose a considerable amount of weight in a short amount of time. Sounds too good to be true, doesn't it?

From what I've learned, the diet itself is limited to 500 calories a day, to which I say – hel-lo, anybody who is limited to 500 calories a day will lose weight; so, why the need for the hormone injections? HCG may help to curb your appetite … but at what cost?

Personally, I think HCG stands for: "HOLY CRAP, GIRLFRIEND!" What are you thinking??!!?? BEFORE taking ANY weight loss drugs do your research. Always check with your health care professional before taking any supplement for weight loss.

There are no shortcuts to losing weight – only hard work and commitment. Not only do we need to change the way we eat, but we need to change the way we think about food. We need to include God in every aspect of our weight loss, our recovery from food addictions and our entire journey to get healthy. This is the only sure-fire recipe for successful weight loss.

Our HCG program should be: *Healthy, Controlled and Grounded* in the Word of God!

The longer I live the less confidence I have in drugs and the greater is my confidence in the regulation and administration of diet and regimen. ~John Redman Coxe, 1800

And we know that the Son of God has come, and he has given us understanding so that we can know the true God. And now we live in fellowship with the true God because we live in fellowship with his Son, Jesus Christ. He is the only true God, and he is eternal life. 1 John 5:20 (NLT)

PRAYER FOR TODAY: *Lord, thank You for common sense and wisdom. Use me to influence others and impart wisdom to anyone who is considering unhealthy approaches to weight loss. Help me to avoid desperate measures when I'm feeling desperate to lose weight. In Your name I ask all these things, Lord Jesus. Amen.*

SEPTEMBER 8
Kick the Kid to the Curb

I've been learning the hard way the last week that if I let my defenses down for even a brief period, the slide back into old habits is subtle and slow, but inevitable. Since my vacation last week, I'm battling some residual procrastination.

When we don't know what we're supposed to be doing we can claim ignorance. However, when we KNOW what we're supposed to be doing and we choose not to do it, then we're just plain stupid. I admit it: I've been lazy and stupid the last week and for no other reason than I'm being rebellious and difficult; as if that terrible two-year-old is about to rear her ugly head once again.

When we've faced some of our emotional eating triggers and we've come to understand why we turn to food, we must recognize we are not completely free yet and likely never will be. We can control our addiction but we can't afford to ever let the voice of the enemy convince us we are completely liberated. We need to discipline that incorrigible little two-year-old living inside us.

Every day is a battle to keep the addiction from breaking down the doors and engaging in a full-fledged takeover. Whether we're doing our best to keep the addiction locked away or locked out, as long as it's not running the show and calling the shots, we stand a fighting chance.

In the meantime, we need to kick the rebellious two-year-old inside of us to the curb *again* and get back on track TODAY. Waiting until tomorrow won't cut it, since our weight loss past is likely littered with failures that all started with *tomorrow, I'll get back on track and get serious*.

If we are serious about losing weight, our commitment needs to begin TODAY, not tomorrow, because for many, tomorrow never comes.

Someday is not a day of the week. ~ Author Unknown

Don't brag about tomorrow, since you don't know what the day will bring. Proverbs 27:1 (NLT)

PRAYER FOR TODAY: *Lord, help me overcome this spirit of rebellion and procrastination that wants to consume me. Help me get back on track TODAY and not be so lazy that I continually put off the hard work until tomorrow. Help me face the hard facts of life today and get busy with the hard work necessary to conquer these weight issues TODAY. In Your name I ask all these things, Lord Jesus. Amen.*

SEPTEMBER 9
He Cares About My Calories Too?

This morning I was spending some time with God, reading the Word and praying and not feeling particularly motivated to come downstairs and attack my menu planner for the day. It started out feeling like one of *those days* when all I could think of is *why bother?*

As I was reading, I came across a Scripture that reminded me of the relevancy of God's Word for my why bother attitude. *Look straight ahead, and fix your eyes on what lies before you. Mark out a straight path for your feet; stay on the safe path. Don't get sidetracked; keep your feet from following evil.* Proverbs 4:25-27 (NLT)

I'm sure when King Solomon penned these words he clearly wasn't worried about straying from his menu plan! Solomon was noted as being one of the wisest men that ever lived and he possessed said wisdom as a direct result of praying and specifically asking God for the wisdom to govern his people.

When reading Scripture – the inspired Word of God, we are reminded that there is a great big world out there and God cares for *the least of these* – meaning people like us. God is omnipotent. He is everywhere, all the time and sees everything that's happening over the earth, under the earth and all around the globe. He cares for us and every problem we struggle with – even something as self-absorbing as our daily diet and calorie allotment.

Taking a lesson from King Solomon, we need to pray for wisdom in *every* area of our life – including help with our daily calorie count. Perhaps God in His wisdom will not only grant us wisdom for the things we ask for, but mercy and grace for the things we *don't* ask for.

Remember this. When people choose to withdraw far from a fire, the fire continues to give warmth, but they grow cold. When people choose to withdraw far from light, the light continues to be bright in itself but they are in darkness. This is also the case when people withdraw from God. ~ Augustine

Give all your worries and cares to God, for he cares about you. 1 Peter 5:7 (NLT)

PRAYER FOR TODAY: *Lord, I know You are everywhere. I KNOW You are listening and You care for me. Help me to share the goodness of God with those that I meet. Help me continue to fix my eyes on you; stay on the path set before me and not get sidetracked. In Your name I ask all these things, Lord Jesus. Amen.*

SEPTEMBER 10
Stupid Never Stops – Stupid Never Sleeps

After the week I've had I'm convinced there's a giant cloud of stupid hovering over the northern hemisphere and no one is immune from it. My husband and I have both had several business dealings with people on the phone this week. Between the two of us it appears that the majority of people we've dealt with have all been infected with this special kind of *stupid*; making for disastrous outcomes. It's like all of these businesses are in cahoots trying to out-stupid one another.

Normally I'd be eating my way through all this frustration, but I'm doing my best to avoid emotional eating. In lieu of mindless snacking, I've turned to my other least favorite bad habit – chewing on my fingernails. My fingers have been reduced to bloody nubbins and I'm running out of emotional outlets.

It would appear as though the enemy has stepped up his assault tactics since I've recently committed to a new ministry. By now I should recognize his plan of attack, as the enemy has resorted to this type of onslaught before. If he can't bring me down one way – he tries another strategy.

The enemy's been firing everything in his arsenal to bring me down. Being a veteran of this type of assault, I've strapped on my armor. I've donned my helmet of salvation; my belt of truth is cinched tightly; my shoes of peace have a little wiggle room, because if I'm still this upset about *stupid* behavior, I'm not walking in total peace yet. I'm wearing my armor of righteousness and doing my best to wield my shield of faith. I've been attacking with the sword of the Spirit (the Word of God), but man oh man … *stupid never stops – stupid never sleeps!*

Some challenges are tougher than others. Resisting the urge to snack through life's challenges is a major victory. If you're like me, however, and you've let the enemy manipulate you with some other bad habit we are a long, long way from winning the war. The world is filled with challenges and stupid people. We cannot let the stupidity be our ruin. The war can only be won, one battle at a time, one stupid at a time.

Maturity is achieved when a person accepts life as full of tension.
~ Joshua L. Liebman

Stay alert! Watch out for your great enemy, the devil. He prowls around like a roaring lion, looking for someone to devour. 1 Peter 5:8 (NLT)

PRAYER FOR TODAY: Lord, I pray for a double measure of peace. Help me to curb my frustration and not overreact to things that are out of my control. Continue to give me strength to conquer those snacking urges so I can not only win the battles but win the war. In Your name I ask all these things, Lord Jesus. Amen.

SEPTEMBER 11
The First Step

The last couple of weeks I've met a number of women who are battling serious food addictions similar to mine. When it comes right down to it, many of us suffer from some sort of crippling addiction. We may as well all be walking around with stickers hanging from our necks labeling us "handicapped."

I'd dare to say that the majority of people we know or pass on the streets are addicted to something, if not food, we're addicted to fear, worry, self-hatred, pity, etc. I've met so many women who are living with the pain of self-loathing so severe it drives them to seek solace in food, alcohol, pills and a whole host of other substances. Life can be so cruel and unfair and there are very few who go their entire lives completely unscathed. Many of us are scarred and hiding something.

I heard one woman say, "I know I need help, but I don't know what the next step is. Where do I start?"

Realizing that we are loved by God feels like the best place to start. Accepting that you are loved totally, completely and exactly for who you are, at the weight you are at and in the body you are in – that's the all-important first step – *in my opinion*. God loves you – even if you've been rejected by your spouse, your parents, siblings, children or every single person in your life – GOD LOVES YOU.

Once we wrap our brains around that truth we can begin to move forward. God is waiting for us to come to Him. He wants to shower His love, mercy and grace upon us, but we must first seek Him. The best way to seek Him is immerse yourself in God's Word. The Bible truly is the *Instruction Manual for Life*. Every answer to every problem can be found by reading and studying God's Word.

Okay, maybe that's two steps: accept that God loves you AND dig into the Word of God. After those two steps, everything that follows are baby steps.

Peace is not the absence of affliction, but the presence of God. ~ Author Unknown

So the LORD must wait for you to come to him so he can show you his love and compassion. For the LORD is a faithful God. Blessed are those who wait for his help. Isaiah 30:18 (NLT)

PRAYER FOR TODAY: *Thank You for loving me unconditionally just as I am. Help me not to question that unconditional love that You have for me – just accept it. I pray for wisdom and boldness to be able to share this knowledge with others who are hurting or who are lost. Use me as You see fit, Lord. In Your name I ask all these things, Lord Jesus. Amen.*

SEPTEMBER 12
Imagine That

An imagination can be a blessing or a curse depending on how far you're willing to let it go. My imagination has served me well in the past as I love to write fiction and tend to be a bit of an overachiever in the imagination department.

I'm fairly good at keeping my imagination under control and out of dangerous situations – most of the time. Last night proved somewhat challenging for me though as I was reading before bedtime, which is my normal practice.

I'm halfway through a Stephanie Plum book by Janet Evanovich and doggone if that Stephanie Plum and her sidekick Lula don't get me in more trouble when I read about their latest adventures. These two girls are constantly eating donuts, pizza, sub sandwiches, fried chicken and a whole host of other assorted highly caloric foods.

When I lie in bed and read about all the delicious baked goods they're enjoying it makes me so crazy I can't sleep without dreaming of jelly filled donuts. Then I wake up hungry for junk food and can't go back to sleep without craving forbidden foods.

The Bible reminds us to constantly renew our minds and to guard our thoughts. As soon as we feel our thoughts starting to wander into dangerous territory, we've got to shore up our minds and put a stop to those wanderings. There's nothing wrong with a vivid imagination as long as it's channeled appropriately and we don't live in the land of make believe.

When we want to think about eating donuts, try chewing on *greater is he that is in me than he that is in the world* (1 John 4:4). We must never forget we have an enemy *roaming about seeking whom he may devour* (1 Peter 5:8). If we don't want to be devoured by the enemy, we would do best to keep our imagination in its place and only let it out once we've tamed it.

Think left and think right and think low and think high. Oh, the thinks you can think up if only you try! ~ Dr. Seuss, Oh, the Thinks You Can Think!

Don't copy the behavior and customs of this world, but let God transform you into a new person by changing the way you think. Then you will learn to know God's will for you, which is good and pleasing and perfect. Romans 12:2 (NLT)

PRAYER FOR TODAY: Lord, help me to control my thoughts and keep me from letting my mind wander into dangerous territory. Be the caretaker of my thoughts and allow them to grow and flourish into things for Your glory and edification. In Your name I ask all these things, Lord Jesus. Amen.

SEPTEMBER 13
Exploding Choices

I was watching a program on the Discovery Science network yesterday about a giant whale. I missed the beginning of the show, but for some reason researchers were transporting this whale on a flatbed semi-truck through some Asian village, moving it to a research facility. Sadly, during transport the poor whale exploded and died.

It was pretty disgusting as tons of blood and various internal parts of this whale spewed all over the street and the fronts of businesses. It was very graphic and very tragic. In fact, it got a little too graphic for me and I changed the channel.

As a "recovering" food addict, I can relate to this tragic whale tale. I've spent many miserable nights with a stomach so full of food, I was certain I was going to explode. Thankfully I haven't had *one of those* episodes in a while. I can only pray that my "gluttony demons" have been conquered, as there's nothing worse than feeling as though you've eaten yourself into a food coma. An overly full stomach makes you feel as though you're going to detonate with the slightest provocation; mere movement brings with it disastrous consequences. The only thing worse is the shame hangover that follows.

I do not live in the land of guilt and shame any longer and whatever sins I've committed in the past have been confessed, forgiven and erased. I'm not too full of pride though that I don't appreciate the occasional reminder of how far God has brought me – even if my reminder comes from a program about exploding whales.

We have the power to choose. We can choose to stick to our plan or we can choose to eat the wrong foods. We can choose to accept the Spirit of conviction and hopefully learn from our mistakes, or we can choose condemnation. If we choose to overindulge we have to accept that we've willingly chosen to lie around in misery worrying that we're going to explode like some giant whale. It's always our choice.

Courage doesn't always roar. Sometimes courage is the little voice at the end of the day that says I'll try again tomorrow. ~ Mary Anne Radmacher

Because we have these promises, dear friends, let us cleanse ourselves from everything that can defile our body or spirit. And let us work toward complete holiness because we fear God. 2 Corinthians 7:1 (NLT)

PRAYER FOR TODAY: *Lord, thank You that You have given me free will to make my own choices and decisions. Help me always to employ common sense and wisdom and not give in to temptation. Help me to stay strong of mind, spirit and body and put my trust in You when I can't trust myself to make the right choices. In Your name I ask all these things, Lord Jesus. Amen.*

SEPTEMBER 14
Life's Multiple Choice

After my quiet time, prayer and meditation this morning I had one of those epiphanies that I can't believe I didn't realize sooner. It was like the consummate *"well – duh"* moment. As I was reading I came across a verse in Proverbs that hit me between the eyes.

Proverbs 18:20-21 reads as follows: *Words satisfy the soul as food satisfies the stomach; the right words on a person's lips bring satisfaction. Those who love to talk will experience consequences, for the tongue can kill or nourish life.* (NLT)

I got to chewing on that for a while and realized how many times I have killed my own success by the words I speak. If I had a dollar for every time I spoke out loud to myself or someone else, *"I'm never going to lose this weight."* Or worse, *"I'm just fat and I need to accept that. I may as well give up and eat whatever I want. It's no use anyway!"*

Our negative talk has the same consequences as if we took a gun and shot ourselves in the foot because we've virtually stopped ourselves in our tracks with harmful words. Our words can hurt us. Our words have the power to kill us.

I actually read this Proverb several days ago and have been meditating on it all week. Part of me argues that I'm not anywhere near as bad as I used to be. But in reality, I'm still a really long, long way from eliminating the negative words from my vocabulary altogether. Replacing a positive for a negative statement may seem like a simple solution, but it's far harder than one would imagine. Especially if you've grown up in an environment that all you ever heard spoken over you or about you was negative.

Life is a multiple choice test. We can either (a) let our words satisfy the soul or (b) we can let them kill our life and experience the negative consequences. When it's spelled out like that is there really any choice? The answer is obvious. Life really is that easy.

Life is like riding a bicycle - in order to keep your balance, you must keep moving. ~ Albert Einstein

Instead, let the Spirit renew your thoughts and attitudes. Ephesians 4:21-24 (NLT)

PRAYER FOR TODAY: *Lord, I pray that You would renew my thoughts and my mind DAILY. Before I speak any negative thoughts running through my brain, I ask that You would snatch them from my thoughts making it impossible for me to voice them. Strengthen my mind and my will to succeed every single day. Help me to stop killing my success with my words. In Your name I ask all these things, Lord Jesus. Amen.*

SEPTEMBER 15
Let's Get Ready To Fumble

My family and extended families are a bunch of sports nuts. No, not even just nuts – we border on the freakish side epitomizing all that the title "fan" encompasses in the word "fanatic." The last few years we've adopted barbecue/ brunch Sundays during football season alternating at each other's homes.

As much as I love these weekly family get-togethers, I'm a little less excited this year because I have been working so hard the last many months to lose weight. It's really tough to make a breakfast brunch healthy when your guests are clamoring for hash browns, bacon and pastries.

The barbecues prove equally as challenging as they usually demand burgers, bratwursts, potato salad and chips. Somehow Egg Beaters or turkey burgers don't have the same appeal to the non-dieting population as it does for someone like me.

Because we drew hosting duties this weekend, we're systematically doing our best to weave in some healthier options. We're barbecuing skinless, boneless chicken and making a large healthy salad. I'm hoping to let some of my healthier habits rub off on the masses, rather than letting their bad habits (and my old bad habits) infiltrate my rock hard convictions to win this battle once and for all.

Lucky for me I don't have to depend on my own will power during mealtime as I'm leaning on the power and strength of the Holy Spirit. While everyone thinks I'm silently praying for our team to win, I'm quietly uttering my prayers for strength to resist the M&Ms my in-laws brought to share.

Surviving an entire NFL football season will undoubtedly require some super strength worthy of a super bowl victory. But then our God is awesome and will never leave us nor forsake us and we KNOW with God ALL things are possible – even resisting *fanatical* football foods.

The reason women don't play football is because eleven of them would never wear the same outfit in public. ~ Phyllis Diller

Dear children, keep away from anything that might take God's place in your hearts. 1 John 5:21 (NLT)

PRAYER FOR TODAY: *Lord, thank You for blessing me with family. I pray for strength to survive the next few months without back tracking and undoing all of the hard work I've put into losing weight. Give me superhuman strength to resist unhealthy foods and help me continue to move forward on my weight loss journey. In Your name I ask all these things, Lord Jesus. Amen.*

SEPTEMBER 16
YOU are NOT the Boss of Me

Recently my husband and I hosted a surprise baby shower as part of our marriage small group. The evening included an amazing potluck dinner and of course – cake. You cannot attend a baby shower without cake; that would be un-American.

As hosts, we ended up with our share of potluck and cake leftovers, *again*. I did my best to delegate and sent a fair portion of high calorie foods to work with my husband today. Most of what I saved was healthy foods such as the remains of the fruit tray and the roasted chicken.

My biggest challenge will be holding on to the big piece of cake I saved for my grandson. I'm thinking this one piece of cake must possess some sort of supernatural mystical power though, because I swear I can hear it calling my name!

I've walked past that piece of cake many times already this morning. With each pass I find myself devising a plan that would allow me to eat that butter cream rose on the top without getting caught. If I remove it, there will undoubtedly be a tell-tale gaping hole. I considered the option of forking the cake to appease my lust. Forking is a verb, which means to help yourself to a sliver of cake by using the straight edge of your fork to smooth off any rough-cut edges. You can systematically fork away a slab of cake without actually cutting a whole piece of cake.

For temptations such as these we've got to pull ourselves together and remember that we do not have to bow down to the cake. The cake does not control us. We can control our thoughts and our actions. The only power cake has over us is the power we choose to give it. Repeat after me: CAKE IS NOT THE BOSS OF ME!

This needs to be my mantra today. Perhaps that mantra should be accompanied by a string of prayer beads crafted out of celery stalks and carrot sticks – at least until the cake has safely left the premises. We can do this if we remember we can do all things through Christ who gives us strength.

Being out of control is one of the worst feelings in the world, sometimes even worse than pain. It is its own kind of pain. ~ Terri Guillemets

I can do everything through him who gives me strength. Philippians 4:13 (NLT)

PRAYER FOR TODAY: Lord, thank You for Your constant presence in my life. Give me the strength I need to resist any and all temptations. Help me not to bow down to the lust of my flesh. Help me to make right choices and recognize that I already have a strong will and a strong mind; I simply need to choose to use them. In Your name I ask all these things, Lord Jesus. Amen.

SEPTEMBER 17
Craving Success

I was reading Scripture last night and came across this verse: *So I say, let the Holy Spirit guide your lives. Then you won't be doing what your sinful nature craves.* (Galatians 5:16) I thought, *yeah, that sounds great in theory* but what do we do when our sinful nature trumps what the spirit wants?

Yesterday's cake was nearly my undoing – especially after attending my support group last night. Because that class has a way of purging my innermost secrets and has me exposing my hidden scars, I tend to feel like I need a treat after all that purging. My feelings and my emotions screamed at me all the way home to go in and show that last piece of cake who's boss. When we listen to our feelings and emotions though, we end up in all kinds of trouble.

I ignored the cake and went to bed, but that one small piece of cake haunted me in my dreams and I slept fitfully, plagued by bizarre dreams waking this morning with a slight shame hangover from indulging in my sleep. While I ignored it in my waking hours, that piece of cake bossed me around in my sleeping hours still causing me shame and guilt and I didn't even consciously do anything.

Oddly enough the topic of discussion at my support group last night was *what does success look like to you?* For years I believed success would be the perfect number on the scale. In the last few months, however, I'm learning success for me is about figuring out what drives me to follow my lustful desires and figuring out why I eat when I'm not even hungry. Success is figuring out WHY my emotions need to be fed. The ultimate success is being set-free from *whatever* that driving force is.

Today is a new day. Hopefully today's challenges will remind us that if we seek help from the Holy Spirit *before* we give in to our sinful nature and its cravings we can avoid those snacking meltdowns.

If at first you don't succeed, you're running about average. ~ M.H. Alderson

The sinful nature wants to do evil, which is just the opposite of what the Spirit wants. And the Spirit gives us desires that are the opposite of what the sinful nature desires. These two forces are constantly fighting each other, so you are not free to carry out your good intentions. Galatians 5:17 (NLT)

PRAYER FOR TODAY: *Jesus, Jesus, Jesus; some days that's all my spirit knows to pray. I need Your help as I'm feeling particularly vulnerable and weak today. Infuse me with Your strength and Your will so I won't have to keep relying on my own will and strength. In Your name I ask all these things, Lord Jesus. Amen.*

SEPTEMBER 18
Magnesium the Magnificent

Last week I was reading a book about food cravings and food addictions and I came across an interesting tidbit regarding supplements. It's not just emotions that drive us crazy and cause us to crave sugar or salty things. Our bodies often times crave things because they are depleted of certain vitamins or minerals.

One suggestion to combat chocolate cravings was to take magnesium tablets. Magnesium helps regulate blood sugar levels, promotes normal blood pressure, and is known to be involved in energy metabolism. Eating a diet that contains a wide variety of legumes, nuts, whole grains, and vegetables will help you meet your daily dietary need for magnesium.

Ideally if we are eating a healthy balanced diet we shouldn't need to add a lot of extra vitamins to our regime. Many health care professionals recommend a daily multi-vitamin. Many of the vitamins we need can be obtained from the foods we eat; but a magnesium supplement may be beneficial to stop chocolate cravings in their tracks.

I was headed to a weekly meeting yesterday and decided to test the magnesium theory as the group hostess always has several bowls of M&Ms scattered about. I never actually believed that restraint was possible, so imagine my surprise when I didn't sample the M&Ms. The magnesium appeared to override my chocolate craving allowing me to resist all temptations yesterday.

Perhaps it was the magnesium doing its job, or perhaps it was the many prayers I prayed beforehand, but the end result was that I bypassed the candy dish. It doesn't hurt to pray for what we want – in fact, I'm certain that prayer makes ALL the difference. Today I am a believer in magnesium, but I've *always* been a believer in prayer. Now *that's* truly magnificent!

Chocolate is like medicine – but as with medicine, the key is the proper dose. Don't overdo it. ~ Edward "Grandpa" Jones

That's why I take pleasure in my weaknesses, and in the insults, hardships, persecutions, and troubles that I suffer for Christ. For when I am weak, then I am strong. 2 Corinthians 12:10 (NLT)

PRAYER FOR TODAY: Lord, thank You for helping me to resist temptation. May I be infused with strength for each day and strength to get me through every temptation. Give me this day, my daily bread. In Your name I ask all these things, Lord Jesus. Amen.

SEPTEMBER 19
Is it Just Me?

Today was a day that had me feeling out of sorts; a day that I questioned – *what is wrong with me?* I couldn't help but wonder: *is there anybody out there who struggles with food addictions as much as me?*

The enemy would like for us to believe that we are crazy and no one is as messed up as we are. Oftentimes he will try to attack us early in the morning before we've barely put our feet on the floor by making us think self-destructive thoughts like, *"What is wrong with me?"* or *"Am I crazy?"*

For those days that we wake up on *the wrong side of the bed* without any apparent provocation, it may be an attack from Satan or it simply might mean that we are fatigued from a restless night of sleep. We need to be wise enough to allow a few minutes for prayer or meditation before we begin our day. Oftentimes merely an unexpected change in schedule can be reason enough to make us feel out of sorts or out of balance.

That was true for me today as I bypassed my morning time with God to run errands. By skipping my prayer and quiet time with God, it was easy for me to slip over into that *"what is wrong with me"* funk making me more vulnerable to Satan's attacks on my mind.

Perhaps it's time to consider a tattoo for each arm as it's likely the enemy will always be looking for an open door with our thought life. We should tattoo the word BALANCE on one arm and *THERE IS NOTHING WRONG WITH ME* on the other. Then perhaps we can shut the door on the prince of lies once and for all and keep him from stealing our peace.

If we had no faults of our own, we would not take so much pleasure in noticing those of others. ~ Francois duc de la Rochefoucauld

So let us come boldly to the throne of our gracious God. There we will receive his mercy, and we will find grace to help us when we need it most. Hebrews 4:16 (NLT)

PRAYER FOR TODAY: *Lord, I cling to the promises in Your Word and ask for favor in resisting temptation. I give You my mind, my body and my will and I pray that You will heal me of my shortcomings, my addictions and my fears. I am Your servant and my desire is to serve You completely with all that I am. In Your name I ask all these things, Lord Jesus. Amen.*

SEPTEMBER 20
Oh No She Didn't!

I have this friend who called me a few days ago to chit-chat. We're not what I call "close friends" but we have a history that takes us back a couple of decades, so we've stayed in touch. She's currently on yet *another* diet and even though she's a bit of a yo-yo dieter like me, she tends to lose weight much easier than I do.

She started bragging about all the weight she's dropped in the last few weeks (over 20 pounds). In a few weeks, she's lost what it has taken me over eight months to lose. As I listened I found my blood pressure rising with each passing minute we spent on the phone. She knows me well enough to know my struggles, but she seems to have no filter on her mouth about speaking her mind and hurting my feelings.

What do we do when well-meaning "friends" speak carelessly with little or no regard to our feelings regarding sensitive subjects?

We aren't supposed to covet what our neighbor has, so for us to be jealous of another's weight loss is very simply – sin. We are also instructed to *love our neighbor as our self* which seems easy when it's someone quite loveable. It's not so easy to follow through with though when our neighbor is altogether unlovable because they speak hurtful words to us.

Not everyone is schooled in proper manners so I've chosen to overlook her careless bragging based on the likelihood that she simply doesn't know any better.

The worst possible thing to do when someone makes you feel this way is to resort to food for comfort. Even though my natural inclination is to want to soothe my hurt, jealous feelings with a bowl of ice cream, I chose rather to go for a walk and air my grievances to God. He's a great sounding board and always cognizant of our innermost hurts. He knows when we hurt and offers compassion through His healing words in Scripture. He is a true friend when you need one most.

Our most difficult task as a friend is to offer understanding when we don't understand. ~ Robert Brault

Friends come and friends go, but a true friend sticks by you like family. Proverbs 18:24 (NLT)

PRAYER FOR TODAY: *Lord, help me not to be bitter or angry with friends who experience success while I cannot. May I be a true blue friend who is supportive and compassionate and offers words of encouragement rather than doubt, despair or pessimism. Help me always to learn from others – be it good things I can duplicate or negative things that teach me a better way. In Your name I ask all these things, Lord Jesus. Amen.*

SEPTEMBER 21
NO – GO – STOP – EAT

Weekends can be tough when you're married to someone who is the opposite of you. My husband is a Type "A" kind of guy who has two speeds when it comes to weekends and that's go, go, go and eat, eat, eat. Unlike me, he doesn't have any kind of weight problem. He thinks go; I think no! He thinks eat; I think STOP!

My husband thinks now that football season is here, football equals food and lots of it. During football season he craves pizza, wings, burgers and hot dogs – all *terrible* foods to eat when you're trying to lose weight.

My husband is working to meet me halfway. He's barbecuing chicken without the skin. We're passing on the deep-dish pizza and settling on the thin crust making sure to skip the extra cheese, pepperoni and sausage.

In a perfect world, I would love to throw caution to the wind and eat to my heart's content during football season. Oh wait, that's what I did last year and my world was far from perfect. "Caution throwing" was not the answer.

If we are still a ways off from achieving the weight loss success we're hoping for, it's best to focus on one day at a time. What can we do today to achieve progress? Don't focus on the one piece of pizza you allowed yourself to have, but rather celebrate that you didn't eat the second piece that you really wanted. If you're going to have the burger, try eating it "bun-less" and skip the mayo. Fill up on salad making sure to stick with lower-calorie dressings avoiding the cheese and croutons altogether.

On days when we feel the most desperate, that's cause to press in and draw closer to God. Don't be afraid to share your burdens with Him, as no one understands your struggles better than God. He knows what temptation feels like and He will help you through this. He's not giving up on us and neither should we.

The road to success is dotted with many tempting parking places. ~ Author Unknown

Don't be afraid, for I am with you. Don't be discouraged, for I am your God. I will strengthen you and help you. I will hold you up with my victorious right hand. Isaiah 41:10 (NLT)

PRAYER FOR TODAY: *Lord, thank You that You hear my prayers and You see my heart. You know that my desire is to serve You and take the best care of my body that I can. Help me to stay the course and not get sidetracked – even by weekends or football. I ask Your help in all areas, but especially for my commitment to get healthy. In Your name I ask all these things, Lord Jesus. Amen.*

SEPTEMBER 22
Deliver Me from Me-vil

Some days I get so tired of fighting with myself over food. The last few days my prayers have been comprised of not even prayers really – but something akin to pleading … *Pleeaassseeee God, deliver me from evil. Deliver me from ME!*

When we pray these kinds of pleading prayers we cannot be unhappy about how God may choose to deliver us at any given time. God delivered me from myself with a nasty 24-hour stomach bug that very effectively kept me from eating most of the day. I was limited to soup and toast with nary a craving for anything other than bland foods.

I'm a firm believer that "If you want specific – you have to pray specific." It really is okay to ask God for specific things when we pray, but that doesn't always mean He's going to answer our prayers exactly as we would like Him to. He knows when we are asking for something that doesn't line up with His plan for us, or if we are asking for something that will hurt us.

Whatever area we're struggling with in regards to our weight loss plan, be it keeping our menu, measuring food portions accurately, or a simple desire to cut out sugar from our diet – it's okay to ask God for exactly what we want. God isn't a genie in a lamp who will answer all our prayers simply because we want Him to. He is a loving Father who knows what we need without even asking, but He is waiting for us to engage our faith by asking Him in prayer.

Over time the closer we become with the Father, the easier it will be for us to ask for things according to His will rather than our will. Prayer really does work – we just need to be careful what we pray for. When we pray, we stand believing in faith and trust that God knows what is best for us and He will answer our prayers according to His will, according to His timetable, not ours.

Prayer is not merely an occasional impulse to which we respond when we are in trouble: prayer is a life attitude. ~ Walter A. Mueller

But when you pray, go into your room, close the door and pray to your Father, who is unseen. Then your Father, who sees what is done in secret, will reward you. Matthew 6:6 (NLT)

PRAYER FOR TODAY: Lord, thank You because I know You hear our prayers. Help me to fix my eyes on You; help me to continue to seek Your presence in my life and to rely on you for strength as I walk this path to freedom. I pray against discouragement and I believe in You for success and victory. In Your name I ask all these things, Lord Jesus. Amen.

SEPTEMBER 23
Waist Management

I was watching an episode of Dr. Oz recently that highlighted the weight loss journey of four different people in New York. Dr. Oz visited them at their apartments and cleaned house, instructing them to throw out all the junk food – which was nearly everything in each of their houses. He took them shopping to replace their bad foods with healthy foods.

His goal was to get them to reduce harmful weight around their mid-sections as extra weight in our bellies leads to heart problems. (Men should be no more than 35" at the waist; women should be 32" or less at the waist.) He gave them a basic exercise plan which involved tracking the number of steps walked each day along with simple strength resistance training they could do at home without joining a gym.

What he suggested are the same things we've been incorporating and practicing since January 1st this year. He gave them the basics without actually getting into the emotional part of why people eat. His program dealt with eating right, reading food labels and balancing physical activity.

This program simply reinforced to me that when you balance healthy eating with moderate exercise – you will lose weight. It's that simple principle of burning more than you take in. It's the science of the human body and it *should* work this way if you apply it to your life.

Clearly emotional issues are harder to deal with than the simple science of burning calories. Rather than losing another 30 pounds in a short amount of time just for the sake of losing weight, it's important to continue this slow uncovering process of what's at the bottom of our emotional heap. In the long run dealing with what-ever's underneath will insure lifelong success because we won't have to worry about recurring issues. Ultimately that's the most important goal we can achieve – healing from the inside out *and* lasting weight loss.

The only disability in life is a bad attitude. ~ Scott Hamilton

It is not that we think we are qualified to do anything on our own. Our qualification comes from God. 2 Corinthians 3:5 (NLT)

PRAYER FOR TODAY: *Lord, I pray that You will give me everything I need to handle whatever situations may come my way. I pray for daily wisdom, common sense, strength, courage and tenacity. May I offer words of encouragement to others and always have a smile on my face and hope in my heart. In Your name I ask all these things, Lord Jesus. Amen.*

SEPTEMBER 24
Duck – Life Comes at you Hard

I love that the God of the universe takes the time to bring us back to reality when we get so caught up in our own little world or our occasional pity party. He's full of mercy to let us know daily He loves us, but yet gently reminds us that He didn't create the sun to rise and set around us. That's a good reminder to get occasionally.

I have a group of friends that are part of the married couples group that meets in my home a couple times each month. One of the gentlemen in our group is at the top of a transplant list in desperate need of both a new kidney and a pancreas. He and his wife got the call to head to the hospital yesterday as both organs were available for him and surgery was scheduled for late last night. I don't know all the details but the message came back a couple hours later that one of the organs was no good so the surgery was cancelled.

This morning I awoke with a spirit of gratitude. My problems – my bum knee, hormonal power surges and my ever present obsession with food, diet and exercise don't even register on the Richter scale of life's problems when compared to a friend needing a double organ transplant.

If we've battled a weight problem our whole life or have a long-standing addiction to food, it's easy to get caught up in our own little world and ignore everything else. Sometimes I DO forget that there are people out there fighting far bigger giants than the ones I fight to lose weight.

Today, why not set aside this day to devote to prayer for others and refuse to think about our weight loss issues. Sometimes it's good to remember that life comes at us hard and all the time spent in selfish pursuit of our own vain "problems" is time wasted.

Some days we have to simply say, thanks for the wake-up call and another reminder that it's NOT all about me, God!

Life is not a final. It's daily pop quizzes. ~ Author Unknown

"God's way is perfect. All the LORD's promises prove true. He is a shield for all who look to him for protection." 2 Samuel 22:31 (The Message Bible)

PRAYER FOR TODAY: *Lord, thank You for reminders that my life is only as good as I choose to make it. Be with my friends who are battling difficulties that are beyond compare and shower them with blessings and mercy. Thank You for all the many blessings in my life I take for granted. Be with me and fill me with Your Spirit daily and help me to be a blessing to others rather than hoarding my gifts for my own selfish needs. In Your name I ask all these things, Lord Jesus. Amen.*

SEPTEMBER 25
Prisoners of Flesh

I watched a Tom Hanks movie recently called *The Terminal* that was made in 2004. Tom's character is a foreign gentleman, who while en route to New York City, learns his country is at war. Upon landing he discovers the country's government has been taken over and the country no longer exists. Tom has no country to return to so the U.S. government won't allow him access into the U.S.

While I was watching this movie I found myself drawing parallels to this poor guy imprisoned in an airport to that of someone who is struggling with obesity. As anyone who has ever struggled with obesity can tell you, there are many days that it is easy to feel imprisoned in these fleshly bodies that we have.

Even though we have the freedom to move around and interact with people, there are many circumstances when we feel trapped in a body that doesn't feel like home to us. Many days we wake up thinking, "Whose body is this? This is not the body of my dreams! Where is my *real* body and when am I going to get it back?"

The main movie character had freedom to move about the airport, he got a job, made scores of friends – but he was still a prisoner in the airport. Many of us have limited freedom at our current weight. Buying clothes becomes a challenge; fitting into a seat on an airplane is difficult; even climbing in and out of the car can leave us winded.

It's important not to give up on your journey to liberate yourself from your prison of excess body weight. Choosing to eat healthy, balanced meals; engaging in moderate exercise; tracking your food portions and sharing your struggles or victories with an accountability partner are necessary keys that will unlock you from your prison of obesity. Fighting for our freedom is up to us.

I don't suffer from insanity. I enjoy every minute of it. ~ Author Unknown

Do not be afraid of what you are about to suffer. I tell you, the devil will put some of you in prison to test you, and you will suffer persecution for ten days. Be faithful, even to the point of death, and I will give you the crown of life. Revelation 2:10 (NIV)

PRAYER FOR TODAY: Lord, I know that You came to set the captives free – of which I am one. Release me from these imprisoning thoughts that bind my mind and have me believing the lies of the enemy. Set me free to be me and help me to appreciate all that You died to give me. Even if I never achieve the "perfect weight" please help me to love myself at whatever weight I am. In Your name I ask all these things, Lord Jesus. Amen.

SEPTEMBER 26
If a Tree Falls in the Forest

If a tree falls in the forest and no one is around to see or hear it, does it still make a loud noise? If you're playing golf by yourself and you get a hole in one and no one witnesses it, does it still count? If you have a perfect day on your food plan and no one is around to see it, was it really a successful day? The answer to all of these questions is YES! (Except the hole in one thing because there are a bunch of PGA rules to follow. Sorry!)

A friend in my weight loss support group struggles at her job to stay away from the vending machines. The combination of unresolved emotional issues and a stressful job push her with an inhuman force to visit the vending machines during the course of her work week.

Last week she asked for prayer to resist the vending machine temptation. She confessed she'd had a good week avoiding the machines but she also said no one at work was aware of her struggle with food. No one noticed she'd practiced restraint. She was disappointed because even though she'd conquered a major foe that week, she was the only person aware of the battle taking place – so did it still matter?

Seldom do any of us have any clue to the inner battles other people are fighting. We need to remember that whatever victory we achieve on a personal level is in fact a victory worth celebrating because it's important to our own personal character development.

If we have a perfect day on our food plan it doesn't matter if anyone else is interested or not. It matters to us and it matters to God. It's okay for us to celebrate our victories especially if we conquer something that's been plaguing us for a long period of time.

The smell of victory is always a heady perfume and it's okay to linger in the aromatic mist of your success. Don't be afraid to give yourself a pat on the back when you resist those temptations or have a perfect day. If a tree falls in the woods and no one hears it, who cares? A perfect eating day … now that's worth celebrating!

Life is a long lesson in humility. ~ James M. Barrie

This is the day the LORD has made. We will rejoice and be glad in it. Psalm 118:24 (NLT)

PRAYER FOR TODAY: *Lord, this is the day You have made and I DO rejoice in it. Thank You for life's many blessings. I pray for a renewed excitement for each day and a servant's heart to follow You. I pray for success in all that I put my hand to and I ask Your favor and grace in times of need. In Your name, Lord Jesus. Amen.*

SEPTEMBER 27
How Now Frau Cow

Several years ago I worked for a large weight loss organization. It was my job to greet the members, weigh them and record their progress. One day a large woman came in – and by large I mean easily six feet tall who fit the description of "big boned." She strode to the desk wearing golf attire, complete with a golf glove, golf cleats, and carrying her 7-iron.

The minute she opened her mouth to speak her German heritage was unmistakable. She leaned over the desk and spoke in her heavily accented native tongue, *"I am on 10th hole tee box; as I lean over ball – my pants – they spleeeet! I am fat cow! Must lose weight!"*

Her commanding presence and her bold proclamation made me want to chuckle. She avoided the litany of excuses that many new members rattle off when joining. She returned the following three weeks in a row, by which time she'd successfully lost between 10-12 pounds.

She informed me she would not be back since she had lost sufficient weight without fearing another pants-splitting episode. She had the knowledge to maintain her weight loss,. She didn't feel the need to continue because she was satisfied. *"I am no longer cow,"* she declared.

Even though this woman referred to herself when she joined as a fat cow, she didn't spend the next three weeks coming to class reminding everyone of what a cow she was. For many of us the temptation to constantly berate ourselves is one we can't resist. Especially if we're dragging around a considerable amount of excess weight; we think with every step, *"I'm such a cow"* or *"I'm such a pig!"*

Along this journey we must be extremely careful about the words we speak about ourselves. We should only allow positive words and thoughts in our mind so that we can speak only positive affirmations. Our words can kill us and impede our weight loss progress. Remember we must ALWAYS think before we speak!

The kindest word in all the world is the unkind word, unsaid. ~ Author Unknown

Take control of what I say, O LORD, and guard my lips. Psalm 141:3 (NLT)

PRAYER FOR TODAY: *Lord, I pray that You will keep watch over the door of my lips and help me to control my tongue, my thoughts and my attitude. Help me not give in to despair and fall victim to self-deprecating words. I pray for a daily rest and renewal of my mind, body and spirit. In Your name I ask all these things, Lord Jesus. Amen.*

SEPTEMBER 28
The Thinks I Thunk

It can be a dangerous thing to spend too much time inside our own head. If you are someone who leans towards being introverted, the temptation to carry on long conversations with yourself can oftentimes lead to hosting a full on pity-party if you're not careful.

As a writer who works from home it's easy for me to spend days holed up in my house communicating primarily through email and instant messaging. That gives me a lot of alone time with me and my thoughts. Too much time in my own head can start me thinking about how much farther I have to go before I will be at a comfortable weight. Those feelings can quickly segue into despair if I'm not careful.

If you are easily susceptible to negative thoughts and attitudes, be on the offensive by keeping positive reminders and affirmations where you can see them throughout your day. Hang Post-it notes with Scriptures in a prominent place like your bathroom mirror, the fridge, your desk or your car dashboard for constant reminders.

Write Scriptures on notecards and carry them in your purse or your pocket so they will be easily accessible to you when you find yourself slipping into negative thoughts or despair; or for when you're faced with temptation. Writing out Scriptures repeatedly helps you to easily memorize them and get them down in your spirit for meditation.

A change of scenery can do wonders for your attitude. If you're stuck in an enclosed office for long periods of time, get up and walk around the floor. If you're in a building with stairs, take a break to walk up and down a couple of stair flights. If you're somewhere that it's convenient to go outside for a few minutes, take a short break; stretch your limbs, inhale long-deep cleansing breaths and clear your head.

Letting our heads become cluttered with too many problems, worries or stresses can derail us and lead to the need to comfort ourselves with food. We've been here too many times before. Before we derail our weight loss journey, we need to stop and examine what's going on in our head. Negative thinking will produce negative responses. If we concentrate on the positive and renew our thoughts with hope, we can quickly regain our footing and stay on track.

I have my own little world, but it's okay - they know me here. ~ Author Unknown

But we must hold on to the progress we have already made. Philippians 3:16 (NLT)

PRAYER FOR TODAY: *Lord, thank You for watching over me and meeting my needs daily. Give me strength to endure this time of testing in my life and bring me through victorious. In Your name I ask all these things, Lord Jesus. Amen.*

SEPTEMBER 29
No Admittance

I've been reading a book written by five health-care professionals that deals with recognizing and conquering our food addictions. Answering some of the questions in the book frequently proves tougher than imagined. One question that has me stumped asks specifics about mealtimes with my family of origin (my childhood family).

For whatever reason I'm having a hard time remembering much of my life prior to the age of 18. A great part of this is because I'd rather forget most of my life prior to that time. My early formative years can best be described as the *anti-Leave it to Beaver* or *Brady Bunch* families portrayed on TV in the 60s and 70s.

I tried so hard to call up anything during that period that I ended up giving myself a headache. Either meal times were so unimportant and boring or perhaps they were so traumatic and stressful my subconscious mind refuses to allow me to remember anything.

One of the questions after relating my feelings about food was "do you think you are a food addict?" To which I replied … "well, duh!" Digging through the muck and mire of my forgotten memories, troubled childhood and embarrassing failed relationships makes me want cookies the way an alcoholic needs a stiff drink or a meth addict needs a quick fix. So yes, I admit I'm a junk food junkie and every day is a battle to talk myself down off the ledge and keep myself from leaping in with both feet to a giant vat of cookies.

Hopefully these last many months have been about more than just losing weight. As long as we are working through difficult emotions and chipping away at those emotions that tie us to food – we are making progress.

We run away all the time to avoid coming face to face with ourselves.
~ Author Unknown

The LORD has given me a strong warning not to think like everyone else does. Isaiah 8:11 (NLT)

PRAYER FOR TODAY: *Lord, thank You for self-discovery. Help me not to hide behind my fears and phobias and the traumatizing events from my past. May I continually move forward with strength and courage to face each day. In Your name I ask all these things, Lord Jesus. Amen.*

SEPTEMBER 30
How About Now – Is that Normal?

What is *normal?* Does anybody really have the answer to this? I find myself questioning that on a regular basis. What is this compulsion so many of us have to establish "normalcy" in our everyday lives. How can we be something that we can't quite define?

Clearly everyone has a different concept of what *normal* should or should not be based on their past or current circumstances. The child that grows up in a home where there is love, security and positive reinforcement on a daily basis automatically believes their childhood was *normal* and everyone grew up that way.

For the child that grows up in a home with daily ridicule, fear of parental figures, alcohol or sexual abuse, or any of the other unspeakable horrors that children suffer – they *believe* that is a *normal* way of life. It's only as they interact with other people that they discover not everyone lives with secrets behind closed doors. They learn that their childhood was in fact the opposite of what normal should be.

For many of us that struggle with addiction, we grew up in homes feeling unloved – or if we were loved, we were loved for inappropriate reasons.

So many life problems can be traced back to *you shall love your neighbor as yourself.* But how do you give away something you never got? Until we can learn to truly *love ourselves* just as we are – it's impossible for us to "love my neighbor as myself."

Identifying the problem is the easier part of this journey. Figuring out what to do with this knowledge is where the hard work kicks in. And yes, it is hard work. Nobody likes pain; which is why we fill ourselves up with food, alcohol, sex or drugs. It's time to let go of the pain and let God fill us up.

The hunger for love is much more difficult to remove than the hunger for bread. ~ Mother Teresa

"'You must love the LORD your God with all your heart, all your soul, and all your mind.' This is the first and greatest commandment. A second is equally important: 'Love your neighbor as yourself.'" Matthew 22:37-39 (NLT)

PRAYER FOR TODAY: Lord, I pray Your mercy as I travel this road on this difficult journey of self-discovery. I pray You will give me strength to walk forward and to face any buried pain so I can deal with it rationally. I ask that You will be with my friends as well; prepare each heart to receive Your healing. In Your name I ask all these things, Lord Jesus. Amen.

OCTOBER 1
The Pants Don't Lie

I keep two pairs of pants in the back of my closet that I pull out and try on when I want to chart my weight loss progress. One pair is a size 16; the other pair is a size 10 that I wore for years but haven't been able to wear in a long while.

On those days when I feel good about life, I get my size 10 pants out to see if I've made any progress. It's been a while since I was able to pull them up over my hips – and even then if they make it that far, the zipper has no prayer of closing. In fact the edges of the zipper aren't even close enough for a polite introduction.

Many health gurus suggest not weighing yourself regularly, but rather use a *clothes-ometer* to gauge your weight. Because many of us have three or more sizes in our closets at any given time, gauging our success by trying on old clothes can be a good idea.

It can be a little unsettling if we "fall off the wagon" and suddenly find that our *fat pants* are now our *skinny jeans* and we must buy new, bigger *fat pants*. To avoid that from happening, consider donning those suddenly too-tight, *fat pants* to wear around the house all day. The binding waist band cutting off your oxygen supply is usually enough of a painful reminder throughout the day to keep your eating in check.

If you're doing well and you've actually decreased a couple of sizes – keep it up! Consider donating those bigger sizes to a charity or to friends. Keeping around too many larger sizes may make it easier for us to slack off and regain our weight. Without options, we learn to live (or eat) within our means.

Let us not forget that most of our weight loss comes from WHAT WE EAT, it's not based on how much we exercise. The pants don't lie! If your *fat pants* are starting to feel snug – the time for action is now!

Success will never be a big step in the future, success is a small step taken just now. ~Jonatan Mårtensson

"But if you turn away and refuse to listen, you will be devoured by the sword of your enemies. I, the LORD, have spoken!" Isaiah 1:20 (NLT)

PRAYER FOR TODAY: *Lord, thank You for every victory, no matter how small. May I always push myself to make forward progress. Help me not to dwell on my failures but to learn from them and move past them. Give me strength for each day and each new challenge. In Your name I ask all these things, Lord Jesus. Amen.*

OCTOBER 2
Perspiration Revelation

I worked as a volunteer caterer for a luncheon outreach today at my church – outside – in the heat; which by October shouldn't be so ridiculously high – but it's Arizona – it's normal. I was on my feet in the heat and now I'm beat, too hot to eat, but maybe a treat, something sweet or filled with meat! Ahhhh … stop me, please!

I was wearing latex fitted gloves for most of the five hours I was prepping and serving food. When I finally was able to remove them my hands were dripping with sweat. I started thinking that perhaps the next time I'm working in the heat I should fashion some sort of latex body suit out of the latex gloves to wear under my clothes. That way when I'm done working, my volunteer service will have accomplished a twofold purpose; serving God to help others, and I could magically sweat off unwanted pounds while I'm doing so much running around.

Sweat isn't a bad thing. Many spas and gyms are equipped with saunas or steam rooms that allow to you to sit and sweat. After researching both dry saunas and wet steam rooms it would appear as both of these sauna types have many of the same therapeutic benefits. They can improve blood circulation, clean and rejuvenate the skin, ease muscle tension and joint pain, promote relaxation, eliminate toxins from the skin, and strengthen the immune system. As with anything, though, be sure to do your research before a visit to either a dry sauna or steam room.

Sweating off a few extra pounds in a sauna or steam room is no substitute for regular diet and exercise. There's nothing like a heart-pounding workout to whittle away the pounds. Weight lost from a sauna visit tends to be a temporary fix. There are no quick or easy fixes when it comes to weight loss; but rather eating balanced meals and good old-fashioned perspiration from hard work. As long as we're perspiring during workouts that's an indication and confirmation that what we're doing is getting the job done!

Statistics can be made to prove anything – even the truth. ~ Author Unknown

Let your roots grow down into him, and let your lives be built on him. Then your faith will grow strong in the truth you were taught, and you will overflow with thankfulness. Colossians 2:7 (NLT)

PRAYER FOR TODAY: *Lord, thank You for opportunities to serve You and give back to others through worthy charitable work. I thank You for a sense of humor and a positive attitude. May You continue to spend me like a coin in Your pocket any way that you wish. May I always be grateful for life's many blessings. In Your name I ask all these things, Lord Jesus. Amen.*

OCTOBER 3
Hollywood Un-Reality

Recently I watch the movie *You Again*. I enjoyed the movie once I got past my rant over the painfully thin women in the movie. Hollywood is the biggest culprit to point the finger of blame at when it comes to our country's epidemic of girls battling eating disorders such as anorexia and bulimia. The young women in the movie looked like they weighed barely more than 100 pounds. If it's true what they say that the camera adds 10 pounds that means those girls probably weigh 90 pounds or less.

The two older actresses in the movie, Jamie Lee Curtis and Sigourney Weaver both near my age – give or take a few years, were impossibly thin for women who no doubt are flirting with menopause. Where are their menopausal midriffs? Their skin, their necks and hands cannot belie their ages so they aren't fooling anyone. Are they simply having all their menopausal fat sucked out through surgery? Do they never eat?

It's infuriating watching scores of actresses portray "normal" wives, mothers and girlfriends that never have an ounce of body fat on their impossibly thin frames that wear size 2. Are we expected to believe that real mothers on the playground look like that? We are real women who battle with weight and menopausal midriffs every single day. Somehow it's comforting to go out in public and see scads of women who look like us.

Our journey to lose weight is about more than simply losing unwanted pounds; it's about getting healthy and learning to love ourselves in the bodies we have. If we can't love ourselves at a size 14 or 16, losing weight and becoming a size 4 or 6 will not magically make us happy. True happiness comes from inside – loving our neighbors as we love ourselves. We are the real women not those fantasy women. Do you hear us Hollywood?

You start out happy that you have no hips or boobs. All of a sudden you get them, and it feels sloppy. Then just when you start liking them, they start drooping. ~ Cindy Crawford

But the LORD said to Samuel, "Don't judge by his appearance or height, for I have rejected him. The LORD doesn't see things the way you see them. People judge by outward appearance, but the LORD looks at the heart." 1 Samuel 16:7 (NLT)

PRAYER FOR TODAY: *Lord, help me to avoid forming opinions about people based on their outer appearance. Please help me to look past my own reflection and not see my flaws and faults. May I always reflect Jesus. In Your name I ask all these things, Lord Jesus. Amen.*

OCTOBER 4
October-Fast

Now that the month of October has arrived, we're coming into the most dangerous time of the year. Typically most organized weight loss class attendance starts to drastically decline during this time of year.

The general attitude of the masses seems to be, "Well, I'll just enjoy the holidays and get back on the weight watching wagon after the first of the year." Hmm ... sound familiar? The retail stores are already overwhelming us with Halloween, Thanksgiving and Christmas merchandise. Now is the time to draw a line in the sand and make a stand and refuse to succumb to the temptations that the majority of people give in to.

Every day we need to get up with purpose and determination and set our minds to be strong. We need to fast from negative thoughts and attitudes and stay prayed up. Group support is more important than ever during this time of year. Don't forego weight loss support groups or meetings because of that *I'm just too busy* reasoning.

The tantalizing temptations available to us between now and Christmas will increase exponentially over the next two and a half months. In order to avoid a total and complete backslide all the way back to start (do not pass go and do not collect $200.00) we must gird up our minds, and practice these three little words until they are ingrained into our brains so we can recite them in our sleep ... NO, THANK YOU! Just saying NO to temptation is tougher than it sounds. It will take super-human strength to resist holiday goodies.

It's time to take stock of what we've learned this year and put everything into practice, kick it up a notch, kick it into high gear and any and other cheeky clichés we can think of. The average person gains between 7-10 pounds during the holiday season! The holiday season is practically upon us – the time is now. Don't become a statistic – become a success!

I may not be there yet, but I'm closer than I was yesterday. ~ Author Unknown

Finishing is better than starting. Patience is better than pride. Ecclesiastes 7:8 (NLT)

PRAYER FOR TODAY: *Lord, help me to put on the armor of God so I can resist any and all attacks and temptations. Help me to stand strong and dig deep and uncover any untapped resolve I may have inside of me. Give me strength for each new day; lift me when I am weak and help me to be an over comer. I can do all things through Christ who strengthens me! In Your name I ask all these things, Lord Jesus. Amen.*

OCTOBER 5
Wonky Excuses

My doctor recently scheduled some routine blood work for me. It turns out my thyroid is out of sorts and acting all wonky *again*. This is not unusual, nor the first time I've battled thyroid issues. The good news is the doctor changed my thyroid medication and hopefully it will kick in quickly and help me get back on track very soon.

On one hand it's nice to have medical confirmation that I'm not completely crazy and my weight struggles are not totally unfounded and there is a reason my body is not responding as I'd hoped. But on the other hand, I can't allow this diagnosis to become a reason to give up completely.

Losing weight and keeping it off is hard work. Perhaps like me you're struggling and don't feel as though there's much progress to be had. If it's been a while since you've had a routine check-up by a medical professional or had routine blood work done, don't put it off. If you're putting in the effort and getting few results perhaps there's a medical reason for why you aren't losing weight.

Identifying the problem is great, but we can't afford to slack off completely and let thyroid issues keep us from putting in the work. Medication can only do so much. Regardless of our health issues, weight will not magically disappear if we're not eating right or exercising.

Wonky thyroid or not – we cannot give up. We should be grateful there are simple blood tests available to identify potential problems quickly. We can only expect doctors, blood tests or medication to do so much. We must do our part and rely on God for all else.

The... patient should be made to understand that he or she must take charge of his own life. Don't take your body to the doctor as if he were a repair shop. ~ Quentin Regestein

Live wisely among those who are not believers, and make the most of every opportunity. Colossians 4:5 (NLT)

PRAYER FOR TODAY: *Lord, thank You for medical experts and blood tests that can give me the knowledge I need to fight my weight issues fairly. Thank You for medication when it's needed. Help me to do the job that I'm supposed to do which means eating a balanced diet, regular exercise and spending time in prayer, meditation and the Word of God. In Your name I ask all these things, Lord Jesus. Amen.*

OCTOBER 6
Friendly Reminders

Over breakfast this morning while channel surfing I stumbled upon a British film about an aging, alcoholic rock star. The movie caught my attention and I was hooked for the next 94 minutes. The story focused on the daughter the rock star never knew he had and a long-forgotten love, mixed with the drama of his out-of-control alcoholic lifestyle and rocker friends.

The reason I was so drawn to the movie was the whole aspect about his alcoholism. With the help of a former band mate he attended AA meetings and was able to remain clean and sober throughout the remainder of the movie. Although he was tempted to turn to whiskey when he hit a particularly rough patch of circumstances, with the help of his friend, he managed to avoid temptation.

I couldn't help but think about the parallels between alcoholism and food addictions. Whenever I've hit a particularly rough patch in my life, my first reaction has been to turn to the thing I could always count on for comfort – food. Food lifted my spirits when I was depressed – temporarily at least.

Unlike the alcoholic though, if we are food addicts we will never be able to be completely "clean and sober" from food. We *need* food to survive.

The one take away point I got from this movie was even though the rock star was a big name and very famous at one time in his life – he wasn't able to pull himself out of the alcoholism on his own. He needed the help of a close friend and a support group.

Some days God sends us little reminders that we cannot conquer our food addictions or issues on our own. We need to rely on the help of friends and a trusted support group. Sometimes it's good to get those reminders, because history has shown us that many of us have failed when we rely solely on ourselves. We all get by with a little help from our friends; for all else, there is God.

A true friend never gets in your way unless you happen to be going down.
~ Arnold Glasow

And let the peace that comes from Christ rule in your hearts. For as members of one body you are called to live in peace. And always be thankful. Colossians 3:15 (NLT)

PRAYER FOR TODAY: *Lord, thank You for the gentle reminders that I cannot conquer these battles on my own. Help me to reach out for help from friends and my support group when the need arises. May I continually be thankful for all of life's many blessings. In Your name I ask all these things, Lord Jesus. Amen.*

OCTOBER 7
One of the These Things is Not Like the Other

It's obvious that God designed men and women completely different from one another. One of the biggest differences has to be the way men and women view the scale when it comes to weighing.

I was reminded of those differences recently when I visited my doctor's office. When I go to see my doctor, I dress in lightweight fabrics. I forego the heavy jewelry and belts and of course wear slip-on shoes to be removed before weighing.

When I worked for a weight loss organization a few years ago, I saw women practically strip down to next to nothing and still stress out about the weight of their wedding rings. One woman even wondered if she should remove her teeth prior to weighing. A man can weigh with $4.00 worth of change in his pocket and heavy work boots on and he doesn't care! Why do we girls freak out over the numbers on the scale? Why does this simple act twist our reasoning and logic?

At my last doctor's visit my twisted denial hung around me like an extra layer of clothing. After removing everything I legally could get by with, I stepped on the scale facing the opposite direction so I wouldn't see what the number registered. I simply explained to the nurse "I'm menopausal and living in denial. Record the number; keep it to yourself." That's pretty *twisted*.

For many of us, regardless of how much weight we've lost, if we're still far from our goal weight we tend to live in the land of make-believe in the neighborhood of denial. If we are still hung up on what the numbers are telling us we've got to find a way to move past that. I have a couple of friends who have avoided their regular annual check-ups for YEARS because they refused to face the facts about their weight gain. We can't afford to indulge our denial by jeopardizing our health. For so many of us *denial* is more than just a river in Egypt. It's time to ditch our twisted sister denials and face the music and face the scale. It's time to change neighborhoods to the land of Freedom!

The person who really wants to do something finds a way; the other person finds an excuse. ~ Author Unknown

Keep me from lying to myself; give me the privilege of knowing your instructions. Psalm 119:29 (NLT)

PRAYER FOR TODAY: *Lord, I pray that You would help me to move out of the neighborhood of denial and face the harsh realities about myself and my weight. Forgive me for my many sins and shortcomings. Help me to move forward with a fresh new attitude. Equip me with the tools needed to fight this battle. In Your name I ask all these things, Lord Jesus. Amen.*

OCTOBER 8
Opposites Distract

The human body is a complicated piece of machinery. It craves foods that aren't good for us. It rejects the good foods that are designed to make us healthier. It wants to sleep when we have a ton of things to do on a schedule with no leeway; it won't let you sleep when you're so bone-weary tired you can barely speak your name. It sends you mixed messages about everything making you feel bad when you should feel good and feel good when you're about to do something bad.

We want to work-out and make our body bow to the demands of vigorous exercise, but when the weather is cooperating, the body won't and when the body complies, the weather prohibits us from setting foot outdoors. Or we're all cranked up and ready to go and the gym is closed or the car won't start. How are we supposed to keep it all together and maintain a well-balanced life when our own body and the universe are conspiring against us?

That's when we need to rely on the clichés of life because even though they're clichés, they still ring true. *Don't sweat the small stuff. Go with the flow. Just do it! You do what you can do and don't worry about what you can't do. You let go and let God. You toe the line; carry the load; put one foot in front of the other … jump down turn around, pick a bale of cotton!* And above all … CHILL OUT!

Don't let these opposite feelings distract you from the mission at hand to get healthy. When our minds, bodies or sleep schedules try to keep us from staying on course, stop; chill out and find a few minutes to regroup. Sometimes all we really need is a cat nap or a good night's sleep. Chill out and lights out when you're out of your mind with opposing feelings.

Insomnia is a gross feeder. It will nourish itself on any kind of thinking, including thinking about not thinking. ~ Clifton Fadiman

In a dream, in a vision of the night, when deep sleep falls on men as they slumber in their beds, he may speak in their ears and terrify them with warnings … Job 33:15-16 (NIV)

PRAYER FOR TODAY: *Lord, grant me a peaceful, restful sleep as I lie down each night. Restore and refresh my mind, my body and my spirit with much needed rest. Be with me and help me to have peace in my spirit. In Your name I ask all these things, Lord Jesus. Amen.*

OCTOBER 9
Age-Old Wisdom

Some days just getting out of bed proves to be a strenuous workout for those of us over the age of 35. Even though logically we may know we're not *that old* – the differences between a 50-year-old body and a 30-year-old body beg to differ with us. Wouldn't it be grand if we could turn the clock back and get those 20 or 30-year-old bodies back, but yet keep our 40, 50 or 60-year-old knowledge and know-how?

If we only knew back then what our bodies would actually look like and feel like in our 50s or 60s we might have worked a little harder at controlling our calorie consumption rather than concentrating solely on exercise to lose weight.

Whether we are someone who has more than just a little problem with food or we simply like to eat, we need to retrain our thinking. We need to maintain healthy eating habits and come to appreciate the true natural flavors of foods that aren't all pumped up with preservatives.

Eating fresh fruits and veggies are so much better for us because they contain so many healthful nutrients, vitamins and minerals that are completely absent from processed foods. Many of us may have realized these truths in our youth, but developed a taste for junk food early on; thinking we could "get by" with eating junk because we were young. Like so many of us we always thought we'd have more time to adopt healthy eating habits.

Facts are facts – we may have the wisdom of a 40 or 50-year-old, but no longer have the body to match and we can no longer tolerate junk food binges. Bingeing wreaks havoc on the stomach both internally and externally adding additional layers to our aging midriffs in record time.

Finding a healthy balance with food that satisfies both our stomachs and our heads is tougher than it may sound. That's where we have to utilize the wisdom of our ages and convince our bodies that our brains really do know better!

The years teach much which the days never knew. ~ Ralph Waldo Emerson

Is not wisdom found among the aged? Does not long life bring understanding? Job 12:12 (NIV)

PRAYER FOR TODAY: *Lord, thank You for the wisdom that comes with age. May I be wise enough to realize that complaining accomplishes nothing, and acting on emotion brings only trouble. Give me common sense and wisdom for each new day and every new challenge. In Your name I ask all these things, Lord Jesus. Amen.*

OCTOBER 10
A Choice Example

When we are children we are subjected to the demands and restrictions of our parents. We're told what we're supposed to eat and when to eat. Growing up in my home we had the standard choices at meal time: *take it or leave it*.

For many years my mother was a single working mother who often worked two jobs so she could keep food on the table. Meals subsisted largely of high carb foods like spaghetti, mac and cheese, tuna casserole, beans and franks or peanut butter and jelly.

We rarely had candy, cookies or chips because those "luxuries" weren't in the budget. Our only candy treats came from Halloween trick-or-treating once a year. Whenever I got any kind of allowance or extra change, my first spending usually included some sort of junk food purchase.

When I became a mom with my first child I was determined not to introduce my daughter to sugar because I remembered how easily I'd been hooked. I wanted to protect her from the addiction of chocolate and sugar. The first two years of her life were easy because we lived 3,000 miles from any family. Once we relocated her grand-parents introduced her to chocolate and it was downhill from there.

We are a product of our environment and how we are raised. Once we reach the age where we're accountable for our own food choices, it then becomes our personal responsibility to eat healthy (or not) and try and pass those healthy habits onto our children (or not).

I can't change all the wrongs I committed while raising my children regarding food choices, but I can do my part to influence them and their children by setting healthy examples now. It's never too late to make healthy choices and undo some of the wrongs we've committed.

If we're not willing to settle for junk living, we certainly shouldn't settle for junk food. ~ Sally Edwards

Let us, therefore, make every effort to enter that rest, so that no one will fall by following their example of disobedience. Hebrews 4:11 (NIV)

PRAYER FOR TODAY: Lord, *help me to consciously make wise choices with regards to the foods I buy, prepare and consume. May I set healthy examples for my children and my grandchildren and not give in to unhealthy food choices simply because they are easier and cheaper to buy and prepare. Give me this day my daily bread. In Your name I ask all these things, Lord Jesus. Amen.*

OCTOBER 11
Animal Instincts

I was watching a wild animal show on National Geographic the other night. The program highlighted a band of three brother cheetahs and how they were forced to work together to hunt for food. They'd been three days without a decent meal and together they managed to attack and bring down a large ostrich. They worked as a team, each did their part and ultimately they all chowed down on giant ostrich drumsticks as a result of that successful teamwork.

I'm sure when a lion is stalking a hyena for dinner they don't look it over and reject the hyena because they're simply not in the mood for hyena. Animals aren't picky when it comes to dinnertime. Somehow they instinctively know how the food chain operates and they eat according to the pecking order. With animals it's either eat or be eaten.

Animals don't eat when they're bored or lonely or stressed out. They don't wake up thinking *I'm hungry and I don't know what I want. I'm in the mood for something different.* Maybe they think, "Ooh, I've got a craving for ostrich for breakfast," and simply ignore a fat warthog strolling by the watering hole because they're not in the mood for warthog. Hel-lo if it's been three days since they've eaten they hunt and kill. It's survival of the fittest with animals.

Clearly we are different from animals. We do have choices when it comes to meal-times. We don't need Oreos and ice cream for our survival but we do need fruits, vegetables, proteins and a diet rich in nutrients, vitamins and minerals and not foods pumped full of preservatives. No we're not animals, but maybe it wouldn't hurt to learn to eat only when we're hungry; and eat to live rather than living to eat.

Animals have these advantages over man: they never hear the clock strike, they die without any idea of death, they have no theologians to instruct them, their last moments are not disturbed by unwelcome and unpleasant ceremonies, their funerals cost them nothing, and no one starts lawsuits over their wills. ~ Voltaire, letter to Count Schomberg, 31 August 1769

Now I urge you to take some food. You need it to survive. Not one of you will lose a single hair from his head." Acts 27:34 (NIV)

PRAYER FOR TODAY: *Lord, thank You that we are different from the animals. Thank You for free will. May I use that free will to make healthy choices when it comes to eating and exercise options. Bless me with wisdom and common sense in every area of my life. In Your name I ask all these things, Lord Jesus. Amen.*

OCTOBER 12
A Loser By Faith

There are days when it may feel as though our begging and pleading with God to keep us from giving in to our fleshly desires to eat the wrong foods, simply isn't working. According to Philippians 4:6-7; if we've prayed and presented our requests to God *with thanksgiving*, we should be walking in peace as soon as we have made our request.

If we are continuing to beg and plead with God for something we've already prayed about – that should be a red flag. Clearly we've NOT followed the Word of God because we're still anxious and distraught if we're begging and pleading. If we are distraught, by very definition that suggests we're not trusting God's Word to be true. Frantic pleas are quite the *opposite* of peace.

I decided to actually apply this Scripture the way that it's written. I prayed and presented my requests to God to help me TODAY to eat healthy foods and not give in to emotional eating. I asked for the strength to resist the temptations for wrong foods today. Once I prayed I offered THANKSGIVING to God for hearing my prayers. And then I asked for the peace of God that transcends all understanding to guard my heart and my mind so that I would not feel anxious about my food choices today.

If we are to believe the Word of God is absolute truth we have to believe the results that are promised will be forthcoming. However, if we don't do our part by *praying with thanksgiving* or if we are still anxious, how can we expect the Word of God to be fulfilled in our life? The Bible is more than just a big book of empty promises; it's the instruction manual for living a successful, joy filled life. Just reading it is one thing; it's an entirely different thing to actually *believe* the Word of God and to *apply* it to your life and to *operate* in faith.

We CAN be big losers by exercising our faith!

Every tomorrow has two handles. We can take hold of it by the handle of anxiety, or by the handle of faith. ~ Author Unknown

Do not be anxious about anything, but in everything, by prayer and petition, with thanksgiving, present your requests to God. And the peace of God, which transcends all understanding, will guard your hearts and your minds in Christ Jesus. Philippians 4:6-7 (NIV)

PRAYER FOR TODAY: Lord, help me to operate in faith and stand on the promises of Your Word. Help me to apply Scriptures to my life daily and not give in to doubt, fear or anxiety. I pray for that peace that passes all understanding and trust that through faith and belief in Your Holy Word, I can do all things that You strengthen me to do. In Your name I ask all these things, Lord Jesus. Amen.

OCTOBER 13
Most Days

In a perfect world we'd all wake up every day have a hard core workout and reach that endorphin high athletes brag about and we'd eat only what's on our menu plan. In a perfect world we'd stick to those plans with perfect precision and go to bed satisfied every night knowing that we had a perfect day. Yeah, in whose world does *that* ever happen? Not mine, that's for sure.

Most of us have very busy lives and we're lucky if "perfection" can be achieved one or two days in a single week – and that's a *good week*. Most days find us giving in to a little pinch of this or little dab of that, and most of the time *this* and *that* aren't on the menu plan for the day. Most days we're lucky if we can find the time to break a sweat with a strenuous workout, since many days the only workout we get is running back and forth to appointments or running errands. Most days we're lucky if we can maintain a healthy balance of that ratio of calories versus exercise-burn.

Most days we *should* be praising God that He's giving us another opportunity to do our best to try and *get it right* even though our track record speaks of everything contrary to *right*. In reality, most days the enemy works overtime to make us feel like a big fat failure even though we should know that our Lord and Savior loves us – every day.

We need to understand that *every day* our God will never leave us nor forsake us. We know that every day in spite of our best efforts to achieve perfection; it's difficult to be perfect in an imperfect world. We know that every day, God continues to love us, uphold us and strengthen us in spite of the fact that we can never truly be perfect.

Most days that's the *most* we can hope for.

Try as hard as we may for perfection, the net result of our labors is an amazing variety of imperfectness. We are surprised at our own versatility in being able to fail in so many different ways. ~ Samuel McChord Crothers

As for God, his way is perfect; the word of the LORD is flawless. He is a shield for all who take refuge in him. Psalm 18:30 (NIV)

PRAYER FOR TODAY: *Lord, thank You for every day and each opportunity to be better. Help me to accept the fact that no matter how hard I work – I can and never will be perfect. Apart from You I can do nothing but with You all things are possible. In Your name I ask all these things, Lord Jesus. Amen.*

OCTOBER 14
Willpower or Won't Power

There isn't a day that goes by that I don't lie down to sleep at night and shudder at the knowledge that I'm a horrible sinner. Before you judge me too harshly – you should know I'm not alone; we are ALL sinners in God's eyes.

It's not that we set out to sin purposely every day; it just sort of comes naturally. The harder we try not to give in to the commands of our sinful flesh, the quicker we generally succumb. Truth be told, we can never stop being sinners under our own power.

Most of us would love to be able to resist tempting foods and simply say "NO" to our flesh and eat only what is on our menu for the day. If only it were that easy. Most of us know from past experience, just saying "NO" when it comes to food doesn't always work. Having willpower isn't always enough.

We can start every day with good intentions and give ourselves the standard pep talk of the day; read some scriptures, say some prayers and that all works great … until we're actually faced with a temptation. So many times in the past we simply fold like a napkin, unable to form the word "NO" on our lips when faced with a gooey, tempting taste treat.

The sooner we accept the fact that we have no willpower because of our sinful nature the sooner we can advance in God's kingdom. Apart from Him, we can do nothing – not even say "NO" to fresh baked, homemade chocolate chip cookies.

Rather than beating ourselves up because we lack willpower, we need to accept that we are weak; we are sinners and willpower is useless against fighting the attacks of the enemy. In the end, it all comes down to turning our free will over to God and giving Him permission to run the show in order to keep us on the right path. Either we will or we won't.

Every morning I spend fifteen minutes filling my mind full of God; and so there's no room left for worry thoughts. ~ Howard Chandler Christy

Do not deceive yourselves. If any one of you thinks he is wise by the standards of this age, he should become a "fool" so that he may become wise. 1 Corinthians 3:18 (NIV)

PRAYER FOR TODAY: *Lord, bless me with wisdom and common sense daily so I can make wise choices and walk upon the path You have chosen for me. Help me to care for this temple You have blessed me with by making healthy choices, not based on my willpower, but according to the power of Your Holy Spirit. In Your name I ask all these things, Lord Jesus. Amen.*

OCTOBER 15
Spare the Change

I've been watching my grandson this week while he's been on fall break from school. This morning we had a Sponge Bob Square Pants marathon. In all honesty, Sponge Bob doesn't do it for me. He grates on my nerves after only a few minutes. It's the combination of his voice and the fact that he's a sponge for gosh sakes.

We were watching an episode of SBSP (Sponge Bob Square Pants) when a weird story line caught my attention. Sponge Bob decided he didn't like his personality because he was too weird. He decided to normalize himself by changing his appearance, his speech, and his mannerisms so he would fit in and be "normal." Turns out his friends thought it was too weird that he was no longer abnormal because he wasn't himself any longer. They liked the weird, abnormal version better.

Most of us have things about ourselves we don't like. One day I decided I'd change the way I talk with my hands. (In my defense I am *half* Sicilian.) I vowed to do everything in my power to avoid talking with my hands. It turns out when Sicilians are deprived the use of our hand gestures, we're rendered temporarily mute and incapable of forming coherent speech patterns or stringing more than three words together in a sentence.

Changing our minds or opinions is far easier than changing a personality quirk. Sometimes it's the "quirks" that make us uniquely who we are. Rather than trying to change ourselves to behave like someone else, we should take a lesson from Sponge Bob: *when we stop being ourselves we stop being the person God created us to be.*

God designed us to be unique individuals with our own personalities. It would be easier to change the things we *can* change about ourselves (like our diets) while leaving the rest up to God. If He doesn't change us, then there must be a reason we are the way we are. Maybe like Sponge Bob, people like the abnormality in us because that's what makes us who we are.

If you would attain to what you are not yet, you must always be displeased by what you are. For where you are pleased with yourself there you have remained. Keep adding, keep walking, keep advancing. ~ Saint Augustine

So God created human beings in his own image. In the image of God he created them; male and female he created them. Genesis 1:27 (NLT)

PRAYER FOR TODAY: *Lord, help me to be comfortable in my own skin and embrace my uniqueness and individuality. Change the things in me that are displeasing to You. Help me to be the best that I can be. In Your name I ask all these things, Lord Jesus. Amen.*

OCTOBER 16
Let's Make A Deal

Yesterday was National Vegetable Day – at least in my house – and I don't mean edible vegetables, but rather *vegging-out* day. I devoted an entire day to a near-vegetative state by the mere fact of my inactivity. For me, that veg-day means I give myself permission to do absolutely nothing for the whole day (unless of course you count watching chick flicks as doing something). In addition, the veg-day means I also take a break from obsessing about my menu and my exercise plans.

Not thinking about exercise is the easier of the two, because let's face it – we humans are quite naturally a lazy breed. Not thinking about or worrying about what we eat isn't as easy as you would think. Because like it or not, even when we're not thinking about our food plans, it's tempting to find ourselves playing caloric *Let's Make a Deal* and opting for trading out one food for another. Some habits are harder to break than others.

Much like any other addict fixates on their addiction, be it alcohol, sex, drugs or whatever – when something controls your thought life it can be virtually impossible to turn it off for even one day, no matter how desperately we want to.

How nice it would be if we could conjure up Monty Hall and really play *Let's Make a Deal* so we could trade our food addictions for what's behind door number three. How lovely it would be if we had a genie in a bottle that would grant us one wish to be able to exchange these obsessions for "normal thinking."

Perhaps our food addiction or obsession is our "thorn in the flesh" if you will. If that thing that controls us continues to hang on despite our best efforts, perhaps it's time to seek God's face and find out the purpose for it. Sometimes it bears considering that the thing that controls us is the very thing tethering us to our constant dependence upon God. As much as I hate the way food controls me, staying continually tethered to God is a deal I *can* live with.

Don't think you're on the right road just because it's a well-beaten path.
~ Author Unknown

That is why, for Christ's sake, I delight in weaknesses, in insults, in hardships, in persecutions, in difficulties. For when I am weak, then I am strong. 2 Corinthians 12:10 (NIV)

PRAYER FOR TODAY: *Lord, I pray for more of Your presence in my life. Grant me freedom to fully enjoy life according to Your plan for me. Strengthen me in the areas where I am weak and grant me wisdom where I'm lacking. In Your name I ask all these things, Lord Jesus. Amen.*

OCTOBER 17
Recalculating the Never Land GPS

For anyone who has ever spent any time in the neighborhood of *Never Land* we need to pay attention if we suddenly find ourselves venturing there more frequently. If it's a neighborhood we're comfortable in, it may be time to *recalculate*.

The Never Land neighborhood is that old familiar mindset that has us thinking things like *I'm never going to lose this weight. I'm never going to conquer this food addiction. I'm never going to fit into my skinny jeans. I'm never going to be "normal."*

We know these negative *I'm NEVER* thoughts are not God's will for us but the work of the enemy who'd like nothing more than to defeat us without lifting a finger. Why should the enemy worry about us when we do such a great job of killing our own visions and dreams with just a few random thoughts in our head?

These *Never* thoughts are not from God. We have a very real enemy that is roaming about looking for someone weak to attack. Keeping our minds and attitudes sharp by daily prayer and the reading of God's Word helps us to ready ourselves for attacks. If the busyness of life interferes with our quiet time with God we may as well paint a bull's eye on our thought life.

If our thoughts are steering us towards depression, despair or a return trip to *Never Land* – we need to check our GPS to see if we've been re-routed. We may be out of balance. When we're out of balance in one area, it leads to a shifting of our emotional axis.

Repeated trips to *Never Land* can find us balancing on a very dangerous precipice of depression that leads to a fall off the edge. Before we fall completely we need to recalculate, reorganize and reset our GPS to point towards God – *again!*

Remember, if you're headed in the wrong direction, God allows U-turns!
~ Allison Gappa Bottke

Give all your worries and cares to God, for he cares about you. Stay alert! Watch out for your great enemy, the devil. He prowls around like a roaring lion, looking for someone to devour. 1 Peter 5:7-8 (NLT)

PRAYER FOR TODAY: *Lord, it's so easy to get myself off course. Help me to stay alert and always at the ready to fight off my enemy. Keep me strong and fill me with wisdom and discernment. If I start to slack off and feel the urge to give in to laziness, gently remind me to stay the course with perseverance and all due diligence. Give me balance Lord! In Your name I ask all these things, Lord Jesus. Amen.*

OCTOBER 18
Diet Jingles

I'm out of things to write and say, about what I eat and what I weigh.
Nearly ten full months have come and gone; my fat remains – it still holds on.
Will I ever lose this weight? Will I stay plump – is that my fate?
Oh dear God I need a break, this endless doubt I cannot shake!

I've lost some weight and gained it back. It's just so hard to stay on track.
It's so much easier to complain; I'd rather eat than to abstain.
Please help me Lord before I fail and stop the climbing of the scale.
I'm such a mess, I'm filled with shame – there's no one but myself to blame.

When I lay me down to sleep, I count my calories instead of sheep.
I'd love to stop this mindless eating; the same mistakes I keep repeating.
I need help, is my confession, to stop this endless food obsession.
Food's all I think of day and night – no wonder all my clothes are tight!

I'd love to be the perfect weight and wear my jeans in a size eight.
Some days it's hard to even smile while I shop the Plus Size aisle.
I'll win the war with what it takes, like Lean Cuisine and breakfast shakes.
I would not, could not, even try it, to give it up and ditch this diet.

Thick or thin, it doesn't matter – (as long as I don't get too much fatter.)
It does not matter what I weigh – my God loves me night and day.
I need to pray and trust the Lord – give up my snacking when I'm bored.
Read the Word and always pray – I'll find success at last one day.

If it takes another year, to lose this weight, I will not fear,
Counting calories is my career – I will not give up, do you hear!

Things could be worse. Suppose your errors were counted and published every day, like those of a baseball player. ~ Author Unknown

"Do not be afraid or discouraged, for the LORD will personally go ahead of you. He will be with you; he will neither fail you nor abandon you." Deuteronomy 31:8 (NLT)

PRAYER FOR TODAY: *Lord, I pray for help today to stay the course, maintain a positive attitude and be a blessing to others along the way. Thank You for always standing beside me, Lord, and carrying me when I am weak and feeling defeated. In Your name I ask all these things, Lord Jesus. Amen.*

OCTOBER 19
An Inconvenient Truth off the Rack

For so many of us the next couple of months promise to be quite busy with parties, school recitals, social engagements or even weddings or graduations. If you're a woman all of those social functions prompt that all important first reaction of, *"Holy cow, I have nothing to wear!"* That thought is generally followed by, *"I wonder how quickly I can lose 20 pounds?"*

For the normal, average size woman this would not present any unusual problems. You go shopping – you try a couple of things on, maybe even grab something off the rack without trying it on and you're good to go. Not so for the overweight or abnormally proportioned woman.

Off the rack is difficult if you're body type is "off the charts" of what is considered "normal." For many of us, the sad harsh reality is regardless of what our current weight is our general proportions rarely change.

Yes, perhaps it is easier to have more shopping options if we are closer to our "ideal weight," but that still can't change our short legs or long legs; wide shoulders or flat bottoms. These bodies that we have, regardless of how out-of-proportion we may think they are – are a gift from God. It's up to us to accept ourselves.

If you're having shopping challenges enlist the help of a friend who can help you pick clothes suitable for your body type. Pick things that make you feel comfortable and things that can camouflage those areas you want to draw attention away from. We shouldn't dress to please others, but aim for dressing in clothes that make us feel good about ourselves. Eliminate your negatives by accentuating your positives.

To be a fashionable woman is to know yourself, know what you represent, and know what works for you. To be "in fashion" could be a disaster on 90 percent of women. You are not a page out of Vogue. ~ Author Unknown

And I want women to be modest in their appearance. They should wear decent and appropriate clothing and not draw attention to themselves by the way they fix their hair or by wearing gold or pearls or expensive clothes. 1Timothy 2:9 (NLT)

PRAYER FOR TODAY: *Lord, I pray You will help me not to stress about my outward appearance. May I always dress for comfort and wear things that please me rather than worrying about what anyone else may think of me. Help me not to be vain or conceited but righteous and holy and a beautiful reflection of the Holy Spirit living in me. In Your name I ask all these things, Lord Jesus. Amen.*

OCTOBER 20
Seven Days to Cheat

Years ago while working for a weight loss organization I saw firsthand what true "cheating" looked like with regards to dieting and losing weight. I thought I was the only one who cheated and manipulated my calories. Apparently "cheating" is a universal trick that many people employ with regularity; it's as much a part of their weight loss program as is menu planning.

The organization I worked for expected members to weigh in once a week and attend meetings meant to inspire and encourage. Many of the members made their weigh-in day, their automatic "cheat day," which usually entailed them skipping all meals prior to weigh-in, followed by a high-calorie lunch out at a restaurant after class dismissed. The attitude and justification was always the same, *"today is my "free day" after weigh-in because I skipped breakfast and I will have seven days to stay on track before my next weigh-in."*

The problem with this kind of thinking is that "What's one more day?" easily becomes "I still have six days to cheat." And, "I've still got *five* days to cheat," and then *four, three, two* … and before you know it you're skipping your support group and weight loss class altogether and are right back where you started! I saw this pattern repeated too many times to count.

This kind of "cheating" logic is what has landed so many of us on the yo-yo weight loss roller coaster for most of our lives. The same way we should stop visiting Never Land we should stop dabbling in *cheater logic* and forget trying to manipulate our menus and calories for the sole purpose of cheating. We are only hurting ourselves. Many of us know from experience that it's only a stone's throw to *once a cheater, always a cheater*, so we need to erase all cheater logic and get off the roller coaster once and for all!

Don't let yesterday use up too much of today. ~ Cherokee Indian Proverb

For we know that when this earthly tent we live in is taken down (that is, when we die and leave this earthly body), we will have a house in heaven, an eternal body made for us by God himself and not by human hands. 2 Corinthians 5:1 (NLT)

PRAYER FOR TODAY: *Lord, I ask that You would help me ditch any kind of cheating logic I may be considering. Help me to make my daily menu plan and stick with it. Help me to realize that trying to manipulate my calories will only hurt me in the long run. Lead me in the path of righteousness. In Your name I ask all these things, Lord Jesus. Amen.*

OCTOBER 21
Come On Let's Get (Trigger) Happy

Iwas doing some housecleaning yesterday and came across a box of forgotten wedding album memorabilia. Inside one of the album pockets I stumbled across a plethora of goodies from my engagement period, wedding showers, wedding ceremony and my first wedding anniversary.

I discovered the printed itinerary from the travel agency that booked our honeymoon trip – even the ticket stubs from our flight to Hawaii. It was a lovely walk down memory lane ... *until* I came across something that proved to be a powerful emotional trigger that wanted to send me straight to the freezer so I could bury my face in a giant vat of ice cream!

Lucky for me the freezer and the pantry cupboards were relatively snack free, so I was unable to do any major bingeing damage. But the very idea that I WANTED to indulge in a binge was a great wake-up call. My trigger turned out to be a card celebrating my first wedding anniversary. The card was from a family member who has longed since passed away – but was someone who was responsible for a lot of the childhood trauma and rejection I felt growing up as a child.

The card contained a hand-written note about some things that sent me over the edge precariously perched on a pig-out precipice. Things I'd thought I'd dealt with, are clearly still major emotional triggers lying just underneath the surface. Because I recognized the trigger for what it was, I was also able to analyze my emotions without turning to food – *before it was too late.*

None of us can ever afford to become complacent or too comfortable in our addiction recovery. Triggers are emotional land mines scattered around where we least expect them and can trip us up at any time – if we let them. The key is to learn how to side-step those land mines *before* they ignite!

Let's not forget that the little emotions are the great captains of our lives and we obey them without realizing it. ~ Vincent Van Gogh, 1889

Even if we feel guilty, God is greater than our feelings, and he knows everything. 1 John 3:20 (NLT)

PRAYER FOR TODAY: *Lord, thank You for reminding me that I can never afford to become complacent with regards to my addiction and the healing process. I pray You will continue to strengthen me and I ask that each day brings me one day closer to healing. In Your name I ask all these things, Lord Jesus. Amen.*

OCTOBER 22
Whittle While You Work

This has been a busy week; so busy in fact, I've barely had time to worry about food. Is that a great week, or what? I spent several days this week painting the interior of my house and I've been volunteering my time preparing meals at church.

Painting challenged muscles I'd forgotten I even had. I discovered I was sore in brand new places that haven't been tested in quite some time. When I had time to stop for brief breaks, the one thought that kept bouncing around in my head was, "I bet I'm burning off tons of calories with all of this not eating! I'm certain I must have just whittled away a bunch of weight!"

Maximizing weight loss with exercise doesn't mean that you have to spend hours in a gym or running endless miles on a treadmill or at the track. Challenging our body doesn't have to be expensive but can be incorporated into our regular, daily activities. Maybe you don't have walls or fences to paint but you can burn calories doing the most mundane household chores.

The next time you have to sweep, mop or vacuum your floors try putting a little gusto into that routine chore. Really stretch those muscles as you reach under furniture or tucked away corners. Use your broom or dust mop to reach high up into the corners of the ceiling to attack cobwebs. When dusting, execute squats up and down or lunges as you bend to reach lower furniture.

Chores don't have to be routine and boring; exercise doesn't have to be a chore. Attack those mindless household jobs with enthusiasm and whittle away the pounds while you work.

Lack of activity destroys the good condition of every human being, while movement and methodical physical exercise save it and preserve it. ~ Plato

No, I beat my body and make it my slave so that after I have preached to others, I myself will not be disqualified for the prize. 1 Corinthians 9:27 (NLT)

PRAYER FOR TODAY: *Lord, thank You for hard work and time given in service to You and Your church. I thank You that I didn't focus on the desires of my flesh this week, but was able to occupy my mind rather than giving into the selfish desires of my stomach. I pray You will continue to strengthen me and give me this day my daily bread. In Your name I ask all these things, Lord Jesus. Amen.*

OCTOBER 23
Diet Choke

My youngest daughter has been taking a medical nutrition class this semester in college. She emails me her concerns regarding areas of my diet that she's identified as problematic. Two weeks ago she gave me a severe lambasting regarding my love and obsession with diet soda. I KNOW diet soda is bad for me – but I don't drink coffee so I need the caffeine!

You'd think we'd all have wised up about the dangers of soda especially after those emails went round the world enlightening us to the multiple uses of cola drinks. When I read that Coke poured into a stained toilet bowl would magically erase unsightly calcium buildup I rushed to test that theory myself. All I got for my efforts was a toilet bowl full of cola. My do-it-yourself Myth-buster test proved *at least one* of those to be false claims.

My daughter did pose some very real concerns about the dangers of eating and drinking diet products though. She wasn't saying that diet soda itself was bad, but the artificial sweeteners used in most diet products are extremely dangerous. Mostly it's the aspartame in diet products that pose severe health risks.

Eliminating products with artificial sweeteners can be fairly challenging. The reason most of us resort to those pre-packaged, preservative-laced products is not because they are so delicious to our palates, but because they're easy!

We're a drive-through, microwave, *want it now* society and apparently we're killing ourselves at a faster than ever pace these days. *Again* … losing weight needs to be about more than just losing weight – it needs to be about getting healthy *and getting smarter*. Are we there yet?

It would be nice if the Food and Drug Administration stopped issuing warnings about toxic substances and just gave me the names of one or two things still safe to eat. ~ Robert Fuoss

Then God said, "Look! I have given you every seed-bearing plant throughout the earth and all the fruit trees for your food. Genesis 1:29 (NLT)

PRAYER FOR TODAY: Lord, thank You for the knowledge given us. Your Word says that Your people perish for lack of knowledge. May I use wisdom and common sense when buying and preparing my food. May I enjoy what I eat and always be thankful for the bounty You have provided. In Your name I ask all these things, Lord Jesus. Amen.

OCTOBER 24
Let's Get Ready to Grumble

Ever had one of those days where all you want to do is cry and you don't know why? Maybe it's just me, but I am a bit emotionally handicapped lately. Especially since my courtship with Mr. Menopause seems to have advanced to the next level. Mr. Menopause appears on the verge of proposing a lifelong commitment of marriage to me (or not) which is why I'm so weepy today.

I'm struggling with physical changes in my body, the winding down of my biological clock and the knowledge that my youth is about to be a faint memory. It would seem all I've got to look forward to are early bird dinners and applying for my AARP card. That tends to make a girl (or old gal, if you will) a tad emotional.

It doesn't pay to grumble. Those that do are the old farts nobody wants to be around because they're so crabby. I'd much prefer to think my best years are still ahead of me because I serve a mighty God who's got a great big plan for my life and He's not done with me yet.

The natural progression of life means changes – BIG changes. From the second we're born till the day God calls us home we are ever evolving and learning and growing. We can choose to grow old with grace and be an example to those younger than us, or we can live in denial and spend all our money on plastic surgery to slow the aging process (which really fools no one).

If we hope to extend our lives so we can be around long enough to become an embarrassment to our children and their children, the time to eat right, exercise and get healthy is now. I'm sure there's an unwritten law somewhere that embarrassing your offspring is a mandatory condition for eligibility for your AARP card. Otherwise, what would be the fun in getting old if not to pester and embarrass your kids? Good health starts TODAY.

Do not regret growing older. It is a privilege denied to many. ~ Author Unknown

I will be your God throughout your lifetime—until your hair is white with age. I made you, and I will care for you. I will carry you along and save you. Isaiah 46:4 (NLT)

PRAYER FOR TODAY: *Lord, thank You for the privilege of growing old. I pray I can enjoy and embrace each new adventure that comes with getting older. Help me never to complain about the changes that come with age. Help me to continue to do my part to eat healthy and exercise so I can remain active and vital and a contributing member of the Body of Christ for a long time to come. In Your name I ask all these things, Lord Jesus. Amen.*

OCTOBER 25
Weebles Wobble, but They Don't Fall Down

This morning was one of those days as I climbed from bed my arthritic posture and uneven gait caused me to bear a striking resemblance to a Weeble. You remember – Weebles wobble but they don't fall down? My Weeble-like movements had me thinking not only do I move like a Weeble, but today I was feeling particularly short and squat and actually looked like a Weeble. All that was missing was a cute little bobbed haircut and a sporty hat to complete my Weeble ensemble.

Of course most of these Weeble feelings stem from the fact that I feel as though I got short-changed in the height department. I'm a mere 5' 4" tall. I've always said I'm not overweight, but under tall. If I was 5'11" tall my weight would be perfect!

Clearly we can't do anything to change our height or the length of our limbs. There is no magic exercise or miracle pill that will make us instantly six inches taller. (No, anti-gravity boots and machines will not stretch you!) But we can change our attitude towards our *Weeble features*. Simply by changing our attitude and extending our carriage when we walk, we can have the effect of appearing taller. Concentrating on good posture and avoiding the slouchies does wonders for a short stature. Walking with elongated or erect posture can also have the effect of making us appear more confident. Who doesn't want that?

Okay – it's not exactly a quick fix cure all – but we Weebles will go to great lengths to avoid falling down. Every pound we chip away at gets us one step closer to success and one step closer to our goals thereby eliminating our wobbly Weeble days. I don't remember if they even made tall, thin Weebles, but if they didn't they should as we short, round Weebles are tired of all the pressure to be thin. Think tall and think healthy!

He who limps is still walking. ~ Stanislaw J. Lec

But the day of the Lord will come as unexpectedly as a thief. Then the heavens will pass away with a terrible noise, and the very elements themselves will disappear in fire, and the earth and everything on it will be found to deserve judgment. Since everything around us is going to be destroyed like this, what holy and godly lives you should live. 2 Peter 3:10-11 (NLT)

PRAYER FOR TODAY: *Lord, I pray You will help me to stick with my exercise and eating program and help me to safely remove this excess weight from my body in order to alleviate unnecessary pressure on my joints. May I not get discouraged and give up, but continue to stay the course daily. In Your name I ask all these things, Lord Jesus. Amen.*

OCTOBER 26
Fried Stuff with Cheese

I had lunch recently with a friend who defies the logic of human physiology. And quite frankly – I'm a little peeved about it. She's had four children and weighs less than 130 pounds, yet she complains about needing to lose weight. She's concerned about her barely noticeable post baby belly resulting from her last pregnancy.

When we went for lunch, my meal consisted of a salad with *light* dressing *on the side*, a grilled chicken sandwich, *sans cheese, sans mayo* on a *whole wheat bun* and water with lemon. My friend indulged in chili cheese fries, fried buffalo wings with a high-calorie high-flavor sauce and some sort of gooey fried cheese thingies with more high-calorie high-flavor sauce for an appetizer AND a soda – *not diet*, BTW.

While I was nibbling my boring lunch, I kept thinking what is wrong with this picture? Somehow I ended up on the wrong end of the genetic lottery and inherited slow, lazy genes that render my metabolism comatose while my friend can eat like a Clydesdale.

When she started reaching for the dessert menu I swear I was close to taking her down and pummeling her with my whole wheat bun! Luckily the momentary insanity passed and I was able to dial down the crazy, but I'm still a little peeved.

When ancestry and genetics align to make you feel as though life's not fair, it's important to keep things in perspective. *Life's NOT fair.* Basically our options are to say the heck with it – give in to all our primal urges and eat desserts, carbs, and assorted fried foods with cheese *or not.*

Sticking with a meal plan that prohibits the intake of gooey cheese sauces and fried things is for the greater good of our cholesterol, our blood pressure and our muffin tops. What's a girl to do? She skips lunch with the *fried stuff with cheese* friend for a while until she can learn to control her animal instincts to pummel her friend or learn to regulate the crazy … whichever comes first.

We should look for someone to eat and drink with before looking for something to eat and drink. ~ Epicurus

So do not be attracted by strange, new ideas. Your strength comes from God's grace, not from rules about food, which don't help those who follow them. Hebrews 13:9 (NLT)

PRAYER FOR TODAY: *Lord, thank You that I have friends whose company I enjoy and they mine. Thank You that every day You provide my daily bread. Please curb my natural propensity for whining and turn it into praise instead. In Your name I ask all these things, Lord Jesus. Amen.*

OCTOBER 27
Game – Set – Match

Recently while running errands I spotted a woman in a parking lot that caught my eye. She was hard to miss because of her size. This woman was so thin I was surprised she had strength to walk through the parking lot. She had the look of one who was starving.

Believe it or not, there is such a thing as *too thin*. For anyone carrying extra weight – we think – *impossible!* Being out of balance in the other direction and being severely *underweight*, is equally as dangerous for our bodies as being overweight.

A woman I knew years ago labored to lose 97 pounds. I always thought it odd that she didn't go for those other three pounds so she could brag about her 100 pound loss. She explained that her body simply wouldn't let her sustain that 100 pound mark. Her body had its own set point and maintaining those extra few pounds was too difficult.

Most of us have a set point that our bodies get comfortable at. When we set our goals to lose weight we may be thinking in our heads that "I'll only be happy when I weigh 125 pounds." In reality our body may not be comfortable there but would be happier at a much higher weight.

Because many of us have abused our bodies with yo-yo dieting; our bodies can end up terribly confused by our radical weight fluctuations. Our set point can get lost in our craziness. We end up playing a dangerous game we can't possibly win once we begin the back and forth match of weight loss/weight gain.

It's important that we establish realistic goals and set realistic boundaries for eating and exercise. It's equally important that we set a realistic pace for losing weight and not hurry the process so our set point has a chance to reset itself. In the weight loss game, the match is really won when we can successfully win the SET point; ultimately making us winners at this *losing* game.

You can't lose weight by talking about it. You have to keep your mouth shut. ~ Author Unknown

Remember, it is better to suffer for doing good, if that is what God wants, than to suffer for doing wrong! 1 Peter 3:17 (NLT)

PRAYER FOR TODAY: *Lord, give me wisdom to make healthy choices and help me minimize my complaining. I pray that each day I can push past the desires of my flesh. Help me listen to my body and ignore the craziness in my head. In Your name I ask all these things, Lord Jesus. Amen.*

OCTOBER 28
Fatty, Fatty Two by Fifty-Four

I thought I was having a good day until I made the mistake of going shopping today. I have a standard rule that I never shop for clothes when I'm hormonal. Because of my current menopausal status, however – I'm *always* hormonal these days. If I wait for the hormones to subside, I'd never get to leave my house.

While I was checking out at the register the cashier who looked barely old enough to drive, asked me if I was a member of the "Tuesday Shoppers Discount Club." When I asked what that was, she cheerily replied that it was the discount available on Tuesdays for those seniors that were 55 and over! (I'm close to 55, but I'm not there yet!) There's nothing worse for our self-esteem than to be mistaken for *older* than we actually are (unless we're 14 and then it's okay).

Even though we're working hard at having positive mindsets, fighting our negative feelings on hormonal days can be a tall order. For those days when we feel fat, really fat, and über fat, (especially "fat, fat, über fat, 55 *and over* fat") it might best serve us and the general retail population to STAY AT HOME until the unpleasantness has passed or at least diminished. I did the only thing a woman in my *senior* hormonal state could do; I came home and ate chocolate. Not a lot of chocolate, mind you – but a Fiber One 90-calorie brownie to take the edge off the crazy. The chocolate was followed up with a dose of magnesium to squelch the sugar cravings that resulted from my hormonal, emotional meltdown.

Not all days are pretty, but if we take a moment to reset our focus and meditate for even a few seconds on one positive thought, we can find something pretty good in every day. For the not so pretty days – at least there is low-calorie chocolate. Thank goodness, God loves us on the not-so-pretty days when we find it hard to love ourselves.

If not for chocolate, there would be no need for control top pantyhose. An entire garment industry would be devastated. ~ Author Unknown

But don't be so concerned about perishable things like food. Spend your energy seeking the eternal life that the Son of Man can give you. For God the Father has given me the seal of his approval." John 6:27 (NLT)

PRAYER FOR TODAY: *Lord, help me not to internalize the words of strangers that might hurt my feelings. I care not what anyone thinks about me other than You. Help me to have a good attitude and speak only what is good and pleasing to You. Help me to remember it's not what I look like on the outside that matters, but rather the condition of my heart. In Your name I ask all these things, Lord Jesus. Amen.*

OCTOBER 29
The Path Less Travelled – The Psycho Path

The human psyche is a strange thing. For months now I've been attending two separate weekly support groups that deal with emotional eating – the causes and effects, etc. These groups focus on digging up the painful memories that are responsible for emotional eating. The stories I've heard in these classes make me want to weep. I leave each class with an almost inhuman need for sugar after sharing my heart and hearing the heartbreaking stories of others.

Luckily I've cleaned out my fridge and pantry and finding illegal foods to eat is extremely tough. Not surprisingly you can still make yourself sick by eating a pound of grapes and a whole cantaloupe in one sitting. When the emotions need to be fed, they'll eat anything in excess.

Whether we are foodies that eat only because we love food or we are emotional eaters that turn to food to pacify unexplained feelings, we must expect that there will be times that food can make us feel absolutely crazy. Some nights my self-discovery is so painful there's no time for reflection or prayer only the need to inhale food at a record speed.

We may feel as though we're still a long way from being liberated from these unnatural food obsessions but we need to keep doing the work. We need to fight any denial we may be holding on to and purge our souls and hearts from any negative emotions that are lingering, just waiting to push us over onto the psycho path. Stay with your weight loss group (if you have one). Some weeks we may think it would be easier to quit altogether and go back to our life of denial. But then, a year from now we'll be right back here where we are today, but most likely we'll be 10 or 20 pounds heavier.

It's time to get off the weight loss roller coaster and kick the crazy out! Get off the psycho path and take the road less travelled that few have the tenacity to walk. Quitting is not an option. Food may make us crazy sometimes, but we serve a mighty God who can calm the wind and the waves. Surely He can calm the crazy and set our feet back on a solid path … one that's not a psycho path!

You can't run away from trouble. There ain't no place that far. ~ Uncle Remus

But by means of their suffering, he rescues those who suffer. For he gets their attention through adversity. Job 36:15 (NLT)

PRAYER FOR TODAY: *Lord, I know that You have a plan and a purpose for my life, but I'm kind of feeling like a failure today. Please heal me of my emotional eating problems. Help me on this journey and give me the strength to face anything left uncovered in my past so I can put these issues behind me and get on with the plan. In Your name I ask all these things, Lord Jesus. Amen.*

OCTOBER 30
Why Am I such a Misfit?

Between my two support groups this week, I've been doing a lot of soul searching. Too many stirred up emotions has left me feeling a bit like a social misfit; a textbook example of a dieting failure. For whatever reason, I kept hearing that song in my head: *Why Am I such a Misfit,* from the classic Christmas story, *Rudolph the Red Noised Reindeer.*

The topic of discussion at one of my groups this week focused on the inner beast inside each of us who battle addictions. The class speaker showed a very graphic clip of the most recent wolf man movie with Benicio Del Toro. The clip was very graphic and very gory. But the clip made a great point.

All it takes is a little push in the wrong direction to trip us up and get us heading along the path less travelled. Before we know it we find ourselves reading the signs along the psycho path wondering how in the heck we ended up there *again!*

Each of us has our own breaking point and our own triggers that set us off. Things that upset me might not upset anyone else. We're all different and we have our own special kind of crazy living on the inside of us.

The one takeaway point from my class was the statement the speaker made: *sometimes we love our sin more than we love God.* That resonated in my spirit and I've been chewing on that for the last couple of days. I hate when I lose control and I especially hate that when I'm in that crazy place, at that particular moment, "I DO love the food more than I love God," (sighed the misfit).

Recognizing the *beast* inside of us is progress, but we need to learn to tame the beast. In a perfect world we'd do more than just tame the beast; we'd eliminate the beast altogether and get to the point where the only real love in our lives is God and not our sin.

A man who is "of sound mind" is one who keeps the inner madman under lock and key. ~ Paul Valéry, Mauvaises pensées et autres, 1942

You keep track of all my sorrows. You have collected all my tears in your bottle. You have recorded each one in your book. Psalm 56:8 (NLT)

PRAYER FOR TODAY: Lord, I'm so glad that You don't think I'm a social misfit and that You love me regardless of what I weigh or what I eat or how badly I fail. I thank You for new perspectives and for whatever emotional or spiritual growth I may achieve each day. Give me strength and wisdom for each day. In Your name I ask all these things, Lord Jesus. Amen.

OCTOBER 31
The Mask of a Which Witch

Halloween is one of those witchy days that have us wondering which way we'll behave today. The urge to eat our favorite snack size candy bars pulls us unnaturally to do the thing we've been avoiding for months now: eat things we're not supposed to eat!

If you are planning on being home to hand out candy to children do not open your candy bags until the last possible second. If you haven't bought candy yet but you want to have candy available for trick-or-treaters (T-O-Ts), do yourself a favor and buy only candy that you don't like! If you've got a weakness for Snickers Bars or Reese's Peanut Butter Cups, by all means don't bring those into your home!

If you have young children and you will be taking them out for T-O-T, enjoy the fun of dressing up with your children. Don't fall into bad habits though and use Halloween as an excuse to indulge in those treats you've been denying yourself. Avoid the temptation to examine your child's goodies "for safety reasons" when in fact all you really want to do is see if they brought home any of your favorite candy. Let your spouse or a friend examine the candy "for safety reasons" if you know you won't be able to resist temptation.

Once your child's candy has been deemed "safe" store it in zippered storage bags and freeze. If you can't be trusted to take on the responsibility of hiding candy in the freezer have your spouse or a friend come over and hide it where you won't find it and be tempted.

Much of this may seem elementary – but if you're someone struggling to lose weight, Halloween can often be the beginning of the upset of balance. Don't let Halloween be an excuse to hide behind the mask of denial. We can survive Halloween by doing what we know to do. Pray for strength; say Scriptures out loud reinforcing your commitment to get healthy; and be successful with God's help!

There is nothing that gives more assurance than a mask. ~ Colette

You used to live in sin, just like the rest of the world, obeying the devil—the commander of the powers in the unseen world. He is the spirit at work in the hearts of those who refuse to obey God. Ephesians 2:2 (NLT)

PRAYER FOR TODAY: **Lord, this is just another day; one that doesn't have to be my undoing if I don't let it. Help me resist all temptations and stand strong on Your Word and my conviction to get healthy. In Your name I ask all these things, Lord Jesus. Amen.**

NOVEMBER 1
Squeeze the Day

My husband had an unfortunate schedule at work recently that required him to work 18 of 20 days without a real weekend. This past weekend was his first Saturday off in three weeks and he had some catching up to do. Naturally because he wanted to squeeze as much weekend into his two days as possible, our Saturday began with an early morning bike ride; followed by an early movie at the theater, shoe shopping, lunch, grocery shopping, church and dinner and more shopping after dinner. With all he squeezes in a single day, he gives new meaning to the words *seize the day*.

My options are to go along peacefully, get dragged along or stay home and sulk by myself. Because I'd had two previous weekends at home by myself sulking, I wasn't of a mind to pick option three. I basically let him drag me everywhere this weekend. Not surprisingly, many of the weekend activities involved snacks and eating. My hubby doesn't have any weight issues, so for him weekends usually mean food and lots of it.

When we live with people who have very few food restrictions we may have a tendency to feel sorry for ourselves and give in to pouting. Oftentimes a pout is only one pucker away from pouncing on a pizza, popcorn or a piece of pie. If we're not careful we can succumb to our fickle feelings and feed our flesh faster than you can say "super-size that!"

We all know by now life's not fair. Rather than ruining time spent with loved ones or friends, we need to focus on *squeezing the day* with activities not centered on food. If that's impossible or unrealistic, plan ahead and pack healthy snacks for yourself; and above all, don't eat if you're not hungry just because someone else is eating!

Just like diets – relationships are not always easy or problem-free. As with diets – we've got to take our relationships one day at a time. With compromise a good diet or a good relationship can help us find peace and contentment. When we rely on Jesus and trust Him to make our journey successful we can *squeeze* more joy out of life.

What counts in making a happy marriage is not so much how compatible you are, but how you deal with incompatibility. ~ George Levinger

Give honor to marriage, and remain faithful to one another in marriage. God will surely judge people who are immoral and those who commit adultery. Hebrews 13:4 (NLT)

PRAYER FOR TODAY: *Thank You, Lord, for friends and family. May I enjoy the relationships I have and learn to practice balance and compromise. Grant me good health to enjoy life's many blessings. In Your name I ask all these things, Lord Jesus. Amen*

NOVEMBER 2
WAIVER STUPID

Have you ever wondered if there's a level of stupid beyond normal, everyday stupid? A couple of days ago my 21-year-old son enlightened me to a whole new level of stupid beyond just your regular everyday garden variety stupid.

My son is away at college currently in his senior year. I called to see how he was doing this week but was unable to talk to him because he was "in the middle of something." He promised to call when he was free to do so. It turns out the "something" he was in the middle of – as a spectator only (thank goodness) – was a hot wing eating challenge.

He was at a restaurant cheering on a fraternity brother who was attempting to break some sort of record for eating disastrously hot (almost suicidal) hot wings. In order to enter the contest, the participants were required to sign a waiver; releasing the establishment of all legal ramifications should they suffer calamitous consequences from eating these sauce covered hot wings of death.

A "normal" person should recognize the stupidity of eating anything requiring a signed waiver. When my son returned my call he couldn't stop laughing recalling his friend's victory. During his challenge the young man was crying, had snot running down his face and vomited as soon as the contest was finished. For his efforts he collected a $25.00 prize.

I've eaten a lot of things in my life that I'd regretted almost instantly. I've never actually received payment for eating anything – but the difference between me and that *special kind of stupid* is I'm smart enough to know that NO amount of money is worth eating something that's going to potentially put me in the hospital.

Many of us may eat for emotional reasons while others for the pure pleasure of enjoying food. If someone ever asks you to sign a waiver BEFORE you eat something and the potential for destroying your intestinal tract is a high probability – don't do it! That, my friend, is a whole other level of stupid ... *that's waiver stupid.*

Wisdom consists of the anticipation of consequences. ~ Norman Cousins

Wisdom is a tree of life to those who embrace her; happy are those who hold her tightly. Proverbs 3:18 (NLT)

PRAYER FOR TODAY: *Lord, thank You for God-given wisdom and common sense. May I always employ both when making choices regarding my health. I pray You will bless all of my children and grandchildren with wisdom, knowledge and common sense and help them to be the voice of wisdom to their friends. In Your name I ask all these things, Lord Jesus. Amen.*

NOVEMBER 3
Four to Six Minute Disasters

Sometimes the road to dieting success is paved with the best intentions but fraught with unexpected pitfalls – as I discovered yesterday. I had an unusually empty stomach yesterday and found myself wearing a path in the carpet back and forth to the kitchen with my frequent trips. Looking – *just looking* … for I don't know what!

While I was waiting for my healthy popcorn to do its thing in the microwave (which only took a few minutes) I was surprised at the amount of snacks I was able to stick in my mouth in a short span of time. Once I finished my snacks I vowed I'd not put another bite into my mouth until lunch. Eventually I opted to ignore the clock on the wall to obey the clock in my stomach. I put a healthy frozen meal in the microwave and waited impatiently for six minutes thinking I was in the throes of starvation while time ticked down agonizingly slow.

When we find ourselves in the middle of an unusually hungry day and nothing seems to fill us, it's important to realize that one can get themselves in all kinds of trouble in a short four to six minute time span while a healthy meal is microwaving.

On days when we feel our hunger level is increased we need to take a few seconds to analyze and make sure there's not something else going on either emotionally or physically. After some thought, I realized I'd only had a piece of fruit before my early morning workout and I'd missed breakfast. My work schedule crowded out my eating which explained my "unnatural" hunger.

To avoid those sudden fluctuations in our hunger levels always keep planned healthy snacks that don't require microwaving readily available. To avoid those four to six minute disasters have four to six ready-made healthy snacks available in a moment's notice in order to avoid microwave meltdown disasters.

Nobody trips over mountains. It is the small pebble that causes you to stumble. Pass all the pebbles in your path and you will find you have crossed the mountain. ~ Author Unknown

May he grant your heart's desires and make all your plans succeed. May we shout for joy when we hear of your victory and raise a victory banner in the name of our God. May the LORD answer all your prayers. Psalm 20:4-5 (NLT)

PRAYER FOR TODAY: *Lord, help me to make a plan for each day with regards to my menu, my snacks and my exercise. Help me to stick with the plan! May I not be tripped up by my own ignorance or weakness. Keep me strong, helping me to fix my eyes on the end goal. In Your name I ask all these things, Lord Jesus. Amen.*

NOVEMBER 4
Teaching Old Dogs New Tricks

Years ago my husband planted a dwarf orange tree in our yard without giving too much thought to the location of the tree's new home. In his excitement to plant something in the yard, he picked the worst spot for this tree. The tree's location upset the symmetry of the yard. Every time I looked out my kitchen window, I'd think, *"That tree looks stupid there!"* I never had the heart to voice my displeasure to my husband, but merely cursed the tree's location to myself. For all the years that tree resided in that unfortunate location, it never produced a single piece of fruit. I can't help but wonder if my negative thoughts interfered with its lack of fruitful production.

Today was a day that required chocolate. I didn't give in to those baser urges, thank goodness – but in my head I ingested massive amounts of chocolate. I sometimes worry that the foods I think about will actually cause me to gain weight. If stress can cause a visible spike in our blood pressure why wouldn't it be feasible for our thoughts about food to add weight to us? If this is possible many of us are in a lot of trouble!

The Bible repeatedly emphasizes the importance of our thought life. We WANT to change to be more like Christ but sometimes changing our thought life feels too hard. For months we've been working on changing our mindsets. It may take years to change our automatic response during stressful times from *food* first to *God* first.

How do we retrain our thoughts to get them off the first response of chocolate or food and on to GOD? We have to retrain our *old dog* mindsets and learn a brand new way of thinking. We need to teach the old dog some new tricks. If our first thought when the stress comes is: CHOCOLATE, we need to retrain our brains to immediately think: GOD HELP ME!

Change won't happen overnight, but forcing our thoughts into a new mindset will eventually kick in if we keep at it. God wants to be our first response and our auto-response, not our *when all else fails and nothing else is working* response! Stress equals God, not chocolate!

You always pass failure on your way to success. ~ Mickey Rooney

Trust in the LORD with all your heart; do not depend on your own understanding. Seek his will in all you do, and he will show you which path to take. Proverbs 3:5-6 (NLT)

PRAYER FOR TODAY: Lord, help me to move past all of these life-long issues that continually trip me up and make me feel like a failure. Please stand beside me and grant me strength and success before I even know to open my mouth and ask for it. In Your name I ask all these things, Lord Jesus. Amen.

NOVEMBER 5
Just Stop Already

Have you ever had someone in your life that once they discovered you were battling some sort of addiction volunteered the unsolicited advice "Well, just stop already!" You know … just stop smoking! Just stop eating sugar! Just stop drinking! Just stop biting your nails! Just stop already!

People who struggle with any type of addictive behavior don't just wake up one day and think to themselves *"Well, duh, I wonder why I never thought of that!"* How could anyone possibly think that people like being addicted to unhealthy substances or habits?

If it were easy to simply *just stop* doing whatever it is that controls us, none of us would ever have any problems. If we never had any problems, though, we'd likely have no need of a Savior. The older we get the harder it becomes to change those bad habits. Even though we may despise our behaviors, we've gotten to be really good friends with our bad habits.

Simply telling ourselves *"just stop eating sugar"* we might as well tell our lungs to stop breathing or tell our brain to simply stop thinking (although that's a weak argument as there are definitely days when we feel like we're incapable of logical thought).

Many of us may know people who've been supernaturally delivered from bad habits like cigarettes, drugs and alcohol – but those people are few and far between. There is no rhyme or reason to why God chooses to supernaturally deliver *some* and not *all*.

Perhaps God has yet to supernaturally free us from our bondage to food because there are days we still believe we can do this *on our own*. We cannot hope to make lifestyle changes without HIM. Our daily struggles remind us we NEED GOD every day, every minute, every second of our life.

Darkness cannot put out the Light. It can only make God brighter.
~ Author Unknown

Temptation comes from our own desires, which entice us and drag us away. These desires give birth to sinful actions. And when sin is allowed to grow, it gives birth to death. James 1:14-15 (NLT)

PRAYER FOR TODAY: Lord, I know You are with me every day. Lord, if You aren't going to supernaturally deliver me from these bondages, then please walk closer to me so I might sense Your presence when I'm floundering and feeling lost. In Your name I ask all these things, Lord Jesus. Amen.

NOVEMBER 6
A Point Well Taken

A couple of days ago, I was having a wonderfully successful day keeping my menu and recording all my calories. As the day progressed I discovered my husband had plans to go to a basketball game with a friend, leaving me all alone to deal with dinner.

Somehow the idea of cooking for one or throwing a frozen meal in the microwave simply held no appeal for me. I did what any free thinking and creative woman does in that situation – she uses her remaining calories to have an unplanned dinner.

I opted for a rare treat for dinner and indulged myself in a small bowl of cereal followed by low-fat, low-calorie ice cream for dinner. I'm not a big ice cream nut as a rule, (I dream about it more than I eat it). I typically save my occasional frozen dessert treats for special occasions.

Because I still had remaining calories for my dinner, I gave myself permission to eat ice cream for dinner. I used most of my remaining calories to indulge in a rare mid-week luxury. The point is – I ate the ice cream; I enjoyed the ice cream and I made the necessary allowances to eat the ice cream without guilt.

I wouldn't recommend skipping dinner in lieu of dessert on a daily basis – but a once in a while treat is just that … a *once in a while treat*. The reason so many diets fail is because they typically restrict certain foods making us feel deprived. Juggling calories to make allowances for something we really want is okay *occasionally* if we plan responsibly. Too many days of calorie juggling can lead to poor nutrition. Eating a meal comprised primarily of fun foods robs us of important vitamins, nutrients and proteins necessary for a healthy lifestyle.

Have the fun meal once in a while – just be sure to get back on course as soon as possible – by the very next meal if at all possible. It's no secret that too much of anything can be a bad thing.

Seize the moment. Remember all those women on the Titanic who waved off the dessert cart. ~ Erma Bombeck

So whether you eat or drink, or whatever you do, do it all for the glory of God.
1 Corinthians 10:31 (NLT)

PRAYER FOR TODAY: *Lord, thank You for a life filled with choices. Give me wisdom to choose wisely when it comes to my health and my eating habits. I pray I won't get caught up in guilt when I veer off course – but give myself permission to relax once in a while when it comes to my health habits. In Your name I ask all these things, Lord Jesus. Amen.*

NOVEMBER 7
Spontaneous Predictability

Spontaneity in one who's predictably *predictable* causes quite the ripple effect to those around us when we act out of character. I woke up feeling blue yesterday because my youngest daughter was being initiated into her sorority. I was unable to attend any of the festivities which included a ceremony and a luncheon. My husband's work schedule conflicted with the events.

For me to go by myself would mean a two-hour car ride there and back – by myself. There was no ignoring my nasty mood because I was missing something important for my daughter. I felt cheated and wanted to do the usual – medicate my disappointment with food.

My desire to be with my daughter was so strong, I was afraid if I didn't go, I'd end up face down in a giant bag of Cheez Doodles. I did something spontaneous and out of character: I went by myself.

The banquet lunch was adequate but hardly memorable, but the look on my daughter's face when she walked in and spotted me was PRICELESS. When we calculate the cost against the greater good of showing love and support to a cherished loved one sometimes the end justifies the means.

Jesus reacted to changes in His schedule with love even when a request was made to detour Him from His agenda. When spontaneous interruptions occur, it doesn't hurt to ask, *"What would Jesus do?"* If we don't know what Jesus would do in our situation, we should ask His opinion. He loves it when we include Him in our decision-making.

When faced with a day of stuffing disappointment with empty calories because I was forced to miss an important event OR the inconvenience of a four hour car ride to attend a one-hour luncheon, I chose the obvious choice: I chose love.

Sometimes it's better to put love into hugs than to put it into words.
~ Author Unknown

Above all, clothe yourselves with love, which binds us all together in perfect harmony.
Colossians 3:14 (NLT)

PRAYER FOR TODAY: *Lord, may I never forget that loving others is one of the single most important things in life. Help me be willing to go the extra mile to serve You and be a blessing to others even if it may not always seem convenient. In Your name I ask all these things, Lord Jesus. Amen.*

NOVEMBER 8
Prevention – Promptings – Purging and Pepto

We learn to appreciate a God who takes the trouble to remind us when we're about to cross a line. His reprimands aren't always pleasant or timely, but we know that our Heavenly Father knows what we need before we even ask for it. Which is why I wasn't surprised that God chose to remind me recently that the last thing my body needs is cake with lots of icing.

I attended a birthday party for a friend that involved two hours of unlimited bowling. By the time birthday cake was served I was feeling as though I'd accomplished a Herculean task by mastering the game with my bum knee which was causing me much pain. *I deserved cake!* Since cake is my own personal Kryptonite, I filled up on Diet Coke, fruit, veggies, meat and cheese *before* cake was served. I was saving my carbs for cake.

After one bite (which was predominately icing), I felt the first tiny rumblings in my stomach warning me that the icing was over the top in the sweetness department. Because of my love for all things cake, I threw caution to the wind and ate a cupcake followed by two antacid chasers.

What followed wasn't pretty. It took about 20 minutes for the cake to ignite to a white hot poker of churning acid in my stomach and the threat for an instant reversal of fortune was imminent. My one cupcake indulgence and the subsequent cupcake purge prompted me to pray all sorts of promises to God if He would only get me safely home and help the *Pepto* do its job.

God's painful reminders aren't always experiences we'd care to repeat, but can be timely prompts that cause us to rethink our food choices. For me, I'm putting my addiction to all things cake on hiatus, even going so far as to ask God to remind me of this incident the next time I am tempted by cake. An ounce of prevention is worth a pound of *Pepto* that tastes just as bad coming up as it does going down. Even cake is not worth that!

Dieting is not a piece of cake. ~ Author Unknown

And may you have the power to understand, as all God's people should, how wide, how long, how high, and how deep his love is. Ephesians 3:18 (NLT)

PRAYER FOR TODAY: *Lord, I pray You will continue to walk this road with me and impart wisdom to me when it comes to making nutritional choices. Give me this day my daily bread and may I remember moderation and balance in all things. In Your name I ask all these things, Lord Jesus. Amen.*

NOVEMBER 9
The Flip Side of Immeasurable Stupid

It's nice to have times in life to gain a little perspective and actually *see the big picture*. It's been a couple of days since I paid the hefty price for my cupcake indulgence and I still find myself treading lightly when it comes to managing my food intake.

Once you've been reduced to floor time in front of the porcelain throne, you're somewhat hesitant to start ingesting *just anything*. Even thinking about eating sweets or foods swimming in grease makes my innards tense up in that auto reflex movement. I can't help but wonder if these reactions aren't divinely designed by God to keep me on the straight and narrow.

Occasional reminders are good for us. Self-control is what separates us from the animals after all. It's sad to think that sometimes the only way God can get our attention is through a trial or a crisis. Seeing my life flash before me from the strategic vantage point of the bathroom floor was indeed an eye-opening experience; one that could best be described as an "Ah Ha!" moment.

You'd think that we humans would learn from these "Ah Ha!" moments and simply stay on course refusing to go back to our self-destructive ways. Clearly that's not been the case for many of us with regards to repeated attempts to lose weight. We need to figure out how to tap into those "Ah Ha!" moments every time we are tempted to reach for forbidden foods.

At some point a person has to cross over the line of immeasurable stupid and come out on the other side to stand up to her addiction and say, "No more!"

Who would have thought self-discovery and freedom could be found lying face down on the bathroom floor? God in His infinite wisdom knows where each of our *stupid lines* are and what it will take for us to cross over to victory. He loves us enough to say, "Ah Ha, are you listening?"

There's a period of life when we swallow knowledge of ourselves and it becomes either good or sour inside. ~ Pearl Bailey

Getting wisdom is the wisest thing you can do! And whatever else you do, develop good judgment. Proverbs 4:7 (NLT)

PRAYER FOR TODAY: *Lord, I believe everything happens for a reason — even eating to the point of misery. For it is only during my misery that I discover clarity and can focus on the direction I should walk in. Stand beside me and continue to guide me daily. In Your name I ask all these things, Lord Jesus. Amen.*

NOVEMBER 10
The Queen of the Club

Life's been pretty good (or tolerable at the very least) lately as I've been a proud member of the *She Looks Pretty Good for Her Age* Club for a while now. This is a far better club to belong to than the *Boy; Has She Let Herself Go* Club.

A good friend of mine, Carol (not her real name) suddenly found herself not only a member of the *Boy; Has She Let Herself Go* Club, but elected Honorary Queen of the club. The transition was so subtle she found herself stymied as to when she bypassed the *She Looks Pretty Good for Her Age Club* to the less reputable club.

For years she'd been a cute, bubbly mom when through no fault of her own, in her early 40s she was unexpectedly wooed by Mr. Menopause. She'd acquired a menopausal midriff, cheek jowls and saggy butt cheeks. Shortly after the birth of her last child she found herself staring at the reflection of someone she described as no longer cute, but "Frieda Frumpy."

The first thing Carol confessed to me after her revelation was, "Dang it, but this excess weight makes me look so much older!" Rather than making excuses, Carol made a choice to stop whining and complaining and get rid of her excess weight.

Carol devised a plan that she began with many of us on January 1st. She chose a healthy eating plan, contacted me about being her accountability partner; she dug into God's Word and uncovered any hidden eating triggers. (She had a few as the result of a painful divorce.) Carol took control and is down nearly 30 pounds.

Carol accepts that she'll never be "young and cute" again, but is looking forward to tearing up her membership in the *Boy; Has She Let Herself Go* Club. She told me with a laugh recently, the only other club after that one is the *Shamu, Buys Her Clothes at the Local Tent and Awning Mumu* Club. Carol got one thing right; she knows when to laugh at herself and when to take action.

Age attacks when we least expect it. ~ Carrie Latet

My child, never forget the things I have taught you. Store my commands in your heart. If you do this, you will live many years, and your life will be satisfying. Proverbs 3:1-2 (NLT)

PRAYER FOR TODAY: Lord, grant me grace to grow old naturally. May I not whine and complain about the changes my body is going through. I pray for a healthy balance in every area of my life to remain healthy and active for as long as possible. In Your name, Lord Jesus. Amen.

NOVEMBER 11
The Most Dangerous Place on Earth

Have you ever stopped to ask yourself where the most dangerous, treacherous place on planet Earth is? If you knew that up front, you'd avoid visiting that place at all costs and wouldn't ever want to a book a ticket there.

I've been learning through a little self-discovery this week that FOR ME, the most dangerous place exists in the 6-8 inches of space between my ears … that squishy orb in my skull – my brain. Some of the things I think in that 6-8 inches of space can be downright ugly. This past week has seen a spike in my negative thoughts thanks to my fight with insomnia. The enemy knows if he can attack us when we're tired, he can win some key battles because we are more vulnerable.

When we notice a sudden change in our thought life that has us reverting back to hurtful jabs at ourselves it might be time for a little self-discovery. Find a trusted friend or therapist and verbalize the mixed up thoughts bouncing around in your brain. Sometimes just putting an actual voice to our mixed up emotions can be cathartic.

Sharing my negative thoughts with my support group helped me to realize what was at the root of my sudden nose dive in the self-confidence department. Fatigue and some un-resolved issues had pushed me over the edge causing me to entertain negative thoughts.

Learning to share with a trusted therapist or friend can get us off the path of self-destruction. If you're like me and suffering from years of stuffing your emotions and covering up pain with food, reach out to people who are fighting the same battles as you are. There is healing and hope in sharing our pain with friends and people who suffer as we do. Sharing is always better than stuffing.

I know well what I am fleeing from but not what I am in search of.
~ Michel de Montaigne

Avoid all perverse talk; stay away from corrupt speech. Look straight ahead, and fix your eyes on what lies before you. Proverbs 4:24-25 (NLT)

PRAYER FOR TODAY: *Lord, thank You for trusted friends that can help me unravel the crazy thoughts in my head. Help me make sense of my emotions until I reach a point of healing. Bless my friends with their healing and help me to be aware of their pain so I can be a friend in return. In Your name, Lord Jesus. Amen.*

NOVEMBER 12
A Perfect Example

On my way out of the house yesterday, there was a show on TV that captivated my attention, causing me to delay my departure. It was a show about Anorexia and Bulimia. The show followed two young women battling these diseases to the point of near death.

One young girl admitted to a therapist that she was purging everything she ate daily until she was only retaining about 200 calories in her body each day. The therapist warned her if she continued on the path she was on, she'd be dead within less than a year. The girl remarked that she'd "rather die than be fat."

Because I've struggled with weight issues since childhood, I understand her desperation. I've crossed the line and binged to the point of eating myself stupid and felt like I wanted to die, but never crossed the line to near-death. Society labels people as obese if they carry 30 or more pounds beyond what is "normal." The very fact that there are young girls risking their health to the point of death because of anorexia and bulimia makes me weep with sadness.

I've seen firsthand how my obsessive behavior about weight and appearances has affected both my daughters. I'm ashamed that I couldn't get a better handle on my issues before my daughters got old enough to observe my dysfunctional behavior.

At this point, all we can hope for is to gain control of our issues and do our best to set an example for younger women from this day forward. That's a tall order seeing as many of us have yet to achieve control in our own lives. We can learn to control our food obsessions now or continue to let it control us; there can't be two winners in this battle.

Appearances are not held to be a clue to the truth. But we seem to have no other. ~ Ivy Compton-Burnett

For women who claim to be devoted to God should make themselves attractive by the good things they do. 1 Timothy 2:10 (NLT)

PRAYER FOR TODAY: *Lord, I ask forgiveness for my obsession regarding weight and appearance. I pray for healing of my obsessive behavior so that I might enjoy a healthy mind and attitude. Help me to set a good example for young women, including and especially my daughters. In Your name I ask all these things, Lord Jesus. Amen.*

NOVEMBER 13
Stupid is the Best Teacher

Every once in a while my faith in myself and my ability to learn from life's lessons is restored. It's nice to know that when I really needed it, wisdom prevailed and I actually used some of my God-given common sense. After my recent birthday cupcake debacle and subsequent face plant on the floor hugging the base of the porcelain throne for several hours last weekend – I'm happy to report that I actually learned a valuable lesson from that horrifying experience.

My husband and I were invited to another birthday party. Before we left the house I went back and reread my cupcake account in my journal from last weekend as a reminder of my stupidity. I wasn't taking any chances, even asking my husband to swear he wouldn't let me ANYWHERE NEAR THE BIRTHDAY CAKE! I practically ordered him to stick to me like glue.

Once the beautiful sugary creation in butter cream with swirls of multi-colored sprinkles and frosting ribbons was unveiled, I felt my resolve begin to buckle. Bless God, it only buckled for a nanosecond and I resisted any and all urges to partake. Not only did I say NO to the cake, but I resisted the M&Ms, the caramel cookie bars, Chocolate Chex Party Mix and chips and dip.

I can't remember the last time I said NO to so many delectable treats. All it took for me to say NO was simply to close my eyes and recall the unbelievable pain I was in from eating one cupcake last weekend. The consequences more than outweighed the miniscule amount of pleasure I received from that one little cupcake. You couldn't pay me to eat cake anytime soon. Sniff! Sniff! Do you smell that? That is the smell of maturity!

If we stick at this long enough and practice everything we've been preaching for the last many months, even those of us who are slow learners eventually can learn and retrain our thinking. Thank you Lord – we're not as stupid as the devil would have us believe. Victory smells better than cake with butter cream icing.

Wisdom doesn't necessarily come with age. Sometimes age just shows up all by itself. ~ Tom Wilson

God blesses those who patiently endure testing and temptation. Afterward they will receive the crown of life that God has promised to those who love him. James 1:12 (NLT)

PRAYER FOR TODAY: *Lord, thank You for allowing me to learn from my past mistakes. Thank You for the realization that I don't need food in order to have a good time. Continue to teach me valuable life-changing lessons every day. In Your name I ask all these things, Lord Jesus. Amen.*

NOVEMBER 14
Keeping Your Delta Burkes Happy

Getting dressed up in something other than my standard housewife uniform (which in the colder months consists of jeans and tee-shirts) is sometimes more trouble than it's worth. Yesterday I went the extra mile and dressed in a nice outfit for a book signing. I was the author doing the signing.

Unfortunately, my new outfit required both pantyhose and a new foundation garment from the Delta Burke collection. I'm on the bubble for Queen Size panty hose, but I don't care – I like the extra room. What surprised me was my eligibility for the Delta Burke club which begins at the 36-D margin. I'm on the size bubble there too, but not complaining, as it's nice to have a bra that doesn't pinch and bind.

Pantyhose most assuredly were invented by someone who enjoys torture. Contorting into pantyhose is a bit like a Cirque du Soleil act. The simple fact that they require a good 10 solid minutes of tugging, twisting, bending, pulling and stuffing just to be able to get them on is proof of that. Donning pantyhose is the best workout I've had in days.

Pantyhose are a necessary evil because they are the only undergarment available that will successfully camouflage mounds of cellulite while strategically squashing menopausal muffin tops. Regardless of the workout required, pantyhose are actually a win-win undergarment.

On the bright side, Delta Burke knows a thing or two about designing bras. Every time I looked down and saw those two perky *twin sisters* staring at me, I kept thinking "Where did those come from and who's hiding in my sweater?

Sometimes we've got to be reminded to stop fighting it. We all get older. We all have body parts that fall, sag and droop. We should dress for our age and embrace our uniqueness and celebrate who we are. Life is short and so am I, so I get a lift from chunky heels *and my Delta Burke's*. My spirits are lifted when I can laugh at myself and enjoy who God created me to be.

They say that age is all in your mind. The trick is keeping it from creeping down into your body. ~ Author Unknown

I thought, 'Those who are older should speak, for wisdom comes with age.' Job 32:7 (NLT)

PRAYER FOR TODAY: *Lord, thank You for the many advantages available today that help us dress for success and look our best. I pray I will always be thankful for all the many blessings in my life. In Your name I ask all these things, Lord Jesus. Amen.*

NOVEMBER 15
Pie is NOT the Answer

My friend Katie (not her real name) called me this morning needing help. Katie is a mom who has a tendency to take her children's problems and make them her own. She can't seem to help herself from that mother hen compulsion. One of her chicks is in the middle of a crisis. Every time this child calls or texts, Katie says she feels her stomach twisting into a hot tangle of knotted worry making her want to eat. She confessed she had a pumpkin pie at home today. Not a good combo – *worry versus pumpkin pie*.

Katie was in the middle of her morning workout when, the phone calls and texts started with her child's crisis. She felt herself reaching for the calming effects of pie. She sliced off a big hunk of pie and buried it under a mound of whipped cream. She crammed a giant forkful of the creamy pie into her mouth when she stopped as she caught sight of her reflection in the microwave mounted above her stove. She froze and panicked.

"In my head and my heart I KNOW that pie will not give me the answers I need for this problem," she wailed. "I KNOW pie is not the answer. But I don't know what else to do," she cried over the phone line. Katie confessed, "My mouth clamped down on the pie in an auto-reflex move like it was attacking that pie with the Jaws of Life! But I don't want to be this way!"

As we talked, I reminded Katie, YOU DO KNOW *what else to do* – why not pray about it? We stopped and did just that. In the end Katie refused to let the pie beat her. She called me and together we took the problem to the Lord and together we chose to leave it there.

Stopping yourself in the middle of a would-be binge when you're already emotionally compromised is sometimes harder than solving the problem that instigated your melt-down in the first place. It can be done, though! If we don't exercise our prayer muscles we'll never build them up! It's time to stop chewing and pray.

God can pick sense out of a confused prayer. ~ Richard Sibbes

Bend down, O LORD, and hear my prayer; answer me, for I need your help. Protect me, for I am devoted to you. Save me, for I serve you and trust you. You are my God. Be merciful to me, O Lord, for I am calling on you constantly. Psalm 86:1-3 (NLT)

PRAYER FOR TODAY: Lord, thank You for your guidance. I know that when I pray You hear me. Continue to help me and guide me on this journey. In Your name I ask all these things, Lord Jesus. Amen.

NOVEMBER 16
Sybil Me This

I think that a lot of women suffer in part from some sort of multiple personality disorder. Part of the time we can be sweet, compassionate and caring individuals who offer warm hugs, sage wisdom and inspirational insight. In the blink of an eye something happens that sends us over the edge and releases our inner *Sybil*.

My *Sybil* sighting today was sponsored by none other than a timely email from a well-meaning friend, who is clueless to the quirks and nuances of interpersonal relationships. That, coupled with the fact that I didn't sleep well again last night and before you know it, I was doing that – *if my husband doesn't stop snoring soon I'm going to smother him with my pillow* – thing. Well … that's reason enough for a little leakage on the crazy valve.

While I don't mean to make light of the story of *Sybil*, which is a movie based on a real woman with a very serious schizophrenic disorder, I'm feeling quite unlike my "normal" self today and fatigue has a way of working the crazy out of us.

After my breakfast and workout this morning, I retreated to my home office to check emails. I have this one friend (don't we all?) that lives in her own little universe where she actually believes the sun rises and sets according to her specific needs. She's the friend who digs herself into trouble and manages to be rescued in the 11th hour coming out completely unscathed. She's the friend who ALWAYS gets everything she wants without paying her dues like the rest of us.

The fact that I still feel this unhealthy need to compare myself to her or anyone else should be a sign that I've still much maturing and healing to do.

It's on days like this it's important to ingest massive quantities of the Word of God to be consumed at regular intervals for pain – *as needed*. When I am done, I'll do the "grown-up" thing and respond politely to my friend and keep my snarky comments to myself. Three steps forward – two steps backs. Any way we slice it, healing is hard work.

After God created the world, He made man and woman. Then, to keep the whole thing from collapsing, He invented humor. ~ Bill Kelly, "Mordillo"

People with understanding control their anger; a hot temper shows great foolishness. A peaceful heart leads to a healthy body; jealousy is like cancer in the bones. Proverbs 14:29-30 (NLT)

PRAYER FOR TODAY: *Lord, today is one of those days I don't even know what to pray for other than help. I need a touch from You in the worst way, Lord. Please help me to relax in Your presence and know that You love me unconditionally. In Your name I ask all these things, Lord Jesus. Amen.*

NOVEMBER 17
Anti-Cheerleader, Real Life Success

While I was cleaning house this afternoon I got sucked into watching an hour's worth of *The Dallas Cowboys Cheerleaders*. I used to watch this show with my daughter because we love anything related to the art of dance.

When I watch this show it's easy for me to imagine that I'm that young, that thin and that talented. The fact that I still have enough imagination to even entertain this ridiculous DCC (Dallas Cowboys Cheerleader) fantasy says a lot about my imagination. I'm so completely opposite of what a DCC is I'm actually the *anti*-DCC.

Even if I were to magically erase 30 years and half my body weight, I'd still have no rhythm and two left feet. But a girl can dream, can't she? It's alright to entertain our imaginations, but before we go too far and get our ticket punched for *Fantasy Land*, it's important to stay grounded in reality.

If we ever hope to achieve success on our weight loss journey we can occasionally indulge in fantasy, but even fantasy needs to be somewhat attainable. Imagining what it would be like to shop for a pair of jeans several sizes smaller is attainable. Competing in a half-marathon is attainable. If we're over 40, being a professional cheerleader is a real stretch of the imagination and highly unlikely.

On any weight loss journey it's important to set *realistic* goals. It's equally as important that we get those mental pictures of what's at the end of this weight loss journey. Maybe we need to be bold enough to paste *realistic* pictures of what we hope to look like when we reach our goal in a place of high visibility so we'll see those images and believe for success. I've still got a pair of size 10 jeans that I keep in the front of the closet to remind me of my goal.

The fact is I may not get there in this calendar year, but I absolutely refuse to give up altogether. I can imagine it or I can do it – but either way, I'm going to conquer this excess weight and this food addiction and get healthy because I am worth it. I may not be a cheerleader, but I can be a success.

If you aim at nothing, you'll hit it every time. ~ Author Unknown

Hope deferred makes the heart sick, but a dream fulfilled is a tree of life. Proverbs 13:12 (NLT)

PRAYER FOR TODAY: Lord, help me to set realistic goals and be willing to work hard every day to achieve them. I pray I can maintain a healthy balance between visualizing my success without wandering over into unrealistic fantasies. May I be balanced in every area of my life. In Your name I ask all these things, Lord Jesus. Amen.

NOVEMBER 18
Anti-Holiday Stress

Here it is a little more than a week until Thanksgiving and the holiday season "officially" begins. The holidays can be a difficult and trying time for anyone who didn't grow up in a house like *The Brady Bunch* or any other fake family depicted on TV where "happy" and "normal" were the main ingredient.

I grew up in the *anti-normal* family. Most of my immediate family remained in denial about our family environment for decades – some even taking that denial to their graves. I've not only accepted the dynamics of my family dysfunction, I'm working through it to overcome it.

With the holiday season just days away I've noticed an unusual amount of anxiety, resentment and anger bubbling up just under the surface of my carefully controlled demeanor. I'm not the only one who suffers from holiday anxiety as I've heard complaints from many friends recently.

The farther along this path we travel; the more we recognize those unhealthy triggers. Once we recognize these triggers, the less damage they cause us. We may still be a ways from overcoming and completely tackling all our issues, but we are in the process of attacking our dysfunction before it beats us.

Over the course of the upcoming holiday season be on your guard and don't be surprised if you have days that make you feel like you've been beaten up emotionally. If that happens, find a release valve that's NOT FOOD and blow off some pent up anxiety or anger. Sometimes all it takes is a good cry over a sappy holiday movie.

Don't tackle your holiday anxiety on your own. Take it from someone who knows, it's not healthy to keep all those emotions bottled up. My advice before the holidays are upon us is, find a trusted friend you can vent with, cry with, or watch movies with and release all those pent up emotions so you can actually enjoy the holidays this year without pain and without excess food.

Family quarrels are bitter things. They don't go by any rules. They're not like aches or wounds; they're more like splits in the skin that won't heal because there's not enough material. ~ F. Scott Fitzgerald

Even if my father and mother abandon me, the LORD will hold me close. Psalm 27:10 (NLT)

PRAYER FOR TODAY: *Lord, thank You for friends who listen and don't judge; who allow me to pour out my troubles and are willing to laugh with me and cry with me. I have much to be thankful for and I pray I never take for granted how blessed my life is. In Your name I ask all these things, Lord Jesus. Amen.*

NOVEMBER 19
One Day and Another and Another …

Do you ever have a day when you've been so exceptionally good on your eating program combined with a fabulous workout and you think … I can do this? And then because you've had one successful day, or maybe two or three successful days in a row, do you wake up in the morning certain that ALL of your excess weight has magically disintegrated overnight and suddenly you're the thin beautiful woman you've always imagined you'd be?

Okay, maybe it's just me, but sometimes I honestly convince myself that a good night's sleep is all I need to wake up and discover that this chubby girl inhabiting my body has just been my imagination. Wouldn't it be lovely if that's all it would take to get rid of the excess body weight?

If we've been battling excess weight for any length of time, we need to wake up and realize these bodies of ours aren't just a bad dream. We're not going to suddenly wake up and get our "real self" back. No matter how unhappy we may be with our bodies when we go to bed at night, it's highly unlikely we're going to wake up after a mere eight hours and find that God has blessed us with a brand new body.

It doesn't mean we'll never have a body that we love again, but we need to accept that it may take us a few more months to get this weight off. We can't magically whittle away this excess weight with anything other than hard work. It makes the journey so much easier if we can learn to love the body we are in right now, regardless of our weight.

Yes, it would be lovely if there were another way, but we can't let all those info-mercials fool us. The only way to kiss this excess body weight good-bye is to have one good day on our program and another good day … and another good day … and so on. One day, one pound, one body, one dream. Don't let your dream die because you're tired of waiting.

Why should a man's mind have been thrown into such close, sad, sensational, inexplicable relations with such a precarious object as his body? ~ Thomas Hardy

Young people, it's wonderful to be young! Enjoy every minute of it. Do everything you want to do; take it all in. But remember that you must give an account to God for everything you do. Ecclesiastes 11:9 (NLT)

PRAYER FOR TODAY: *Lord, thank You for each and every good day I have on my wellness program. Help me to repent for the bad days and do what I can to learn from my mistakes. Lend me Your strength so I can grow in wisdom and knowledge daily. In Your name I ask all these things, Lord Jesus. Amen.*

NOVEMBER 20
Give a Little – Get a Little

A little bit of success can be a dangerous thing. I had a fairly good week on my eating plan. I had a great week with my exercise program this week. The best I've had since I had knee surgery this past summer. Last night when I slipped on my jeans and they were a smidge looser than they'd been the previous week, I thought "YEAH! This is progress!"

So why is it when we have even a modicum of success, we feel the need to *reward* ourselves with *food?* Dressed in my slightly looser jeans my husband offered to take me on a dinner date to *celebrate* my successful week at a nice all-you-can-eat salad buffet (AYCE buffet).

I gave myself the standard pre-dinner pep talk about the dangers of AYCE buffets and promised myself to eat in moderation. The real hidden dangers of the AYCE buffets are the pasta salads, especially tuna salad which is generally made with *all the fat* mayo. Pastas are full of carbs and overall something you should avoid if you're watching calories.

Eating out can prove to be extremely challenging and until one has a firm grasp on this healthy eating lifestyle, it would best be avoided until you're on more solid footing. However, a healthy lifestyle shouldn't completely limit or inhibit your lifestyle to the point that you become reclusive and unwilling to leave your home for fear of the food temptations out there.

Maintaining a balance is possible as long as we use wisdom, common sense and a certain amount of restraint. We can have a healthy social life that involves food, but doesn't revolve around food. Limiting our calories at breakfast and lunch in order to save calories for a night out is a great way to plan ahead so we can say "Yes!" to some of those dinner invitations. As with anything if we give a little to get a little, we can and will succeed.

If you keep doing things like you've always done them, what you'll get is what you've already got. ~ Author Unknown

"Look at the birds. They don't plant or harvest or store food in barns, for your heavenly Father feeds them. And aren't you far more valuable to him than they are?" Matthew 6:26 (NLT)

PRAYER FOR TODAY: *Lord, thank You for this week's successes. Help me not to completely forget the failures, but rather help me to learn from them. Thank You for standing by me and guiding me on this difficult journey. Continue to walk beside me and help me when I am weak. In Your name I ask all these things, Lord Jesus. Amen.*

NOVEMBER 21
More than Rats and Garbage

A couple of days ago I watched a program on TV about a woman and her son who lived in Cambodia. The program followed them as they were out scavenging for their daily food. The son had already spent time at the local dump scouring the piles of garbage looking for anything edible or something worth selling so he could make extra money for his family. His mom finally managed to catch and kill a rat which she barbecued for their only food that day.

You can't watch a program like that and not be changed by it – even a little bit. After watching that show, it reminds me of all the food available to my family. It saddens me to think of the food we let go to waste and end up throwing out when there are so many people starving all over the world; in our country and even in our own cities.

I'm doing my part this week to make sure that the meals I plan for myself are minimal and healthy. I'm making a vow to eat only what I prepare and measure, not allowing anything to be thrown away or wasted.

With obesity at an all-time high and practically an epidemic in our western culture, it's sad that there are people around the world forced to catch and kill rats for their daily food as their only means of survival.

As individuals we can't cure world hunger by ourselves, but we can all do our part by not being wasteful with what we've been blessed with. It's a moral decision what to choose (or not) to do to benefit those less fortunate. We can volunteer our time to a local food bank or donate to programs that feed the hungry or sponsor a child or families with a monthly donation.

As we approach Thanksgiving, take a minute every day to find something to be thankful for. Remember to make a menu plan, stick to it and endeavor to avoid wasting food. Look for something to be thankful for every day.

**If the only prayer you said in your whole life was, "thank you," that would suffice.
~ Meister Eckhart**

And let the peace that comes from Christ rule in your hearts. For as members of one body you are called to live in peace. And always be thankful. Colossians 3:15 (NLT)

PRAYER FOR TODAY: *Lord, I am thankful for all of the many blessings in my life and my family. May I never take for granted how blessed we are to have food to eat and we never go to bed with empty bellies. Give me a heart for the suffering and help me do my part to feed the hungry either by donations or volunteering my time. In Your name I ask all these things, Lord Jesus. Amen.*

NOVEMBER 22
Stepping Thanks

Today I am thankful for hard work. I worked my fingers to the bone today with normal "housewifey" duties. My husband and I just found out two days ago we are hosting Thanksgiving at our house this year. Needless to say I've had lots of cleaning to do like carpet shampooing; scrubbing toilets and a host of other duties to keep me busy.

I wore my pedometer in order to chart my activity level. My morning workout and my hours of housework all combined to equal way more than the recommended daily total of 10,000 steps.

Squeezing in planned meals was challenging, but after the story about the mom and her son and their rat dinner yesterday, I decided, *less is more* with regards to my calories. I volunteered my time at church in the afternoon and ended the day exhausted but feeling satisfied that today I did my part.

Ten hours on my feet and I'm unbelievably thankful that even though I limp terribly and every muscle in my body aches – I can still work hard and accomplish a full day's work. When I think of the many people who are either house bound, or handicapped and unable to be on their feet for extended periods of time, I'm grateful that God has blessed me with a fairly healthy body. I'm grateful I'm able to contribute and fill my days up with serving my family, my Lord and my church.

There's a slight chance I won't be able to get out of bed tomorrow – *but today* – I'm thankful for hard work! God is good!!!

What we're really talking about is a wonderful day set aside on the fourth Thursday of November when no one diets. I mean, why else would they call it Thanksgiving? ~ Erma Bombeck, "No One Diets on Thanksgiving," 26 November 1981

Devote yourselves to prayer with an alert mind and a thankful heart. Colossians 4:2 (NLT)

PRAYER FOR TODAY: *Lord, even though my whole body aches tonight, I'm thankful for strength of mind, body and spirit to be able to do physical tasks. Thank You for providing for all of our needs and may I be ever mindful of the needs of others and give unselfishly to those in need. In Your name I ask all these things, Lord Jesus. Amen.*

NOVEMBER 23
Healthy Reminders

Today I am thankful for good health. I have two friends in the hospital. I have another friend who is going through cancer treatments. I have several other friends who are either suffering from some sort of illness themselves or have loved ones who are sick and in the hospital. Sickness doesn't take a break just because the holidays are upon us. Disease is a frequent flyer travelling on the accumulated points of the masses. Illness travels at our expense.

If we're one of the lucky ones that enjoy good health, we should take a minute to realize that it is a gift we shouldn't take for granted. I have mild health issues and general aches and pains that come with age. Overall, I'm far better off than so many others and I promise never to forget that. Whenever I start to complain about my bum knee, God arranges to send someone across my path that is in a wheelchair, paralyzed or has no legs at all. I'm reminded regularly that things could be worse and I've got it pretty good.

Because of the availability of medications and doctors in this country, we are blessed to be able to get immediate attention if there is something amiss. Even if we can't agree on the current health care changes, we still have much to be grateful for compared to health care in many other countries which is frequently non-existent.

During this week of Thanksgiving, many of us have much to be thankful for. If we have food to eat, heat in the winter and hot water for showers, we're better off than a large percentage of the world. We can't fix all of the world's problems; some days we can barely handle our own problems. That being said, look to God when problems come your way and be thankful for a Savior who loves us unconditionally and provides for our needs when we seek Him.

As we express our gratitude, we must never forget that the highest appreciation is not to utter words, but to live by them. ~ John Fitzgerald Kennedy

"But giving thanks is a sacrifice that truly honors me. If you keep to my path, I will reveal to you the salvation of God." Psalm 50:23 (NLT)

PRAYER FOR TODAY: *Thank You, Lord, for life's many blessings. I am thankful to enjoy good health each and every day. I appreciate those gentle reminders that my life is pretty good and I have no valid reasons for whining or complaining. Continue to make me ever mindful of the needs of others. In Your name I ask all these things, Lord Jesus. Amen.*

NOVEMBER 24
Low on the Crap-o-Meter

Some days are easier than others to come up with things to be thankful for. On any given day most of us are only a phone call, a text message or an email away from the next disaster. Because life is subject to change in the blink of an eye – even when you're having a really crappy day – if you try hard enough, it's still possible to come up with *at least one thing* to be thankful for.

Today was a moderately crappy day on the crap-o-meter scale of life, but I'm not complaining. I'm actually thankful things aren't any worse than they are. In the grand scheme of life my problems, while huge and challenging to me, are still barely a blip on someone else's crap-o-meter scale. Say … someone who is in the hospital fighting for their next breath.

I'm certain most of my problems are the direct result of pre-Thanksgiving stress and planning a sit down dinner for 24 that has me weepy and on edge. I had to reach way down deep today to find something to voice my gratitude for. Today's gratitude candidate is: *family* (even the ones creating all this Thanksgiving dinner stress).

You may be thinking *family?* Really? In many circumstances, it's my family that pushes me over the edge and pushes me towards an untimely food binge. Some of you may have families worse than mine; some may have better families; and some may have no family. Some family members are easier to love than others. Some we love because *we have to.* Some we love even when we think there is nothing fundamentally loveable about them. We love because God is love. He loves us even though many of us are unlovable.

I love my family in spite of my pre-Thanksgiving craziness as I prepare to host our holiday get-together. My sanity and balance are in question as all I want to do is eat chocolate to combat the pre-Thanksgiving family stress. Now if only that chocolate was calorie-free, life would be near to perfect.

Thanksgiving is America's national chow-down feast, the one occasion each year when gluttony becomes a patriotic duty. ~ Michael Dresser

Be thankful in all circumstances, for this is God's will for you who belong to Christ Jesus. 1 Thessalonians 5:18 (NLT)

PRAYER FOR TODAY: *Lord, sometimes I think You must have the most bizarre sense of humor based on the way You put families together. While many of us have difficult family members, help us to see that sometimes WE might be the difficult family member in the family dynamics. I pray peace upon my entire household and all my family – both immediate and extended – and may we all get along and appreciate one another. In Your name I ask all these things, Lord Jesus. Amen.*

NOVEMBER 25
Holy Calories, Batman!

You gotta love a day set aside for the sole purpose of eating surrounded by family members. Unless of course you're suffering from some sort of eating disorder, food addiction or hail from an extremely dysfunctional family. It's difficult to find families that can co-exist under one roof for several hours without resorting to physical blows, cynical sniping or hurtful repartee.

The Thanksgiving meal itself can be fairly legal and healthy if you put in the effort. Turkey is good for you as long as you avoid the dark meat and the skin. Potatoes can be made to be creamy and delicious if you avoid using lots of butter, sour cream, whole milk or salt and don't overdose on gravy. I always volunteer to make several bowls of steamed veggies, which not only provide low-cal options for diners, but also add color to your Thanksgiving table. Offer to contribute one or two healthy dishes to the holiday menu so you can guarantee some healthy options.

It may surprise you to know that the average caloric content of a typical holiday meal can be anywhere from 2,500 calories to just over 4,500 calories. Yowza! For many of us, 2,500 calories are more than our allotment of calories for an entire day! With careful planning we can reduce that number significantly, but it will take lots of effort.

My Thanksgiving downfall is usually the rolls and butter. The average dinner roll with butter is right around 310 calories. Look for whole wheat rolls and lower calorie butter substitutes. If you remove your "healthier" butter option from its original container and place it in a decorative bowl in lieu of butter, your company will be none the wiser.

When it comes to desserts, we know we need to approach them with moderation. There are lower calorie options available for pies as well. Consider a "crust-less" pie. Do your research to avoid falling off the wagon for this one meal. Be prepared and be thankful that we don't have to be mindless eating machines on Thanksgiving just because everyone else is. We can undo a lot of hard work on this one day, so eat responsibly!

An optimist is a person who starts a new diet on Thanksgiving Day. ~ Irv Kupcinet

They sang, "Amen! Blessing and glory and wisdom and thanksgiving and honor and power and strength belong to our God forever and ever! Amen." Revelation 7:12 (NLT)

PRAYER FOR TODAY: *Lord, thank You for family and friends this week. In spite of the work necessary to welcome people into my home, I am thankful for the home You have provided. May I be continually reminded of how much life has to offer and how truly blessed I am. In Your name I ask all these things, Lord Jesus. Amen.*

NOVEMBER 26
Another Lap around the Friend Zone

A friend of mine approached me not long ago asking my opinion about "Lap Band" surgery for weight loss. This is a young woman in her early 30s who is 125 pounds overweight, suffers from hyper-tension and has a BMI of 41. She suffers from anxiety/panic attacks because she's afraid she's going to have a heart attack because of her weight. Yet she still has a difficult time managing her emotional eating.

I'm not an expert who can counsel anyone with regards to weight loss surgery. I am however, an expert at suffering, pain and hopelessness when it comes to being overweight. Based on my first-hand knowledge from that perspective, I advised her to check every detail from insurance, to surgery (pre and post) and of course long term side-effects.

Many insurance companies are opting to pay for the procedure these days because obesity is a precursor to many fatal diseases, such as heart disease and diabetes. After doing some minimal research, the Lap Band is a vast improvement over what used to be considered state-of-the art "Stomach Stapling" surgery for obesity.

Upon further investigation, I learned that for all lap band surgeries extensive pre-op testing and counseling is mandatory, as well as post-surgery testing and counseling. My friend said she would be required to undergo regular weekly counseling before and after the procedure so she won't continue to perpetuate her eating disorder without uncovering the emotional causes.

My advice to my friend and anyone who might ever ask me: seek medical advice, do your research and get all your questions answered before you pursue surgery. Because my friend is doing all of these things, I support her and pray she will choose wisely. I pray whatever she decides she can live a life free from her self-destructive food addiction.

Judge not lest you've walked in another's shoes. I've never been 125 pounds overweight, so it's impossible for me to know exactly how my friend feels. I love her so I will do whatever I can to support her and help her. We love because *He first loved us.*

In giving advice seek to help, not to please, your friend. ~ Solon

The godly offer good counsel; they teach right from wrong. Psalm 37:30 (NLT)

PRAYER FOR TODAY: *Lord, thank You for friends. Help me always to be a good friend by not offering advice unless asked. Help me not to overstep my boundaries, but to offer love, support and respect when the situation calls for it. I am blessed to be a friend and have many friends. May I always continue to learn and grow and be the best person I can be. In Your name I ask all these things, Lord Jesus. Amen.*

NOVEMBER 27
I Feel Pretty

Just when you think you've seen everything on TV, some stupid show pops up confirming your worst fears. Our society is most definitely circling the drain – all that's needed is one giant flush to eliminate what's got to be the worst idea for a reality show of all time. I saw a preview for a reality show called "Bridalplasty" about brides competing for the ultimate fantasy wedding that also includes their dream plastic surgery makeovers.

Most of these brides are early to mid-20s, with the oldest bride only 32. One of the brides is just 20 and has *11 things* about her body she'd like surgically changed. Each bride has a laundry list of all the things they don't like about their bodies they want changed. The bride with the fewest items on her wish list only wants four things surgically changed on her body. One bride wants as many as *15 things changed*.

The thing that's so surprising about these 12 women is they are all very attractive women. They are all engaged to be married but clearly they must all suffer from some sort of low self-esteem issues. What's worse, their fiancés were required to sign releases stating they won't see their brides until the wedding day. They'll see their brides with new faces and bodies at the same time the viewing public sees them.

Is this a healthy way to begin a marriage? No wonder there are so many young girls out there suffering with eating disorders and killing themselves to be thin and "perfect." The *role* models projected on TV are all surgically implanted, botoxed, liposucked, tummy tucked, siliconed fake Barbie™ dolls! Worse yet, the men out there are all looking for a Barbie™ doll to marry.

If women like us don't make our voices heard and set an example to our daughters, nieces, granddaughters and young women everywhere we are merely perpetuating the problem. We "real" beautiful women need to encourage the young girls in our circle of influence to love themselves as they are and embrace the unique beautiful individuals God created them to be. Beauty begins at home.

**Beauty… when you look into a woman's eyes and see what is in her heart.
~ Nate Dircks**

He will delight in obeying the LORD. He will not judge by appearance nor make a decision based on hearsay. Isaiah 11:3 (NLT)

PRAYER FOR TODAY: *Lord, thank You that Your Holy Spirit dwells in me and that I am not loved based on my appearance. Help me to see myself as You see me. Help me to accept that I am beautiful because I am Your child and I reflect YOU. May I always be a positive example to others who struggle with a poor body image. In Your name I ask all these things, Lord Jesus. Amen.*

NOVEMBER 28
The Four "F's" of Thanksgiving

Waking up this morning and the prospect of entertaining a houseful of people, and today I'm thankful for the four "F's" of Thanksgiving: *family, friends, food and fun!*

Because we're expecting a couple dozen people at my house there's a good news/bad news scenario for the day. The good news is last minute cleaning and preparation is good for burning a couple hundred calories. In addition, my family is somewhat competitive and several, rousing games of bocce ball, ping pong and bean bag toss are planned for later in the day. Somehow my family has a way of making any game a contact sport so there will be ample opportunity to burn off some of those Thanksgiving carbs.

The bad news is, most Thanksgiving meals include generous portions of desserts and assorted baked goods and the temptation to sit and nap after a big meal is oftentimes too much to pass up. I have a whole contingency of relatives who spend their post-holiday meal relaxing on the couch cat-napping to the traditional holiday football game. That can look pretty good after the many days of marathon housecleaning prior to the start of today. However, that won't burn off those extra calories.

Today is a day to give thanks. If you're in a panic about how you're going to manage your calories, stop and reflect. You don't have to bow down to the whims of your flesh today. You don't have to let pies, cakes and cookies boss you around.

Cut calories where you can. Begin your day with a small meal or a low-cal breakfast shake. Get busy and offer a helping hand so you won't have time to sit and think about food. If you're really worried about your calorie intake today, wear an outfit that is a little snug in the waistline to remind you that you don't have a lot of wiggle room for extra calories.

Let this be a day of celebration to enjoy family and friends. If you stumble, pick yourself up, dust yourself off and remember to be thankful this day only comes once a year. There is always something to be thankful for each and every day.

We can only be said to be alive in those moments when our hearts are conscious of our treasures. ~T hornton Wilder

I will offer you a sacrifice of thanksgiving and call on the name of the Lord. Psalm 116:17 (NLT)

PRAYER FOR TODAY: *Lord, today is day to give thanks; not a day for complaining. May this be a peaceful day filled with the goodness of You, Lord Jesus. Help me to be joyful and thankful to those I share a meal with today. In Your name I ask all these things, Lord Jesus. Amen.*

NOVEMBER 29
Black Friday, Black Moods

You have to wonder if part of the reason they call the day after Thanksgiving "Black Friday" is because your mood is so foul, dark and black from eating too much food the day before. Many of us wake the morning after feeling like a giant engorged toad too fat to even move.

I practiced considerable restraint yesterday and I still woke up feeling like a slug. I could hardly move this morning because of all the carbs slowing my system down. In spite of my restraint, I still indulged in a "small bite of this" and "a tiny pinch of that." Not to mention "just a nibble of something else."

When you've denied your flesh tons of sweets and sugars for any length of time and suddenly you reintroduce them to your system – you're headed for an intestinal grudge match. The consequences of consuming a bunch of carbs in a short span of time is bound to cause some stomach upsets and some definite imbalances in your system.

On the bright side, I've not been able to walk farther than a mile and a half in the last three months since my knee surgery – but today because I felt so sluggish, I made myself walk, and walk and walk A LOT today.

Because holidays can be so emotionally draining it's a great idea to schedule some healthy exercise, if only to restore sanity and balance to your emotionally drained psyche. A little exercise can go a long way towards lifting your Black Friday mood and holiday eating regrets! A holiday dedicated to the singular purpose of pigging out is sure to produce a certain amount of regrets. Rather than sitting around stewing in your regrets stew in a little sweat instead.

The funny thing about Thanksgiving, or any huge meal, is that you spend 12 hours shopping for it and then chopping and cooking and braising and blanching. Then it takes 20 minutes to eat it and everybody sort of sits around in a food coma, and then it takes four hours to clean it up. ~ Ted Allen

You prepare a feast for me in the presence of my enemies. You honor me by anointing my head with oil. My cup overflows with blessings. Psalm 23:5 (NLT)

PRAYER FOR TODAY: *Lord, thank You for the gift of exercise, the gift of life, the gift of time and the gift of love. My cup overflows with all the goodness and mercy You've bestowed upon me. Help me to always let Your blessings flow from me to others. In Your name I ask all these things, Lord Jesus. Amen.*

NOVEMBER 30
Yo-Yo Statistic or Success Statistic

This morning I woke up thinking about my friend who is considering Lap Band surgery for weight loss. My spirit is heavy as I pray for her because I know how hard she's tried to lose weight the traditional way. I've seen the hours she's in the gym and watched how carefully she weighed and measured her food portions. But I've also seen her when she's lost all hope and eaten herself sick. How desperate must someone be to consider surgery for losing weight?

I know that for my friend she's looking at this surgery as a lifesaving procedure. She's got nowhere else to go. She'd even considered sending in a tape to be considered as a contestant on that TV reality show, *The Biggest Loser*. Both the TV show and Lap Band surgery are very extreme solutions. Reality shows aren't "real" in the fact that you're taken out of your "real" life for months at a time but eventually you have to go home.

When any weight loss program promises you dramatic weight loss in a short amount of time, your brain and your emotions usually don't have enough time to significantly deal with the related issues that caused the weight gain in the first place. Many people who are significantly overweight eat because of unresolved emotional issues.

If your reasons for losing weight don't involve long-term commitment and maintenance, you're likely to end up in the 95% category of people who lose weight only to quickly regain it. You'll just be another "yo-yo dieter." You'll be a statistic.

If however, you've got long range goals on how you're going to maintain a slimmer, healthier you then by all means, seek medical approval and start a weight loss program, join a gym, get a workout buddy, or even perhaps research a Lap Band surgery to see if you meet the necessary criteria. Do what you need to do to get healthy. Don't be a statistic – be a success.

Never confuse a single defeat with a final defeat. ~ F. Scott Fitzgerald

Show me the right path, O Lord: point out the road for me to follow. Lead me by your truth and teach me, for you are the God who saves me. All day long I put my hope in you. Psalm 25:4-5 (NLT)

PRAYER FOR TODAY: *Lord, thank You for the many options available for losing weight. Help me not to become a weight loss failure statistic, but an overcomer and a success story. May my success and positive attitude be an inspiration for those who are struggling. In Your name I ask all these things, Lord Jesus. Amen.*

DECEMBER 1
Wasted Oxygen and Misspent Molecules

Yesterday turned out to be a real "slug fest" for me. No, I wasn't physically beating people senseless, as the only *physical* thing I did yesterday was moving from the bed to the recliner to the bathroom and back to the bed again.

I awoke feeling icky all over. I had to wake at the crack of dawn to send my youngest daughter back to college with hugs and tears at an ungodly hour. After crying off and on for a little while, it became apparent the pounding in my skull wasn't simply from emotional saturation, but the beginnings of either a nasty cold or a sinus infection.

My son woke up a couple of hours later that he too had to make the return trip back to school. After another round of tears and tantrums – mine – not his, I said good-bye to my son and watched another child drive away.

That's where the rest of the day got kind of hazy, but I know there was definitely cold medicine involved. You know the kind that promises to take care of your *achy head, runny nose and aching body so you can rest* stuff. It definitely lived up to its promises.

Fighting a cold is not the time to fixate on extra calories. Cold medicine has a tendency to make us a little foggy-headed so menu planning and counting calories is tougher during illnesses and should not be our first priority. We need to take care of ourselves.

We don't have to be undone by a simple cold. Staying on top of our healthy program may feel impossible when we are sick. Even if we feel we're losing ground by consuming high-calorie juices or eating empty carbs like toast or crackers, it's important to remember this is one minor battle, not the entire war.

For every defeat there is always a Savior who can help us fight these battles—big or small. Thank goodness He never sleeps, He never gets sick and He never takes a holiday. Jesus is just a prayer away!

To give vent now and then to his feelings, whether of pleasure or discontent, is a great ease to a man's heart. ~ Francesco Guicciardini

My eyes are blinded by my tears. Each day I beg for your help, O LORD; I lift my hands to you for mercy. Psalm 88:9 (NLT)

PRAYER FOR TODAY: *Lord, I know You hear my cries and see my pain and collect my tears in a bottle. I pray Your mercy, Lord, and ask that You would send Your Holy Spirit to be a healing balm to my troubled heart and aching body. In Your name I ask all these things, Lord Jesus. Amen.*

DECEMBER 2
The Sweatpants Don't Lie

One of the hidden pitfalls of too much time off over a long holiday weekend during the cold winter months is just that – *too much time off*. Eventually the weekend wraps up and we have to get off the couch, ditch our sweatpants and hope that when it's time to reintroduce our self to society – our pants still fit.

For the past couple of days – I've pretty much been living in my sweatpants. Sweatpants can lull you into a false sense of comfort because you don't have the restrictions of zippers and buttons to remind you that you've exceeded reasonable limitations with your food intake. Sweatpants drawstrings don't really constitute a binding, per se, as people rarely bother to tie them.

The need for sweatpants is more emotional rather than physical. For me – sweatpants are the "comfort food" of my wardrobe and I rely on them when I'm out of sorts emotionally. There are days when in spite of my best efforts, my body simply feels fat. I'm not gonna lie to you – I've had several days of just *feeling* plain fat. Again this is all merely hormones and I expect this *feeling* will pass in four to six days.

I've got several obligations and commitments this week that necessitate the need for real pants and I trust I will still be able to zip and button when the time arrives. Thankfully the holiday leftovers have been eliminated from the house and I started my day with vigorous exercise.

Now that December is here, social calendars fill rapidly and the need for holiday party wear becomes an incentive to stay on track with our menus and exercise programs. As lovely as it would be to attend all functions in "party sweatpants," that's a *lazy attitude* that won't get any of us to our goals!

It's time to ditch the sweatpants, dig in our heels, kick it up a notch and get ready to look our best. New week, new month and renewed attitudes and hopefully we can all agree that this is *the most wonderful time of the year!*

What lies behind us and what lies before us are tiny matters compared to what lies within us. ~ Ralph Waldo Emerson

For we are God's masterpiece. He has created us anew in Christ Jesus, so we can do the good things he planned for us long ago. Ephesians 2:10 (NLT)

PRAYER FOR TODAY: *Lord, thank You for time off to rest and regroup. During this new month I pray You will increase my commitment to succeed. Please continue to help me and walk this road beside me. In Your name I ask all these things, Lord Jesus. Amen.*

DECEMBER 3
Just Say NO, Again

The next few weeks have the potential for utter destruction with any "normal" eating plan. So much so, that many diet companies are already gearing up to start a barrage of advertisements targeting those New Year's resolutions for losing weight.

The month of December holds the promise of holiday foods; sweets and baked goods which equal a whole lot of trouble – especially for those of us that see all things sugar as our Achilles heel.

In order to safely navigate our way through the holidays without adding an additional 7-10 pounds of holiday weight (the average holiday weight gain), we've got to strategize. We need to have a workable plan in place that will guarantee our success rather than causing us to fall victim to the statistics.

My advice: the most important tip for avoiding holiday weight gain … JUST SAY NO! I know it sounds too simple to be of any real help, but try saying NO once in a while. You don't have to sample everything. Drink lots of water and avoid alcohol as not only does that add a lot of empty calories, but it lowers our inhibitions and causes us to not give a flying fig about calories.

At social gatherings, fill up on veggies; avoid rich creamy sauces, dips and desserts. Avoid mindless nibbling just for the sake of something to do. If you don't like to engage in witty repartee, make a game of sizing up the guests and imagine funny stories about what they're talking about with others. That way you'll be so busy you won't have time to eat.

Holiday parties do not have to equal holiday weight gain. Be prepared to be tough with yourself and don't let months of hard work losing weight and getting healthy all fall apart over the course of the next few weeks. Enjoy … but be smart!

The only way to keep your health is to eat what you don't want, drink what you don't like, and do what you'd rather not. ~ Mark Twain.

"Therefore, be careful to obey every command I am giving you today, so you may have strength to go in and take over the land you are about to enter." Deuteronomy 11:8 (NLT)

PRAYER FOR TODAY: *Lord, help me to relax and enjoy the holiday season without adding stress and anxiety to my already full plate. Grant me wisdom and knowledge to grow and mature daily so I can fulfill the plans You have for my life. In Your name I ask all these things, Lord Jesus. Amen.*

DECEMBER 4
Lord, I Want to be a Loser

A recent discussion with a group of my peers spawned an age-old debate regarding nutrition and weight loss. One of my friends was talking about her recent lack of success with weight loss. She was actually quite frustrated because she was adamant that she'd cut way back on her sugar intake and was eating only once a day.

Her one daily meal was usually late in the day after putting in a ten-hour day at work. Her typical daily meal was a marathon with her consuming a full day's worth of calories in one sitting. Yet, she couldn't understand why she wasn't losing weight. In addition, she complained that by the end of the day she had little or no energy and would come home and find herself with barely enough strength to eat her one meal before she fell into bed.

Many people simply don't understand that in order to lose weight successfully, it's imperative that you eat to lose … and that means you need to eat frequently. It's suggested that whether you're losing weight or maintaining weight loss or monitoring diabetes, four to six *small* meals a day are highly recommended.

Your body needs food as fuel to keep you properly energized. If you're eating only once a day, your body holds on to whatever calories you give it thinking that you're starving. If you save all your calories for one meal, your body will be depleted of energy because you've denied it nutrients all day long.

Life is predictably unpredictable and there may be times in life when skipping a meal occurs whether by accident or design. If you're serious about losing weight; if you're maintaining a successful weight loss or if you're managing diabetes, you must eat regularly.

Fuel your body five or six times a day with SMALL, healthy meals; weigh and measure your portions; exercise four or five times a week for a minimum of thirty minutes and before you know it – you'll be the best kind of loser and you'll do it by engaging in something as simple as eating. Now that's a plan I can get on board with!

He conquers who endures. ~ Persius

Better to be patient than powerful; better to have self-control than to conquer a city. Proverbs 16:32 (NLT)

PRAYER FOR TODAY: *Lord, thank You for wisdom and knowledge and the maturity to know when to use them. Help me continue to stick to a healthy eating program and not give in to the many temptations that come across my path daily. I thank You for success, regardless of how small or insignificant it may seem sometimes. In Your name I ask all these things, Lord Jesus. Amen.*

DECEMBER 5
Eventually, You Get It

I was thinking back to when my children were babies and needed to be "trained" in certain things – like walking and potty training. There were times when they needed to be "broken" of certain things as well, like "breaking" their habit of breast feeding, bottle feedings and/or pacifiers. As stressful as those times are for parents – now that I think back on them, my kids eventually got the hang of whatever we were trying to teach them and moved on to the next stage of life. Instinct kicks in at a certain point and they simply "just got it."

That's how I've started to look at this whole healthy eating lifestyle. I know as much or more about nutrition than the average person; the same applies for exercise. So my question to myself is *"When are you going to really get this, girl?"* Honestly, I still have my share of "off" days.

Many of us are more lazy than stupid. Some days it's just too hard to apply everything that we know. The law of averages would suggest that when we possess this much knowledge, instinct will kick in for us and we're going to wake up and "just get it."

Until we do "just get it" we need to make an effort every day to get up with the intention of eating healthy, sticking to our food plan, exercising and making sure we get in our *Play 60* time of exercise each week. We need to continue doing what we CAN do and let God take care of the rest. Eventually, *I KNOW we'll just get it!"*

God gives us dreams a size too big so that we can grow in them. ~ Author Unknown

Obviously, I'm not trying to win the approval of people, but of God. If pleasing people were my goal, I would not be Christ's servant. Galatians 1:10 (NLT)

PRAYER FOR TODAY: *Lord, I ask that each day You would help me to grow in wisdom and knowledge so that one day I can wake up and just "get this" based on instinct. Help me to set goals every day and then do my best to achieve those goals. Thank You for sticking by me through this journey. I ask that You would continue to walk this path with me because I know I cannot succeed without You by my side. In Your name I ask all these things, Lord Jesus. Amen.*

DECEMBER 6
Fighting Colds and Feeding Drips

Thanksgiving last week gave me something for which I'm not too terribly thankful – an annoying cold. This cold has been in the incubating stages for about eight days now and only recently has taken up residence in both my chest and now my head. Yuck and double yuck!

Colds and sinus ailments wreak havoc in your head, nose and chest and if you're amongst the "norm" it eventually leads to your stomach. I'm currently in the stage of this incubation where my head is so filled with mucous that everything I eat tastes gross because it's followed by a mucous chaser. Nothing tastes good, which really makes eating a pointless waste of time. It's time for toast and crackers.

Why is it when you get going on a successful weight loss plan, the enemy and/or Mother Nature and dumb luck all conspire to mess you up so you blow it with a sleeve of crackers? I've been doing my best to flush this nastiness out with lots of water and hot tea, but the annoying drip remains.

Sometimes our bodies have a mind of their own and regardless of our careful planning and dedication to our healthy eating program – *stuff happens* that usurps our best efforts. This is cold and flu season so it just makes good sense to carry a travel-sized bottle of anti-bacterial hand-washing solution. Make good use of those stores that offer anti-bacterial hand wipes for swabbing down your shopping cart as you enter the store.

We have to take the necessary precautions to avoid colds and flus. If at all possible, a flu shot can be a good preventative weapon for staving off flu germs. Colds don't last forever. Be sure to drink plenty of water and fluids to help flush your body of both germs and any excess carbs you're eating to "starve your cold." Starve your cold, feed your drips but more importantly, remember to get right back on the weight loss wagon as soon as you're feeling better.

About the only time losing is more fun than winning is when you're fighting temptation. ~ Tom Wilson

My health may fail, and my spirit may grow weak, but God remains the strength of my heart; he is mine forever. Psalm 73:26 (NLT)

PRAYER FOR TODAY: Lord, I pray You will help me to stay physically and mentally strong during attacks on my body. Help me to eat right and get the necessary rest so I may do battle against this foe. Continue to stand beside me and help me through the tough days. In Your name I ask all these things, Lord Jesus. Amen.

DECEMBER 7
What's that Rotting my Bones?

Last night I went for a walk with my hubby and for every lap I was able to walk, I praised God. Seeing as how I spent the better part of the year confined to the *Lazy-boy*, every lap I walk is a victory lap. There was a time not so long ago; I was worried I'd never walk for exercise again.

Last night towards the end of our walk, a young girl happened along who was singularly focused on breaking land speed records, as she could run like the wind. During our walk, this girl who looked to be a teenager, about six inches taller than me and a good 60 pounds lighter, never broke her stride. She ran like a championship thoroughbred with a long, lanky gait; steady, even breathing and a sense of purpose.

Even in my prime at the peak of my youth and healthiest body weight – I could never run like the wind. It's never been in the genetic cards for me to be a runner. God did not design me for running or endurance sports.

At times my heart and my head have tried to convince me that I've got an athlete's spirit, but that's where all comparisons end. Even last night I found myself *wishing* I could just take off and run and not stop for several miles. I know a woman who runs 8-10 miles four or five days a week! Why can't I be *that* girl?

The sad truth is, we can wish all we want, but life is what life is – and no amount of wishing will change our genetic disposition. Letting ourselves get sucked into that "wishful" mindset or giving in to jealousy or envy will *attack your bones*. At least that's what the Bible says.

I have mild arthritis and occasionally I find myself wondering if that's an ailment caused by the envy that's creeped in and attacked my bones. Perhaps it's time to cast all those wishes away in the well of bygone days and accept the facts – I can walk two miles with only minimal pain now and that may be as good as it ever gets. Walking, even slow walking, beats paralysis any way you slice it.

Envy is the art of counting the other fellow's blessings instead of your own. ~ Harold Coffin

A heart at peace gives life to the body, but envy rots the bones. Proverbs 14:30 (NIV)

PRAYER FOR TODAY: *Lord, thank You for the progress I'm making with regards to my activity level. Help me not give in to envy and jealousy. Help me always count my blessings rather than comparing my circumstances to others. In Your name I ask all these things, Lord Jesus. Amen.*

DECEMBER 8
Tip Top Temple

The human body is an amazing machine. To the scientist that's what the human body is – a machine that can be repaired when damaged by disease, accidental injury or even our own stupidity. To those of us that are more spiritual than scientific – the body is a *temple of the Most High God*. At least it's *supposed* to be a temple. Unfortunately many of us spend years abusing our temples with out-of-balance lifestyles.

We've spent the better part of the last year doing our best to eat healthy, balance our exercise and think happy positive thoughts. But we've got to ask ourselves, "Are we *all in?*" Meaning have we really been doing *everything* within our power to clean up our temples and get rid of the damaging habits, poisonous foods and self-destructive thinking?

If I really examine myself, I know there are areas where I could be doing more – trying harder, and working at a whole other level – if *I really wanted to*. So I have to ask myself, do I want to find that whole other level or am I still living in the neighborhood of make-believe and maybe I simply can't push through to that other level?

Bottom line, we should want our "temple" to be healthy inside and out. No matter how hard we try to sweep it clean, there might yet remain an unlimited amount of debris hiding in the corners. Maybe sweeping out the temple takes more than one year – and that's okay. In the end, regardless of how long it takes to get the "temple" in tip-top order, we are the temple's caretaker. We are each only responsible for our own temple. No one is going to do this for us.

There's no statute of limitations on healing. Getting healthy takes as long as it takes.

The trouble with always trying to preserve the health of the body is that it is so difficult to do without destroying the health of the mind. ~ G.K. Chesterton

Don't be impressed with your own wisdom. Instead, fear the LORD and turn away from evil. Then you will have healing for your body and strength for your bones. Proverbs 3:7-8 (NIV)

PRAYER FOR TODAY: Lord, thank You that Your mercy is new every day – because quite frankly, I need a fresh dose of mercy DAILY. I pray You will help me to press in and get to the bottom of my food addictions so I can move forward and enjoy great physical and mental health for as long as You see fit to let me inhabit this temple. In Your name I ask all these things, Lord Jesus. Amen.

DECEMBER 9
Compounding Stupid

Being sick in any way, shape or form really stinks. My cold has lingered past what I thought should be the expiration date. Finding the energy for anything requires superhero strength – for which I have none, but life goes on and I've got responsibilities.

Not listening to our bodies is like compounding stupid on top of stupid ... and well – that's just plain super stupid! We need to listen to what our bodies are telling us and react accordingly. Even though I wanted to exercise this morning, to have done so would simply have been stupid. I can barely breathe without pain, but for some reason I thought I needed a good cardio workout huffing and puffing my way through 10 miles of torture. Why? Because I'm afraid to slack off and undo all my hard work. A noble attempt – but stupid. I can't breathe for crying out loud!

When we're sick we need rest and we need to listen to our bodies. We live in a world fraught with germy germs and odds are good at some point, we may catch something icky. Clearly we need to pick and choose when we listen to our bodies. When our bodies tell us they don't feel like working out because working out is too hard – well, you can bet your bottom dollar your body is simply being lazy.

When you're exhibiting dangerous symptoms such as shortness of breath, profuse sweating and heart palpitations when walking from the kitchen to the *Lazy-Boy* well, then LISTEN UP! Your body is trying to tell you something important. We can't let our bodies dictate our every action or decision because clearly sometimes our bodies are lazy or are operating on feelings alone.

We know ourselves better than anyone else knows us and we should know ourselves well enough to know the difference between being sick, being lazy and being stupid. Today I'm listening to my body that wants rest, Ibuprofen, minimal physical activity and hot tea and chicken soup. Today the cold speaks louder than the stupid! Hmm ... maybe I am getting smarter.

I am my own heaven and hell! ~ J.C.F. von Schiller

Teach us to number our days, that we may gain a heart of wisdom. Psalm 90:12 (NIV)

PRAYER FOR TODAY: *Lord, thank You that even when I'm not feeling well, You've still instilled wisdom and common sense in me. Help me to have sense enough to rest when I'm sick and to push past simple sluggishness when I'm feeling lazy. May I always have the understanding to separate my feelings and operate with maturity and God-given wisdom. In Your name I ask all these things, Lord Jesus. Amen.*

DECEMBER 10
What's in Your Head?

I spent some time talking with a friend of mine recently and as is my habit – the conversation got around to weight loss and dieting. This girl is significantly overweight. She confessed that most of the time, she feels like a little girl. The mental picture she has in her head makes her think she's about my size. "It's only when I look in the mirror I'm reminded that I'm overweight," she confessed.

I couldn't help but think how odd that I'm exactly the opposite. Most times I feel like a large overweight person and when I look in the mirror I see a large overweight person. I know based on the actual number on the scale, I'm only slightly overweight. I know other people see me as a "normal-sized" woman.

What goes on in our brain that makes us hear voices telling us one thing when it's so obvious we're oftentimes something altogether different? Do we believe the voices in our head or what we see reflected back at us? The truth is likely somewhere in between. We'd all do better not to live inside our heads so much of the time!

If we're battling a weight issue, living in denial isn't healthy. Yet telling ourselves we're larger than we really are isn't healthy either. Every day we need to get up and take a good look in the mirror and love ourselves exactly where we're at. We need to be willing to put in the hard work if we don't like what we see. That translates to a few more laps around the track and pushing back from the table when we've eaten our allotted calories.

We won't just somehow magically fall into good health or the perfect body weight. To achieve successful weight loss and then maintain that weight loss we have to do our part. Our part is to eat healthy, use portion control and exercise. Most importantly, we need to pray about everything, read Scripture daily and keep a positive attitude.

Getting healthy and staying healthy doesn't have to be as hard as we make it! We have to do what *we can do* and trust God to take care of the things *we can't do*. It's not easy, but worthwhile in the end.

A good laugh and a long sleep are the best cures in the doctor's book. ~ Irish Proverb

Trust in the LORD with all your heart and lean not on your own understanding; in all your ways submit to him, and he will make your paths straight. Proverbs 3:5-6 (NIV)

PRAYER FOR THE DAY: *Lord, help me to see myself clearly and not walk in denial or suffer from a skewed perception. Help me to concentrate on changing the things about myself that I can change and be willing to leave the rest to You. In Your name I ask all these things, Lord Jesus. Amen.*

DECEMBER 11
Ho-Ho-Holy Cow Life is Fun!

Last night my husband and I attended the first of several Christmas parties we have scheduled this month. In order to mingle and fit in at parties without feeling like you're walking around with a giant scarlet "A" (for food "Addict") on your forehead, careful planning is necessary if you want to enjoy yourself without feeling deprived.

Simply walking in the door to last night's party candy dishes were scattered strategically about overflowing with Hugs and Kisses (the foil wrapped chocolates) and an enormous table was set up with a catered gourmet meal. There was another large table overflowing with every kind of dessert confection imaginable. Aww … but life is hard sometimes!

My pre-party planning started at breakfast yesterday – hours before the party. I had a low-cal high protein, high-fiber shake for breakfast that filled me until well into the afternoon. I made sure to exercise. I scheduled a late lunch (around 3:00) so I wouldn't be starving by dinnertime. I stayed busy all day which helped to take my mind off food so I wasn't mindlessly snacking.

The first thing I did upon arrival at the party was accept a bottle of water from my hostess. I made myself drink the whole bottle before dinner started. My stomach was quite full before I filled my plate. I had another bottle of water with dinner and another one later in the evening.

At dinner time I found myself in line behind a woman only a few years my junior who has competed AND WON several women's bodybuilding competitions. I watched her fill her plate with greens and salad avoiding the bread basket and the pastry covered chicken. I copied her because she looks fabulous for a woman near my age! I kept my portions to a bare minimum.

I didn't make a pig of myself. I stayed engaged in conversation and didn't focus on the food. Like anything, socializing when there's food involved can be unbelievably hard. Arm yourself with a plan, focus on fellowship and remember, it's a party, so try to have some fun.

Life is really simple, but we insist on making it complicated. ~ Confucius

In their hearts humans plan their course, but the LORD establishes their steps.
Proverbs 16:9 (NIV)

PRAYER FOR TODAY: Lord, thank You for friends, fun, fellowship and food. Grant me common sense and wisdom to balance it all. I pray You will be with me for each function I attend and grant me success for healthy eating at each. In Your name I ask all these things, Lord Jesus. Amen.

DECEMBER 12
A Plethora of Parties and Fun

People-watching is one of my favorite pastimes. My husband and I attended another Christmas party where there were a bevy of bodies to focus on with roughly 350+ people in attendance. The event was business casual/semi-dressy which for me is always a comical spectator sport. People who aren't normally used to "dressing up" act very different from their "day-to-day" selves when you put them in suits, ties, heels, sequins and you stick a cocktail in their hand.

Dinner was a standard "one-size fits all" banquet fare with a take it or leave it menu. Most of it, I chose to leave, making my food choices very simple. Sometimes it's better all the way around if reasonable choice is taken from us – thereby protecting us from temptation.

For those of us millions of diet-obsessed individuals counting calories, we miss a lot of life going on around us because we're stuck in these "it's all about me" struggles. We may look "normal" on the outside, but inside our heads is another whole dimension of craziness taking place while you're talking to us at a party making polite chit-chat.

The career dieter thinks things like, "I'm going to a Christmas party tomorrow. How can I lose 10 pounds overnight and how am I going to eat what I want and keep it legal?"

Most of the food struggles end up being resolved with the standard response of, "Oh, the heck with it! It's Christmas and I'm going to eat what I want! I'll get back to my diet after New Year's!" Most of us would likely say, "Been there – done that."

We can continue to "Go there," and "do that," or we can make this holiday season different. We can choose to focus on the joy of the season and spend time cultivating friendships or we can obsess over calories. The choice is ours to either continue in old mindsets or finally get off the hamster wheel and make this year our success story. This can be the year about fun, not food!

What I don't like about office Christmas parties is looking for a job the next day. ~ Phyllis Diller

Bring joy to your servant, Lord, for I put my trust in you. You, Lord, are forgiving and good, abounding in love to all who call to you. Psalm 86:4-5 (NIV)

PRAYER FOR TODAY: *Lord, thank You for opportunities to spend time with friends and relax and enjoy an evening out. Thank You for watching over me and helping me to eat healthy and make wise choices even in holiday party settings. Continue to walk beside me and give me strength when I am weak. In Your name I ask all these things, Lord Jesus. Amen.*

DECEMBER 13
Stronger than Kisses

This last two weeks of the year can make or break even the most stalwart diet conscious individual and cause us to do the unthinkable, which is eating ourselves stupid and right back into our *fat* pants. Everywhere we go whether we work outside the home or not – there is an abundance of holiday treats and foods beckoning us to succumb to temptation.

This last two weeks of the year during the Christmas season is the time, when if we're serious about getting healthy, we've got our work cut out for us. The average individual gains from 7-10 pounds during the holidays. Many of us give in to the temptation of holiday goodies promising ourselves we'll "get back on track *after the holidays*." Do we really want to add an additional 10 pounds to a body we're already struggling with? Are cookies and candy really worth it?

Just say "NO" becomes even more important these last two weeks of the year. There is always going to be another holiday right around the corner. The cycle is never-ending and we'll never get off this treadmill of yo-yo dieting if at some point we don't stop giving into our stomachs.

If you are born again and call the Lord Jesus Christ your Lord and Savior, you have the power of the living Christ dwelling on the inside of you! There is power in the name of Jesus which will give you the strength to resist the pull of a box of candy.

Tap into the power of God and draw on that unlimited strength to give you the wherewithal to fight off temptation. Those Christmas cookies are not the boss of me or you! The Lord of the Universe is stronger than a bowl of holiday foil-wrapped *Hershey's Kisses!* If we don't call on that power we are letting the *Kisses* win! There is power in the blood, not the *Kisses!*

He brought peace on earth and wants to bring it also into your soul – that peace which the world cannot give. He is the One who would save His people from their sins. ~ Corrie ten Boom

So when you are assembled and I am with you in spirit, and the power of our Lord Jesus is present. 1 Corinthians 5:4 (NIV)

PRAYER FOR TODAY: Lord, thank You that I have the power of the Holy Spirit alive in me and at work in me daily. Give me strength to withstand temptation not just during the holidays – but every day. May I be willing to suffer slight discomfort if it means being set free from my destructive addiction to food. In Your name I ask all these things, Lord Jesus. Amen.

DECEMBER 14
No Trying – Just Doing

My friend who is considering having lap band surgery for weight loss asked me to accompany her to a consult this morning with the doctor who would be performing the surgery. It was a very eye-opening visit. I learned way more about the procedure than I was expecting. I asked questions my friend hadn't thought of so that by the time we left the appointment we were both well-informed. Sadly though, my friend cried all the way home because she's worried about the procedure itself. It is a radical solution for her and *surgery*, after all. She's also smart enough to realize that she's not yet really addressed the emotional reasons for why she eats and worries that the surgery won't fix what's going on in her head.

Most of us know there's more to excess weight than just the number on the scale. When someone is morbidly obese, nine times out of ten there are underlying emotional reasons for the excess weight problem.

My friend has not made a decision yet regarding surgery. After today's visit and getting all of the "gory details" of what to expect before, during and after a procedure such as this, she wants to revisit some other options. She's scared of surgery, yet she's scared of gaining more weight. I have promised her I will support her 100% *whatever* she decides, but I am also encouraging her to give diet, exercise and therapy another try before she opts for very expensive surgery.

As anyone who's ever tried to lose 10 pounds or 210 pounds will tell you – there are no easy quick fixes. Losing weight and maintaining that weight loss needs to be a total lifestyle change, not just something you try for few weeks or a few months.

The supply and demand principal for quick fixes makes weight loss a mega bucks industry. Weight loss manufacturers target consumers who are looking for the short cuts and easy solutions. When it comes right down to it, even surgery is a far cry from a quick fix and definitely not an *easy* (or cheap) solution. We need to get it through our heads—losing weight and maintaining a weight loss is nothing but W-O-R-K and lots of it!

When the world says, "Give up," Hope whispers, "Try it one more time."
~ Author Unknown

So let's not get tired of doing what is good. At just the right time we will reap a harvest of blessing if we don't give up. Galatians 6:9 (NLT)

PRAYER FOR TODAY: *Lord, I ask for wisdom and direction with my commitment to lose weight and exercise. Help me to be strong for others who look to me for help and support. May I continually be learning and be willing to work hard in order to achieve lasting success. In Your name I ask all these things, Lord Jesus. Amen.*

DECEMBER 15
The Dizzy Life

The last two weeks of the year seem to speed by faster than any other months of the year. The holiday season finds many of us complaining, "I'm getting dizzy and would like to get off, now, please!" There's simply not enough time to get everything done! With all of these demands on our time is it any wonder our priorities for diet and exercise get moved to the bottom of our list?

Our priorities are bound to shift and lives are going to be hectic during the Christmas season. But nothing has changed! Eating right and making sure we exercise and monitor our food portions still needs to be a major priority. Otherwise, we're in serious danger of succumbing to the failure statistics and we can quickly regain the weight we have worked so hard to lose this year. Most of us know that weight that took months to lose can come back faster than it takes a five-year-old to unwrap Christmas presents.

We need to practice restraint and exercise our voice by commanding the enemy to "get thee behind me, Satan!" When the enemy whispers that life is so busy, *relax, you deserve a break from all this weight loss stuff. Who has time for exercise?* That's when we need to remember that the enemy is a liar and greater is He that is in ME than he that is in the world.

After Jesus fasted for 40 days the enemy quickly swooped in and tried to negotiate with subtle attacks on His character. The first thing Jesus did was quote Scripture to the devil. We need to follow that example so that when the enemy whispers those lies in our ear; we need to be ready with a Scripture that will have him backpedaling.

We need to call on the name of the Lord Jesus to give us strength and help us find our inner peace so that not only can we survive the holidays … we can enjoy them, without adding additional weight to our body. Make your health a priority this Christmas. What better gift to give to your loved ones than a happier, healthier you? Let's get dizzy with joy so we can make it through the season as holiday losers.

Perhaps the best Yuletide decoration is being wreathed in smiles. ~ Author Unknown

No, in all these things we are more than conquerors through him who loved us. Romans 8:37 (NIV)

PRAYER FOR TODAY: *Lord, I am grateful for the wonder of this amazing season that celebrates the birth of Jesus. Help me to prioritize and keep the things that really are important at the top of my list and not stress over the things that aren't so important. I pray I won't compromise on the things that matter. Help me to remain steadfast and diligent in my commitment to get healthy. In Your name I ask all these things, Lord Jesus. Amen.*

DECEMBER 16
Blasting Belly Fat

A friend of mine is halfway through her first pregnancy. I started thinking about how amazing the human body is in the fact that it can house another entire person (or persons) inside it for an entire nine months. Watching my friend's belly grow the last few weeks boggles my mind.

I'm equally amazed when the reverse happens – as in massive weight loss. Another friend of mine has lost 125 pounds over this past year. Watching her body shrink has proven to be equally fascinating.

Watching our body stretch and grow can make us step back and reflect on what a huge responsibility caring for our bodies truly is. We have the power to reshape and re-sculpt our bodies simply by the choices we make with our food and exercise intensity.

While our bodies aren't exactly made of *Silly Putty* and we can't mold them into the exact shape we would like (oh, if only), we still retain that control when it comes to managing our basic figure. Genetics and DNA determine our body structure, height and bone construction; unfortunately we can't do much about that. But we can do our part in maintaining a healthy diet and making sure we have a healthy balance of exercise as well. Adding a regimen of either free weights or machines can do wonders for targeting problem areas and help to re-sculpt those areas we despise.

I'm ecstatic that my belly fat is slowly disappearing into the weight loss cosmos. I wonder where that excess body weight has disappeared to? In all honesty I wish those "saddle bags" clinging to my upper thigh and buttock region would hurry up and pack up and follow suit. In all likelihood, it probably won't happen this year, but next year is just a couple of weeks away and another opportunity to send those saddle bags packing.

Man cannot remake himself without suffering, for he is both the marble and the sculptor. ~ Dr. Alexis Carrel

Commit your actions to the LORD, and your plans will succeed. Proverbs 16:3 (NLT)

PRAYER FOR TODAY: *Lord, I am blessed to see actual changes in my body as I work hard to remake myself into a healthier version of me. Please continue to guide me and direct me until I experience complete success with my weight loss program. In Your name I ask all these things, Lord Jesus. Amen.*

DECEMBER 17
Win Some – Learn Some

The holiday season can provide more than ample opportunity for us to "fall off the wagon," with regards to our eating or exercise program. Over the course of the last year we've been retraining our brains to learn new habits with our eating, our exercise programs and our thought life.

In the "old days" when we fell victim to a sudden munching meltdown we would have fallen off the wagon and lay there whining while the stupid wagon backed up and rolled over us again – repeatedly. Hopefully, we are feeling stronger and more confident about our chances for success now and when faced with tempting treats it's getting easier for us to turn and walk away.

After nearly a year we've gained enough insight and knowledge to know that if we have a slip-up with our eating plan we don't have to wait until tomorrow to get back on track. We know that kind of logic is merely a delay tactic – one conveniently arranged for us by our enemy. That guy is roaming about looking for weak-willed individuals who are not fully suited-up with the full armor of God in place. We need to rely on the truths of God's Word to combat those destructive lies the enemy fires at our thought life.

If we have a slight "holiday meltdown cookie binge" or any other sort of binge we need to remember that it is not the end of the world. We can stop – step away from the cookies and hit a reset button by telling ourselves that even though we may have faltered, we will get right back on our healthy meal plan immediately.

Some days we win some battles; some days we lose some battles and some days we learn what we are made of and what it will take to overcome failure. We must learn how to quickly climb back up on that wagon and keep on rolling instead of letting it flatten us while we are down.

A man should never be ashamed to own he has been in the wrong, which is but saying… that he is wiser today than he was yesterday. ~ Alexander Pope, in Swift, Miscellanies

LORD, save us! LORD, grant us success! Blessed is he who comes in the name of the LORD. From the house of the LORD we bless you. Psalm 118:25-26 (NLT)

PRAYER FOR TODAY: *Lord, thank You for the knowledge gained through lessons learned. May I continue to accumulate wisdom and common sense and apply them liberally when situations call for them. Help me to be a help and an encouragement to others who are struggling. Help me have a willingness to share my failures without feeling shame. In Your name I ask all these things, Lord Jesus. Amen.*

DECEMBER 18
The Birth of a Great Idea

I have a friend who was pregnant this past year and gave birth in the spring. She is in her early 30s and has few health issues, the most worrisome being Type II Diabetes. She's been diabetic for several years now, not just during pregnancy. She's just over six feet tall with some excess weight, but she isn't obese by any means.

I watched in awe throughout her pregnancy as she became a nutrition expert, monitoring her blood sugar frequently every day. She hoped to avoid adding additional medications during her pregnancy. Just past the halfway point in her pregnancy her hormones increased creating conflict with her diabetes.

The doctor cautioned she'd need to add another medication or restrict her diet even further. She opted for stricter eating restrictions. She admitted that where she used to take a bite of a cookie, she no longer could. The few M&Ms she planned daily was reduced to zero. The pastas and breads she loved became a thing of the past; no room for debate. She had amazing self-control.

By further restricting her diet she weighed 30 pounds less the day her son was born than on the day he was conceived. Losing weight was crucial for her health and the safety of her unborn child.

Most of us may know eating certain foods is detrimental to our health, yet there are times we choose to ignore restrictions. Our health should be every bit as important to us as caretakers of these earthly vessels as a woman incubating a growing baby.

Life is short and I'm grateful for the reminders and wisdom God imparts to us regularly. It's up to us to open our eyes and ears and let the wisdom be birthed in us.

The power of love to change bodies is legendary, built into folklore, common sense, and everyday experience. Love moves the flesh, it pushes matter around.... Throughout history, "tender loving care" has uniformly been recognized as a valuable element in healing. ~ Larry Dossey

In a loud voice she exclaimed: "Blessed are you among women, and blessed is the child you will bear! Luke 1:42 (NLT)

PRAYER FOR TODAY: *Lord, I am grateful for continued good health. Help me to eat right, maintain a proper balance between work, play, sleep, exercise and food. May I learn from my mistakes and make wise choices daily when it comes to eating. Help me resist the temptations of the foods that are bad for me and truly enjoy the flavors of the foods that are good for me. In Your name I ask all these things, Lord Jesus. Amen.*

DECEMBER 19
Hoarding the Truth

The last few days have filled my backpack of life with innumerable life lessons – thanks in part to a 91-year-old widow lady. My husband has been caring for this widow for the last 25 years; helping her out around the house, doing small home repairs and shopping for her weekly. Sadly she passed away last weekend, leaving a giant void in my husband who thrives on servant-hood.

Many years ago the widow appointed my husband Executor of her estate because she had no family. Together he and I spent days at her house cleaning, sorting, boxing and discarding a half century's worth of "stuff" from every room in her house. It became clear this woman had the makings of a full-fledged hoarder. She grew up during the depression era and adopted a "never toss anything," mentality, which is not unusual for that generation.

After hours of sorting junk, when I got home I took one look around my home and started worrying that perhaps I was guilty of the same hoarding habit. I may not hoard old mail or jelly jars, but what other things might I be hoarding?

After days of de-cluttering and disposing of old junk, I decided I don't want to be a hoarder of any sort. Many of us might not be aware of it, but we may be guilty of hoarding things besides newspapers or canned goods. How many of us have been hoarding negative mindsets and opinions that we really should dispose of? How many of us hoard fear, worry or jealousy? Hoarding ANYTHING is unhealthy.

It may be time for an anti-hoarding mantra for the upcoming year – *if we don't need it – donate it or pitch it* before someone stages a hoarding intervention. Now if we could just get our excess body fat on board to adopt the same anti-hoarding mantra – life would be infinitely less cluttered.

There are no perfect men in this world, only perfect intentions. ~ Pen Densham, Robin Hood: Prince of Thieves

You will keep in perfect peace those whose minds are steadfast, because they trust in you. Isaiah 26:3 (NLT)

PRAYER FOR TODAY: *Lord, I am blessed to be shown a better way to do things. Help me to be willing to let go of harmful mindsets and attitudes so that they cannot poison me or prolong my healing. Please continue to guide me and direct my steps. In Your name I ask all these things, Lord Jesus. Amen.*

DECEMBER 20
Addicted to Losing

My husband and I attended yet another holiday party last evening. It was smaller and more intimate, but large enough that the hostess couldn't see me pass up her homemade family recipe main dish. It was a dish that didn't register a blip on my interest level. If I'm going to spend 400-plus calories on an entree – *it better be worth it.*

If you're like me, you're likely counting down the days until this whole holiday season is behind us. It's becoming increasingly more difficult to control my portions and limit my calories. Just in the last four days, in addition to the dinner party last evening – we've been invited out for lunch or dinner FOUR TIMES. The average weight conscious individual can only take so much.

I'm getting pretty good at saying "NO" for the simple reason that the more I say no, the better the number on my scale is becoming. I've been doing so well, I fear I may have crossed over and swapped my food addiction for another addiction. I've become addicted to losing.

I watched a friend of mine last year when she got to this point and it can be a very dangerous tightrope to walk. My friend did so well with her weight loss that the closer she got to her goal weight; the more she cut her calorie intake – almost to the point of what was considered unhealthy.

We need to enjoy success but remember to keep our calories balanced without consuming too many or too few. As our bodies adapt to less weight, we will require fewer calories to sustain us, but we must not be so addicted to the losing part of weight loss that we put our health at risk.

Once we finally reach our goal weight, we need to adopt a lifestyle that will allow us the freedom to maintain that weight. That's going to require a little trial and error on our parts as we retrain our habits yet again so we can go from being "Losers" to "Doers."

May Peace be your gift at Christmas and your blessing all year through!
~ Author Unknown

I will maintain my love to him forever, and my covenant with him will never fail.
Psalm 89:28 (NIV)

PRAYER FOR TODAY: *Lord, help me to be an encouragement to my friends – and always help me to be a good listener. I pray You will continue to help me resist temptation and make wise choices in every aspect of my life – whether it's in choosing friends or making decisions about taking care of my body. In Your name I ask all these things, Lord Jesus. Amen.*

DECEMBER 21
Giant Slayer

One of my favorite stories in the Old Testament is the story of King David, before he actually was a king. As a young boy, David was famous for slaying the giant, Goliath. The story in its entirety can be found in 1 Samuel, Chapter 17. It's a great read.

That story got me thinking about some of the giants I've faced in my lifetime. One of the toughest giants this past year has been the giant of *excess weight*. Some days I get tired of standing up to the giant that's been trying to best me all these years. Some days I knock him down a few pegs. Some days, the giant flat out kicks my behind.

We are 10 days from the year-end expiration date and we may be feeling a certain amount of "giant" defeat if we haven't reached our goal yet. If we're still a ways from our projected goal we need to resist the urge to feel like failures. We need to look back over the year and acknowledge some of the "lesser giants" we were able to conquer.

Maybe we didn't fell our Goliath, but we likely got in a few well-placed shots. If we've made it through the year and we are feeling more at home in our bodies that is a good thing. If we are happier with ourselves regardless of the number on the scale, that is a great thing.

Next year – we can work on perfecting our giant-slayer skills and aim for the heart of the matter. It's time to get on with being about the Lord's business and as long as we're holding onto any buried pain, hurts or addictions, our giants will still have the power over us. It's time to kill some giants, not just knock them down. We want our giants dead, decapitated and buried!

Give thanks for what you are now, and keep fighting for what you want to be tomorrow. ~ Fernanda Miramontes-Landeros

As Goliath moved closer to attack, David quickly ran out to meet him. Reaching into his shepherd's bag and taking out a stone, he hurled it with his sling and hit the Philistine in the forehead. The stone sank in, and Goliath stumbled and fell face down on the ground. 1 Samuel 17:48-49 (NLT)

PRAYER FOR TODAY: *Lord, thank You for each and every victory I've had this year, no matter how small they may have been. I pray that I can continue on this path and not let the holidays interfere with my commitment to succeed. May I learn from all my failures; and press forward to total victory in the upcoming year. In Your name I ask all these things, Lord Jesus. Amen.*

DECEMBER 22
Baby Stepping to Success

This morning as I was in the middle of my 12-mile bike ride, I paused to take stock of the progress I've made this year. I began the year nursing a hip injury from a fall six weeks prior to the New Year. My year started with chronic pain and a considerable limp. The year went radically downhill from that point, as the pain increased it created problems leading to my torn meniscus.

While waiting for doctor's visits, insurance claims and surgery, a good portion of my year was spent practically sedentary, confined to the *Lazy-Boy*. I was forced to abandon all physical exercise. Thank goodness for the warm summer months as swimming for exercise was the only thing that got me through a long hot summer.

As we count down towards the end of our year, we should all pause and take some time to reflect on any progress we have made this year. The year shouldn't be solely about the number on the scale. Have we increased our activity level this year? Has our blood pressure or cholesterol levels changed at all? Can we climb the stairs without stopping midway for a nap?

I'm one who likes to record my struggles and successes in a written journal. I experience the most success when I've faithfully chronicled my emotions, my triumphs and my defeats. Having a written journal comes in handy when I'm suddenly facing familiar trials. A journal gives me a point of reference to find answers for how I previously dealt with situations.

We may not have conquered all of our weight loss giants this year, but be thankful if we've conquered the exercise giants or the blood pressure giants or diabetes giants. As we look towards a New Year, if we're going to continue on this journey, we need to remember to set reasonable, realistic goals when it comes to exercise and diet. We do what we can and don't beat ourselves up if we're not perfect – and above all celebrate our victories, no matter how insignificant they may seem. There are no small victories, just baby steps to success!

Pray that success will not come any faster than you are able to endure it. ~ Elbert Hubbard

Pay careful attention to your own work, for then you will get the satisfaction of a job well done, and you won't need to compare yourself to anyone else. Galatians 6:4 (NLT)

PRAYER FOR TODAY: *Lord, I am grateful for my progress and the ability to work out again. Help me to listen to my body and not push it beyond its limits. Help me to take care of the temple You've blessed me with. In Your name I ask all these things, Lord Jesus. Amen.*

DECEMBER 23
Shields Up!

This is *supposed* to be the happiest season of the year; one we're supposed to look forward to with joy because we're spending all kinds of time with loved ones. I can appreciate the joy of the season – but I'm not exactly looking forward to the next 10 days with much joyfulness.

My children will be arriving home from college today and tomorrow and my grandson and oldest daughter will be here as well. The combination of my children, my husband and my grandson all here together under one roof for the next 10 days will most definitely create some food challenges.

For most of us, the next week may prove to be a test of exactly how much we've learned over the last year. These last days leading up to Christmas right on through until New Years are probably the busiest days of the year. Our resolve is weakened; our defenses are down because we get all caught up in the emotion of the season. We're spending time with people we might not get to see throughout the year; we're doing a lot of socializing at events that are centered on food!

We need to continue to practice restraint and don't let well-meaning family or friends push us off the weight loss wagon. It's very easy to undo a year's worth of hard work in only a few short days. Form a battle plan before your next eating event. Spend your calories wisely. Before you eat anything ask yourself, "Are these calories really worth it?" Remind yourself, "Nothing tastes as good as being healthy feels."

We need to strap on our armor and renew our minds HOURLY, not just daily. Polish up our Swords of the Spirit and wield those positive affirming Scriptures like we're battling a beast intent on our destruction. Our enemy would like nothing better than to see us felled because of our love of all things sugary.

Shields up! Full steam ahead! Trade in those "I think I can do this," attitudes for "I KNOW I can!"

I will honor Christmas in my heart, and try to keep it all the year. ~ Charles Dickens

Yes, and the Lord will deliver me from every evil attack and will bring me safely into his heavenly Kingdom. All glory to God forever and ever! Amen. 2 Timothy 4:18 (NLT)

PRAYER FOR TODAY: *Lord, I am thankful for family and friends. Grant me grace to say NO to all eating temptations. Help me to enjoy time with my family and not live with daily regrets. Help me to remember the real reason for this blessed season. In Your name I ask all these things, Lord Jesus. Amen.*

DECEMBER 24
'Twas the Night Before Christmas

'Twas the night before Christmas, and here's my rendition
of my family's idea of a holiday tradition.
It's the night before Christmas and all through my house
my kids are all squeezed on the couch with my spouse.

The Chinese food take-out still litters the table.
A *Christmas Story* plays, non-stop on the cable.
During commercials we laugh and we all reminisce
of Christmases past and of the family we miss.

The stockings are hung on the mantle with care,
they're crammed full of snacks and junk for our hair.
The "magic" has changed with kids that are grown.
The toys that they want are *X-Box* and *iPhone*.

If only I'd known I'd have savored the past.
How could I know my kids would grow up so fast?
Since they are grown, they've moved out on their own,
but no matter the miles, they still call this home.

We celebrate Christ and we eat lots of food.
We hang out with family; we're a big happy brood.
We play lots of games. We all love to compete.
Each year is a challenge to see who we will beat.

The day has one purpose; our objective is clear.
To love one another and spread lots of cheer.
So Merry Christmas to all; it's a heavenly night,
to share in the joy of Christ's joyous light!

Wishing you a joyous Christmas celebrating the birth of our Lord and Savior!

Christmas is a time to open our hearts to God and his gifts. Just like the rest of the year. ~ Author Unknown

"Glory to God in highest heaven, and peace on earth to those with whom God is pleased." Luke 2:14 (NLT)

PRAYER FOR TODAY: *Glory to God in the highest and peace and goodwill to everyone everywhere. I am thankful for life's many blessings and my wonderful family. I ask Your blessings on my family and friends at Christmas and for the upcoming New Year. In Your name I ask all these things, Lord Jesus. Amen.*

DECEMBER 25
Counting Blessings, Not Calories

Christmas morning dawned bright and early, as all the kids gathered around the tree to open presents. A brand new Wii Fit package to help me get in shape in the upcoming year promises to provide hours of entertainment and fun. I'm likely to provide great big belly laughs with my two left feet and no sense of balance or coordination.

I'm going to enjoy the day and not stress over my food and embrace the warm feeling of being surrounded by all my kids, grandson, husband and extended family.

Today is a day to enjoy family and friends and celebrate the birth of our Savior. Today is a day to count our many blessings and not our calories. Enjoy the day without guilt. God did not send His Son to earth so that we could feel guilt on this holy day.

If food is a big part of our day, we can enjoy that too, but we don't need to go crazy just because it's Christmas. Use wisdom and common sense when it comes to eating today. Endeavor to make the day about being with loved ones rather than stressing out about what goes on our plates.

Christmas blessings to one and all!

Three phrases that sum up Christmas are: Peace on Earth, Goodwill to Men, and Batteries not Included. ~ Author Unknown

God decided in advance to adopt us into his own family by bringing us to himself through Jesus Christ. This is what he wanted to do, and it gave him great pleasure. Ephesians 1:5 (NLT)

PRAYER FOR TODAY: *I pray people the world over can experience the love of Christ our Savior on this day of celebration. May there be peace on Earth and goodwill towards men. In Your name I ask all these things, Lord Jesus. Amen.*

DECEMBER 26
The Fun Hangover, Laughter Diet

Forcing my eyes to open this morning was a bit of a chore as I'm suffering from a bit of a fun hangover. Christmas day was so much fun that today I'm feeling some uncomfortable side-effects of having imbibed in an abundance of laughter and merriment.

I'm moving at a slower than normal pace – barely able to make my sluggish body find a gear other than *toad-slow*. My blood flowing through my veins feels somewhat "sludge-ified," causing me to misfire on all cylinders. If only we could flush our fleshly bodies as easily as we flush a radiator. There must be a tea for that sort of flushing.

Every muscle in my body is experiencing a new level of pain and discomfort as a result of a Wii-Fit overdose compounded by too many family games last evening. My stomach hurts from so much laughing!

The day after a holiday may find many of us regretting food or drink choices made the previous day. If we overdosed on fun, food or alcohol during our Christmas festivities, we shouldn't waste time beating ourselves up. No good comes of regret. If we wallow in our failures it will only take us that much more time to recover. Proverbs 23:7 in the Amplified version reminds us: *"For as he thinks in his heart, so is he."*

Today is a new day. If we didn't do as well as we hoped with all of our Christmas eating, we need to pull ourselves right back up on that weight loss wagon and begin anew today. This is where so many people falter. We can't afford to wait until after New Year's. That's how that whole downward spiral slowly begins.

We need to get out our measuring cups today and practice portion control starting with breakfast. Write down what we plan on eating the rest of the day and stick to it. If leftovers are a problem, package them up and stick them in the freezer until we find that self-control again.

Spend some quiet time with God today if you're able. Confess your weaknesses, your worries and your fears. God's always got time for us and wants to see us succeed at this journey to get healthy. We know what we need to do – so let's get doing.

Difficult things take a long time, impossible things a little longer. ~ André A. Jackson

So now there is no condemnation for those who belong to Christ Jesus. Romans 8:1 (NLT)

PRAYER FOR TODAY: *Lord, I am grateful for the gift of laughter and the joy of spending time with people I care about. May I store the events of a wonderful Christmas away in my backpack of happy memories. Thank You for life's many generous blessings. In Your name I ask all these things, Lord Jesus. Amen.*

DECEMBER 27
Double Down on Bloatiness

You know you're in a little bit of a pickle when you get dressed and your underwear feels tighter than usual. You rings feel tighter and you suddenly need a little help introducing one side of your zipper to the other. You start to feel as though a conspiracy may be brewing when you slip into your shoes and your feet are begging for mercy because even they are tight. The evidence of your Christmas *fun hangover* has settled into your body and you feel as though you're in trouble!

It's devastating to come to grips with the hard cold facts of reality that in a matter of two days, it's quite conceivable to undo months of hard work. If we've been really monitoring our eating and avoiding salty foods like nuts, crackers, chips or holiday hams and we suddenly indulge, we may be suffering from water retention problems. Drinking endless glasses of diet soda can also add to any bloat we may be feeling as there is quite a bit of sodium in diet sodas.

Sudden bloating may be looked at as a good thing in the fact that this is our body's way of letting us know that we don't *need* all that extra sodium in our diet. Body bloating is a great reminder to us that it's time to go back to drinking lots of water instead.

Today I'm excited by the bloatiness because this is proof that I've been on the right track and my body can no longer tolerate too much sodium. What the bloatiness is telling me is, "Girl, you're doing great! Salt and sodium no longer agree with you, so get back to basics and keep doing what you know is the right thing to do!"

It's nice when our bodies communicate in terms that we can understand and not misinterpret. The next time you wake up and your underwear and your shoes are suddenly too tight – stop and listen … your body is trying to tell you something! Don't ignore the bloat!

The body never lies. ~ Martha Graham

Young people, it's wonderful to be young! Enjoy every minute of it. Do everything you want to do; take it all in. But remember that you must give an account to God for everything you do. So refuse to worry, and keep your body healthy. But remember that youth, with a whole life before you, is meaningless. Ecclesiastes 11:9-10 (NLT)

PRAYER FOR TODAY: Lord, I thank You that I'm smart enough to listen to the signals my body is sending me. Help me to be smart enough to act on the signals and to adjust my food intake accordingly. Help me to gain wisdom and apply it so that I can be as healthy as possible and be a great caretaker for this body entrusted to me. In Your name I ask all these things, Lord Jesus. Amen.

DECEMBER 28
Shut Up Already

I had an opportunity to golf yesterday and I went in spite of the warning signals my body was trying to send me. I could feel the clawing anxiety and irritability common with PMS and hormones, but I ignored them. I was golfing with three men who I'm related to by either blood or marriage. Right away these guys started our day by bragging that while they've been on vacation this week, *they're losing tons of weight from all the exercise they're getting!*

One guy has been running three miles daily; something he can't do during a normal work week. Another was saying he eats a lot more food while at work and he's dropped a bunch of weight this week since he's been home. The other was complaining that he's not working and there's nothing to do BUT eat, but he simply cannot gain weight. (Can you see my eyes bugging out of my head at this point?)

In my head I'm screaming at the top of my internal mental lungs shut up! Shut Up!! SHUT UP!!! Needless to say, golf went far downhill after that. I was sniping at my golf cart partner, slicing every shot and every other word bouncing around in my skull was some sort of longshoreman, guttersnipe, trash talking four-letter word. At that point I simply needed to remove myself from the situation before I started brandishing my pitching wedge as a weapon of mass destruction and risked pummeling my male family members to unrecognizable pulp.

We should remember that men and women lose weight differently. God designed us to be completely different and men will usually lose weight more quickly than women. If we over-indulged during this past week, our male counterparts can likely recover rather quickly compared to us girls. Don't let the enemy convince you otherwise. We've got to dig in, stop our whining (oh wait, that's probably just me), and get busy doing the hard work, again. This will likely never get easier, but it can become routine which is almost as good as easy.

Can you imagine a world without men? No crime and lots of happy fat women. ~ Attributed to both Marion Smith and Nicole Hollander

A wise woman builds her home, but a foolish woman tears it down with her own hands. Proverbs 14:1 (NLT)

PRAYER FOR TODAY: *Lord, I ask Your forgiveness for the times I stumble. Give me balance in all areas of my life, but especially with my moods and temperament. Help me learn from my mistakes so I don't repeat them or cause harm or discord amongst my family. In Your name I ask all these things, Lord Jesus. Amen.*

DECEMBER 29
Blessings of the Positive

For the last couple of months I've adopted this attitude of gratitude that I try to employ from the minute my eyes pop open every morning. As soon as I'm awake, I thank God for the blessings in my life. I'm always grateful for my warm bed, a climate controlled environment that affords me blankets when it's cold and a working furnace this time of year.

After I've named several things I'm thankful for, I've been proclaiming a positive confession for all the things I'm believing for. I thank God for my healthy body and my self-control. I thank Him for protecting me from disease and that I am losing weight and that I am beautiful because I am made in His image.

I feel it only fair to share that I don't always feel all of these things I've been confessing, but the enemy cannot read our thoughts the way God can. The enemy can hear the words that come out of our mouths though. The more I say these things, the more I believe them so it's only a matter of time before the enemy will believe me as well and leave me alone with all of the attacks on my mind and my self-esteem.

Since I began this process of thankfulness I'm feeling much stronger emotionally. I believe that once we've prayed for healing we don't need to keep hounding God about our prayer. The Word of God tells us that God hears our prayers (2 Chron. 7:14). I choose to thank God for hearing me and I ask that He will bring about the manifestation of that answered prayer.

We serve a big God who loves us and cares about what happens to us (1 Peter 5:7). As we end this year and are on the threshold of beginning a new one, why not purpose in our hearts to start the year with thankfulness and trust God to set us free this year from whining, worrying and stressing over every detail of our life? If the Son sets us free, we are free indeed (John 8:36)

Sometimes the littlest things in life are the hardest to take. You can sit on a mountain more comfortably than on a tack. ~ Author Unknown

If you make the LORD your refuge, if you make the Most High your shelter, no evil will conquer you; no plague will come near your home. For he will order his angels to protect you wherever you go. Psalm 91:9-11 (NLT)

PRAYER FOR TODAY: *Lord, I am thankful for so much in my life. Help me to develop an attitude of gratitude and end this year with thanks and begin the next one the same way. Stay with me, Lord and continue to walk this journey by my side. In Your name I ask all these things, Lord Jesus. Amen.*

DECEMBER 30
What Works for One

Exercise has been my saving grace this past week. The only thing separating me from the craziness of having my daily routine disrupted by having so many people underfoot has been my daily exercise. The holidays may come and go, but unless we get off the couch and start moving our Mr. or Mrs. Potato Head bodies – obesity is for a lifetime. The more excess weight we carry – the shorter those lives are certain to be.

This past year, if it's taught us anything is that we are all different. What works for one of us may not work for all of us. I need regular exercise. I need portion control with my food and I need to keep track of everything I'm eating by way of keeping a food journal and tracking my calories.

Perhaps my way hasn't been your way and you've tweaked things to find a plan that has worked for you. We are all created as individuals and a certain amount of trial and error is necessary for us to achieve the success we are seeking.

Jared Fogle became the face of *Subway* sandwich shops and reinvented himself and found a new career as a TV spokesperson when he found a way of life that worked for him. A *Subway* diet might not work for everyone. Any of the other popular weight loss programs may or may not work for each of us. We may be on the same journey, but there may be several roads leading to the same destination.

The good news is the Statute of Limitations on getting healthy won't expire any time soon if we're willing to keep doing the work and continue this journey. Here we are staring down the barrel of another loaded New Year. How many of us are going to keep repeating stupid unhealthy habits that steal our energy and our joy of life? How many of us are willing to say – enough already? Let's find out what works for our success.

I may not have gone where I intended to go, but I think I have ended up where I intended to be. ~ Douglas Adams

The LORD directs the steps of the godly. He delights in every detail of their lives. Though they stumble, they will never fall, for the LORD holds them by the hand. Psalm 37:23-24 (NLT)

PRAYER FOR TODAY: Lord, I thank You for getting me through another full year and for the self-discoveries I've made. Thank You for the progress I've achieved and for standing beside me throughout this oftentimes difficult journey. I pray You will bless me with another full year of rich discoveries and progress. Above all, I pray that my walk with You will draw me closer to becoming the person You created me to be. In Your name I ask all these things, Lord Jesus. Amen.

DECEMBER 31
Happy You Near, Again
Pay It Forward

The turning of the calendar and welcoming in another year is a great time for reflection for me personally. I like to spend the first couple of days of the New Year in prayer and examining the past year to see where I may have stumbled with things; as well as meditating on things that I may have done well over the year that brought me great happiness or success.

Even if we didn't achieve 100% success with our weight loss this past year, hopefully we've learned that there is more to losing weight than just shedding pounds. This has been a year of self-discovery, revelation and learning to love the person on the inside as much as the outer persona we present to the public.

If we didn't achieve all that we'd hoped to this past year, there's no reason why we can't begin again. In fact, I encourage everyone to set new goals this year and push yourself even that much harder to be a better you.

Now that we are ready to embark on another trip around the sun why not consider a challenge to *pay it forward* and share your successes and become a source of encouragement to others. Don't be shy about sharing your failures either because there is always something to be learned from both success and failure.

We can end the year the same way we began by reinforcing this simple logic: Include God in ALL your plans – be it losing weight, getting out of debt or whatever your resolution may be this year. God wants to be part of EVERY aspect of your life! If you want to lose weight … PRAY, PRAY, PRAY! And after you've done that – pray some more. Hopefully, by incorporating all these suggestions into your life you will achieve your New Year's goals and you'll uncover a brand new you. This year can be different! Don't fail at another a resolution for a Happy New Year; but realize there's a Happy You Near!

Be always at war with your vices, at peace with your neighbors, and let each new year find you a better man. ~ Benjamin Franklin

"LORD, remind me how brief my time on earth will be. Remind me that my days are numbered — how fleeting my life is …" Psalm 39 4: (NLT)

PRAYER FOR TODAY: Lord, thank You for all that I've learned this year – both good things and bad, because I know You never waste pain and disappointment. Please help me to continue learning and growing in all areas. Help me to walk in love and share with others and to continually be a source of encouragement and support to others. In Your name I ask all these things, Lord Jesus. Amen.

Diet Nuggets and Wisdom Appetizers
is the third book for author, Kathleen Kurlin,
who is the author of two inspirational fiction novels entitled
Her Father's Eyes and *The Name*.

You can visit her website at **www.kathleenkurlin.com**
and share your comments on her guestbook.
Thanks for reading!